ADMINISTRATION OF CONTINUING EDUCATION

GEORGE B. STROTHER
Graduate School of Business
University of Wisconsin–Madison

JOHN P. KLUS
Department of Engineering
University of Wisconsin–Extension

Wadsworth Publishing Company
Belmont, California
A Division of Wadsworth, Inc.

Continuing Education Editor: Nancy Taylor
Production Editor: Donna Oberholtzer
Designer: Adriane Bosworth
Copy Editor: Margo Quinto
Technical Illustrator: Lois Stanfield

Printed in the United States of America
1 2 3 4 5 6 7 8 9 10—86 85 84 83 82

Library of Congress Cataloging in Publication Data

Strother, George B., 1918–
    Administration of continuing education.

    Includes index.
    1. Continuing education—Administration.
I. Klus, John P.   II. Title.
LC5219.S76   374   81-11401
ISBN 0-534-01066-0   AACR2

The Wadsworth Continuing Education Professional Series

POWER AND CONFLICT IN CONTINUING EDUCATION: SURVIVAL AND PROSPERITY FOR ALL? Sponsored by Wadsworth Publishing Company and the National University Continuing Education Association

ADMINISTRATION OF CONTINUING EDUCATION by George B. Strother and John P. Klus

The Wadsworth Series in Continuing Education

ARE YOU A TARGET? A GUIDE TO SELF-PROTECTION, PERSONAL SAFETY, AND RAPE PREVENTION by Judith Fein

PCP: THE DEVIL'S DUST—RECOGNITION, MANAGEMENT, AND PREVENTION OF PHENCYCLIDINE ABUSE by Ronald L. Linder, Steven E. Lerner and R. Stanley Burns

Phillip E. Frandson, Consulting Editor
Dean of Extension, University of California, Los Angeles

CONTENTS

FOREWORD   viii

PREFACE   x

A NOTE ON SEMANTICS   xiv

CHAPTER ONE: THE CHALLENGE OF ADMINISTRATION   1
The Goals and Objectives of Administration   1
Determining the Scope of the Program   4
Lessons from History   7
The Immediate Future   10
Bibliography   14

CHAPTER TWO: ASSESSING CLIENTELE NEEDS   17
Understanding Needs and Incentives: The First Step   17
Assessing Needs: Identifying the Client   21
Assessing Needs: Asking the Client   27
The Costs and Benefits of Data   37
Bibliography   42

Contents

CHAPTER THREE: PROGRAM PLANNING   45

The Planning Process   45

Approaches to Planning   58

Tools for Effective Planning   62

Factors Affecting Outcomes   68

Bibliography   71

**CHAPTER FOUR: DELIVERY SYSTEMS,
METHODS, AND MEDIA   73**

Choosing a Strategy   73

The Design of Instructional Systems   76

Packaging the Educational Contents   79

The Uses of Educational Technology   83

Selecting Media and Methods   95

Bibliography   98

CHAPTER FIVE: PROGRAM PROMOTION   101

Defining the Market   101

Effective Selling Techniques   107

Selecting Marketing Channels   110

Managing the Marketing Function   117

Bibliography   121

CHAPTER SIX: PROGRAM EVALUATION   123

Some Uses of Evaluation   123

Setting Objectives   124

What Is Evaluated   127

Who Evaluates   129

The Dimensions of Performance   132

Designing and Carrying Out Evaluation   133

Evaluation in Action   141

Bibliography   143

CHAPTER SEVEN: CURRICULAR PROGRAMMING   145

Curriculum in Continuing Education: A Perspective   145

Types of Offerings   150

Modes of Earning Credits   153

Curriculum Development   156

Special Problems   159

Bibliography   161

CHAPTER EIGHT: ORGANIZATION   165

How Organizations Are Put Together   166

Alternative Organizational Structures   171

Bases of Departmentation   180

Interagency Organizations   183

Bibliography   185

**CHAPTER NINE: DEVELOPING FACULTY
AND ADMINISTRATIVE STAFF**   189

Meeting Staffing Needs   190

Staffing Structures   196

The Personnel Functions   197

Increasing Staff Effectiveness   201

Bibliography   204

CHAPTER TEN: BUDGETS AND FINANCE   207

Budgeting Fundamentals   207

Program Planning and Budgeting Systems   212

Developing the Budget   216

Fund Management   224

Budget Defense   226

Bibliography   232

Contents

CHAPTER ELEVEN: STUDENT SERVICES   235

Establishment of Essential Services   235

Admissions Services: Getting Them In   239

Other Essentials: Facilitating Their Learning   244

Bibliography   253

CHAPTER TWELVE: PUBLIC RELATIONS   257

The Scope of Public Relations   257

Identifying and Relating to Significant Publics   261

Public Relations Strategy   272

Channels of Communication   274

Bibliography   281

**CHAPTER THIRTEEN: THE FUTURE:
PROSPECTS AND PROMISES   283**

Forecasting and Futurism   284

What Does the Future Hold?   289

Confronting the Future   293

Program Emphases in the Future   295

Bibliography   297

INDEX   298

FOREWORD

At no time in the history of extension and continuing education in America's colleges and universities has there been a greater crisis in leadership. This critical situation has resulted from a number of factors. First, an unusually large number of experienced deans and directors in the field have recently retired from programs and institutions—small and large, public and private—that have been highly innovative in a variety of programmatic ways. Second, many deans and directors are being newly appointed in these institutions where chief administrators have retired and by institutions who, for the first time, are beginning continuing education programs. Many of these persons have limited background and experience in the administration of extension and continuing education. Third, there is little research or written materials on administration directly applied to this field at the higher education level.

Considering that extension and continuing education is the fastest growing segment of higher education today, it is timely, even overdue, that a book on administration be available. This book will be valuable to all administrators, particularly for the large number of new and relatively inexperienced personnel who have direct administrative authority and responsibility, yet have virtually no published material to assist them in the great variety of tasks they are called upon to perform and the short- and long-term decisions they have to make.

The responsibilities for outreach of an extension or continuing education program is as broad as that of the college or university itself. The chief administrator is responsible for the development of an appropriate mission in extension and continuing education for the institution and for developing a staff capable of fulfilling this mission. The dean or director must be able to assess community needs for which the institution is uniquely qualified to provide educational services. Given the fiscal constraints on most institutions today, the chief administrator must be both knowledgeable and experienced in budget planning and know how to use the budget process to assist in achieving the goals identified for the college/university. In addition, the chief administrator must be sensitive to the wide variety of support services necessary to achieve a high quality program; e.g., student services, including adult and career counseling programs, marketing resources which assist staff in a variety of ways from adult needs assessment to surveys, direct mail, the use of media and so forth. There is no easy course of study which prepares one for a job with such diversity. Until now there has been no single work available which covers these broad areas of administrative responsibility.

This is the first such book to address these subjects and as such is valuable to any administrator, whether new or experienced, who must confront these myriad responsibilities at a time of rapid change. Both George Strother and John Klus are uniquely experienced and qualified to present this work. They have been directly involved for many years with the extension program of the University of Wisconsin, one of the oldest and most prestigious institutions in the country. As administrators they have confronted the problems and diversity of jobs discussed in this book. They write from experience and present important subjects in a way that will be useful to administrators in a wide variety of institutions — public or private, rural or urban, well-established or new to the field of extension and continuing education.

> Phillip E. Frandson, Dean
> University Extension
> University of California at Los Angeles

PREFACE

WHY THIS BOOK?

The job of the administrator is viewed by some as that of the facilitator—the procurer of resources, peacemaker, and coordinator of activities, whose responsibility it is to bring about meaningful encounters without being a direct participant. The administrator is seen by others as the entrepreneur or the leader whose function is to plan and to direct. A more modern view of administration emphasizes "uncertainty processing"—orchestration of the complex and ever changing relationship between the organization as a system in equilibrium and a dynamic external environment. In this view, administration is a balancing act performed under conditions of risk and uncertainty. As such, much of the job of the administrator must be learned on the field of action. If so, then the question naturally arises, "Why a book on how to administer?"

The answer is that there is a new professionalism in continuing education and extension. Today's administrators of continuing education and extension have often grown up with their organization. Many began their careers with budgets in the thousands and are now dealing with budgets in the millions. The administrators of the end-of-the-century organization will be of a different breed, often moving up the ladder in an already large and mature organization. Management will become more and more a team function.

The new professionalism does not mean that the common body of knowledge now forming will grow inflexible as it becomes more solidly established. It does mean that the art and science of continuing education and extension administration will be more clearly defined, and will be acquired less by trial and error and the exchange of personal experience at annual meetings and more by specialized training and systematic learning.

Authors of management textbooks in bygone years have written about the universality of the principles of administration and, to a degree, it is true that planning, organizing, procuring resources, coordinating, directing, and controlling are functions common to administrators. Yet when this book was first discussed, one of those consulted as to its potential value asked, "How can you write a useful book on administration of continuing education in view of the tremendous diversity of programs, organizational structures, goals, and problems confronting different administrators?" It is a legitimate question. A brief catalog of types of institutions suggests something of the range involved.

1. Land-grant universities
   a. Cooperative extension
   b. General extension
2. Other public colleges and universities
   a. State universities
   b. Municipal universities
   c. Community colleges
   d. Vocational schools
3. Private not-for-profit colleges and universities
   a. Large multi-purpose universities
   b. Private four-year liberal arts colleges
   c. Two-year private institutions
4. Proprietary institutions
5. Trade and professional associations
6. Community agencies
   a. Service agencies (e.g., YMCA)
   b. Elementary and secondary schools (e.g., Mott Foundation and Michigan Schools)
7. Business and industry
   a. In-house programs
   b. Programs for customers
8. Government agencies
   a. Federal schools and training programs
   b. State and local programs
9. Consulting firms
10. Commercial producers of educational materials

While such a diversity of agencies cannot be brought within the scope of a single book of manageable proportions, the following overview of topics to be covered here will suggest the many common issues.

THE PLAN OF THIS BOOK

Chapters 2 through 6 discuss production; that is, the processes of planning, executing, and assessing programs. The remaining chapters deal with general administration and support.

Chapter 2, "Assessing Clientele Needs," defines the needs to which programs must respond. In business management terms, it deals with market research: who will buy what and in what kind of package? Chapter 3, "Program Planning," discusses how to design a program and plan its content. Given the validity of the needs identified, how do we go about developing the program that will best respond to those needs? Chapter 4, "Delivery Systems, Methods, and Media," covers what delivery systems and methods to use, which are best suited to the content and clientele, and how best to use these systems. Chapter 5, "Program Promotion," suggests ways to inform potential participants about programs and to get them to participate. Chapter 6, "Program Evaluation," offers assistance in determining how well we have done. Did the program indeed accomplish its objectives?

The foregoing topics deal with the responsibilities of administrators at all levels. In the remaining chapters, we turn to the general management and staff functions that are the necessary underpinnings of successful overall effort.

Chapter 7, "Curricular Programming," discusses the planning and execution of sequential programs that culminate in a degree, a diploma, or a certificate. Chapter 8, "Organization," describes how to organize the total operation for it to function most effectively and the advantages and disadvantages of various kinds of organizational structures. Chapter 9, "Developing Faculty and Administrative Staff," concentrates on the procurement and management of human resources: recruitment, selection, classification, promotion, and job security. Chapter 10, "Budgets and Finance," reviews the essentials of financial planning, the budget process, and money management, not as separate staff functions, but as the basic responsibilities of top administration and as integral aspects of program planning. Chapter 11, "Student Services," emphasizes support services for students—the special needs and characteristics of the part-time student, the problems of counseling and advising, and financial aids. Chapter 12, "Public Relations," suggests ways of adjusting to a complex external environment: hostile, neutral, or supporting and how an administrator can influence various publics in furtherance of organizational goals. Chapter 13, "The Future: Prospects and Promises," examines the implications of future events for future action. Plans of action must deal with unfolding events and contingency plans must be ready if events unfold differently than anticipated.

These functions comprise the administrator's craft: managing a diverse collection of human and material resources in a constantly changing environment in order to produce and market needed educational programs in the most efficient and effective manner possible.

Each administrator must reinterpret this common body of knowledge for his or her own organization, and change it where personal experience proves it inappropriate or where the changing world renders it invalid. The process of learning to manage will always be a continuing one.

No preface would be complete without our thanks for the contributions of a number of people who helped make this book possible: Pat Gritzmacher and Susan Jensen, whose typing and retyping of the manuscript went beyond careful transcription and helped bring greater order and sense to the final product; Lorne Parker and David Jensen, who read portions of the manuscript and contributed information and insight; Robert Ebisch and Judy Jones, who helped materially in editorial and research aspects of preparation. In particular we wish to thank Darrell Petska, whose help in overall planning, editorial decisions, and information gathering made a major contribution to the final product. Finally, we wish to acknowledge gratefully the help of Nancy Taylor of Wadsworth and Morton Gordon of the University of Michigan, Lowell Watts of Colorado State University, Harold Miller of the University of Minnesota, Mildred Bulpitt of Maricopa County Community College District, John Buskey of the University of Nebraska–Lincoln, and Larry Kavanaugh of the College of the Redwoods who reviewed the manuscript and whose own professional experience and critical competence gave additional breadth and depth to the final product.

A NOTE ON SEMANTICS

Professionals in the area of university outreach have long been divided as to a name for their calling. Some of the terms in current use are *extension, general extension, cooperative extension, continuing education, distance education, adult education, university outreach, public service, nontraditional study,* and *lifelong learning.* Each has its special connotations and each implies a set of exclusions to some listeners. Small wonder the public is confused. Fred Harvey Harrington, in *The Future of Adult Education,* seems tempted by *extension* and *continuing education* but opts for *adult education.* Many who have served long in the Cooperative Extension Service favor *extension* as the generic term but also tend to think of all extension as *Cooperative* Extension. Others who work in *general extension* have tended in recent years to favor *continuing education.* The term *general extension* occurs less and less frequently, its apposition to Cooperative Extension increasingly felt to imply some kind of undesirable dichotomy of functions. It is not only the public that is confused.

We were tempted, therefore, to try controlling the language by edict, with one all-encompassing term. The best prospect was *extended education.* Today's educational systems are being extended: beyond the traditional period of formal education; into adult life, working life, public service, and society at large; to the remote countryside, the commuter train, and the employees' lunchroom. Neither age, locale, nor occupation sets limits. But the likelihood of general adoption of *extended education* seems remote.

Adult education had to be rejected outright as misleading in two ways—most full-time post-secondary students are also adults, and conversely, many of those served by higher education outreach programs are not adults.

We have opted for using *continuing education and extension* in tandem, feeling that the combination of terms would convey to most readers something of the full range of activities that are included in university outreach and public service programming.

Extension, whether cooperative or general, has some connotation of a college or university bringing its resources to bear directly on problems external to the institution. *Continuing education* generally carries the connotation of organized instruction for part-time students. We should add that in some contexts other terms have seemed more appropriate and, relying on Emerson's dictum against a foolish consistency, in those cases we have used other terms.

CHAPTER ONE

THE GOALS AND OBJECTIVES OF ADMINISTRATION

Better Uses of Resources
A Well-Defined Mission
Identifying Significant Problems

DETERMINING THE SCOPE OF THE PROGRAM

A General Philosophy
The Program Content
Choice of a Vehicle

LESSONS FROM HISTORY

Origins and Transition
The Cooperative Extension Model—A
Problem-Solving Approach
Recent Developments

THE IMMEDIATE FUTURE

The Economics of Progress: The Problems
of Competition
New Markets for New Products
Changing Patterns of Leadership

THE CHALLENGE
OF
ADMINISTRATION

THE GOALS AND OBJECTIVES OF ADMINISTRATION

Better Uses of Resources

The major concentration of knowledge in contemporary society lies in the human and material resources of educational institutions. Yet, in a large measure, these resources are put to only limited use. Full-time students are more concerned with acquiring knowledge than with using it. What they are learning is thus mostly a deferred benefit to themselves and to the larger society of which they are a part. Furthermore, what they are motivated to learn is more immediately determined by the values of academia than by any considerations of utility.

Those outside the academic community who might make immediate application of this knowledge or who want to enrich their lives by some esthetic or intellectual activity are frequently given only limited and often grudging access to campus resources. With the notable exception of the Cooperative Extension Service, there has never been any sustained support on a national scale to provide mechanisms for public access to the resources of colleges and universities. Unlike fossil fuels and metals, knowledge is a renewable resource. More than that, this resource grows with use, and the public benefits of increased access should be self-evident.

While underutilization of these resources continues, there has also been an increasing effort by academia in recent years to provide better general access. Under such names as adult education, extension, and public service, a greater number of programs exist today than ever before. More people are touched by academic outreach programs than there are full-time students. An Illinois study completed in 1978 claimed that one-third of all the people in the state were reached by some programs. All this is encouraging to those concerned with better utilization of educational resources, but the nagging question remains: "Is this the best we can do?"

A Well-Defined Mission

The scope of continuing education and extension can be as broad as its institutional base is varied. This is not always a virtue. Just as uncontrolled cell growth turns functional tissue into cancer, so unrestricted program development can sap the energy of the institution. An institution may try to do things it is ill equipped to do, it may duplicate the efforts of competing institutions, or its resources may not be put to the best use. There is a temptation to ride off in all directions. This tendency is limited somewhat by the growing scarcity of financial resources in nearly all institutions; but scarcity may also drive institutions to program where the most money is rather than where they can serve best. Even though the programs in question may produce a paper profit (euphemistically known in some academic circles as *budget relieving income*) there are often hidden costs and side effects that make profit a mere illusion.

The scope of an educational institution's program is defined by three constraints: the intended mission of the institution; its capabilities; and the resources it can tap to expand the use of these capabilities.

If, for instance, an institution includes continuing education in its mission, the last of these constraints may imply several different things: it may mean no more than inviting the public to on-campus events; it may mean staging activities that produce supplemental income, for example, summer programs that use excess space; in still other institutions, it may signal the intent to give equal emphasis to residence teaching and research and to extension or public service.

By implication, the institution's commitment to this full spectrum is limited by the commitment of its staff—are they able and do they *want* to be involved? A research professor working on learning disabilities may have truly useful findings but lack the motivation, aptitude, or means for moving these findings out into the stream of use.

To achieve a linkage between intent and practice may thus require additional resources and resources of a different kind. An institution that intends to include continuing education in its mission, must first possess the capability for doing so or be able to acquire that capability. This may seem self-evident, yet many institutions stumble blithely into the trap of attempting what they are unable to do. A parallel and a warning can be found in the bankruptcy records of business firms, where failure often results from a misguided effort to diversify into areas outside the capabilities of the firm. For example, an institution that does not have a school of pharmacy is likely to handle the continuing education of pharmacists rather badly and should under most circumstances leave this to better-qualified institutions.

On the other hand, if there is an unmet community need for pharmacy programs, it may be desirable to develop that capability. This may only require arranging for help from outside, or it may require a deliberate expansion of services or a redirection of resources away from areas where needs have declined. In some cases, the community need for continuing education in a subject has been a spearhead that is later followed by development of capacity for residence teaching and research in that subject.

In all cases, sound development is motivated by emergent needs and controlled by the limits of capability, resisting the temptations to embrace fads and targets of financial opportunity. A state university may find fleeting success in courses on wok cookery and home tailoring, but it may also find legislators voting down public funds for adult education. In addition, the program may be of poorer quality than can be obtained at a local community college where programs for chefs and tailors are part of the regular curriculum. The caveat against the hasty embrace of new directions is, however, only a guideline and not a categorical imperative. A course in wok cookery may be relevant to a larger program dealing with nutrition; home tailoring may fit a program in consumerism for low-income families; a fad may signal a need.

Having cautioned against a heedless branching out in new directions, the remainder of this discussion will consider the wide range of activities that might be included in a broadly based and well-supported program.

Identifying Significant Problems

There is a persistent and unfortunate tendency among many adult educators to approach programs from the perspective of formats rather than the needs of their clientele. This tendency has manifested itself often in the organization of adult education activities into administrative units such as correspondence study, classes, educational broadcasting, and conferences. The scope of the program becomes a by-product of format. Planners may ask, "How many conferences should we have?" rather than, "What problems should we tackle?"

The range of the continuing education needs or problems of people can be grouped into four major areas:

1. the problems of daily life—management of personal finances, conservation of energy in the home, child care, and other activities through which the individual or family manages its basic resources;

2. the responsibilities of membership in society—from the social role of the immediate family through the neighborhood and the local community up to the problems of the fragile planetary ecosystem;

3. increasing human potential—the enrichment of leisure time, better opportunities for minorities, the physically handicapped, the elderly, and women, and the universal problems of fuller emotional, intellectual, and physical development; and

4. gainful employment—preparation for new careers, reentry into the labor market, maintaining and upgrading job skills.

Continuing education and extension programs will prosper most when they start with these needs.

This approach to planning might be stated as a three-stage development:

1. What is the problem?

2. What is the objective, in terms of audience, content, and result?

3. What methods will be most efficient and effective in achieving the objective?

3

One caution that should be kept in mind when thinking of adult education as problem solving is illustrated by the possibly apocryphal statement of a British educator: "You Americans are always talking about solving problems; we British talk of coping with situations." The danger in presuming to solve problems is that one can wind up peddling nostrums. There is some wisdom in thinking in terms of coping rather than of problem solving. We may solve some problems—eliminating polio or smallpox, for example—but many of society's problems—such as juvenile crime or aging—can only be made less burdensome.

DETERMINING THE SCOPE OF THE PROGRAM

A General Philosophy

While trying to avoid hawking cure-alls, most continuing education practitioners have an evangelical zeal with respect to their profession. Their commitment is underlaid, explicitly or implicitly, by two premises. The first follows from Abraham Maslow's hierarchy of needs theory: under favorable circumstances, people will pursue self-actualization, the exercise of the highest order of capacities that the individual possesses; and education is a powerful aid in this direction.

Second, the individual is an integral part of a larger society. As John Donne put it in his *Devotions:* "No man is an island, entire of itself . . . ." The fullest degree of self-actualization is achieved when the self is seen as continuous with the community and the world. These are high sounding words, but people who are truly dedicated to adult education in its fullest sense have internalized these values. Their broad objective is to help people function at their highest possible level with a broad view of what their community is by increasing knowledge and understanding, releasing creative energies, and developing skills.

These concerns are not confined to the land-grant institutions or to the larger public institutions in general. The nature and size of the service niche involves all organizations. The larger private institutions may confine their activities to those areas of endeavor that provide dollar in-dollar out return, such as continuing education in the professions. Small private institutions may confine themselves to only one or two program areas. For example, one small private institution located within a few miles of two Indian reservations has given one of its two principal community services emphases to off-campus programs held on the Indian reservations. Because it also has a major emphasis on environmental studies in its residential degree program, its other major emphasis is on outreach programs dealing with regional environmental issues. Community colleges may give as much emphasis to part-time students' needs as they do the needs of full-time students. Trade and professional associations may quite appropriately confine their activities to a narrowly defined programmatic base. However, whether public or private, not-for-profit or proprietary, large or small, all dealers in continuing education are providers of a service. All have in common both the need to identify their most appropriate niche and the responsibility, within the confines of that niche, to live up to their commitments to their clientele.

The Program Content

A focus on self-actualization and community service then underscores the wide-ranging concerns of continuing education: a better life from day to day, social development, and increased human potential. The who, what, and how of these elements determine the potential scope of the program. Who is served, by what, and how, become the questions that define the goals of continuing education programs.

We will discuss the "who" in Chapter 11, focusing on the broad range of potential students. The premise is that anyone who can benefit from access to institutional resources is a potential student. The limit for any audience is whether the institution has something relevant to offer. If it is relevant to specialists, the chances are it has some kind of relevance for others. One successful example has been Cooperative Extension's translation of current knowledge about nutrition into an action program for low-income families.

"What" is the question that identifies the range of subject matter: daily living, social development, and human development. This range can be wide in the more comprehensive programs, as illustrated by the following examples of innovative or significant programs.

A. Daily living
   1. Family life: the single parent home
   2. Consumerism: product liability and product safety
   3. New careers: training legal aides
   4. Professional development: a professional development degree for engineers
   5. Business management: financial statements for small businesses
   6. Retraining: refresher course for nurses returning to practice
B. Social development
   1. Environmental issues: energy alternatives in the twenty-first century
   2. Community development: planning and promotion of mass transit
   3. Politics and government: political action for minority groups
   4. Health care delivery: hospital cost containment
   5. Employment problems and issues: the Occupational Safety and Health Act
   6. Services to business and industry: marine extension advisory services
C. Human development
   1. Problems of minorities: a special two-year college program for Spanish-speaking students
   2. Philosophical issues: foundations of civil disobedience

3. Liberal education: arts and humanities sabbaticals for business executives
4. Physical education: lifelong sports for older adults
5. Mental health: dealing with stress
6. Physically handicapped: classes for the deaf

The range of possibilities is limited only by the creativity of the faculty and administration. Reliance on proven programs is sound fiscal policy, at least in the short run, for institutions that need a stable revenue source, but the most successful institutions allocate some portion of their scarce resources to innovative programming. Development costs and failure rates in any field of endeavor are high, as any director of research and development will testify. But even with a fairly small success ratio, testing the limits through innovative programs increases institutional vitality.

Choice of a Vehicle

And now we come to the "how" of adult education—the delivery systems. The range is as broad as the range of content. Skillful experimentation with these systems characterizes the most successful institutions. The following outline is intended to suggest how varied the choices are.

A. Organized instruction
   1. Skill development: clinics and workshops
   2. Dissemination of knowledge: classes and lectures
   3. "Distance education": correspondence study, study through newspaper, telephone, television
   4. Computer-based and programmed instruction
B. Action programs
   1. Community action groups: inner city community development
   2. Special purpose groups: homemakers clubs
   3. Demonstrations: energy conservation in a model home
   4. Applied research: feasibility studies for new industry
   5. Testing facilities: soil testing for farmers and home gardeners
   6. Technical assistance for business and government
C. Person-to-person activities
   1. Advisory and counseling services
   2. Tutorial study: learning contracts
D. Guided experience
   1. Internships and apprenticeships
   2. Personnel exchanges
E. Information services
   1. Information retrieval systems
   2. Dial access
   3. Mass media: broadcast, publications, films, telephone

4. Exhibits, fairs, and festivals
5. Traveling libraries

LESSONS FROM HISTORY

Origins and Transition

The idea that extension is a central part of the academic mission has been slow to gain acceptance. According to some authors continuing education originated in the early nineteenth century. But it is only in recent years that colleges and universities have begun to give any significant priority to the service function. The origins of the external degree go back to the founding of the University of London in 1836, but adult education as an organized activity arose first largely outside of higher education and was brought under university auspices later, as was the case with farmers' institutes in the 1880s and the adaptation of the Chautauqua movement by William Rainey Harper when he became president of the University of Chicago in 1893. Many campuses today still see continuing education and extension as an auxiliary enterprise like the bookstore and the food service, useful for supplementing faculty income, improving public relations, or recruiting new students, but academically suspect at best. From the viewpoint of enthusiasts, the rate of change has been agonizingly slow; from the standpoint of staunch traditionalists, the gains have been alarming.

Most university presidents have never worked in extension and many have never worked in universities where it was emphasized. Administrators whose careers have advanced in at least a limited climate of outreach commitment are more willing to take real steps to increase the commitment to continuing education and extension. As some of these carry a personal commitment through the years and into senior administration, they may supply the evolutionary pressure needed to raise continuing education and extension to the status it deserves.

The Cooperative Extension Model—A Problem-Solving Approach

Certainly the Morrill Act of 1862 represented a revolutionary idea—that proper universities could teach useful things. Likewise, the substantial federal funding of the Cooperative Extension Service, begun with the passage of the Smith-Lever Act in 1914, represented a milepost in the redirection of the mission of higher education.

The Act provided federal funds to land-grant colleges on a matching fund basis. The match came from state and local sources on a dollar-for-dollar basis. Formula funds were linked to the filing of a state plan of work, and the combined funds supported state subject matter specialists and local agents. Historically, this scheme has contained a built-in ratio of extension to research funds: one estimate is that for every dollar it has spent on agricultural research, the federal government spends fifty cents to promote the utilization of that research. The ratio in areas other than agriculture is incredibly low by comparison—1 or 2 percent by one estimate.

Over the years, the sphere of operations of the Cooperative Extension Service has been broadened from the family farm to commercial agriculture and agribusiness in general and then to a concept of total resource development in the rural community and finally to include urban problems as well. In the meantime, the community problem-solving concept has gained deeper roots as a part of continuing education programs in a number of other settings, usually with the help of some kind of extramural funding.

Witness the application of a formula of problem identification, program objectives, and choice of delivery system, in the Pico-Union Neighborhood Project in Los Angeles as described by Phillip E. Frandson, Dean of University Extension at the University of California–Los Angeles.

> In the shadow of on-and-off access ramps where two of our most heavily traveled freeways cross and meet, Pico-Union is an area of complex ethnic background. In the economic sense it was a "poor" neighborhood, a low-income neighborhood of run down buildings and depressed small businesses. But Pico-Union was rich in community spirit, and its diverse ethnic groups lived in considerable harmony. Its people loved their homes, and maintained a strong family spirit.
>
> Suddenly all this was threatened as urban planners rattled the sabres of major redevelopment. The people turned to UCLA Extension for help and with the support of Title I funds, an extension "pilot project" became a near-perfect example of the large public university responding to community needs.
>
> With Extension acting as the central coordination core, we brought together the people's own visions of what their neighborhood could and should be, and the knowledge and resources of the University of California. Expertise in law, real estate, architecture and urban planning, business management, economics, educational and recreational specialties were brought to bear on the problems that seemed to be inviting urban renewal. The process of change was lengthy, including not only extensive consultation among Extension, campus, and the community, but also our joint appearances at hearings before Los Angeles City and County government officials. Here are a few of the things we accomplished together:
>
> 1. repair, restoration and renewal of neighborhood facilities including housing, the community school and a vest pocket park; training of residents as teachers aides and child care center operators; acquisitions of Small Business Administration loans for existing and new small businesses in the community;
> 2. transformation of the community from unorganized powerlessness to a skillfully led and cohesively organized neighborhood, with an understanding of their governmental and economic system and knowledge of how to influence it;
> 3. application of this new knowledge at city hall in public hearings on what people wanted for their community, with UCLA Extension testifying to Pico-Union's new potential as a sound community.
>
> Community effort and UCLA Extension support paid off. Redevelopment plans were crossed off and the family community of Pico-Union was preserved and immeasurably reinforced by all they had learned and accomplished together. As a valuable by-product of this joint community-Extension-campus effort, the university was able to offer participation in the project to graduate students in several of its schools, with excellent opportunities for action research.

The University Extension at the University of California–Los Angeles receives no state funding for current operations, yet by various external fund-raising efforts (in this instance Title I of the Higher Education Act), it has been able to operate a broad spectrum extension that includes a highly diversified content and clientele as well as a variety of delivery systems. In addition to people-to-people action, the Pico-Union project was approached with organized instruction, media, applied research, and exhibits.

The UCLA experience is one of many that support the idea that colleges and universities can work with local communities on demonstration, planning, and action programs outside of the classroom. Technical assistance projects such as Iowa's CIRAS (Center for Industrial Research and Service), Penn State's PENNTAP (Pennsylvania Technical Assistance Program), and Wisconsin's Business Development Center have flourished and receive varying degrees of support from local, state, and national sources. Arts and humanities outreach has been supported by two well-funded national endowments.

Recent Developments

Recent reports by leaders in higher education—the Carnegie Commission, the Newman Report, the Commission on Non-Traditional Study, to name a few—have prophesied a new era. The American Council on Education's 1974 report on financing part-time students proclaims the "new majority"—the part-time student.

The movement to consolidate a variety of public service programs under a single administrator and to provide this administrator with budgetary clout continues in many colleges and universities. Beginning with the University of Missouri in 1960, a number of states have merged their cooperative and general extension services into a single unit under a vice-president or chancellor. This type of unified operation has sometimes resulted in cross-fertilization; however, a majority of these mergers are loose federations rather than integrated operations. Whether the result in the long run will be hybrid vigor, interspecies sterility, or both remains to be seen.

The so-called SCOPE report (Kearl, 1959), its successor, *A People and A Spirit* (1968), and a series of reports by the National Advisory Council on Extension and Continuing Education (e.g., 1972, 1975) have called for greatly increased emphasis on service to nontraditional clientele. Funds have not increased in proportion to their demands.

On the positive side, today's flow of words seems to be a harbinger of tomorrow's current of events. The community college movement has an openness and growth rate that provokes imitation. The enrollment decline of eighteen to twenty-two year-olds in the 1980s prompts an intensified search for new academic markets in many institutions. In spite of the hardiness of Cooperative Extension programs and such longstanding, large scale, fee-supported programs as those of New York University and the University of California, the further rise of extension and continuing education may be more like a glacial advance—slow to take form, vast in dimension, moving irresistibly before the pressures of social need.

Chapter One

THE IMMEDIATE FUTURE

The Economics of Progress: The Problems of Competition

Two significant factors affecting the immediate future of continuing education and extension are the population projections for the 1980s and the trend toward mandatory continuing education as a condition for recertification and relicensure. As the number of people of traditional college age declines by 25 to 30 percent between 1980 and 1990 and the proportion of older people increases, higher education institutions will face painful adjustments. Departments with 90 percent or more tenured faculty will consider alternative modes to maintain employment and to provide alternatives to growth as a source of vitality.

One obvious response is to provide more extensive and more varied services to older people and to part-time students in general. They are being accepted more fully as members in good standing of the academic community. Some institutions are abandoning the separation of evening from day school and retreating from discriminatory fees and cost allocations. New standards of admission and new measures of achievement are being adapted to the nontraditional students. Credit for experience, learning contracts, external degrees, and continuing education units for part-time students are being more widely accepted as alternative measures of academic accomplishment. The long lines, complex forms, lockstep curricula, large lecture sections, and courses taught by untrained teaching assistants have been endured by full-time students, a captive audience. They are not tolerated by part-time students and are being replaced by formats and content that appeal to those whose primary commitment is to a job or to a home and family: weekend colleges and classes on commuter trains are examples of the new note of responsiveness. Higher education is moving more into the free-market economy. But an emerging competitive environment has bred problems.

The growing competitiveness of postsecondary education has been met with an increased effort by government to minimize conflict and wasteful duplication of effort. This effort has led to an establishment of coordinating councils, federally mandated regulatory commissions, and the mergers of separate systems under unified boards of control. None of these has fully comprehended the scope of the problem, which transcends state boundaries and public and private, proprietary and not-for-profit charters.

Not only is there duplication and conflict among public institutions—community colleges, vocational schools, four-year and graduate colleges and universities—and between them and their private counterparts, but a number of proprietary schools and diversified corporations are also expanding offerings to service the same markets. In a recent unprecedented development, as one example, the Department of Public Instruction of the State of Massachusetts has extended accreditation to a master's degree program offered by a public accounting firm, and Minnesota has granted recognition to the doctoral program of a proprietary institution. Furthermore, groups such as the YMCA and the Jewish Community Center have extensive programs. In-house training by individual firms or consortia of firms continues to increase in kind and number. Many professional and trade associations have extensive offerings. For example, the

American Management Association offers more than 2200 programs a year throughout the nation and in a number of locations overseas, awarding continuing education units and bringing to bear a large reservoir of marketing knowhow and membership support, and their fees are generally competitive with academic programs servicing the same clientele.

Two important points should be noted. First, many programs developed by nonacademic organizations are backed by greater resources in terms of money and specialized staff. Second, they have a skimming effect; that is, they service those with ability to pay. In the long run this means that academic institutions face formidable competition in the areas where profits are to be made. Such competition undermines the ability of academic institutions to apply the Robin Hood principle, where income from high tuition programs helps support programs for people who cannot afford to pay as much. By specializing in the profitable areas and committing more money, private-sector programs can concentrate better staff, software, and marketing knowhow in carefully chosen courses, leaving academic programmers with reduced income to meet the need for subsidized programs. Recertification and relicensure requirements and an increased emphasis on credentialing in general provide further incentives for expansion of educational programs in the private sector. Economically marginal types of programming in the public and not-for-profit sector are thus coming under increasing competitive pressures.

A growing number of occupations are requiring continuing education as a condition for retaining one's credentials. In the accounting profession, for example, the number of states requiring continuing education as a condition for retaining certification as a public accountant increased from one in 1968 to twenty-five in 1978. At least ten of the occupations requiring college-level training in one illustrative state now require or are in the process of implementing requirements for continuing education. The number of people who may be affected as the trend continues has been estimated at over six million.

Furthermore, as price and cost competition increase, program content and standards become more of an issue, too. Problems arise as to what constitutes valid continuing education. How does one control the problem of courses with no measure of achievement? What about the problem of people who sign in and then spend the remainder of their time on the nearby golf course?

The development of the continuing education unit, which is discussed in Chapter 11, has not succeeded in providing a uniform yardstick of educational quantity or quality because its use has not been universally accepted. Indeed, there exist self-serving operations that simply sell credentials, credits, and degrees for a price.

How can the educational equivalent of Gresham's law, which states that bad money drives out good money, be avoided? Educators and licensing boards are not the only ones wrestling with these questions. The Internal Revenue Service has shown an increasing and demonstrably legitimate interest. Controls will come. The main question is one of the extent to which they will be externally imposed.

Many of these activities may be viewed with equanimity as healthy processes of the free-market economy. Natural selection may determine which programs will flourish and which will languish or die. The implications for the administrator, however, are that the problems confronting institutions will increase. More than ever, environmental sensing, political action, marketing research, intelligence operations, cost control, and product design become essential tools for a once genteel and scholarly occupation. References to the halls of ivy and the ivory tower have an increasingly quaint and archaic ring.

New Markets for New Products

If academic institutions are to meet the full range of needs, they have a lot to learn about the new academic markets that would be served by a more open and competitive system of higher education. The growing body of literature on external degrees and nontraditional studies provides a false sense of security, an exaggerated feeling that academia is moving ahead in significant new ways. The truth of the matter is that most academic institutions have changed their basic philosophies of instruction very little since St. Thomas Aquinas lectured at the University of Paris in the middle of the thirteenth century. In far too many cases the new external degrees are simply old wine in new bottles.

More imaginative approaches must be developed. New academic markets have to be reached by different scheduling patterns—weekend courses, for example—that require different teaching techniques. Meeting the needs of the culturally deprived requires imaginative approaches. Reaching people who have been academic dropouts requires an understanding of why people drop out. Prisoners are a different kind of audience than their free-roaming counterparts. Young couples with parallel careers need complementary study schedules. Most older people do not resume their education merely because they are told they will be welcome in the classroom. There is need for greater understanding of the anxieties, learning problems, motivational patterns, and situational constraints that characterize these new markets.

Changing Patterns of Leadership

Changes in participation patterns and the support base of postsecondary education have accelerated the rate of change in the role of the administrator. As with transportation, communications, and energy production, the problems of the administrator seem to have increased exponentially. The image of the academician as stuffy, eccentric, and dodderingly irrelevant comes from the time when colleges and universities were considered to be havens for lone wolves and off-beat personalities, monasteries of learning. Administrators still tended to be *primus inter pares*—professors crowning their careers with an interlude of presiding over a faculty.

World War II, Korea, and Vietnam have given birth to a new breed. Modern administrators tend to be entrepreneurs and managers who can launch and control large-scale projects and programs and dispose wisely and diplomatically of the larger monies with which society now supports its centers of learning. They wield greater power and bear greater pressure, but are more dependent on the good will of the average citizen. Today's administrators' guild is no longer the learned society but rather the association of career administrators.

Continuing education administrators have developed along parallel lines, but they have a job that is in many ways more complex than that of residence administrators. Clientele are more diverse and in many ways more demanding. There is more variation in the forms of services provided, the locations at which they must be supplied, and the ways in which instruction is dispensed. Program cycles are frequently shorter and therefore require more administrative attention than residential programs. The lockstep approach dictated by the semester or quarter, the interchange of academic currency between institutions, and regulation by a multitude of accrediting agencies have a homogenizing influence on the traditional programs. But these factors can bring a comforting uniformity that the extension administrator lacks. He or she must develop new specialized organizational structures.

The new administrators might be classed in two categories: those originally trained to do research and to teach traditional disciplines in the residence format, and those trained specifically for adult education. Those crossing over voluntarily from traditional disciplines usually do so because they have discovered greater satisfaction in nontraditional clientele and delivery systems.

A growing number of administrators, however, come into continuing education and extension not through the teaching ranks but through degree programs in adult education. They differ from the other group in having made a much earlier and more general commitment to this comparatively new specialty.

One early result of this demand for special expertise in general extension was the development of specialists in delivery systems—institutes, evening classes, and correspondence study. A somewhat comparable pattern in the Cooperative Extension Service was what might be called geographic specialization. County agents were originally considered generalists who served everyone in their counties; their specialty was the land and the people they served. Now, as problems become more complex and clientele more sophisticated, method and geographic specialization are being modified more and more by a shift to problem or subject matter specialization. The administrator today, whether at the project or at the middle management level, combines competence in methods of delivery with competence in problem solving and subject matter, presiding over collaborations between experts on form and experts on content.

As in any field of endeavor, the nature of the job changes with the level of administration involved. Since continuing education and extension require more administration at more levels than in the usual academic residential program, there is no clear separation of administrators and nonadministrators. The distinction is more likely to be between project administration, program administration, and general administration. Whereas the project administrator may work on a refresher course for nurses who have not practiced for years, the program administrator may oversee the whole program of continuing education for nurses. The administrator in charge of several program areas—the health care professions, for example—has a still broader responsibility, which we call middle management. Middle management may also entail

13

responsibility for a support function such as finance or personnel. The duties of top management include general planning, organizing, directing, and controlling for the entire operation or a major subdivision.

The difference between project administration and top administration is like that between a platoon commander whose responsibility is tactical and an army commander who formulates strategy. The effective project administrator deals with detail, often has few if any staff under his or her supervision, and works directly with clientele. The top administrator deals with the general public, the political power structure, internal politics of the parent organization, and the procurement and allocation of resources for the project managers. In this book, written primarily to help practicing administrators, we need to deal with problems of both strategy and tactics because only a fine line separates the two. Today's tactician may be tomorrow's strategist.

BIBLIOGRAPHY

American Council on Education, Committee on the Financing of Higher Education for Adult Students. *Financing Part-Time Students: The New Majority.* Washington, D.C.: American Council on Education, 1974.

Apps, Jerold W. *Problems in Continuing Education.* New York: McGraw-Hill, 1979.

The Carnegie Commission on Higher Education. *A Digest of Reports.* New York: McGraw-Hill, 1974.

The Carnegie Commission on Higher Education. *The Fourth Revolution: Instructional Technology in Higher Education.* New York: McGraw-Hill, 1972.

Drucker, Peter F. *The Age of Discontinuity: Guidelines to Our Changing Society.* New York: Harper & Row, 1969.

Harrington, Fred Harvey. *The Future of Adult Education.* San Francisco: Jossey-Bass, 1977.

Hesburgh, Theodore M., Paul A. Miller, and Clifton R. Wharton, Jr. *Patterns of Lifelong Learning.* San Francisco: Jossey-Bass, 1973.

Hightower, Jim. *Hard Tomatoes, Hard Times: the Failure of the Land Grant College Complex.* Washington, D.C.: Agribusiness Accountability Project, 1972.

Houle, Cyril O. *The Design of Education.* San Francisco: Jossey-Bass, 1972.

Houle, Cyril O. *The External Degree.* San Francisco: Jossey-Bass, 1977.

Kearl, Bryant. *A Guide to Extension Services in the Future: The Scope and Responsibilities of the Cooperative Extension Service.* Raleigh, N.C.: North Carolina State College, 1959.

National Advisory Council on Extension and Continuing Education. *Fifth Annual Report of the National Advisory Council on Extension and Continuing Education.* Washington, D.C.: U.S. Government Printing Office, 1971.

National Advisory Council on Extension and Continuing Education. *Sixth Annual Report of the National Advisory Council on Extension and Continuing Education: Pursuant to Public Law 89-329*. Washington, D.C.: U.S. Government Printing Office, 1972.

Newman, Frank. *Report on Higher Education*. Washington, D.C.: U.S. Department of Health, Education, and Welfare, 1971.

Newman, Frank. *The Second Newman Report: National Policy and Higher Education*. Cambridge, Mass.: MIT Press, 1973.

Peters, John M. et al. *Building an Effective Adult Education Enterprise*. San Francisco: Jossey-Bass, 1980.

Shannon, Theodore J. and Clarence A. Schoenfeld. *University Extension*. New York: McGraw-Hill, 1972.

United States Department of Agriculture and the National Association of State Universities and Land Grant Colleges. *A People and A Spirit*. Fort Collins, Colo.: Colorado State University, 1968.

CHAPTER TWO

**UNDERSTANDING NEEDS AND INCENTIVES:
THE FIRST STEP**

Understanding People's Needs
Modifying and Satisfying Needs

**ASSESSING NEEDS: IDENTIFYING
THE CLIENT**

Census-Takers and Statisticians
Environmental Scanning
Expert Opinion
Government Agencies and Foundations
National Associations

ASSESSING NEEDS: ASKING THE CLIENT

An Overview of User Needs
Sample Surveys
Direct Assessment and Trial Balloons
Advisory Groups
Inquiries and User Feedback

THE COSTS AND BENEFITS OF DATA

The Cost of Information
Estimating Course Attendance
The Decision to Participate

ASSESSING CLIENTELE NEEDS

An enterprise survives in large part by satisfying the needs of several groups of people. It must satisfy not only the needs of consumers of its goods or services but also the needs of employees, suppliers, and those who exercise the rights of ownership—public or private. Subsequent chapters will deal with some of these important others. Here we will consider the consumers of educational services who provide the justification for their continuation.

This chapter will deal with the assessment of clientele needs beginning with what we know about motivation in general and then proceeding to specific ways in which we can identify the educational and informational needs of part-time students. These specifics are dealt with under two main headings: first, how we can assess needs by getting information *about* our prospective students and, second, how we can get information *from* them. Finally, this chapter will show how needs assessment translates into course attendance.

UNDERSTANDING NEEDS AND INCENTIVES: THE FIRST STEP

Understanding People's Needs

We motivate people by identifying their needs and by offering the appropriate incentives to satisfy those needs. The assessment of needs is a basis for program planning. The important needs relating to education fall into that general group we call social needs, which are primarily the product of an individual's experience.

Maslow's theory, mentioned in Chapter 1 and outlined in Figure 2.1, describes a hierarchy of needs. His theory holds that the higher order needs such as esteem and self-actualization become operational only when lower order needs, such as those

Figure 2.1. *Maslow's hierarchy of needs*

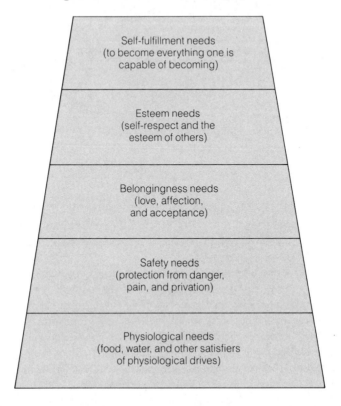

related to survival, have been satisfied. Those needs related solely to survival are not relevant for continuing educators. A starving man needs bread—not a course on how to bake.

Because they are the product of the individual's unique past, social needs also differ most from one individual to another and are most subject to modification by subsequent experiences. A study done some years ago (H. A. Murray et al., 1938) generated a list of twenty such needs. Since the publication of this study a great deal of work has been done within Murray's framework. Some of the needs the Murray group listed can be useful in identifying the motives for continuing education and the development of appropriate incentives. Table 2.1 lists these and the authors' definitions.

A few examples may serve to illustrate how programs are designed to appeal to some of these needs. The need for achievement has been studied extensively and it has been shown that people with a high achievement need are motivated by challenging situations in which they have a reasonable probability of success. Executive development programs are usually designed to appeal to the achievement need. People with a high exhibition need are attracted to programs that foster the opportunity for display: programs in public speaking, the performing arts, and the visual arts. A high under-

Table 2.1. *A catalog of needs*

n Abasement	To surrender. To comply and accept punishment. To atone. Self-depreciation.
n Achievement	To overcome obstacles, to exercise power, to strive to do something difficult as well and as quickly as possible.
n Affiliation	To form friendships and associations. To cooperate and converse sociably with others. To join groups.
n Aggression	To assault or injure another. To belittle, harm, blame, accuse, or maliciously ridicule a person.
n Autonomy	To resist influence or coercion. To seek freedom in a new place. To strive for independence.
n Counteraction	Proudly to refuse admission of defeat. To select the hardest tasks. To defend one's honor in action.
n Defendance	To defend oneself against blame or belittlement. To justify one's actions. To offer explanations and excuses.
n Deference	To admire and willingly follow a superior. To cooperate with a leader. To serve gladly.
n Dominance	To influence or control others. To persuade, prohibit, or dictate. To lead and direct. To organize the behavior of a group.
n Exhibition	To attract attention to one's person. To excite, amuse, stir, shock, thrill others. Self-dramatization.
n Harmavoidance	To avoid pain, physical injury, illness, and death. To escape from danger. To take precautionary measures.
n Infavoidance	To avoid failure, shame, humiliation, ridicule. To refrain from attempting to do something that is beyond one's powers.
n Nurturance	To nourish, aid, or protect the helpless. To express sympathy. To "mother" a child.
n Order	To arrange, organize, put away objects. To be tidy and clean. To be scrupulously precise.
n Play	To relax, amuse oneself, seek diversion and entertainment. To have fun, to play games. To laugh, joke, and be merry.
n Rejection	To snub, ignore, or exclude another. To remain aloof and indifferent. To be discriminating.
n Sentience	To seek and enjoy sensuous impressions.
n Sex	To form and further an erotic relationship. To have sexual intercourse.
n Succorance	To seek aid, protection, or sympathy. To cry for help. To adhere to an affectionate parent. To be dependent.
n Understanding	To analyze experience, to abstract, to discriminate among concepts, to define relationships. To synthesize ideas.

SOURCE: Adapted from H. A. Murray et al., *Explorations in Personality* (New York: Oxford University Press, 1938)

standing need can motivate participation in programs that deal with history, natural science, and social issues. It becomes evident, as one searches for examples, that any one activity may satisfy more than one need. It also seems safe to conclude that effective need assessment should begin with an awareness of the broad social needs in operation rather than with specific topics. One way to limit the infinite range of possible programs to manageable proportions is to think of them first within the context of generalized need satisfaction.

For example, planning a set of general liberal arts types of programs might start with a consideration of the needs that such programs are likely to meet: affiliation, deference, exhibition, play, sentience, and understanding. Each of these may in turn suggest more programs or program themes. *Affiliation* may suggest a study tour by bus of geologic highlights, *deference* may suggest a series on great leaders of history, *exhibition* a course in interpretive reading, *play* a course in folk dancing, *sentience* a course in baroque music, and *understanding* a course on the problems of strategic arms limitations.

Modifying and Satisfying Needs

Needs are not static. They increase or decrease in strength as a result of ongoing experience, reward and punishment, social approval and disapproval. David McClelland has demonstrated, for example, that the achievement need can be increased as a result of planned classroom experiences and that subsequent behavior will change in predictable ways as a result of these experiences. It has also been shown that needs can be inhibited by failure or by lack of reinforcement. While direct reward—a good grade, a pat on the back, or a promotion—may be a powerful reinforcer, important generalized reinforcers such as membership in a social group also raise the level of motivation.

People will differ furthermore in the perceived value of a reward. A certificate suitable for framing may have incentive value for some and may be totally inadequate for others. Paraprofessionals such as dental hygienists attach considerable significance to the display of visible evidence of their credentials. On the other hand, people who have just completed a course on adjusting to divorce are not likely to frame their certificate of completion.

One of the problems with incentives is that their perceived value is to some degree dependent on their immediacy in point of time. Independent study programs, which are so often plagued with very low completion rates, suffer from the double disadvantage of limited social reinforcement and the low frequency of feedback in comparison with daily classroom recitation.

In a 1975 study, James Hertling and Robert Greenburg found that certain categories of courses were more likely to be devalued after completion than others. For example, people who participated for social reasons were considerably more likely to find that a course met their expectations than were people who took a course to reach a personal goal such as increasing their competency in some area of endeavor. Part of the problem may be the delayed payoff which many achievement-oriented activities have, but part of the problem may also be the result of unreasonable expectations fostered by the exaggerated claims made in promoting the program. The devaluation of an outcome will be in direct proportion to the gap between expectations and the perceived outcome. Some of this difficulty can be avoided by a more realistic presentation of the objectives of the program.

If unrealistic expectations are a hazard in promoting programs, it should also be noted that skillful promotion can create specific needs by building on an understanding of basic needs. As John Kenneth Galbraith points out in *The Affluent Society,* modern marketing techniques have created a desire for specific shampoos, deodorants, and analgesics where no desire existed in the first place. Much of this is accomplished by persuading the potential user that the product will enhance social esteem or sexual attractiveness. To some degree the use of these products becomes a self-fulfilling prophecy. If use of the product makes one feel better, so the reasoning runs, it must be because of the efficacy of the product.

But not all created needs are frivolous or spurious. Many people, under the illusion of immortality or indestructibility defer estate or retirement planning until the time for good planning is past. A program that made people in their thirties and forties aware of the need to plan for their later years would build on their need to avoid future harm and thus would render a useful educational service.

Likewise homemakers who are only vaguely dissatisfied because of the void created in middle life by the decreasing dependence of their children may benefit by having that vague feeling converted into a conscious need, activating a systematic search for new outlets.

ASSESSING NEEDS: IDENTIFYING THE CLIENT

In the simplest terms, there are two sources of information about the needs of potential users of educational services: the intended user and sources that tell us something about the intended user. In a 1973 survey of continuing education administrators, Hertling reported their attitudes toward the value of various sources of information. According to his study, practitioners valued direct contact with potential user groups most highly, generally gave an intermediate rank to secondary sources, and ranked questionnaires at the bottom of the list. Since the study reporting these facts was based on a questionnaire, one might be tempted to question the results.

There can be little argument, however, that data gathered by personal interview, conducted by skilled interviewers, provide a richness of information that cannot be duplicated by large scale sampling techniques. The danger in generalizing from small samples to large populations, however, is a definite disadvantage of the interview. Furthermore, there is a danger of comparing good interviews with bad surveys. Perhaps the only safe conclusion that can be drawn is the computer programmers' slogan: "garbage in—garbage out." No method is infallible; bad data cannot be made to yield good conclusions, and good data are no guarantee that the user will draw the right conclusions. A general maxim for those who must stand or fall by providing the right programs based on their diagnosis of needs, is that a sale only results when the right buyer is confronted with the right product. Need assessment is the process of identifying the potential buyers and the type of product that they will want. The more good information the programmer has and the better he or she uses that information the more likely there will be a sale.

From a practical standpoint some of the most inexpensive, most readily available information comes from external sources. While such information does not directly reflect the needs of potential clientele it permits some rather strong inferences about those needs and it helps define the parameters of the target audience. We will deal in this section with major sources of information *about* potential participants and in the following section with ways of obtaining information from the potential users themselves.

Census-Takers and Statisticians

Among the numerous agencies producing various kinds of population data, the Federal Census Bureau, the Bureau of Labor Statistics, and the National Center for Educational Statistics are three of the most useful in helping programmers to follow population trends. Other data bases are also readily available both through the Government Printing Office and in most major libraries. The basic questions that can be answered from these sources are:

1. What is the population in the primary service area?
2. What is the age distribution of that population?
3. What is the breakdown by sex?
4. What are the levels of income, education, and employment in the area?
5. What is the breakdown by occupations?
6. What significant trends are indicated in employment, labor force participation, and shifts in occupation?

The answers to these questions give some indication of the potential for different kinds of programming in terms of both the size of target audiences and the likelihood of their involvement. A few trends that are likely to be significant in most areas are suggestive. The increase in the number of people over sixty is reflected both in the participation rate and in the kinds of programs that attract. The growing number of women in the labor force, accounting for half of all new jobs in 1977, and the breakdown in the traditional lines between "women's jobs" and "men's jobs" have significant implications. The declining employment opportunities in teaching, journalism, and the practice of law and concomitant growth in the health care occupations, accountancy, and computer science coupled with the estimate that over one-third of the labor force are either making or considering a job change give some idea of the population dynamics that any observant planner will turn to advantage.

In a less direct way, several other statistics are worthy of note: the rate of increase in participation in part-time study is five times as great for women as for men; recent figures indicate that people with college degrees are eight times as likely to participate in continuing education as people who lack a high school diploma; participation rates double as base income increases by 50 percent, and the recent growth in nondegree oriented part-time study is nine times the growth rate in part-time degree credit programs.

These are a sample of the kinds of national population statistics that have implications for identification of significant areas of need. While they are useful in a general way, there are enough differences between one area and another so that local conditions need to be studied to the extent figures are available. The behavior of subsets of the population can provide a substantial basis for inferring patterns of need.

As one practical consequence of these figures, consider the needs of middle class women in the forty to fifty year age bracket, who have college degrees with only minimal work experience but who have now decided to enter the job market. How should they direct their energies? Where can they find jobs commensurate with their abilities? What are their learning needs? A combination of statistics and imagination can suggest a number of program possibilities.

The Continuum Center for Women at Michigan's Oakland University capitalized with substantial success on the needs of this particular market segment, providing counseling and identifying educational opportunities for this group. Another program registering success is the Displaced Homemaker Program. With government support several colleges such as Bergen Community College in New Jersey and Valencia Community College in Orlando, Florida, are able to attend to the special needs of women.

Environmental Scanning

Active observers of ongoing events are quick to note the political and economic disasters that result from failure to respond to new developments: a firm specializing in the manufacture of steam locomotives failed because they underestimated the impact of diesel engines; a number of small manufacturers of wooden boats were put out of business by the advent of fiberglass construction, and the move of many American automobile manufacturers to compact cars was a belated one. These are only three examples of insufficient sensitivity to developments in the environment. Unfortunately, a large part of the so-called knowledge explosion is an explosion of paper, making the job of separating the informational wheat from the chaff exceedingly difficult. Nevertheless it seems likely that most of the failures to respond adequately to change are less the result of information overload than they are the result of failure to utilize information that was readily available.

The most effective kind of environmental scanning goes beyond the immediately and obviously relevant. The administrator who is too busy to read anything but inter-office memos and too busy to break away from the daily brush fires for some dreaming is likely to be no more than a competent caretaker and may end up the caretaker of a cemetery.

How then does one go about the business of doing an effective job of environmental monitoring? There are two general aspects that need to be considered: what lies directly ahead and what lies beyond the bend in the road. The first aspect is mainly a matter simply of adequate data gathering and interpretation; the second aspect involves imaginative interpretation of data and ingenious use of forecasting methods. Needless to say, the first place to look is at the road ahead. Professional and trade journals, information clearing houses such as the Educational Resources Information Center (ERIC), publications of the Government Printing Office, and conventions and professional meetings are good sources. In the latter instances the sessions in the bars and corridors may be more productive than the formal sessions, which are apt to be overcharged with self-congratulation or self-pity.

Best of all the daily paper, perceptively read, provides early notice of significant developments. A forward-looking programmer in the relatively recent past might have seized on the programmatic possibilities of a variety of issues ranging from the discovery of the Qumram scrolls to changing interpretations of the First Amendment, to the history of civil disobedience, to the 35 million-year-old anthropoid remains found in Burma, to the Shakespeare cycle on public broadcasting, to say nothing of the more obvious issues of politics and technology.

When dealing with the question of what lies beyond the next turn in the road the base of search widens. At this point literate, nontechnical periodicals become useful points of departure. Some examples of wide-ranging and provocative types are *The Futurist, Scientific American, Science, The Wall Street Journal,* the *Sunday New York Times Review of Books, Psychology Today,* and the *American Humanist* as well as a number of good, out-of-the-way publications by state historical societies, academies of the arts and sciences, and some of the better house organs. In addition to articles of interest, book review sections in a number of publications can help to reduce the time spent in browsing in book stores where the stock of significant books is often half-buried among the merely topical.

Two examples, using all the wisdom of hindsight, may make the role of environmental scanning clearer. A reader of the *Scientific American* a century or so ago might have pondered the significance of the discovery of oil in Titusville, Pennsylvania, or the patents granted to Mr. Thomas A. Edison and might have been able to turn that pondering into an early response to a whole new set of human needs.

One final suggestion for the environmental scanner, is to ask the compulsive gamblers' favorite question: "Where can I find the action?" Talking with the decision makers and the style setters and with those somewhere on the outer edges of society—economically, intellectually, or socially—can provide fresh perspectives and new insights.

Several universities saw such an opportunity in the often destructive and ill-focused resistance to the Vietnam war and sought to provide needed insight and direction by offering courses in the historical and philosophical foundations of civil disobedience.

Expert Opinion

In almost any field of continuing education there are specialists who know something about the potential clientele that even the clientele themselves may not know. Many of these specialists have graduated from being users themselves to being producers of educational services or buyers of these services for others. They are employers, administrators, consultants, or coordinators and instructors. They are frequently people with a surplus of ideas beyond those in which they feel a proprietary interest. Because they enjoy trafficking in ideas they are surprisingly accessible and willing to talk at length in spite of their often very demanding commitments. As a source of information they can be tapped in three principal ways: individual contacts, advisory groups, or as an offshoot of some other activity.

Individual contacts may be made either as the result of a deliberately planned and scheduled program of periodic field calls—a device that is used by a number of continuing education practitioners—or by what professional sales people call a *cold canvass*. The latter may begin with a stop at the office or a telephone call, preferably based on prior acquaintance, with a request for a few minutes of time or an invitation for lunch. The use of experts in advisory groups may involve combining them with users or keeping them separate from user advisory groups. There may be some advantage to separation since the level and perspective of discussion will probably differ for the two types. More will be said about advisory groups as such in the following section.

Expert opinion may also be obtained as the incidental result of some other activity—joint membership on a task force, for example, with the opportunity for off-hours discussion. It should be noted in passing that the use of Spartan sleeping accommodations at a meeting can be false economy since it precludes holding impromptu meetings in one's room where a before-dinner cocktail or a nightcap may result in the most productive discussion of the entire occasion.

An example of this kind of need assessment came out of a routine series of field calls on owners of small businesses in which it became evident that one of their major frustrations was an inability to get sufficient financing for expansion or new product development. Further inquiry indicated that part of their problem was the result of their inability to prepare adequate financial statements. The upshot was a successful series of classes on the preparation of financial statements for small businesses.

New York University recently started a program in business skills for people in publishing after contacting former participants in their long-standing publishing program. The participants also identified such specific employee problems as punctuality and general lack of personal discipline. These contacts with former students thus opened up a whole new area of programming.

Government Agencies and Foundations

In their multiple roles as grantors, regulators, and purveyors of information, government agencies, especially the federal establishment, are rich potential sources of information both through their publications and through direct contact with their staffs. The Government Printing Office has already been mentioned. Such print sources as the *Commerce Clearing House,* the *Federal Register,* and the *Congressional Digest* are additional examples. With respect to personal contacts a great many staffers in a wide variety of agencies are both accessible and well-informed as to developments and impending developments. Likewise many large foundations, through publications, sponsored activities, and staff contacts afford reasonably open channels of communication as to what is going on within their field of interest.

By way of illustration, consider the case of a continuing education administrator at a national meeting who got into casual conversation with two people from a federal agency. The conversation centered around the agency's programmatic interests and the administrator's capability. The outcome was federal funding of a program that became a major program of the institution.

Another program that developed from ideas provided by a government agency is the Energy Management Diploma program. The Department of Energy was contacted to help support a Boiler Improvement program. After reviewing the college's broad course offerings, they suggested that a critical need existed for energy managers and by structuring a certificate or diploma program—most of the courses were already available—this objective could be met without a great deal of extra cost and effort.

On a more premeditated basis, many members of Congress have knowledgeable staffers who are willing to map out and help set up a series of calls for the inquiring educator who wants to find out what's new in the nation's capitol in the arts and humanities, health, science and technology, or transportation; and agencies in turn have people whose principal job it is to serve as liaisons. This applies not only to funding programs but also to gaining an overview of issues and activities.

National Associations

Professional staff in many national associations are another valuable source of information. Fortunately for those interested in developments in postsecondary education a large number of these associations are concentrated in one building in Washington, D.C.—1 Dupont Circle—where, to mention a few examples, the American Association of State Colleges and Universities, the American Council on Education, the National Association of State Universities and Land Grant Colleges, the American Association of Community and Junior Colleges, and the National University Continuing Education Association are all housed. In addition, a number of other education-related associations are headquartered at other Washington, D.C. locations. Just a few include: American Association of University Affiliated Programs, 2033 M St. NW; Institute of Lifetime Learning, 1908 K St. NW; National Association of Independent Colleges and Universities, 1717 Massachusetts Ave. NW; and the Adult Education Association of the USA, 810 18th St. NW. Trade and professional associations, such as the American Society of Civil Engineers, can also be of tremendous value in identifying needs and as sources of information. The Encyclopedia of Associations, Gale Research Co., Detroit, Michigan, 48226 contains a wealth of information. One must be cautious in evaluating information from trade associations in that often they also provide continuing education, and like universities in the same situation may be unwilling to help.

There are no generally accepted rules of thumb about how much time should be spent in exploring the foregoing external sources of information about clientele needs.

In a number of instances their value as a resource for need assessment may be intertwined with their value as a funding source or a public relations ally. There may be less need for this kind of wide-ranging exploration of needs if the organization is primarily involved in undergraduate correspondence study courses for degree credits for example, than if the organization has a major commitment to institutes and conferences dealing with advanced technology. But even the institution with the most stable and well-run programmatic base would do well to remember the lesson of the Baldwin (steam) Locomotive Company—do not underestimate the impact of new technology.

ASSESSING NEEDS: ASKING THE CLIENT

The most efficient barometer of continuing education needs is interest voiced by the buyer with money in hand. The labor leader who comes into the continuing education office in search of a collective bargaining course for his union stewards is a strong signal that such a course is needed; particularly if he has already identified twenty potential students and established a budget to support the course. The same is true of the public works director who wants his building inspectors to sharpen their professional skills, or the manufacturer whose plant engineers are weak in air conditioning technology.

Unfortunately, needs assessment is seldom that simple. The horizons of individuals and organizations would grow very little if institutions responded only to concrete proposals from some ready user group. As every practicing continuing educator knows, in most instances we tap a very small percent of the total target group. One problem is that it is frequently difficult to define the potential user group. Who, for example, are the potential participants in a course on the American novel since 1900?

The job is made even more difficult because the potential user is frequently unable to articulate needs or is even totally unaware of certain needs. This is especially likely to be a problem when working with groups that are outside the socio-economic mainstream. Need simply does not imply demand. The outsider may recognize a great need for low-income minority youths to acquire marketable job skills. It does not follow that there is a corresponding awareness of their need on the part of the young people themselves. Most of the voting public recognizes the need for courses in public administration yet few courses are well attended.

An Overview of User Needs

In 1971, the Commission on Non-Traditional Study was created to find out how well the structure of today's education system fits into society. The Commission's report included philosophical and policy-oriented recommendations based largely on results from studies of the need for continuing education and nontraditional instruction.

The Commission conducted a major survey to determine overall adult education activity, perceived needs, reasons for not being involved in continuing education, and other related information. With a sample of approximately 4000, the study covered a broad cross section of people in the United States. Approximately 77 percent indicated that they had a need to know more or would like to learn something better.

Individuals who expressed an interest in learning were listed as *would-be learners,* while *learners* were those who had participated in a continuing education experience during the previous year. Important differences were shown to exist between the two groups. Almost half (41.8 percent) of those who actually enrolled had taken courses in hobbies and recreation but only 13.4 percent of the would-be learners expressed such an interest. Apparently, a better academic background is something many people want, but when the registration form is in hand, they may opt for courses that are fun. Credit also functioned differently for learners than for would-be learners. The would-be learners were much more concerned with credit than were the learners. Learning is the main objective of continuing one's education, of course, which may explain why those who actually got involved were less concerned about certificates and credits than those who said they would like to participate but who in fact did not. This is in keeping with the disproportionately greater growth in not-for-credit courses.

Besides understanding the positive motivations for learning, we must also be aware of obstacles that may prevent learning. Cost, time, job and home responsibilities were primary obstacles cited by would-be learners. Some individuals feared they were too old to begin studies again or no longer had confidence in their ability to succeed at learning. Others met with transportation and child care constraints. The essential point is this: with a clearly articulated understanding of the motivations and obstacles involved in learning, we can more closely tailor course design to fit clientele needs.

Because overall needs studies, such as the Commission on Non-Traditional Studies project, are of a general nature, the results may not apply to an individual discipline, age group, or other, narrower grouping; but they do suggest that all areas have a great potential for expanded services. More narrowly-focused needs studies can provide useful guides in assessing the general receptivity of a community to a given level of continuing education activity. In one community of about 70,000 people, a survey of this sort gave a good indication of the kind and degree of increased continuing education offerings that the community could absorb without some danger of saturation. It answered questions as to how many people were interested in doing more, what they could afford, what kinds of offerings they would like, at what level they should be set, and what locations, times, and duration would be most attractive.

Continuing education is provided by a number of organizations including industry, community organizations, religious institutions, government agencies, and museums as well as academic institutions. To avoid competing with ongoing courses, be sure to seek the involvement of other organizations or at least query them about their course offerings.

Sample Surveys

The art of public opinion polling has progressed considerably since the famous *Literary Digest* presidential poll of 1936 that predicted the election of "Landon by a landslide." Modern survey research experts are much more aware of the problems of sampling and questionnaire design. For the expert and for the well-meaning amateur the warning is still there: misuse of sample survey methodology can lead to massive errors. On the other hand, it is equally clear that carefully gathered information about what people *say* they will do can be highly predictive of what they *will do*. Larger institutions such as the Pennsylvania State University support professional staff to do surveys and make extensive use of the results. Smaller institutions can also make good use of survey data on a smaller scale and can almost always find some kind of expert help near at hand to assist. This discussion is not intended to make instant experts out of would-be surveyors but to suggest some of the considerations that may be of value in working with the experts.

Expert help can be expensive and one way to keep costs down is to do most of the preliminary planning before going to the experts, relying on the experts primarily for advice and help in avoiding errors. The following discussion might be thought of as a guide to preliminary planning and to the intelligent use of expert help.

OBJECTIVES   The first question to ask is, "What would I hope to accomplish by a survey?" The answer may range from an ambitious effort to determine the continuing education needs of a nationally distributed and numerous professional group or of the total adult population of a large urban area at one extreme, to the determination of the needs of a relatively small group in a limited geographic area—for example, all of the court reporters in one city with a total population of 200,000—at the other extreme.

THE TARGET POPULATION   Frequently the target population can be readily identified and a list of names obtained at little or no cost. Many associations publish membership lists that may be purchased economically or obtained free. In some cases the classified telephone directory may be a good source. Government records can be useful. For example, lists of property owners in a resort area or lists of newlyweds can be obtained from the county courthouse. Sometimes, these sources can be less adequate than they appear to be at first glance; in the case of the court reporter population, for example, some classified telephone directories provide a list of free-lance reporters but do not include those in public employment. In other instances, published membership lists or government records may be badly out of date, leading to incomplete sampling of the current population and, in a mail survey, a number of costly undeliverable returns. In brief, the identification of the target population includes not only an informed judgment about the parameters of the population but also a feasible means of reaching it.

DRAWING THE SAMPLE   Sampling experts are quick to observe that amateurs do not understand the difficulties in drawing truly random samples. For example, the common method of drawing the sample by taking every tenth (or hundredth) name on a list does not meet the criteria of true randomness. In most instances, however, such a simplified method may be quite adequate and considerably more economical than using a computerized system for random sampling. The main question to be addressed is whether the list from which names are drawn or the sampling method itself is likely to be a source of bias. The famous *Literary Digest* poll, for example, drew its sample from telephone books and in 1936 more Republicans than Democrats owned telephones. Assuming that the list itself covers the population or is truly representative of the population, the bias may come from the way the sample is drawn. For example, if the sample is all people whose names begin with the letter *F*, there may be an ethnic bias because of systematic differences in the frequency of last name initials due to national origins.

The problem is further complicated by the fact that there are no handy lists available for many populations. How, for example, would one go about sampling the general population of first-line foremen in a large city with a considerable number of firms varying greatly in size and type of product? In this case, some sort of stratified sampling is necessary and this, too, can be a source of error when the characteristics of the population are not well-understood. In the foregoing example it may suffice to break the sample down by size and by product line, but such simplified approaches should be used with caution.

However, sampling errors that could be disastrous in predicting the outcome of elections may be unimportant for purposes of need assessment. The reason for this is that the objective of a need survey is to identify clientele needs and a 5 percent error may not be particularly significant in deciding on the feasibility of programs but could easily result in picking the wrong winner in an election.

Another question that must be considered in drawing a sample is sample size. Theoretically, perfect prediction would result from a 100 percent sample, all other things being equal. Since the cost goes up in more or less direct proportion to the size of the sample after preparation costs are covered, it follows that the smaller the sample needed to get the accuracy desired, the better off the sampler is. With this as a general guide, two things need to be considered: the larger the sample, the smaller the sampling error; second, the more one may want to subdivide the sample for analysis, the larger the initial sample needs to be. In the earlier example of a broad survey of the continuing education needs in a large metropolitan area, if one goal was to find out how many working mothers with less than a high school education would be interested in high school completion, it would require a larger general population sample than if one only wanted to know how many people in the population lacked a high school diploma.

METHODS OF DATA-GATHERING   There are four commonly used methods to gather survey data:

1. *Mail surveys:* questionnaires are sent to the sample population by bulk or first class mail.

2. *Distribution channels:* questionnaires are distributed at a meeting or by internal channels such as intraoffice mail.

3. *Telephone interview:* trained interviewers ask questions and record answers by telephone.

4. *Personal interview:* trained interviewers gather the data in face-to-face con-

tact either at some common gathering place (such as the office or the church), at the home of the interviewee, or at a special interview site.

Several things govern the choice of method. Cost, the richness of the data desired, and the accessibility of the sample group are some of the principal considerations. Mail surveys are relatively low in the cost per contact but limit the range of possible responses to any given question and are plagued generally with relatively low response rates. Face-to-face interviews are the most costly but generally result in the richest variety of responses and a low number of nonrespondents. One strategy is to combine two of the above methods: for example, doing a small number of personal interviews to get a feel for the population and then using a mail survey in order to get a wider sample.

DESIGN OF THE INSTRUMENT The survey instrument may at one extreme be a highly structured questionnaire that can be completed entirely by making checkmarks. At the other extreme, it may take the form of an almost completely open-ended interview with the interviewer recording the respondent's verbatim answers to a few questions such as "What kind of educational programs would be of the greatest value to you on your job?" The checklist type of questionnaire is easy to process but is not designed to get at any nuances of response and, at its worst, may so limit the range of responses as to lead to serious distortion. Open-ended interviews, while permitting a much wider range of response, may suffer from interviewer bias or from coder error when the responses are reduced to usable form. In addition, as noted earlier, and as will be discussed in more detail in the section on the cost of information, they are much higher in cost per respondent. One middle of the road strategy is to combine the checklist questionnaire with space for written comment by the respondent.

Whichever of the foregoing methods is used, a wise precaution is to pretest any questionnaire or interview on a small sample to insure that there are no unforeseen problems in either the design or content of the survey instrument.

PROCESSING THE DATA After the responses are returned or recorded, the results must be reduced to a usable form, the end stage of which is a set of tables or figures ready for interpretation. If a checklist form of questionnaire is used, the processing may consist chiefly of transferring information either manually to paper or mechanically to punch cards or tapes. If the responses are open-ended—remarks made during interview or written statements—they must be coded into various response categories for summarization. Coding changes the data and the user should insure that the coding categories and the decisions of the coders do as little violence to the basic data as possible. One safeguard is to have two or more competent judges set up the coding categories and to have two or more independent coders do trial runs before freezing the categories.

Finally, unless data are processed manually, the duly coded and recorded data are ready to feed into the computer. The computer must be told what to do with the data. First of all it can provide tabulations of responses: "How many people checked each of the following choices?'' or ''How many of the respondents fall into the following age brackets?'' But some of the best information comes out of what survey researchers call the cross-tabulations, that is, the breakdowns into cross-referenced categories. For example, how many of the people who have more than two years of college work but no degree indicated a preference for noncredit courses and how many indicated a preference for degree credit? The right cross-tabulations can give a much clearer picture of the needs of important subpopulations. But cross-tabulations need to be thought out in advance. There is a temptation to program a high-speed computer to print out every possible cross-tabulation. If the survey is very detailed, the result is informational overkill—more information than can be managed. It is better to determine carefully in advance which cross-tabulations can produce useful information, resisting the temptation to play statistical roulette.

INTERPRETING THE DATA   The basic assumption behind any sample survey is that what people say is a reliable indicator of what they will do. Everyone knows that there are many situations in which people do not do what they say they will, and the problem is confounded in surveys by sampling errors and several kinds of systematic bias. Nevertheless, well-done surveys can be effective predictors. If the response rate is small or if the subject being investigated is one that relates to conventional attitudes about socially acceptable behavior, interpretations need to be made with greater caution. Memory and mood play tricks, too. All of this is considered in the use of well-done surveys but the problem of the utility of the results is still haunted by the remembrances of failures: the conference that the survey showed would be attended by a hundred people when only fifteen registered or the conference where only fifty were expected and four hundred sent in registration forms.

Because it is almost impossible to narrow down the number of factors that contribute to the decision to participate, the need survey generally is an effective predictor in the same way as are actuarial or epidemiological statistics. That is, it predicts something about a small proportion of a large population. The only notable exception to this general rule is the case of the closely-knit interest group surveyed under the sponsorship of a membership organization that commands a high degree of member loyalty or that is able to invoke sanctions for nonparticipation. In these special cases, the survey may effectively predict the behavior of a large part of a small population. More commonly though, surveys deal with predictions in situations such as the following: in a sample of 600 drawn from a population of 10,000, sixty people, or 10 percent of the population indicated a strong or very strong interest in a program in estate planning. The implication for actual attendance will be dealt with in more detail in the concluding section of this chapter. It should be noted, however, in the case of the foregoing example, that with a breakeven point of thirty registrations the inference would be that a thousand are interested and that the program has a reasonable chance for success.

The following is illustrative of the steps that have been outlined in this section. These steps will be reviewed now to indicate how they may be applied.

    1. *Objective.*   Get a general overview of the continuing education needs of the

adult population in the four counties that constitute the southeastern corner of the state in order to plan a substantially increased continuing education program in the area.

2. *Population*. The population was defined as all adults between the ages of twenty-five and fifty-nine. These somewhat arbitrary limits were set in order to exclude both college age and younger people and to eliminate people whose ages might minimize their participation.

3. *Sampling*. The sample of about one thousand was drawn randomly by computer based on telephone numbers; the desired numbers of male and female respondents was based on population data and screening was done by the interviewers to insure that the criteria of age and sex were met.

4. *Method*. As indicated above, the method used was a telephone interview; in a prosperous area of the state, the telephone sample would introduce only a moderate possible bias and the response rate is far higher than for most mail surveys, thus reducing the possible bias from those failing to respond.

5. *Design*. The questions asked were suggested by a number of staff members who indicated what information they might find useful; the general format was intended to insure a logical flow of questions and to eliminate unnecessary questions (for example, if the answer to the question about present employment is ''not employed'' then detailed questions about nature of job, employing firm and the like, are readily skipped).

6. *Processing the data*. The data were fed into a computer; instructions to the computer included the basic printouts required (such as distribution by age or educational level) as well as analytic printouts (cross-tabulations) such as number of people with various levels of education who would be interested in college work (e.g., how many with a high school diploma only as compared with number having some college and number who already held a degree).

7. *Interpreting the data*. Given the information obtained from the computer, the users had to draw conclusions or inferences; for example, since the total population sampled was approximately 200,000 and 1 percent of the sample indicated an interest in courses in business, the total number of interested people is projected to be 2000. Other information about the sample (e.g., ''How far would you be willing to travel to take a one night a week course of sixteen weeks duration?'') provided further indications as to how many of this interested group might take a course under a given set of conditions.

To be sure, some subjective estimates based on past experience or intuitive judgments have to be made. However, survey data can take much of the guesswork out of the need assessment process.

Direct Assessment and Trial Balloons

Of all needs assessment methods, the most nearly ideal is direct observation of the clientele in action, in order to quantify the strength of their educational background in each area. This approach was applied to continuing medical education needs at the University of Wisconsin, where assessors actually went into the doctors' offices and analyzed their practices based on discussions and examinations of records. The first step was to find what percent of that practice was devoted to cardiac disorders, trauma, infectious disease, and so on. Then the physician was given a diagnostic examination to identify discrepancies between the demands of practice and the areas of competence. Thus, empirical need identification helped the physician to plan his or her continuing education and the university to prepare appropriate courses.

Although direct observation is far more accurate than survey, it has the drawback of higher costs in time. The disruption of a practitioner's normal routine must be added to the time and effort invested by the assessor. The method would be nearly ideal in a world of unlimited resources and selfless desire to improve, but in this less-than-ideal world it can be regarded only as a model.

As systematic as direct assessment is for understanding real need, the *trial balloon* is not. The method involves simply offering a course largely on the basis of the program director's intuitive judgment to see if it attracts clientele. Probably 70 percent of all new courses are born beneath a trial balloon. Not only is this method widely used, but it is sometimes the most economical. A market study may cost $5000, whereas setting up a program and advertising may require less than $2000. It is a wonder the trial balloon method is not more fully recognized as a needs assessment tool.

One programmer got the idea from a part-time instructor in weaving that courses in crafts were beamed too exclusively toward women. He felt that often men hesitated to take courses because they supposed that they might be looked at askance or feel isolated as the sole male in a class. To test the market, he and the instructor devised a plan to offer a course in weaving for men only. It was promoted by having a burly football player pictured sitting at a loom and a feature story that played up the value of handcrafts as hobbies for men. In this instance, the trial balloon was a success in itself but the numbers responding were such as to suggest that such courses should be offered sparingly if at all in the immediate future.

Advisory Groups

Advisory groups may serve a variety of functions other than need assessment. On the input side, they may also provide help with program content, possible speakers, scheduling, teaching methods, fee schedules, and visual aids. On the output side, they may stimulate enrollment, be a source of formal sponsorship, and provide an aura of authenticity and respectability. We are concerned at this point mainly with their contribution to need assessment and will return to some of the other functions in the chapters on program planning and on public relations.

The makeup of the group should vary according to the kinds of functions that the group is to perform. If the group is to have a great deal of interaction and to do detailed planning, a small, closely knit group may be desirable. If the group is intended to represent a sample of those to be served and is expected chiefly to generate a variety of more or less random ideas a larger group may be desirable. It is also necessary to allow for attrition. Even a closely knit, highly motivated group will have some absentees and, in spite of careful planning, the shrinkage may be a third or more in less closely knit groups. Generally, if the purpose is primarily to assess the needs of a particular group by consultation with representative members of the group, a larger group may be desirable in order to have adequate representation and in order to provide a critical mass for stimulating the flow of ideas. Brainstorming groups commonly have twelve to fourteen members in order to serve the latter purpose but this may be insufficient to meet the goal of representativeness and a good group leader can work effectively with still larger groups.

If, for example, one wanted to put together an advisory group to gain better insight into the needs and interests of older people, a representative group might need to include people selected on the basis of geographic distribution, living patterns, sex, race, income, education, and marital status and it might be necessary to have a sizable group in order to include all of the desired perspectives. However, advisory groups may be less useful in dealing with such broad areas as the problems of the elderly than in dealing with groups that have a better defined educational focus such as occupational groups or the handicapped.

Unlike surveys, where some approximation of a random sample is the goal in selecting respondents, advisory groups must be constituted on the basis of representativeness. That is to say that one is looking for people who not only can provide a certain point of view but who can also be expected to articulate that point of view reasonably well. In the example of a group designed to help get at the needs of the elderly, the participants need to be representative not only by virtue of their group membership but also in the sense of speaking effectively for the group. The danger, of course, is that many who speak up on behalf of a group do not accurately reflect the views of the group.

Once the general composition of the group is determined the intended membership must be persuaded to participate. A letter of invitation followed by a telephone call will produce better results than either alone. When the desired number of acceptances have been received, and a meeting scheduled, background material can be sent in order to make the meeting more productive.

All too often such meetings end up with a great deal more telling than asking and so fail to get the desired input from the group. An effective discussion leader will maximize group involvement by using such techniques as brainstorming, buzz groups, or adaptations of Delphi, which will be discussed in Chapter 3, or nominal group techniques with only such leader input as is needed to define the task and to keep the group on track.

The group may be an ad hoc group that meets only once and is then dissolved or it may be a standing committee. Continuing advisory groups become a problem when they need to be shaken up without undesirable side effects and it may be well to have some rules for planned turnover in order to insure that the group will retain its usefulness. Whether the group is ad hoc or continuing, its value will be enhanced by the right kind of follow-up: a letter of thanks, a summary of the discussion, a request for additional input by telephone or letter, and of course a mailing of any resulting program announcements.

The primary value of an advisory group in the need assessment process is less to give a systematic picture of clientele needs than to bring out needs that might otherwise be overlooked or to test hypotheses about needs on a group of potential users as a preliminary to or follow-up of other methods of assessment.

For example, an advisory group working with staff in the area of health care finance came up with a number of ideas for broadening the enrollment base for programs. One of these ideas was that many supervisory personnel in areas other than finance felt a need for more technical knowledge in accounting and finance, and promotion was broadened on a trial basis to test the market among nonfinancial managers. The special expertise of members of the advisory group thus became a guide to a successful expansion of the program into a related field of activity.

Some problems with advisory groups are that they (1) can be expensive to maintain, especially if they only confer on one course; (2) become so possessive of the course that new inputs or changes will not occur without a lot of extra work—if at all; and (3) will not allow courses that have passed their useful life to just die because they feel a sense of responsibility to keep it going. Careful instructions in setting up the advisory committee and reminders at each meeting will help alleviate these problems and make an advisory committee useful and efficient.

Inquiries and User Feedback

Many successful programs have started as the result of a single inquiry. Conversely, good program ideas have been lost through failure to keep a record of unsolicited inquiries. Unsolicited requests and suggestions can also uncover areas of overlooked or emerging need. It is good practice to respond to such contacts with a letter or a telephone call since people who take the initiative in bringing up program ideas can be a continuing source of help. Even a totally impractical suggestion can be dealt with in such a way as to encourage future suggestions.

Some of these contacts may result from crisis situations that nevertheless signal a significant need and program opportunity. In the larger continuing education operations it is well to have enough leeway so that prompt response can be forthcoming in those comparatively rare instances when a crash program appears to be warranted in response to an inquiry or request. For example, the Cooperative Extension Services in several states diverted resources to deal with the sudden threat of southern corn leaf blight's becoming epidemic in the spring of 1971. Other situations such as plant shutdowns, natural disasters, new legislation, and energy shortages may give rise to a program need and the first indication may come from an unexpected outside contact. Receptiveness to such unsolicited inquiries or suggestions can lead to significant programming.

In business and industry similar opportunities may come out of court cases, grievances, and strikes when a situation arises that reveals an underlying problem or a significant change in direction. The Supreme Court's ruling in the Bakke case prompted managers and executives in a number of organizations to ask what the implications were for their affirmative action programs. An inquiry or two at that time might have been a strong indication that a prompt program response was in order. It would be fatuous to suggest that every inquiry or even two or three inquiries should lead to a program. Obviously, in the final analysis, professional judgment has to be exercised. Response should be based on the best assessment that can be made in keeping with considerations of timeliness.

Another means of assessing needs is to include an "other" category in newspaper advertisement coupons or direct mail promotion postcards. Attendees at ongoing programs are another good source of ideas. End of course evaluations can include questions such as, "What other subjects would you want covered in future programs?" or "What other topics would you have liked to have covered in this program if there had been more time?" Participants may also be a valuable source of ideas as to what kinds of programs their friends or associates might need.

THE COSTS AND BENEFITS OF DATA

Organizations that lose touch with their external environment are doomed. An essential element in environmental awareness is some kind of needs assessment. The crudest and most costly method is to stay with a given program until it dies a natural death and then through trial and error to stumble onto some viable program opportunities. At the other dangerous extreme is the organization that uses so many of its resources for need assessment that it significantly reduces program capability. Although few organizations err in the direction of this second extreme, the threat is real. It occurs in rare instances usually in units where there is considerable pressure within the organization for research and publication and need assessment becomes a thin disguise for bootleg research. This is a reversal of the desirable kind of relationship in which need assessment can hitchhike on research that is externally funded.

How much of a continuing education operation's resources should be allocated to need assessment? The answer will vary with the mission of the unit. Pennsylvania State University, for example, estimates that it spends about 7 percent of its total budget directly on need assessment. In many other organizations, need assessment is only an indirect cost and almost impossible to estimate. However, the foregoing discussion of need assessment implies that cost considerations are important and this section highlights some of the cost considerations in relation to the expected benefits.

The Cost of Information

Information about needs costs money in either direct outlay or indirectly through time and materials consumed. However, misinformation or the lack of information can be still more costly. Few people realize the full cost of information until those costs are broken out and then the reaction is likely to be one of shock, but when the issue is faced squarely as it is more likely to be in business and industry, it becomes evident that this form of research and development is a necessary cost of doing business. As is true in business and industry, the amount of resources that should be allocated for this purpose is dependent on the product mix. Systematic need assessment should be a major concern in such areas as continuing medical education or in engineering and the applied sciences. It may properly receive a lower priority in areas with a more stable subject matter and a more homogeneous clientele—the closer one is to any given field of endeavor, however, the less evident it is that it is one of the stable areas. The need for continuing assessment is a fact of life in almost all areas of continuing education and the real issue is the choice of strategies—not the question of the necessity of assessment. There are four basic strategies and any given organization must elect one or more of these:

1. Assessment is done as a secondary responsibility shared by many within the organization.

2. It is a contributed service as is the case when it is done by graduate students as part of their degree requirements or when it is done as a part of funded research.

3. Services are purchased, either internally as through a survey research laboratory or through outside consultants.

4. A formal research and development function is established within the organization.

Even when the work is done by staff specialists with that specific responsibility, there is a cost in the time of program staff since studies done with close liaison with program staff are more likely to have impact on programs. Small operations may therefore be better off to do most of their own need assessment as a secondary responsibility of program staff, garnering what outside help they can get on a catch as catch can basis, just as their counterparts in small business do. There comes a point, however, as organizations increase in size, where a formal assessment staff should be considered. When this point is reached, two alternatives are faced: one is to create a separate "thinktank" operation divorced from day to day concerns and the other is to create a direct service type of operation that is closely linked to the everyday concerns of program staff. If the goal is to scan distant horizons a separate thinktank may be the answer, but for most units, for which long range planning is defined as one to five years, the closely linked service unit will be most productive and the scanning of distant horizons can be left to carefully orchestrated annual retreats.

Such a service unit might have a narrow mission—for example, conducting relatively standard surveys—or it may have a broader responsibility for using all possible assessment techniques. One argument favoring the latter approach is that it focuses on the end to be attained—the best possible assessment of needs—rather than on the means. However, it is always more difficult and usually more expensive to find broad-gauged staff than it is to find specialists.

If the decision is made to create a unit devoted to need assessment, it may still be desirable to keep that unit small but broad and to provide the unit with a budget so that it can purchase specialized services. Furthermore, it is better to start small and expand as the results warrant than it is to create a large staff unit and then find that it is not worth the investment. It is difficult to state a rule of thumb to guide investment in need assessment but there may be some validity to a comparison with market research expenditures in some types of service businesses where 1 percent of sales is common.

We can be a bit bolder in discussing costs of specific assessment methods although there are wide variations in these costs, too. Direct assessment methods are almost always costly because they involve direct contact with clientele usually over a considerable period of time. The basic techniques are similar to those used in work sampling and in job analysis with the further complication that larger samples are necessary. The small samples that are relied on for better or for worse by industrial engineers will not give an adequate picture of the complexities of professional occupations. So, while direct assessment is the ideal method to get a complete picture of the needs of a professional group it must be used sparingly because of the high cost of a satisfactory sample.

Surveys can yield usable results at considerably lower cost. Lower cost, however, is a relative term and it may come as a surprise to people who have not used surveys to find what the unit costs are. Five or six dollars per usable response (including design, printing, mailing, and data processing) would not be unusual for a mail survey. The cost for telephone surveys will run more than double this amount and the cost of personal interviews done under favorable conditions (limited geographic spread and previously trained interviewers) can easily amount to forty dollars per usable response. Direct costs can sometimes be held down by resorting to various expediencies such as making a survey mailing part of another mailing or getting studies done by taking advantage of staff slack time that might otherwise be poorly utilized. Also, of course, unit costs go down somewhat for larger samples because the fixed costs of preparation and planning are spread over a large number of units.

Other than for direct assessment and sample surveys, it is not practical to use rule of thumb guides to estimate the cost of need assessments. The costs of advisory groups, for example, vary with such significant side issues as whether they receive a complimentary meal, whether travel expense is covered, or even whether an honorarium is provided. The basic fact is that all forms of assessment involve a cost but that excessive thrift is false economy when it results in an information deficit.

Estimating Course Attendance

Making course attendance projections is tenuous at best. Projections must nonetheless be made for a budget, room size, supplies, handouts, and various other enrollment factors. Sometimes, market research data from other institutions and programs is available. If generalizable, it may lead to accurate, useful projections.

The following example reveals how relevant information can be gathered and utilized to derive a projection as accurately as possible. A one-week short course in specification writing was being proposed for members of the Construction Specification Institute (CSI) from throughout the country. How many times should it be offered and what would be the expected attendance?

A survey of the CSI's 11,000 members indicated that approximately 11.5 percent of them had major responsibility in specification preparation. An additional 10.8 percent indicated a general interest in specifications, amounting to an interested clientele base of about 22 percent. Based on (1) the response to questionnaires, and (2) attendance at prior meetings and continuing education courses, the maximum number of members involved in continuing education was estimated by geographic regions. Assuming the course was to be offered in region 6, an optimistic estimate of members attending courses was 15 (in all interest categories). Assuming 25 percent interest in the membership, four people would most likely attend from region 6. Because the survey also showed as many nonmembers as members involved in specification activities, enrollment of four nonmembers could be anticipated. Extrapolation from past enrollments in other regions suggested that national advertising would increase participation by 300 percent. Hence, there were 8 estimated enrollees from region 6 and 24 from the rest of the country, for a projected total enrollment of 32. A year later, the course was offered and the attendance was 37.

The Decision to Participate

According to the motivational model described at the beginning of this chapter, needs provide force and direction for behavior when an appropriate incentive is present or expected. There is a kind of universality of basic needs—a finite number of needs can describe a wide range of human behavior. However, people differ in the strength of any given need and in the personal mixture of strong and weak needs. Nevertheless, through need assessment, it is possible to predict, with reasonable accuracy, the percentage of people who will respond to the appropriate incentives.

Some confusion may be created by the fact that, at the secondary need level—specific needs that are an outgrowth of basic needs—the need and the incentive tend to be called by the same name. That is to say, that a need for professional education responds to the incentive of professional education opportunities. However, the response is complicated by several conditions: (1) a number of needs are operational at any time and some of these needs pull the individual in opposing directions; (2) needs operate at different levels of awareness and therefore differ in their effectiveness as directional forces apart from their basic strength; (3) some needs respond to the attractiveness of an incentive and others are needs to escape or avoid; (4) the value of an incentive is not inherent in the object but rather depends on how it is perceived. Good food may be rejected because it appears unattractive and junk food may be sought because of the way in which it is presented. Small wonder that need assessment is a complicated process and charged with uncertainty.

The problem becomes acute when dealing with the hard-to-reach or when dealing with small circumscribed groups where a small percent response spells program failure or early exhaustion of potential. Fortunately for most programmers, they are dealing with large enough numbers so that a small percent response spells success. There is an offsetting advantage for those trying to reach small groups. Small groups are usually homogeneous so that once the right formula is derived the participation rate becomes highly predictable.

In the final analysis, group response is the summation of a number of individual responses so it is well to speculate a bit as to what goes on in the individual's mind as he or she wrestles with the decision to participate. Consider a final example.

Ellen Teagarden feels stranded in a blind alley job. She has always had a high achievement need but felt compelled, as the only child, to drop out of college in her sophomore year when her widowed mother was disabled by a stroke. She is restless, discontented, but lacks any clear sense of direction. Because of her mother's continuing disability and the cost of care, she feels she cannot quit work to return to school. The incentive value of a college degree earned on a part-time basis is substantially diminished by the remoteness of the goal: one course at a time for so many years! To say nothing of the accumulated cost of several years' tuition.

Even her vaguely felt need prompts a search process. She starts reading the job opportunities advertisements in the classified section of the daily paper, talking more and more with her friends about the rewards of their jobs, even reading the print inside the match book cover because on the outside it proclaims "SUCCESS WITHOUT COLLEGE" in capital letters. Little slogans begin to dance in and out of her consciousness: "Earn good money as an accountant," "Select a new career," "Become a mechanical engineer," "Success without college," "Study at home."

Ellen, however, is a very practical person. She knows her own mind better than most do. She also knows some important facts about the job market. She knows, for one thing, that she is quite gregarious and that it would be very difficult for her to be satisfied with home study as a method for learning. She also knows that in her state she cannot become a CPA through home study. She also likes the idea of getting out and away from her sick mother but wants to avoid the feeling of guilt that sometimes rises up when she is away "for purely selfish reasons." Given this ferment, a vocational counselor or a perceptive friend might ask, "What sorts of things have you enjoyed doing in the past?" Ellen might recall the fun she had going door to door when she was in high school soliciting sponsors for her walk for development and she might then further recall a number of other experiences that formed a cluster of similar interests: persuading people to buy something or to give money.

At this time, her attention is drawn to an article in the daily paper describing a new course offering whereby, with one evening of study each week for one semester at the nearby community college, she can qualify to take an examination for a license to sell real estate. She discusses this possibility with friends and with a neighbor who sells real estate. She gets some idea of the earning potential, the employment opportunities, and the working conditions. She then refreshes her memory as to the tuition charges, which she only vaguely recalled as being reasonable, consults her own psyche as to the probability that her need for achievement, autonomy, and affiliation fit the job as she understands it, and goes on opening night to enroll.

There are several possible endings to Ellen Teagarden's story. One is that she could not find a parking place and so went back home only to enroll later in a different program at a different institution. Another is that she arrived only to find the class filled and so enrolled in a course in interior decorating instead. Another is that the instructor was an incredible bore and so, after the second week, she dropped the course and got a 60 percent tuition refund. But we will leave Ellen at the moment of decision since the purpose of this narrative is only to illustrate some of the complexities of the decision to participate and to show how a variety of needs and incentives enter into this decision. We will return to the decision to participate in the chapter on program promotion.

BIBLIOGRAPHY

Commission on Non-Traditional Study. *Diversity by Design*. Samuel B. Gould, Chairman. San Francisco: Jossey-Bass, 1973.

Cross, K. Patricia. "Adult Learners: Characteristics, Needs and Interests," in *Lifelong Learning in America,* Richard E. Peterson et al. San Francisco: Jossey-Bass, 1979, pp. 75–141.

Hertling, James and Robert Greenburg. "Determining Continuing Education Needs and Interests." *NUEA Spectator,* March 1974, pp. 7–14.

Hertling, James and Robert Greenburg. "Goal Expectations and Accomplishments of Adult Non-Credit Course Enrollees." *NUEA Spectator,* September 1975, pp. 29–34.

Katz, Israel. "Higher Continuing Education," in *Handbook of College and University Administration—Academic*. Edited by Asa Knowles. New York: McGraw-Hill, 1970, pp. 5-35 to 5-59.

Knowles, Malcolm S. *The Modern Practice of Adult Education: Andragogy Versus Pedagogy*. New York: Association Press, 1970.

Murray, H. A., et al. *Explorations in Personality*. New York: Oxford University Press, 1938.

Pennington, Floyd C., ed. *Assessing Educational Needs of Adults*. New Directions for Continuing Education No. 7. San Francisco: Jossey-Bass, 1980.

Reith, Jack. "Group Methods: Conferences, Meetings, Workshops and Seminars." In *Training and Development Handbook,* 2d edition. Edited by Robert L. Craig. New York: McGraw-Hill, 1976, pp. 34-1 to 34-24.

Tough, Allen. *The Adult's Learning Projects*. Research in Education Series No. 1. Toronto: Ontario Institute for Studies in Education, 1971.

CHAPTER THREE

THE PLANNING PROCESS

The Elements of Effective Planning
Decisions to Consider
Implementation and Supervision

APPROACHES TO PLANNING

The Individual Planner
Advisory Committees
Staff Planning
Delphi and Nominal Group Techniques

TOOLS FOR EFFECTIVE PLANNING

Gantt Chart
Checklist
Critical Path Method

FACTORS AFFECTING OUTCOMES

The Clouded Crystal Ball
The Principles of War

PROGRAM PLANNING

This chapter deals with specific, short-term planning that may include next year's total evening class program at one extreme or a single one-day conference at the other. It does not deal with the five-year plan of the total organization. Overall and intermediate-range program planning are dealt with mainly in Chapter 10. A view of the long range is the subject of Chapter 13.

This chapter also discusses the general planning process—the elements of planning, what to include in the plan, and how to move from blueprint to action. It then goes on to consider some approaches to planning: planning by individuals, by advisory groups, by staffs, and by such techniques as Delphi and nominal group processes. The use of Gantt Charts, checklists, and critical path techniques are discussed. Finally the chapter looks at planning under conditions of risk and uncertainty and closes with a nod toward the planner as strategist.

M. S. Knowles's book, *The Modern Practice of Adult Education* and Cyril Houle's book *The Design of Education,* discuss planning models in a narrower context, but include a much broader concept of philosophy and assumption. In this chapter, models from other disciplines with some different techniques will be discussed.

THE PLANNING PROCESS

Planning may be viewed as a form of behavior that needs to be explained (nonrational models) or as a skill that can be learned (utility models).

The essence of one planning process, the organizational process model of explanation, is that outcomes are the result of the structure and manner of functioning of the organization. The planners are constrained by available channels of information, organizational routines, and the physical limitations and biases of the people on whom they depend. Thus the outcome is primarily determined by what might loosely be termed the habit patterns of the organization. For example, the data processing facilities and staff or the director of the conference center may dictate the range of possible outcomes. Administration controls can also be factors, as is the case, for example, when a dean of the graduate school decrees that credit courses must be held on campus. These constraints are internalized as organizational givens and decisions must be within this framework.

Another planning process, the bureaucratic politics model, sees the organization as composed of a number of cliques or political enclaves, with decisions being the outcome of a bargaining process that G. T. Allison describes as "compromise, coalition, competition and confusion among government officials who see different faces of an issue." It is a game, he says, and the players are people in jobs. The bureaucratic politics model leads to satisfying explanations of planning outcomes when planning is constrained by territorial imperatives—"You can't program for this group because they belong to Department A''—or when two parties vie for prime time on the educational television network.

The importance of this brief look at the nonrational models of the decision-making process lies in the need to recognize that the planning process takes place at best under conditions of what Herbert Simon calls "bounded rationality" and at worst under conditions that represent a flight from rationality altogether. Indeed the would-be rational planner must couple rational planning skills with high frustration tolerance, political acumen, and a talent for getting around procedural barriers and for climbing out of organizational ruts. Given this preparation, we are now ready to consider the utility models.

There is no single planning model that is universally accepted, partly because there is no one model that is universally applicable. There are, however, several elements that are common to most utility models:

1. a statement of objectives;

2. the systematic gathering and evaluation of facts;

3. the analysis of the situation in terms of strengths and weaknesses;

4. the use of appropriate tools such as statistics, flow charts, and computers for decision-making;

5. a major search effort to identify the complete feasible set of solutions or alternative courses of action;

6. a systematic testing of alternative decisions with a projection of probable outcomes for each;

7. a timely decision;

8. effective and efficient execution of the plan.

The following outline is an example of this model applied to an external degree project in long-term care administration.

A. The Objective: to provide a predominantly off-campus program of study leading to a Bachelor of Science degree in long-term care administration in order to increase the number of well-qualified administrators of nursing homes and other long-term care administrators.

B. Facts (For illustration, the fact-finding process is outlined in the form of questions needing to be answered rather than in the form of the answers themselves.)

   1. What is the present situation in terms of quantity and quality of practitioners in the field?

   2. What is the demand for practitioners?

   3. What are the licensing requirements in typical states?

   4. What are the things that a LTC administrator needs to know (1) to be fully effective, (2) to meet licensing requirements?

   5. Where are the students, what kinds of preparation do they have, how motivated will they be to pursue a degree as opposed to shorter routes to licensure and practice?

C. Strengths and weaknesses (a partial listing)

Strengths	*Weaknesses*
Increasing aging population	Existence of less-than bachelor's
Growing concern with health care	degree certification
Potential for federal funding	Competition from relatively
Favorable job market	low-cost, short-term programs
Competent available faculty	High expected dropout
Adequate existing office facilities	Barrier of high nonresident tuition
	Variation among states in licensing
	requirements
	Number of small, low-paying
	institutions
	Problems with accreditation

D. Analytic tools

   1. Probability analysis of demographic data

   2. Breakeven analysis

E. Courses of action

   1. Scrap the project

   2. Correspondence study format

   3. Off-campus classes with independent study

   4. Short-term residence plus independent study

   5. Group study

   6. Mediated instruction: audiocassettes, telephone and electrowriter network, programmed instruction

   7. Others

F. Testing alternatives (A detailed analysis is needed; the tests given here are simply illustrative.)

1. Development costs for this method
2. Evidence of its effectiveness
3. Continuing costs
4. Relation to existing resources and expertise
5. Attractiveness to students
6. Acceptance by the academic community and accrediting agencies

G. Decision: to offer a five-year course of study on a lockstep basis (enrollment accepted once a year, class progresses through the cycle as a parallel group) with three weeks of residence each year combined with independent study modules using study guides supplemented by audiocassettes and monthly progress tests.

H. Execution: detailed decisions as to curriculum, standards, staffing, marketing, and so on. Essentially execution answers the questions as to who will do what, when, how, and to whom. For example, "one item in the curriculum will be accounting and finance; this unit will consist of five modules on (1) basic accounting methods, (2) preparation and analysis of financial statements, (3) third-party reimbursement, (4) budgeting, and (5) cost control." It requires identification of the instructor(s), preparation of study materials, decisions regarding the servicing of the course, preparation of examinations, and all other decisions regarding the conduct of the unit.

The Elements of Effective Planning

The planning process begins with a problem situation—a perceived challenge or opportunity. In continuing education programming the problem is usually stated in terms of an unmet need. The objective then is defined as a desired future state of affairs that will have reduced or satisfied that need. Although it is not always possible to define objectives as precisely as we would like, they should be stated in terms of measurable outcomes: numbers of people to be reached, level of accomplishment intended, or dollars to be saved. Well-conceived objectives do not include such weasel words as *try, seek, hope,* or *attempt.* The objective also should specify the kind of learning outcome that is sought. Basically learning outcomes can be classified under three main headings:

1. *Knowledge.* English is one of the few Indo-European languages that does not have two separate words to distinguish between formal knowledge and what Elton Mayo has called "knowledge of acquaintance." In German, for example, one says *ich weiss* (I know about) history and *ich kenne* (I know about) my friends. Much learning involves acquiring formal knowledge of facts, understanding of theories, and other kinds of abstract mental operations.

2. *Skill.* Basically, skills are knowledge of acquaintance: familiarity with tools, dexterity in using them, and facility in dealing with people and situations. The

ideal measures of these kinds of outcomes are in what a person can do rather than what he or she can say or write.

3. *Attitudes.* Attitudinal learning has to do with values, beliefs, interests and the ways in which people react because of them. A program designed to increase citizen participation in politics seeks to increase interest in the political process with the expectation that as a result more of the participants will vote, or run for office, or otherwise become politically involved.

Many educational programs are intended to increase knowledge and skill as well as to change attitudes, but usually the primary emphasis is on one of the three. The program plan as to content, method, and staffing will differ as a function of intended outcome. Teaching people to assemble their own hi-fi sets is quite different than teaching people something about the influence of Albert Einstein on modern scientific thought, although both may be taught by physicists.

The objective is not cast in concrete. It initiates and gives direction to the decision-making process, but the end result may be abandonment of the objective, a decision to defer, or a review and restatement of the objective. Objectives are statements of purpose that are fundamental to any undertaking. As Peter Drucker warns, if we are to succeed we first need to know what business we are in.

The second stage of planning—the gathering and evaluation of facts—is subject to two main diseases both of which reach epidemic proportions in many organizational settings. The first is the jump from an objective to a decision without sufficient considerations of the intervening steps, and the second is the overintellectualization of the decision process because of the need for certainty. People tend to differ in their decision-making style. Those with a strong aversion to risk and uncertainty will put off decisions until the intended action has to be scrapped for obsolescence. As Lord Halifax once said, "He that leaveth nothing to chance will do few things ill, but he will do very few things." The impulsive decision-maker will be up to his or her hips in the swamp before concluding that it would have been a good idea to test the ground before going ahead. Figure 3.1 is a simple graphic representation of the time to decide. That time can be defined as the point at which the descending curve of decisional obsolescence (when time reduces the value of a decision) intersects the ascending curve of certainty. What it suggests is that there needs to be a balancing of risk against timeliness. The slope and form of the two curves may differ, the time coordinates may vary from one situation to another, and conflicting priorities may dictate deviations but, in general, the best decisions are those that result from the best possible factual foundation that can be attained within a reasonable span of time.

The passage of the Occupational Safety and Health Act of 1970 provides a ready example. The Act was far-reaching in its consequences for business, government, and labor and was a complicated piece of legislation. There was a clear need to develop educational programs that would inform people about its effects. It was evident, however, that the market for such programming was limited and timing was important. Those with a strong academic base responded early with programs and established their audiences and their reputations. Latecomers found the market in a state of decline.

Figure 3.1. *The time to decide*

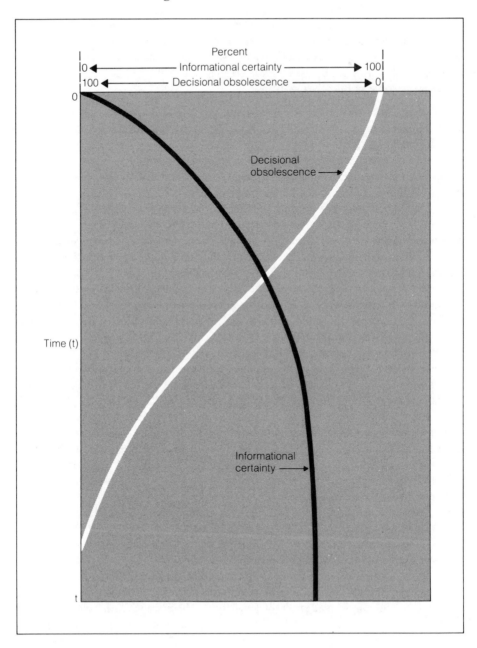

What kinds of facts are needed? This will vary greatly from one situation to another, but there are a few main categories of facts. They involve some knowledge of the characteristics of the target audience, the availability of course materials, the lead time on promotional materials, the availability of speakers, accommodations for meetings, overnight and meal arrangements and other factual data both of a general nature and also some that may be specific to the program and target audience. For example, in many communities it is important to know that people from Podunk are very disinclined to attend activities held in Endsville and vice versa. It is important to remember that retail merchants will not turn out for a program between Thanksgiving and Christmas and that foremen in northern Minnesota will not be available on the opening day of deer season or of trout season.

After the essential facts are marshalled it is helpful to set up a balance sheet of strengths and weaknesses to help in formulating program strategy. The purpose of such a balance sheet is to help answer two complementary questions: (1) What are the strengths that we can build on? and (2) What are the weaknesses that we need to correct or to build around? For example, we may conclude that we have on our staff the leading authority in the country for this topic but that he is a notoriously bad lecturer, or we may want to capitalize on our excellent videoplayback equipment and avoid the dangers of nondelivery of a film that is in high demand.

More will be said about some decision-making tools later in this chapter. Generally the sophisticated tools of decision-makers—statistical decision theory, operations research, PERT and the critical path method (CPM), and game theory have limited value for planning the typical continuing education project, although they may have considerable utility for large-scale program planning. Perhaps the most useful tool for simple project planning is a good management information system that can produce data about registrations in previous similar programs, the number of registrations that result on the average for programs held in a particular location, or the response to programs that had certain cosponsors. Also when survey data are available and when there is a background of experience in using survey data with particular audiences, some applied probability theory may be preferable to intuitive judgments.

Survey data can, for example, establish the size of the total possible audience in a given geographic area for a bilingual course in American history for Spanish-speaking people; it can then provide some indication of the extent of interest among this group, what fee they are willing to pay, and what time and place would be most attractive. By identifying the age, educational level and other demographic factors associated with individuals with the highest level of interest, survey results can help with selection of location, timing, fee-setting, and, as is often especially important in dealing with ethnic groups, who might best cosponsor the program.

Students of the decision-making process seem to agree that the most common shortcoming of problem solvers is that they allocate insufficient time and effort to the search for alternative solutions. The ideal search process is one in which all feasible alternative solutions are identified. All too often decision-makers either arrive at this stage with a predetermined solution in mind or they drop the search prematurely. The common expression "jumping to a conclusion" aptly describes this behavior. Simple logic tells us that the odds of making a ''best'' decision are dependent on the completeness in the listing of alternatives, and experience with brainstorming tells us that the best solution may come out fairly late in the process. Programmers in continuing education are probably at least as prone to jumping to conclusions as are most other planners. They tend to favor certain formats and ways of doing things. Programmers who start with the premise that they need to plan a conference to meet a given need have already foreclosed the possibility that a videocassette or a self-study course may better accomplish the basic objective.

The search for alternative courses of action will result in a number of alternatives that can be ruled out readily after some reasonable consideration. They can be ruled out because upon close examination they will not accomplish the objective or are not feasible due to cost, availability of resources, or time constraints. The remaining alternatives are the ones that need to be weighed in a cost/benefit analysis and in a kind of mental war game where the impact of competition and other external circumstances can be systematically considered.

The final stage in the planning phase is the execution of a course of action. This will be discussed in the section, ''Implementation and Supervision,'' but there are details that must be considered before execution. Some of these may have already entered into the planning process and some bridge the gap between the decision and its implementation.

Decisions to Consider

There are a number of decisions that have to be made as a project moves from the initial idea to the final implementation. We have divided some of the most important into two major categories: primary considerations, which affect the basic decision to go or not go, and secondary considerations, which are part of any program plan and which allow a fairly wide range of discretion as to how to proceed. These two sets of items bring the planner face-to-face with the decisions that spell success or failure.

PRIMARY CONSIDERATIONS   We have divided the primary considerations into eight topics. Some have been touched on in the preceding section but are re-examined here because they bridge the gap between planning and execution of the plan, and because they will need to be developed in greater detail in the implementation phase.

Assumptions   In military strategy manuals, assumptions are defined as conditions that must be met if a plan is to succeed. Urban dwellers are not greatly bothered by the assumption that they will survive the morning rush hour in order to begin the day's work. In planning, however, there are assumptions with a higher level of probability that need to be made explicit, since they relate to events that require contingency plans. There are a wide array of assumptions to be concerned with, such as philosophical and environmental, but most are implied. For example in northern latitudes programmers make assumptions about the weather in the snow months. Crucial speakers become ill regardless of weather and climate. Events such as these have a high probability of occurrence, so they need to be considered in advance and provision made to deal with them.

To continue with the example of an external degree in long-term care administration, one of the basic assumptions might be that a minimal input of thirty students with an average annual attrition of no more than 10 percent would be maintained, this assumption being essential to adequate funding and program continuity.

Audience   While the audience has been considered in the need assessment and initial planning stages, a closer look is required as the detailed plan unfolds. Do we need to restrict the audience in any way: an enrollment limit, special qualifications or exclusions, or the achievement of some desired mix of participants? What level of sophistication will they have? Can we reasonably expect that this group will make any advance preparation? Are there certain topics that they will want dealt with? Too many programs fail because of insufficient information about the characteristics and pre-occupations of the audience.

In the long-term care administration program, several audience characteristics might emerge as central considerations in program planning. An example would be weakness in quantitative subjects. Another would be reluctance of practitioners to work at what they perceive to be purely theoretical subjects. Thus in planning courses in accounting, computer science, and statistics, care needs to be taken to make the material seem as directly relevant as possible. Lifting materials bodily from an existing general undergraduate course is likely to significantly increase course attrition.

Competition   Continuing education offerings are a form of consumer goods. Markets become saturated, prices get cut, some packages are more attractive than others. The response to any program is directly related to the conditions in the market place, especially when more than one agency is operating in the same area. The word *competition* conveys an image of an adversary relationship, which is sometimes the case. In other instances it may simply be a matter of insufficient communication. Whatever the problem, precautions are necessary to insure that two or more programs do not cancel each other out.

The planned program in long-term care administration has to be looked at in terms of the limited market potential. The number of similar programs in the expected market area needs to be surveyed. How many programs are there, at what price, of what duration, and at what quality level? Trade journals, trade associations, and accrediting agencies can provide a reasonably complete picture and will indicate that there are an adequate number of acceptable opportunities available if one disregards the added value of the degree and the attractiveness of the opportunity to pursue that degree while fully employed. The programmer might find that there is no competition for this type of program in the proposed market area.

Content   The identification of a need and the decision to proceed with a program may still leave a great many specifics undecided. After the decision is made, for example, to offer a program for the recently divorced or separated person, the topics that should be dealt with need to be identified. The programmer is in danger of overlooking important topics or may be overwhelmed with more ideas than can be managed within a reasonable time frame. Some consultation with advisory groups, conversations with experts and potential participants, and scouting of the competition may be needed to put the final program together. It most often is necessary to brief speakers on topics that they should include in their presentations or to indicate topics that will be dealt with by someone else.

As noted in the preceding section, the presentation of course content can be the key to the success of the program. The long-term care administration student will be faced in most institutions with a set of requirements that are imposed on the program planner by general institutional policy and requirements. There may be no choice as to whether computer science or statistics will be required. The key to survival may lie very largely in adapting formal requirements to needs as perceived by the students. Fortunately, there are texts for basic introductory courses that are designed for various occupational specialties, and study guides can be developed that relate other text materials to the particular group. If there is no suitable text in introductory statistics for nursing home administrators, there is one for people in the health care system, and study guide development can complete the process of adaption to the clientele.

Cost   The curse of cost overruns is not peculiar to contractors. Costs have a habit of escalating in any but the simplest kinds of programming. The speaker who cost a few hundred dollars in 1970 may ask for a four-digit fee today. The computer terminal hookup may be essential but it may be expensive. The team of presenters may include someone who expects to travel first class from the other side of the continent. Cost factors will affect not only the final planning details and the pricing decision but also the decision in some instances as to whether to go ahead with the program or not.

The plan for the program in long-term care administration will include a budget proposal that covers all expected costs—overhead, instructional staff, promotion, travel, secretarial—in short, the whole cost of operation. Decisions will need to be made about using a toll-free number and its cost, the cost of recording and reproduction of audiocassettes, the preparation and reproduction of study guides, mail costs, and other items that are a part of the external degree plan.

Methods   The decision as to the method relates to general program format: class, conference, workshop, clinic, broadcast, independent study, personalized instruction, demonstration, and so on. As was noted in the preceding section, programmers have a tendency to fall into habit patterns with respect to their choice of program formats. It is wise to consider several program formats, especially as this relates to the program objectives. It makes little sense, for example, to refer to skill attainment in the statement of objectives and then to run the program entirely by a lecture discussion method.

The basic choice of methods in the example of long-term care administration was made as part of the general decision to proceed. However, as the detailed plan is developed, further consideration must be given to methods employed. Should we use a speech compressor for the audio tapes; how should the progress examinations be handled; how shall we handle the laboratory part of the computer science course; how will we synchronize the necessary visual materials with the audiocassette presentations? The problem and, to some extent, the advantage, in a full degree program as contrasted with a single offering, is that a variety of approaches may be needed not only to sustain interest but also to adapt the instructional methods to the various course contents.

Staffing   We have touched on the question of staffing in the context of the initial planning stage and as it relates to cost. Getting the best possible staff goes beyond either the identification of potential staff or cost. It involves careful checking with knowledgeable people on the names and track records of several possible candidates, and finally it involves competent preparation for this particular program. The programmer's job is one not only of good selection but also of providing orientation for the instructors.

The special problem in staffing an entire external degree program is that many people with appropriate subject matter expertise cannot present it in terms directly applicable to the students' special interest. Most students are not terribly imaginative in making the transfer from an example, say, of a scheduling problem in a paint factory to a problem in a nursing home, and instructors who have not worked in a health care setting may have equal difficulty in adapting their examples to this setting. The program coordinator may have to search for teaching staff on the basis of a combination of academic competence, relevant experience, and adaptability. One instructor may be married to a doctor or a nurse, another may have worked in a hospital, another may be a consultant to the health care industry. There are more of these happy combinations than one might guess. Other instructors have a talent for adapting to a specialized need. The coordinator can accomplish a great deal in the latter instance simply by adequate briefing of the prospective instructor. Such helps can include a reprint or two of relevant articles from a trade journal, providing copies of relevant cases from the Intercollegiate Case Clearinghouse, or by having the instructor talk with one or two members of the professional advisory group.

Timing   We discussed timing considerations as part of the fact-gathering process. The selection of a best time goes beyond merely avoiding bad times. It includes decisions about season of the year, days of the week, time of the day, and the relationship between the proposed program and outside events as well as the fit with other activities within the unit. Unless the planner has exceptional knowledge of the proposed audience, a few visits or telephone calls may be a good safeguard against unexpected problems. Who outside of the target group could have foreseen that budget hearings would affect the attendance of social work supervisors on a particular date in October?

The timing of our program in long-term care administration may involve care, for example, in the selection of a time for the three-week residential period on campus. Admissions tend to drop off during the summer months, there tend to be fewer crises of care, there is a lull in the visits of licensing agencies, and a breather in Medicare-Medicaid reports, Social Security, and Workmen's Compensation submissions. This may also be a good time, in some localities, to make some of the family's summer vacation expense tax deductible. July 12–26 may, upon investigation, be an excellent time to hold the on-campus residential program. One does not plan to attract certified public accountants between January 15 and April 15, or hunters on the opening weekend of deer season.

SECONDARY CONSIDERATIONS   After the primary decisions have been made, and once the program is going forward with the basics decided, there are several secondary decisions that need to be made. Seven of these will be dealt with briefly in this section.

Amenities   Small items can do a great deal to enhance the program. Should we have an informal gathering before the program begins? Coffee and doughnuts at the break? A dinner meeting? Shall we ask the Dean to give a few words of welcome at the opening session? Do we want to have some simple closing ceremony? Who will give out the certificates of completion? What time limit should we set on the Dean's welcome? What briefing does the Dean need in order to say some of the right things?

Duration   The length of the program, number of hours or number of days is usually determined in part by the content and number of speakers, but the length of the program should be reviewed as the final pieces are being fitted together. Inexperienced programmers are prone to put too many topics and speakers into too small a time frame. As a result the participants either feel they are being rushed through each stage, or the program runs constantly behind schedule. Among other undesirable side effects is the disgruntled speaker whose carefully prepared presentation has to be pruned drastically near the end or who faces a dwindling audience as people leave to catch their planes. In this final review of the program's time span the time may need to be increased or the number of speakers and topics reduced. The length of the instructional day also needs to be considered, both to fit work and travel schedules of participants and to provide for whatever discretionary time participants need for programmatic or personal reasons.

Location   Frequently the programmer has little discretion with respect to where a program is held. If it is possible to select a location—to remain on or to go off campus, for example—location decisions may have a great deal to do with a program's success. When the participants' expenses are fully reimbursed or tax-deductible, a ski resort or seaside hotel may increase attendance. It may also increase the distractions. Moves to untried resorts or hotels may also increase the number of things that can go wrong. Anyone who has tried to lead a discussion of prenatal care in the room next to a Tupperware sales meeting, or tried to find a replacement bulb for the overhead projector when miles away from home base, knows that outside locations need to be checked out very carefully.

Media In spite of the media revolution proclaimed by the Carnegie Commission, a great many programs fall short of expectations because the use of media has not been well planned in advance. A program intended to develop interviewing skills, for example, may fail to take advantage of readily available videoplayback equipment. Transparencies suitable for an audience of twenty may be projected for an audience of two hundred, with the speaker saying, "I know you can't read most of that so I'll read it to you." There may be a last minute scramble for masking tape to attach flip chart sheets around the walls of the room. Or at the other extreme, overenchantment with audiovisual displays may lead to overuse of equipment, the content becoming swallowed up by the media.

Pricing There are two major pricing considerations: what it will take to break even and what the traffic will bear. Added to these two considerations may be a profit objective. In some operations breakeven may mean recovery of expenses that are paid out for the course, excluding salaries and facilities and other costs that are already paid for; this often is called out-of-pocket expenses. In others the breakeven point may include recovery of indirect cost. In subsidized operations there may also be a breakeven point that is less than out-of-pocket costs. Failure to meet the breakeven point on enrollments may require that the program be cancelled or a decision be made to take some loss with the expectation of recovery on more successful programs. The criterion of what the traffic will bear brings in the second figure in the equation: how many people can be expected to enroll at various fee levels? How the equation is set depends to a degree on what constraints are imposed. If, for example, the intent is to limit enrollment of a maximum of thirty people and a minimum of twenty, then the fee might be set so that the breakeven point would be an enrollment of twenty. The number over twenty would then provide some discretionary dollars for program improvements or for carryover to some other purpose.

Procedures A number of procedural details have to be included in the planning process if the program is to run smoothly: arrangements for registration, room reservations, meals, name cards and tags, inscribing certificates, recording credits, preparation of handouts, and general logistics. In a professionally run conference center many of these are taken care of automatically by the center staff. Even in the best-managed operations, however, the participants will rightly hold the program coordinator responsible if things go wrong. Checklists and checkups are part of the planning process.

Promotion As part of the planning process promotion needs to be considered primarily in relation to the ability to reach the target audience and the cost of doing so. The specifics of this phase of planning will be covered in Chapter 5.

Implementation and Supervision

The execution of a plan may involve a task force of considerable magnitude or it may be carried out entirely by one person. In either case, the basic tasks are the same. The essence of a good plan is that it has left nothing to chance in the development of the blueprint and specifications. However, the final building can be a mess if the assignment of tasks, the coordination and timing of activities, and the quality assurance functions are not carried out continuously. If implementation is to be a team effort, assignments need to be made and the assignees need to be given the necessary instructions as well as supplies and equipment required for getting their jobs done. Omitting these elementary steps toward implementation is a common cause of failure with the best of plans.

An old familiar adage traces events from the loss of a nail in a horseshoe to the loss of a battle. In a somewhat similar vein a nearly catastrophic program failure occurred in one institution when a major bulk mailing got lost somewhere in the postal service. A simple check of one or two names on the mailing list would have revealed the problem early on. "A simple check" in this instance means that someone should have been assigned that responsibility and notice taken that the check had been made.

When the essential tasks have all been determined, with assignments made and action begun, administrative responsibility moves to the control phase. The elements of control are feedback, measurement of results against standards, and corrective action. Enrollments are illustrative of this process. The possibility of having to cancel the program must be kept in mind. If the promotion has been chiefly through direct mail advertisements, there will usually be a pattern of returns—a few early ones, a buildup to a peak, and then a tapering off. As the deadline for cancellation nears, a daily report on returns is needed to see what the pattern is. The standard may be simply an expectation based on experience, but whatever the standards, a significant deviation may signal the need for corrective action—a second mailing, telephone calls to potential enrollees, or an effort to reach other target groups than those reached in the first promotion. Planning tools that can help in the supervision of the plan will be dealt with later in this chapter.

APPROACHES TO PLANNING

Some planners go by the book, methodical down to the last detail. At the other extreme are planners who proceed almost entirely on intuition. The former may get lost in a maze of detail and the latter may be destroyed by an excess of loose ends. On the other hand, both may be successful, the main difference between them being, simply, the extent to which they do their planning activities on paper or in their heads. The danger of keeping the planning process in the head of one planner becomes evident in large-scale planning. Planning done on a large scale requires teamwork, and planning that can rely on a strong staff backup requires a more explicitly methodical approach since it requires communication with others. But not everyone directs a sizable staff.

Some lone programmers are grateful to have even part-time secretarial help, and for them planning is largely a solitary activity of necessity relying more on an intuitive approach. In this section we will deal with the planner as an individual and with some approaches to planning in group settings.

The Individual Planner

The requirements for becoming a successful individual planner are not too different from those of the planner who operates in a group setting. The chief difference is that all of these qualities must be incorporated in one body. In some ways the individual planner has an advantage since he or she does not have to contend with some of the pathologies of group action: the formation of cliques, the digressions that lead nowhere, the tendency to belabor the obvious, or to conclude that more study is needed. Individual planners are better able to keep a clear objective in mind, to use methods of planning that they are comfortable with, and to close the gap between thought and action more quickly. They pay the price however of operating usually with a smaller information base, a narrower perspective, and without the checks and balances that characterize effective group action.

There is a greater burden on the individual planner to foresee how the plan will work. There is a greater danger of overlooking some important considerations and there is the everpresent problem of having only two hands and two feet at times when four or more of each are needed. The wise individual planner will offset some of these difficulties by using volunteer help whenever possible. This volunteer help may be an advisory committee, cosponsors, volunteer helpers, or a combination of these. Some volunteers will work for recognition alone and others will be attracted by a complimentary registration. Many will bring more enthusiasm and energy to the task than someone else's salaried staff.

Advisory Committees

Advisory committees may comprise people from outside the organization, from within it, or both. We have discussed advisory committees in the context of need assessment. The same advisory committee can also serve as a planning group, or a separate committee may be needed since the inputs related to need may be quite different from those involved in planning the program. An advisory committee may provide input as to content, speakers, location and timing, and methods. They cannot be held responsible for the working blueprints but are likely to be most helpful in developing the specifications or in serving as a reactor panel after the working drawings have reached the first draft stage.

An advisory group will function best if the program's objectives are kept before the members at all times, and if the chief planner provides only enough structure to the meetings for the group to accomplish these objectives. There is a tendency on the part of many people who work with advisory groups to spend too much time briefing the group and too little time listening. A minimum of background information followed by a series of well-framed questions is the best approach to insuring the group's success.

Staff Planning

Business and industry in recent years have made extensive use of task groups for product development. A borrowing from military planners, the task group concept has been corrupted in some instances into nothing more than another name for a committee. As the name implies it is considerably more than that. A task group in its strictest sense is a staff group that has been assigned a specific task to perform. In industry it is commonly created to carry a product from the idea stage to the production and marketing stage, or alternatively to the point where the idea is finally scrapped. Such groups are set up so that a combination of talents can be brought to bear on the task. Membership will typically include someone from each of several departments: research and development, finance, production, and marketing. They are usually detached from their day-to-day responsibilities and instructed to devote their full attention to the development of the new product. Upon completion of the task they are made available for reassignment. This type of team action has proven highly successful in a number of businesses and industries.

The application to continuing education is appropriate when dealing with major program efforts but can also be used in modified form for lesser efforts when task group membership is a part-time rather than a full-time assignment. The membership is determined by the appropriate mix of skills needed to carry out the project. It clearly presupposes a reasonable diversity of available staff specializations. Such a task group might consist of someone with special competence in program content, another with special knowledge of the target audience, another with expertise in program promotion, and still another with specialization in methods and media.

A staff planning effort of this sort was carried out in one institution when the decision was made to do a pilot effort using cable TV. The task group was composed of three kinds of people—those with special media expertise, those with subject matter or clientele expertise who had used similar media in the past, and those with experience in providing support services. The problem was to produce enough quality programming at a given maximum cost to constitute a fair test of the medium as a future vehicle for programming. The cable channel was available, the budget was set, and the task group was given full authority and responsibility for planning and executing the program. Some courses had already been developed totally or in part for cassette, videotape, or film presentation. Additional courses or presentations were developed as part of the overall plan, and the administrative functions of promotion, registration, and student contacts were assigned to members of the task force or farmed out to the appropriate departments. In this case, in spite of what everyone agreed was a reasonable effort and a limited success, the conclusion was that future time and effort could be better spent on other kinds of programming.

Such an outcome is not evidence that staff task forces are likely to be ineffective. Their value, as in some industries, is probably greatest when new product development is the goal and, as always, the development of truly new products is charged with uncertainty. As with oil well drilling, the result may be a strong flow, a trickle, or a dry hole but only through such exploration can significant new resources be developed.

In addition to the direct value in program development, the task group has two important secondary benefits: first, each member of the group has a vested interest in the program (something they do not have if they merely serve as outside consultants), which becomes a significant source of motivation; and second, task group involvement becomes a valuable training and proving ground for staff development.

Delphi and Nominal Group Techniques

Every planner who has worked extensively with group planning knows that a well-constituted group is not enough. Frequently the remaining challenge is to use the group productively. Productive use may be defined simply as sending the members away better informed or as having induced them to put their seal of approval on a predetermined course of action. More often the goal is to garner their collective wisdom in order to have a better program. Since the group operates under a time constraint, the challenge is to find a way of maximizing group input within the available time. We have earlier mentioned the use of subgroups for this purpose. This use of subgroups has been around for quite some time under such names as *buzz groups* and *Phillips 66*. The Delphi and nominal group techniques are of more recent vintage, having come into extensive use as planning techniques only in the decade of the seventies. There are a number of variations on both, and a detailed treatment on their use can be found in *Group Techniques for Program Planning* by A. L. Delbecq and associates. In simplified form, however, they can be used without elaborate preparation. The following account is intended to provide enough information so that the planner could experiment on his or her own.

DELPHI TECHNIQUE   Named after the Greek oracle at the temple of Delphi who could foretell the future, the Delphi technique was developed at the Rand Corporation in the 1960s as a tool for technological forecasting. The wider application to planning in general came in the 1970s. The Delphi technique does not use face-to-face interaction. In an illustrative example, a staff group prepares a questionnaire and sends it by mail to a selected group of respondents, for example, absentee landlords identified by tax rolls. The respondents are asked to complete the questionnaire and return it without consulting anyone else. The staff group summarizes the responses and prepares a second questionnaire, which may be simply a set of true-false statements, based on the first set of responses. The summary and the second questionnaire are then sent to the respondents, with the request that they now independently re-evaluate their original responses and vote their preferences or priorities on the ideas included in the second questionnaire. After the second or maybe the third or fourth set of responses are received, a summary is made and sent to the decision-makers and the respondents.

One obvious advantage of the Delphi technique is that people can be involved who would be difficult to bring together in a face-to-face group because of cost and time considerations. A difficulty equally obvious is to obtain a significant response rate. In program planning the most feasible use of Delphi would be in a situation where a highly committed, geographically dispersed group of experts were sought for the planning phase: a planning committee appointed by the officers of a national professional association, for example.

NOMINAL GROUP TECHNIQUE   Unlike the Delphi technique, nominal groups are face-to-face groups. The difference between the nominal group and other face-to-face groups, and the reason for the term nominal, is that in the initial stage the members of the group do not interact with one another. It is thus at this stage a group in name only. Each member of the group writes down his or her ideas. After a period of time, commonly five or ten minutes, the recorder goes around the room taking one idea from each participant in order and repeating this procedure until none of the participants have any more ideas to offer. Each idea is written on a flip chart or blackboard. After all ideas have been recorded, they are discussed by the group. Once the discussion is completed each member votes independently on priorities and the group decision is the composite rank-ordering or rating of the members.

Both Delphi and nominal group techniques can be used with lay advisory groups or with staff planners. Both have the virtue of encouraging independent thinking by the people involved and, under the best of conditions, insure a higher level of individual input than is usually obtained from unstructured groups. They also reduce the likelihood that the group will be dominated by the discussion leader or by a few individuals. In addition, the nominal group technique or a variant thereof can be used as a fallback procedure if an advisory group does not seem to come to life as expected.

TOOLS FOR EFFECTIVE PLANNING

Despite the fact that no one universally applicable planning model or set of approaches exists, we have been able to identify a number of considerations that have proven important to many successful planning efforts. In the same way, no one planning tool could possibly fit all program situations. In the following, we discuss three commonly used tools that, when appropriately employed, are useful in facilitating effective program planning.

Gantt Chart

A Gantt Chart is a simple means of identifying tasks and indicating their duration on some kind of time scale. It can be useful for simple programs in which timing is critical. Because a Gantt Chart is easy to explain to others, it is also an aid in selling a program to superiors or to funding agencies. Figure 3.2 illustrates how the Gantt Chart can be used to depict typical activities for planning a course. The planner should keep

Figure 3.2. *Gantt Chart for planning an evening course starting April 15*

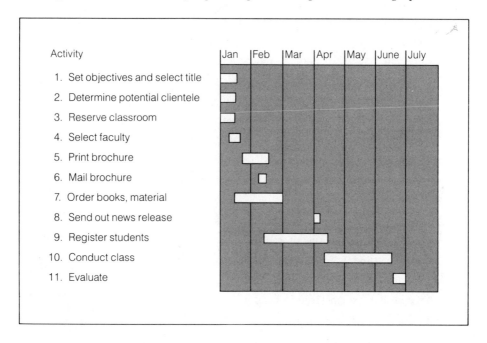

in mind that, from the stage of setting course objectives to that of evaluating results, the involvement of many other persons may be necessary.

The Gantt Chart effectively shows the critical nature of a planner's time schedule, and the need for completion of activities by specified dates. To enhance effective use of the Gantt Chart, some planners use differently colored lines to indicate progress being made on and completion of the particular activity.

Keeping programs on schedule and understanding time limitations are very important aspects of planning. If the program becomes extremely complex, however, other tools are available to assist the planner more effectively.

Checklist

In developing any program, a planner must be sure to consider every element necessary to a successful completion of the program. When problems arise, the cause is often the neglect of apparently insignificant details. For instance, the fact that someone has forgotten to order a projector on time may detract considerably from what otherwise would have been an outstanding lecture. Having a checklist helps prevent such occurrences and therefore can function as a good tool for organization.

To insure that the list is actually checked, the checklist and its use can be assigned to a secretary or program aide who can make it a high-priority item on the work schedule. The following is one such itemization of activities that typically occur during the last two weeks preceding a short course, in what might be called the final preparation stage. The list should be reviewed each day until all items are completed.

- Make tentative arrangements with a restaurant
- Order all visual aids and equipment required by speaker
- Make arrangements for session breaks, either self-service or served
- Duplicate all material identified for handout purposes
- Send materials to be assembled in notebook form
- Tell personnel about materials to be prepared
- Confirm that certificates are ordered
- Check on the use of a final exam
- Contact workshop assistants
- Revise and construct biographical outlines for "Meet Your Staff"
- Make hotel reservations on request
- Send hotel literature and reservation card to speakers
- Prepare instructional approval form
- Prepare handout material in handout form
- Prepare "Meet Your Staff"
- Sign certificates
- Finalize computer arrangements
- Finalize restaurant arrangement: place cards, head table, P.A. system, bar
- Confirm luncheon arrangements
- Inform instructors of make-up of participants
- Secure visual aids
- Assist in preparation of exam
- Deliver required materials to location of meeting
- Check final room set-up and equipment
- Check registration set-up
- Check break set-up
- Make arrangements for messages to be sent to meeting room

Checklists are most effective when they do not have activities needing to be done at different times. For example, a list that has an item, "Make auditorium reservations," which occurs six months before another item, "Check the lectern lights before lecture time," will often not be used. It is better to break the checklist up into weekly activities. If the activities can be completed in one week, the checklist will be more effective; the person responsible can look ahead to see what needs to be done, and then use that same list at the end of the week to assure that everything has been done.

Critical Path Method

The Critical Path Method (CPM) is probably the most used tool in formal planning today. It is also called Precedence Network, and it can be applicable to both small and large programs. When the system becomes extremely complex, a computer can be used to determine the critical path and, in some cases, draw the network. CPM determines minimum completion time and cost. There are techniques for scheduling activities to adjust for limited manpower availability. In educational programs, however, this is seldom required.

The guiding idea of CPM is to arrange activities in such a way that they form a network revealing the critical path, in fact, the shortest time in which the program can be completed. Developing the network requires (1) identifying all activities that need to be completed to carry out the program, (2) determining the sequence of activities, their timing and relation one to another, (3) determining the minimum duration of each activity, and (4) the cost of that activity. The method most commonly used is a series of arrows intersecting circles. In organizational charts and other kinds of diagramming, the circle usually signifies an event or person; whereas in CPM the line between the circles is the meaningful activity. The circles mean little in and of themselves. Very often, however, the circles are numbered, and these numbers are used in the computer program, which later determines the critical path, shortest time, and cost.

The network of Figure 3.3 reads from left to right, with the earliest time on the left so that the first activity is to select the planning committee and plan the preliminary program. This activity generally requires about eighteen days and costs approximately one hundred dollars. The second activity is to conduct the program planning meeting, at which time the soundness of the program idea is determined. Here the date is selected, speaker suggestions made, and program content discussed.

In Figure 3.3 the activities that can take place next are, "Plan final program," "Reserve room, meal, break at center," or "Reservations for dinner." Once the program is made firm through the activity "Plan final program," then speakers may be hired. After that, the program can be prepared. In other words, develop the brochure. It should be noted that the reservations for dinner must be completed before the program brochure is prepared, since it contains the location of that dinner. This is why the "Reservation for dinner" arrow ends just before the activity "Prepare program." And so it goes on throughout the network. Studying Figure 3.3 for a time will provide the sense of what is taking place. It must be remembered that the lines are the activities, and the circles simply starting and stopping points.

Notice also that the critical path in this figure lies along the straight line shown. What it tells is that once one activity is completed, the other activity on the critical path should be undertaken. When moments of freedom occur during that period, one can get involved in other activities not on the critical path but still having to be done in order to complete the program. For instance, printing the program requires thirty-one days. While this work is being done by a printer, the program director can turn to activities that are not on the critical path, including ordering mailing lists and envelopes, filing instructional approval forms, sending letters to speakers, and printing certificates.

Figure 3.3. *Two-day institute planning network (Department of Engineering, University of Wisconsin Extension)*

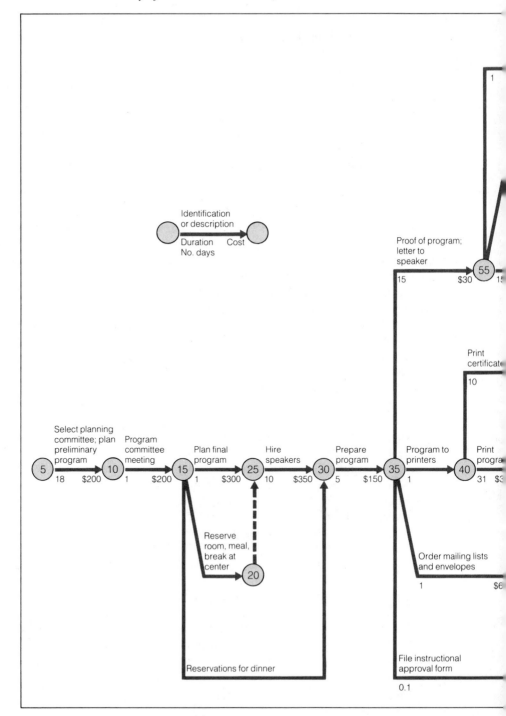

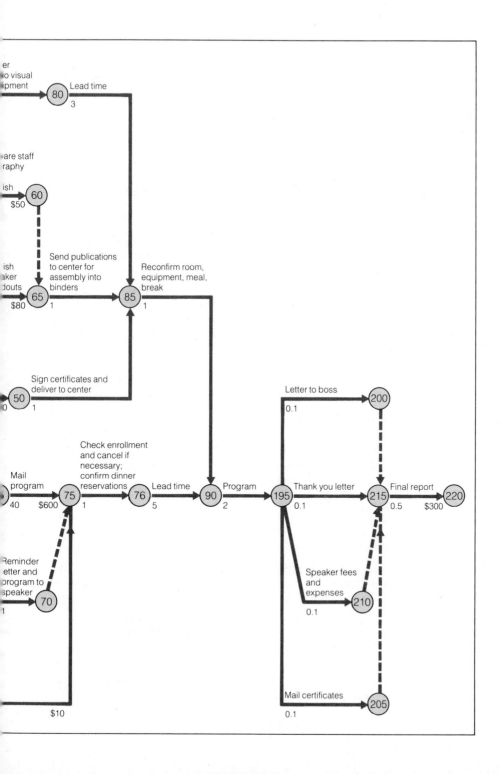

As programs become extremely complex, involving a hundred or more activities, a computer may be useful in determining the critical path. However, the logical, sequential development by the planner is still required to determine what activities may precede other activities.

Because people tend to do the things they enjoy, tasks that are on the critical path are quite often not done. This can delay the entire program. The critical path defines those tasks that must be completed in sequence, and those tasks that can wait without affecting the completion date.

This very logical sequencing of activities constitutes one of the advantages of using the critical path method for planning and scheduling. It forces the planner to think in this manner, and helps to eliminate the possibility that certain activities may be forgotten or overlooked. This particular sample network has been used in a general way for many programs of different subject content. Use of this sample network makes it easy to schedule programs and keep track of progress that is being made prior to conducting the program. The network also serves as a training tool that can be given to someone not familiar with sequencing of activities or program planning in general. Another advantage of the network becomes evident in the event that the program director is required to suddenly turn over responsibilities to someone else. The existing network readily shows the progress that has been made and the exact status of each one of the programs under the director's responsibility.

A more sophisticated method developed by the military is the Program Evaluation and Review Technique (PERT). It uses the same principles as CPM but allows a probability factor to be included in projecting the time, which makes the time planning more detailed and more accurate.

FACTORS AFFECTING OUTCOMES

Murphy's Law, Robert Burns's lines about the best laid plans of mice and men, and some perverted logic, have explained away too much bad planning. The ghost of Aristotle should haunt the believers in this strange syllogism.

Some good plans turn out badly.

This plan turned out badly.

Therefore it is a good plan.

Most planning failures are not the result of the strange and inscrutable ways of Fate. They are human failures. This is especially likely to be the case in short-range planning. This chapter, as noted earlier, is concerned with the immediate future, which encompasses a variable span of time. For a simple program, a two-day workshop for example, the span of a few months from concept to completion is a period of minimal risk. On the other hand, a building program is a short-range planning program with a life cycle of three to five years and subject to all the uncertainties of cost overruns, strikes, changing technology, legislative or donor caprice, and economic and social change. The longer the span the greater the uncertainty.

One difference then between the successful and the unsuccessful planner lies in the ability to contend with risk and uncertainty. Contending with risk and uncertainty does not imply avoidance of either. Some very successful planners have a significant number of failures simply because they allocate a portion of their effort and resources to innovative experiments and count on a favorable payoff ratio of successes over failures. And even their failures are instructive. Thus a primary difference between successful and unsuccessful planners is in the relative difficulty of their undertakings as well as in the number of successful completions. The remainder of this chapter deals with some of the factors that make the difference between successful and unsuccessful planning.

The Clouded Crystal Ball

Plans may fail because of what lawyers call ''acts of God.'' Broadly construed this might include anything that cannot be foreseen or controlled by the planner: blizzards, floods, and tornadoes. Just this side of the unforeseeable lies another category of events that resist but do not totally defy prediction: the outcomes of elections, energy shortages, strikes, revolutions, and the acts of government. Most other planning crises are defects in the planning process or in the execution of the plan: human errors. This latter group of problems are, to a significant degree, under the control of the planner; and to the extent that they are not the result of poor planning procedures, they are most likely to be the result of poor forecasting.

There are lengthy books written on forecasting, and a number of very sophisticated techniques are available to the scientific forecaster: weighted averages, exponential smoothing, time series analysis, to name a few. These will receive more attention in Chapter 13. Most people can deal quite well with their short-term plans using less formidable armament. We will confine our present comments to only one hazard and two techniques that can be used by nearly everyone who gambles on planning outcomes.

One hazard, the mishandling of assumptions, may take two forms: (1) making assumptions instead of getting the facts and (2) mistaking assumptions for facts. The first of these results from the unnecessary substitution of personal judgment when good data are reasonably obtainable. For example a programmer may assume that ten o'clock in the morning would be a good time to start a three-day institute, although a check of airline arrivals would clearly have shown that 1:00 P.M. would be preferable. Some assumptions however may have to be made because the facts are not available. The danger is that, if these assumptions are treated as facts, contingency plans will not be made. An example familiar to veteran programmers would be the case in which the star speaker calls on the morning of the second day of a three-day institute to say he is snowbound in Schenectady. The planner who treats the speaker's appearance as an assumption rather than as a fact will have given thought to a contingency plan.

The simplest of all forecasting techniques is persistence forecasting and, while at best a fallible technique, it may still be the most generally useful technique we have. It is nothing more than a forecast that past events will repeat themselves. The effectiveness of persistence forecasting depends on the quality and quantity of available data, and good judgment as to their applicability to the new situation. Unfortunately for many planners the records they need have been poorly kept or have not been kept at all. A record, for example, of the size of past mailings and the number and timing of the returns may provide the best available basis for deciding on a second mailing or the cancellation of a program. In such recurring situations, persistence forecasting may prove the most useful method.

The second technique with almost universal applicability is the use of subjective probabilities, which in its simplest form consists of making a judgment that there is a given percent probability that an event will occur. It differs from purely intuitive judgment in several important respects. First, it forces the forecaster to assign a numerical value to the forecast; second, it then provides an opportunity, based on judgment or experience, for discounting the forecast on the basis of the characteristics of the forecaster; third, it permits pooling of judgments where more than one competent forecaster is available; and fourth, it provides a reference point for analysis and evaluation of the bases for the forecast. The Delphi technique can be employed as one means of getting at these results. The use of discounting is simply the adjustment of the forecaster's probability upward or downward on the basis of any known tendency toward a systematic bias such as habitual optimism or pessimism.

If this method of forecasting in the absence of factual data is used systematically it can be a valuable aid in predicting outcomes. For example if a pool of experienced people is available and if three of these predict attendance at each program, a base of experience can be built such that systematic differences can be allowed for, the increased accuracy due to pooling noted, and the effectiveness of different forecasters measured. The logical basis for a systematic use of subjective probabilities lies in the fact that the human brain has enormous data processing capabilities, and that what we call sound intuition is a kind of subconscious application of this potential to situations that cannot be cranked into a computer. Neither persistence forecasting nor subjective probability should be used when better means are available, but both on the average will provide better predictions than simple "guesstimates."

The Principles of War

Successful strategic planners in peaceable occupations have certain qualities in common with military commanders in time of war. The principles of war in military strategy are a distillation of the wisdom of successful commanders from ancient to the most recent times. The usual strategic considerations are: the objective, simplicity, cooperation (or control), the offensive, maneuver, mass, economy of force, surprise, and security. Volumes have been written about these principles. It is not our intention to deal with them in detail but only to make a few points about their applicability to effective planning.

In essence, an effective strategist is a person who formulates clear goals, keeps plans as simple as possible, has a good sense of timing, allocates forces for maximum results at minimal cost, adapts readily to change and, perhaps most important of all, takes the offensive whenever possible. This translation leaves out the elements of surprise and security. While their relationship to peaceable activities is less evident they apply in the sense that creative programming does depend on strategic and tactical surprise *vis á vis* the competition.

Many years ago Admiral Byrd said of his successful conquest of the North and South Poles, "It has always been my habit never to leave anything to chance." An unattainable ideal, yet as an ideal his statement is a good description of effective planning in any setting. But beyond the requirement of an orderly approach, that which separates planning touched with genius from effective routine planning is the view of planning as the formulation of imaginative strategies in an environment of change and uncertainty.

There is no one best planning system but planning is in its very nature the process of taking a systematic look at the present with the view to deciding on actions that will bring about a desired future state of affairs. From among a great number of planning models this chapter has selected a few to describe. Like the navigator of a ship the planner may choose to develop his or her own model, but also like the navigator's model, it will have to deal with the same essential elements as any other successful model. It must include decisions about all the essential elements that go into a program and fit these elements together into a workable set of blueprints and specifications. Furthermore, because any plan confronts some degree of risk and uncertainty, the planning process must seek to reduce the area of uncertainty by drawing on the capabilities of skilled individuals and on those of groups. In the case of planning groups their productivity can be enhanced by being well-constituted, by providing staff support, and by the use of such techniques as brainstorming, Delphi, and nominal groups. The emerging plan can be strengthened further by the use of checklists, Gantt Charts, and critical path techniques, as well as by recourse to modern forecasting methods. Finally the effective planner is one who views planning as a form of strategy, who conceives of plans as a proactive response to an unfolding situation—who acts with the wisdom of foresight rather than reacting with the wisdom of hindsight.

BIBLIOGRAPHY

Allison, G. T. "Conceptual Models and the Cuban Missile Crisis." *American Political Science Review* 63 (1969): 689–718.

Burman, P. J. *Precedence Networks*. New York: McGraw-Hill, 1972.

Delbecq, A. L., Van de Ven, A. H., and Gustafson, D. H. *Group Techniques for Program Planning: A Guide to Nominal Group and Delphi Processes*. Glenview, Ill.: Scott Foresman, 1975.

Houle, C. O. *Design of Education*. San Francisco: Jossey-Bass, 1972.

Knowles, M. S. *The Modern Practice of Adult Education*. New York: Associated Press, 1970.

CHAPTER FOUR

CHOOSING A STRATEGY
Clientele
Content
Cost

THE DESIGN OF INSTRUCTIONAL SYSTEMS
Technical Assistance Models
The Open University
Learning Resource Centers
Geographic Dispersal Plans

PACKAGING THE EDUCATIONAL CONTENTS
Institutes and Conferences
Short Courses
Classes for Part-Time Students
Correspondence Courses
Self-Study and Tutorial Methods

THE USES OF EDUCATIONAL TECHNOLOGY
Television and Radio
Audio and Video Recordings
Computers
Laboratories and Simulators
Telephonic Communication

SELECTING MEDIA AND METHODS
Costs
Motivational Factors

DELIVERY SYSTEMS, METHODS, AND MEDIA

The late Marshall McLuhan's most often quoted aphorism is "the medium is the message." In a world where technology has moved within this century from Marconi's first wireless message to communication with the outermost planets of the solar system, it is easy to fall in with the fallacy of McLuhan's catchy phrases and to become enamoured of the medium at the expense of the message. Although television has captured the global eye to an almost unimaginable extent since its advent as a laboratory toy in the 1920s, print technology is still alive and flourishing more than five centuries after Gutenberg's press turned out its first book.

People who plan educational programs have to decide how to get a given content across to a particular audience at an acceptable cost. The range of choices is greater today than ever before, but the problem of matching the message to the medium is as old as the cave drawings of the Cro-Magnons at Altamira and Lascaux. Thus, the three C's of educational design are clientele, content, and cost, and the basic choice of strategies is threefold: (1) bring them in, (2) go to them, and (3) use media. A fourth alternative is to use a mixed strategy incorporating elements of all three basic strategies.

CHOOSING A STRATEGY

Clientele

The following are some considerations that determine the strategy for reaching a given clientele.

1. *Numbers.* How many people do we want to reach? Broadcast television

may be the preferred means for serving a thousand students and totally inefficient for ten.

2. *Mobility.* How free is our intended audience to move about? Many people such as small business owner-managers, homemakers with children, and people with physical handicaps are unable or unwilling to travel away from their business or home for any great length of time. Others may simply lack access to convenient means of transportation.

3. *Time factors.* Job requirements make it difficult for some people to attend regularly-scheduled classes; other people such as commuters have regular blocks of time that they can make serve double duty.

4. *Dispersal.* Some potential clientele groups—hospital dietitians in non-urban areas, for example—-are numerous enough to form viable educational targets but are thinly dispersed over a wide geographic area.

5. *Financial constraints.* As travel costs escalate, it becomes increasingly difficult to motivate people to travel long distances; net cost is often lower if they are served by bringing the program to them physically or via media.

6. *Behavioral factors.* What is the strength of the extrinsic or intrinsic motivation to learn? What are the habit patterns of the group? What kind of prejudices, interests, hopes, and expectations characterize the group? For example, one survey of small business owners and operators showed that they did very little job-related reading; it seemed unlikely that a conventional correspondence course would be the right vehicle to teach them the analysis of financial statements.

Content

Content can dictate strategy in a variety of ways. The following are a few considerations that may govern the choice.

1. *Learning outcome.* Whether the desired end result is information, skill, or behavioral change relates to the question of how content can be imparted. While music appreciation may fairly readily be taught by radio, musical performance requires a more intimate interaction between student and instructor.

2. *Facilities.* If certain kinds of physical facilities are required—access to a computer, for example—the choice of methods is more constrained than if only voice and two-dimensional visuals are needed. A cardiopulmonary resuscitation course would be most inadequate without hands-on experience.

3. *Interaction.* Feedback requirements act as a limiting factor. For some content, one-way communication may be sufficient. For other content, two-way voice interaction may be enough. In still other situations, learning to ski or to swim, for example, a complex pattern of instructor-student interaction is required.

4. *Process.* Learning may vary from simple rote memorization to mastery of complex skills. The practice required, the distribution of instruction over time, the

interdependence of successive sessions, and the sensory modalities involved may all bear on the choice of methods.

5. *Social factors.* Some kinds of learning are inherently dependent on social reinforcement. For example, attitudinal learning may be significantly enhanced by role-playing; recreational and cultural courses may either benefit from or require an interacting group.

The interplay of variables, some of which are sketched above, is complex; the choice of strategies requires careful balancing of possible approaches, some of which must be rejected outright and others weighed against costs.

Cost

In this age of mass production, inflation, and high taxes, the cost of education does not often permit bold and risky educational experiments. Practical administrators must consider the means to their educational ends on a far more constrained basis. Given an intended course content, a target audience, and a desired educational outcome, the administrator must decide on the most efficient manner in which this content can be conveyed to the audience. Efficiency in this context implies four things: (1) the income the program can be expected to generate, (2) the costs of alternative deliveries, (3) expected results of the various options, and (4) affordability. The decision is not determined by what will yield the best possible result but rather by what will give the best result given the funds available.

Experimental and unconventional packaging of educational content has been more readily accepted by continuing education practitioners than by educators working in traditional modes. Many traditional educators are not well-informed about new educational technology and many, especially in graduate schools, reject nontraditional methods on the basis of an assumed adverse effect of media on quality. There are legitimate grounds for skepticism—for example, many such programs do not deal well with the question of access to library resources. On the other hand, some of the reservations of conservative educators seem to stem from nothing more substantial than a belief in the value of living in a community of scholars and the consecration brought about by a laying on of hands, a sort of doctrine of the Apostolic succession in academic garb. The real issue, of course, is the comparative effectiveness of various methods or, in some instances, the extent to which a less effective educational method is preferable to none at all. The evidence regarding the relative effectiveness of various methods and media is equivocal and conflicting. Methods that have been hallowed by long use tend to be taken for granted in the world of postsecondary education. New methods are greeted with skepticism or a presumption of ineffectiveness. Perhaps the most tenable generalization at this stage is that there is very little conclusive evidence on which to base a preferential ranking of educational alternatives. To put it more positively, there are good reasons for believing that the quality of an educational outcome is more a function of the skill that goes into the execution of the program than it is of any specific method or medium employed.

THE DESIGN OF INSTRUCTIONAL SYSTEMS

The delivery of instruction can be viewed as the design of a general instructional system, as a way of packaging specific learning content, or as the use of educational technology. In a progression from the general to the specific we will move in this and the following sections from a look at some of these general systems for delivering content, through consideration of some of the commonly-employed instructional for-, mats, and close with a look at the uses of technology.

There are four general systems that provide some insight into the building of integrated delivery systems. The most extensive in terms of public expenditure and numbers reached is the technical assistance model, exemplified by the Cooperative Extension Service but also incorporated into business, industrial, and government technical assistance programs in Iowa, Pennsylvania, and Wisconsin which in some instances grew out of such federal legislation as the now defunct State Technical Services Act and such other legislation as the Sea Grant Act.

The other three general delivery systems to be described briefly thereafter are the open university model, pioneered in a large measure by the British Open University, learning resource centers, and geographic dispersal plans.

Technical Assistance Models

This model in its general sense is not confined to the Smith-Lever Act or to the land-grant system. In its broadest outlines it is a model that has been employed on a smaller scale in various business advisory programs. It offers direct assistance to individuals or groups, providing advice and information. Probably its most distinctive method is the demonstration—a process of conveying educational information by putting a concept or technique into practice in one or more working models so that dissemination comes about when others observe the effectiveness of the practice as applied to the model. A familiar example from times past was teaching farmers to use contour plowing to prevent erosion; an "early adopter"—a farmer who tries new things more willingly than most—became the instrumentality for the demonstration.

Six factors account for the historic effectiveness of the Cooperative Extension Service as a technical assistance system.

1. The service has deep roots in local people and local government. It is, to a very great degree, as it purports to be, a partnership between federal, state, and local interests. Using federal matching funds as a lever, it has mustered substantial support from state and local governments and has sought to merge local concerns and national policy in its programmatic thrusts.

2. It has faculty or academic staff out in the local community where the problems are, identifying the problems and reaching back to the campus for needed resources.

3. It has faculty on campus who serve as experts in scanning research and interpreting it for community-based staff.

4. These scanners and interpreters are closely linked to the research faculty, often moving from the scanner-interpreter role to the researcher role and back again, and in the most successful institutions housed with and working with a total faculty.

5. As part of an international network of scholars this team can reach out almost anywhere in the world for needed information. Because of university ties, Cooperative Extension workers are able to quickly obtain research results—including translations if needed—from almost anywhere in the world, a feat university people tend to take for granted but that few other institutions can so readily do.

6. The Cooperative Extension model promotes continuous feedback between the community-based staff member and the research scholar. The payoff is not one that neatly divides between pure and applied research, but affects the whole range of agricultural research. In one university for example, the development of an anti-coagulant and rodenticide came about in part because field workers were encountering an animal disease that had them stumped. Cattle were dying from internal bleeding. Investigation linked the internal bleeding with the eating of fermented clover. Research isolated the causative agent. The net result was prevention for the cattle, death to the rodents, and important practical and theoretical contributions to the biochemistry of blood.

Other technical assistance models such as Pennsylvania State University's PENNTAP operate along somewhat similar lines but without the benefit of federal funding. The basic pattern is a person-to-person type of assistance supplemented by some group instruction, some use of media, and interaction between client, field staff, and campus specialists. Urban problems outreach has also been tried under the Urban Observatory rubric and in isolated instances under Title I of the Higher Education Act. None of these has had either the level of financial support or the continuity of funding that has buttressed the Cooperative Extension Service since 1914 but on a smaller scale several have achieved sustained support. The small business assistance centers funded under the Small Business Development Center Act of 1978 offers yet another hope of continuity for technical assistance programs.

The Open University

The most familiar example of this system concept is the British Open University. In varying degrees, the Regents University of the State of New York, the University without Walls, Minnesota's Metropolitan State University, and the University of Mid-America based in Lincoln, Nebraska, are other examples. All have in common the concept of an institutional commitment to the part-time student. Unlike the Cooperative Extension model all are oriented toward granting degrees. Their basic approach is one of bringing the campus to the student rather than the student to the campus; all (in some cases, a consortium of institutions) have in common a degree of commitment not only to nontraditional methods of instruction but also to nontraditional academic standards for admission and accomplishment.

While other more traditional institutions have become involved in this type of education as an experimental or secondary emphasis, the idea of open education as a central, organizing concept for an institution is still in its early developmental state. We will deal with some of the specific concerns of this type of delivery system in Chapters 7 and 11.

Learning Resource Centers

In the broadest sense, every campus is a learning center. By using this term to describe a major delivery system concept, however, we are referring to the special purpose centers that are designed as sites where the independent learner or part-time student can pursue educational goals with minimal supervision. There are, of course, learning centers for part-time students that rely primarily on conventional instructional methods—the Quad Cities Center in Moline, Illinois, or the New England Center for Continuing Education in Durham, New Hampshire, for example. Although quite different in design and tradition, they both serve the part-time student. But learning centers that have as their primary purpose making learning resources available to part-time students have not yet become numerous, although several successful examples exist.

The learning resource center usually provides library resources, cassettes, viewing equipment, some advising and tutorial services, meeting rooms, laboratory facilities, and a place to complete examinations under controlled conditions. Such a center may be an elaborate facility with extensive equipment and considerable space such as the Miami-Dade Community College Center or a minimal facility provided by a trailer and an itinerant tutor as in the case of the North Island College Mobile Study Center in British Columbia.

Centers housed in special-purpose buildings are economically feasible in areas of reasonably high population density where a fixed facility may serve sufficient numbers. The use of a mobile center has the advantage of being able to reduce the geographic barriers but can provide only a very limited range of equipment and services. A unique rural learning center is Kirkwood Community College in Iowa. They serve a seven-county area through a combination of (1) area coordinators, (2) classes by television and telephone, and (3) short courses, seminars, workshops, and conferences.

One important advantage of the learning center concept is the ability to adapt the pace of instruction to the needs of the student. Bunker Hill Community College in Charlestown, Massachusetts emphasizes the use of self-paced modules and a mastery concept to serve 1700 to 1800 students each month on an individualized basis. Through the use of learning modules their learning center has been able to mount highly effective remedial, credit, and continuing education courses at a fraction of the cost of traditional classroom methods.

Geographic Dispersal Plans

As noted in the opening paragraphs of this chapter, there are three basic strategies. The one of bringing instruction to the student by moving the instructor out into the countryside has succeeded over a long span of time. The original University of Wisconsin Extension had itinerant instructors in the early 1890s. A number of community colleges have used the itinerant instructor method of reaching outlying areas, and the University of Southern California offers on-location programs to businesses, custom designing programs to serve specific needs. Geographic dispersal plans have the dual advantage of reducing cost in time and travel expense for participants and in utilizing locally available space often at little or no cost to the institution. The principal drawbacks of this form of delivery are the added staffing needed to serve generally smaller groups of students, the travel expense incurred by the institution, and the wear and tear on itinerant staff. Charter and institutional airplanes have been used to reduce staff travel time. When schedules are synchronized so that an itinerary can be arranged to deliver several instructors along a circuit, a fairly wide geographic area can be served with reasonable efficiency by this means.

These general systems for delivery may utilize some or all of the media and methods described in the following sections, although the media and methods may be used on a piecemeal basis quite apart from any general delivery system. Both the general systems and the following subsystems may also operate as part of a master system serving both nontraditional part-time students and traditional full-time students. The multi-purpose facility or system may be the ideal when the result is maximum use of resources. The 8:00 A.M. to 3:30 P.M. campus operating at near capacity for only thirty-two weeks a year is an anachronism that has been extraordinarily resistant to change. As many community colleges know, a successful community college operation can be both a traditional teaching facility and a learning resource center.

PACKAGING THE EDUCATIONAL CONTENTS

The Commission on Non-Traditional Studies did a survey of preferences for different kinds of instructional methods. It found a strong preference for lectures and classes—not surprising since this is the method that most respondents were accustomed to. Probably students who were most familiar with some other method would indicate that they preferred that method. Preferences tend to reflect a satisfactory past experience and skepticism with respect to untried methods; apart from student preferences research evidence does not, in general, support claims for the superiority of one type of learning over another. A possible exception that receives support from a number of studies is Keller's Personalized System of Instruction which is covered briefly later in this chapter.

The term *method* as used in this section refers to an instructional format rather than to a teaching technique. In this sense the choice of a method refers to an administrative choice. Within the general format methods may include lecture, discussion, case study, role-playing, and many other teaching techniques. In term of formats, the most extensively employed are: (1) institutes and conferences, (2) short courses, (3) special classes, (4) correspondence study, (5) self-study and tutorials. These will be dealt with in the following subsections.

Institutes and Conferences

Although institutes can be broadly defined as entire educational colleges or programs (e.g. Environmental Studies Institute), in this particular context it refers to the short-duration, generally one- to three-day, single-topic program. A conference is treated here as essentially a synonym for institute. With the fast pace of technology and the widespread information explosion, these updating experiences play an important educational role. The institute is often a state-of-the-art program incorporating two or more speakers discussing the latest developments in areas such as building design systems or public health methodology. In this form it emphasizes keeping people up-to-date, with the expectation that periodic refresher courses will be needed as the field changes. In other instances it is designed to provide basic information for a particular type of person—fundamentals of supervision for nursing supervisors, for example.

Some organizations, such as the American Management Association, offer their institutes and conferences at a number of metropolitan centers, including such overseas locations as Caracas and Singapore; colleges and universities more often bring clientele to the campus. Many such programs attract a worldwide audience and large numbers. For instance, the University of Wisconsin-Extension Engineering Department annually offers approximately 200 institutes that serve about 10,000 people representing every state in the United States and approximately thirty foreign countries. To the extent that institutes are distinguished from conferences, it is in part a matter of audience size and consequently of the way in which the group is handled. For example, the American Association of Community and Junior College's 1980 conference titled "Energy and the Way We Live," affected over 1200 communities.

Short Courses

The short course is generally from one week to six weeks in length, incorporating material that will provide an individual with a new skill or understanding of material. State-of-the-art material constitutes a relatively low percentage of short course content. The short course can be the condensation of an undergraduate course or graduate course into a format convenient to working individuals. The material must be designed to meet the new requirements and the faculty equipped to deal with new problems and questions. This format, one of the most common in continuing education, seldom requires large investments and need not always be involved with massive programs. Any institution can be doing one or one hundred depending on the size of their staff, facilities, or interest.

Probably the oldest example of a short course is the ''Farm Short Course'' started in several states in the 1880s. Farmers had the opportunity to spend several weeks on the campus of a land-grant college to learn the latest farming technology and operations.

Classes for Part-Time Students

The classroom lecture-discussion is one of the oldest methods of continuing education. Most often such classes are an extension of daytime courses for working students who are pursuing a degree. Generally following the format of courses for full-time students, these classes incorporate lecture and discussion, examinations, and grading. The principal difference is typically in the scheduling of times; in addition to being scheduled at nonworking hours, these classes usually meet for several hours at a time instead of for the traditional single hour. The length of classes may vary from three hours a week to twelve hours once a month. Part-time student class formats, however, provide access not only for students who are pursuing a degree but also for those interested in continuing education. Such courses may carry credits toward a degree or may result in some other form of recognition such as a certificate or continuing education units.

Correspondence Courses

Correspondence courses have been in use since the last half of the nineteenth century. They exist in great variety, with many institutions and organizations offering them to the willing student. This instruction method is unique: it brings the instruction directly to the student—anywhere—and is flexible in permitting the students great freedom in deciding when, where, and how they will study. This flexibility can also be a disadvantage, of course. Less persevering students may not be able to handle the freedom. But studies do show, that overall, highly-motivated correspondence students who complete their courses learn subjects more thoroughly than students who learn in the classroom. The National University Continuing Education Association (NUCEA) issues a publication listing nearly all of the collegiate correspondence courses available. Among university correspondence study programs the University of Nebraska reports the highest number of annual registration with nearly 15,000 enrolled in 1980. They offer approximately 250 courses and grant an accredited high school diploma as well as college credits.

Courses are based on a well-written textbook, and may include slides, audiotapes, or other materials. A study guide clarifies lesson content and gives assignments to be written and submitted. End-of-course examinations are usually included. Most courses cover basic subject matter, rather than state-of-the-art, so that they may have a useful life of three to five years or more. There is not a great deal of flexibility for content change. The student completion rate of correspondence courses generally runs about 30-40 percent; the other 60 or 70 percent of enrolled students complete portions of the assigned course work. The cost of course development ranges from $3000 to $8000 depending on length and complexity.

Modular course design has the advantage of holding down costs of updating courses and can serve students who may be interested in only one part of a course. Modular design has the additional potential of using a mastery learning concept that seeks student mastery of each module before progressing on to the next module. In modular design, one or more units can be updated as the necessity arises while retaining other modules for longer periods of time.

Lesson grading is usually done by graduate students and ad hoc instructors, but if enough students are likely to take the course—say a thousand over the life of the course—computer grading may be a viable alternative. The examination must be well-designed, and computer instruction for mistaken answers must be well thought out to further the student's understanding. This may take up to one month's time for the writer, but after development costs are recovered, the per lesson grading costs should be less than half the cost of manual grading and the results, on the average, as good or better from the viewpoint of the students. The key factor is sufficient volume to amortize the development costs. During the early days of computer grading, the United States Armed Forces Institute tested the reaction to computer grading and found favorable student response. The computer printout comments for incorrect answers were as complete and helpful as the best efforts of the faculty graders. When a student had difficulty, a faculty member interceded. The most significant measure of success was an increase of about 50 percent in the course completion rate.

An effective correspondence study operation requires a fairly high volume of participation. The fixed costs of course development (writing, editing, and publishing the study guide), and the logistics of handling and grading lessons, arranging for examinations and recording results, as well as promotion of courses generate a high support requirement and therefore substantial fixed costs, which must be spread over a large enrollment base if per student costs are to be kept at an acceptable level.

One adaptation of the correspondence course utilizes newspapers as the vehicle to get material to students. Enrollment figures indicate it can be successful. The courses by newspaper project launched by the University of California at San Diego has involved 450 papers and 300 colleges and universities with thousands of enrollments. Another newspaper course on energy has been used throughout the country.

In another variation of the correspondence course, part of the study material was published in a monthly trade magazine and monthly self-exams and a final exam were given by the cooperating university. For a given course clearly directed to a particular readership, and given an abundance of new information, the experience can be worthwhile.

Self-Study and Tutorial Methods

For individual learners without access to a computer, programmed learning texts can guide the student in much the same way that computer-based instruction does, using branching techniques to take the learner through a series of choices to the point of mastery. It is most effective for factual subjects that lend themselves to a step by step breakdown such as mathematics or a foreign language. A good programmed learning text requires considerable skill and time to prepare and must therefore generate high enrollments if cost recovery is important.

Individuals with specialized interests, where no self-study package is available, may be served by assigning a faculty member to work with a student on an individual basis. The faculty member designs a course of study for either an undergraduate course or a special study project that can adequately guide a student toward his or her objectives. In many schools this procedure is called independent study; it may require one visit in the beginning to outline the course of study and receive the study material, and a final visit to assess the student's understanding. If the project extends over a long period of time, it may be necessary to have discussion at least once a month to insure progress along the way and to respond to questions as they develop.

The Keller Personalized System of Instruction, a variant on the tutorial method, is receiving increased attention. In its barest details it provides varied forms of access to instructional materials, leaves the option of how to learn up to the student, lets the student set his or her own pace, and provides frequent feedback through the use of challenge examinations. The student is able to take an examination over a unit of content when he or she feels ready; failure to reach the passing level for that unit simply sends the student back to the books (or tapes or classroom), preferably with diagnostic information about the reasons for not passing. The student may then take an alternative form of the examination after further preparation and will receive credit for the unit when the standard is met. Nearly all studies of the method show it to be equal or superior to conventional methods.

When all is said and done, 90 percent of what is being presented in all the methods and formats described is available in textbooks, trade journals, and professional journals. Therefore highly self-motivated individuals might learn everything required for an undergraduate or even for some graduate degrees through a combination of home study and library work. The textbook and library material are still the most cost effective continuing education opportunities in existence. The educator merely attempts to provide guidance in making the educational experience more efficient and meaningful. The use of independent readings may be linked to short periods of time on campus and to examinations, with a degree as the ultimate objective. The University of Oklahoma's Bachelor of Liberal Studies program generally follows this format.

THE USES OF EDUCATIONAL TECHNOLOGY

Although the number of courses and students utilizing television and other media are small, it is important to know what is available. The administrator must know also about the limitations of educational technology in order to evaluate its use. The following sections will survey some of the present and imminent future opportunities for using media.

Large mediated systems require large capital investments and should be approached with caution. The book, *New Educational Media in Action: Case Studies for Planners*, contains some excellent case studies of large systems in action. Relative costs and system effectiveness are explored. Another significant book on educational technology in postsecondary education, *The Fourth Revolution*, published in 1972, predicted such impending developments as the following:

> Fewer students will study on campus, as more elect to pursue their studies off campus and get credit by examination. This will reduce enrollments on campus below the levels they otherwise would reach.

> The library will become the center for the storage and retrieval of knowledge in whatever form and thus will become a more dominant feature of the campus. New libraries will be planned as information storage and processing centers rather than simply as book depositories.

> New buildings will have to be built with electronic capabilities for search, review, and computer retrieval with access on a twenty-four-hour-a-day basis.

> New configurations will take place to the extent that students are dispersed as consumers and as some faculty members and many technicians are concentrated as producers.

> New professions of multimedia technologists are being born.

> Prospective high school teachers and prospective college and university teachers will need to be trained in the use of the new technologies for instruction. Prospective teachers who are in college now will still be teaching in the year 2000 when the new technology will be in general use in educational institutions.

> Many more and better tests will be required to evaluate the progress of students who learn through the new forms of instructional technology.

> Some of the informational technology, thus far, seems better at training skills than at general education. The better it is at training skills, the more general education may suffer as a result—particularly if students move off campus and become content with skill training. But instructional technology, represented by such media as television and film, can also contribute to general education and to the teaching of concepts.

> Some equivalent of the university press, or an expanded university press, may eventually be necessary to produce videocassettes and other instructional software that can be used with the new technology.

The study now seems optimistic in light of the rate of research investments and the first few years of experience. Faculty reluctance to accept it and the expected reduction in student population further reduce the likelihood of general use of instructional technology by the year 2000 that was predicted, as shown in Figure 4.1.

Whether the Carnegie Commission's timetable is met or not remains to be seen. The fact remains that the hardware needed to implement these projected changes already exists. As the Carnegie Commission foresaw, the ultimate effect will be to shift education from a highly labor-intensive industry to a significantly more capital-intensive one. As in the Industrial Revolution, in addition to the almost universal response of generalized resistance to change, there is already evidence of fear of technological unemployment (machines will take jobs from people) and increased obsolescence for people who fail to master the new technologies. But, as in the Industrial Revolution, the most likely outcome is that educators will be doing not less

Figure 4.1. *Estimated use of electronic technology (computers, cable television, videocassettes) in higher education (Carnegie Commission on Higher Education)*

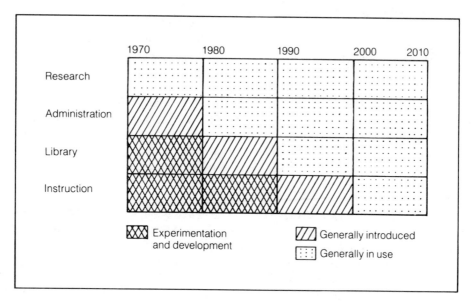

but rather different things. In the remaining sections of this chapter we will take a look at some of the newer technologies that are likely to have increasing impact on the job of the educator with the underlying assumption that the challenge will be to use technology rather than to be used by it. The major technologies that will be surveyed are: (1) television and radio, (2) audio and video recordings, (3) computers, (4) laboratories and simulations, and (5) telephonic communications.

Television and Radio

BROADCAST TELEVISION Broadcast television using regular commercial and public channels has up to now fallen short of its full potential for continuing education. Educational broadcast channels are more often used for regular courses in most other countries. Generally to obtain university credit, the broadcast is supplemented with an appropriate text and examination schedule, thus effectively reducing the contact hours of professors while giving students flexibility in their programming. The study material must be extremely well-designed for this self-study method. Broadcast television can have a high dropout rate similar to correspondence instruction unless people are pursuing degrees or have other motivational factors influencing them. Nonetheless, there are many examples of successful broadcast television experiments and programs, most notably in Britain's Open University.

In the United States the "Sunrise Semester" has been one of the most successful recent examples and the Chicago City Junior College started televised credit courses as far back as 1956. It was possible through the Chicago program for students to get an entire associate degree program by television. Over 1000 students completed degrees and the televised courses accounted for approximately 145,000 student credits. Other experiments have used commercial broadcast channels or public broadcasting facilities. Such use, generally confined to off-hours, must generate large enrollments—a thousand or more on a one-state basis—to be economically feasible, if broadcast quality standards are to be met.

One exception to large enrollment nonprime time constraints has been the development of courses designed around ongoing prime time broadcasts. The broadcasting of Shakespeare's plays by the Public Broadcasting System provides one such opportunity. Also, the Coast Community College District's "History of Mexico" television course was a success on their own TV network based in Costa Mesa, California.

CLOSED CIRCUIT TELEVISION   Closed circuit television (CCTV), often referred to as Instruction Television Fixed Service (ITFS), has been used with good results. A good example of a closed circuit system is the Stanford System in the San Francisco area. When several firms in that area were interested in having their members take courses without having to go to campus, a closed circuit television system was established by Stanford University. The system was started around 1967 and has been operating ever since. Although originally designed to provide credit instruction for people pursuing master's degrees, it now provides noncredit continuing education as well. In fact, the use of noncredit programming has made the system more cost effective and financially successful.

In costing a closed circuit system, one must consider the convenience of students in the process. The initial capital cost of a closed circuit system can be very high and if compared to a live classroom can show astronomical per student cost. However, if the convenience and the time of students are taken into account, this will significantly reduce the real cost. However, such a system can only be cost effective if utilized for a long period of time and at a high daily use rate. Therefore, a sustained enrollment is necessary in order to justify the system. Numerous examples have shown interest to peak in the first couple of years, with enrollments decreasing significantly thereafter so that the educational programmers have found themselves designing programs simply to keep the system in operation.

Another form of closed circuit television which has seldom been used by educational institutions is a national hookup. Boxing events and other entertainment programs have been shown at theaters throughout the country, serving tens of thousands of individuals. Although the base cost is high, if large numbers are served this system can be cost effective. Closed circuit TV has also been used as a means of preserving something of the small class atmosphere in large enrollment programs where a featured speaker may appear "live" in one room, or even circulate from room to room, while the main part of the discussion is carried out by section leaders in each room.

CABLE TELEVISION   The development of cable television with potential access to community, educational, and local government groups, has produced another opportunity for the use of television in education. Again, courses using television, closed circuit or otherwise, require a large enough audience to make the per student cost reasonable. Basic courses required in most university disciplines—freshman English, for example—may have a reasonable enrollment. Meteorology, a freshman elective that draws over 300 each year and has a high interest in the general population, did not have satisfactory enrollments when offered on cable TV in Madison, Wisconsin (population: 250,000). Cable or educational channel courses to help adults obtain at least two years' college credit are most likely to succeed if the colleges and universities hold the number of courses down and avoid a wide offering of electives. A phantom audience for televised programs always exists. Those who watch but never enroll has been recognized as an additional benefit to society. However, for both credit and continuing education courses, there should be a scheduled lesson with an instructor so questions can be answered and student progress evaluated on a systematic basis.

Although operators of major cable television systems are not now required by federal law to provide access to educational or other groups, state and municipal governments have the franchising authority to require cable companies to provide public access channels and many cable operators welcome the activation of such a channel. Even though the channels themselves may be available at little or no charge to the educational programmer, the cost of broadcast quality programming is a deterrent. Merely broadcasting regular classes has not proved successful in most instances. Two other considerations need to be checked: the number of cable subscribers in the area and the capability to produce the critical mass of programming needed to maintain an adequate viewing audience.

RADIO   The radio has been one of the greatest influences on cultural standards, reaching even those for whom the printed word has little or no significance. Although it has been losing ground to television for national and international news it continues to be one of the conveniences found in cars, homes, and in the work place. The convenience has allowed people to learn while doing other things not requiring their full mental concentration. In the United States radio is not a common tool of modern continuing education. Internationally, many countries are using radio in conjunction with correspondence courses to upgrade the national educational level. In this context, it is very cost effective. A major national effort to combine correspondence study and radio broadcasts in Kenya resulted in a significant upgrading of elementary and secondary school teachers.

Radio has, however, been used with some limited success in the United States, to provide general interest credit and continuing education programming by taking advantage of the commuting time of large numbers of people. It is not a very practical means for reaching small specialized subgroups of the commuter population.

Because of the difficulty of access to existing broadcast channels, special broadcast channels can also be used. It is possible to obtain a Subsidiary Communication Authorization (SCA) from the Federal Communications Commission. This permits as many as three special broadcast signals to function essentially as overrides on the basic frequency. These special signals require relatively low-cost special-purpose receivers and are thus mostly suitable for transmitting to groups gathered in relatively few locations. They are not a practical means for bringing educational radio into every home, but a prime example of its use is Minnesota Educational Radio's offering of information for the blind, seventeen hours per day, seven days per week, via the SCA channels.

SATELLITES   The use of satellites for transmitting television signals and its influence on continuing education may be significant. It has already made possible international television and the recording of history-making events as they occur. Its use for educational purposes, however, is still in the trial and error stage. Early international education attempts found that programming, content, instructional design, language, and costs caused more failures than did technical hardware. Just as content transportability is considered a problem in going from an undergraduate course to an adult course, it is an even more critical problem in going from one country to another. Language and cultural barriers, time zone differences and political differences are complicating factors. The satellites, which have already substantially changed television news and entertainment, offer great promise for continuing education. It is conceivable that large companies, or a government in conjunction with consortia of universities, will form a viable combination to disseminate technical information to pockets of engineers or pharmacists on a global basis. For example, it has been proposed that global continuing education be programmed to reach public health personnel wherever they are. Because of the widespread use of the English language among peoples throughout the world, the language barrier for selected audiences would not be as great as might be imagined. Furthermore, more than any other world language, English lends itself to simplification for international use. Through the developments pioneered by Charles K. Ogden and I. A. Richards in creating a Basic English it is possible to use a highly teachable version of English that literate nationals in all parts of the world can learn in a comparatively short time.

Audio and Video Recordings

Television and radio can, of course, be transmitted live or recorded. The purchase of increasingly sophisticated home recording devices at fairly low prices is now also making home recording a more likely prospect for the development of continuing education applications. If one has a home television recording device, one does not have to stay home or stay up until dawn in order to see an instructional program. The machine will do the job just as the oven timer assures the afternoon bridge player that dinner will be ready at five-thirty or six.

With home recording and playback equipment it also becomes possible to check out video as well as audio recordings for home use just as one would library books. The biggest single obstacle to growth of this technology is the high fixed costs of quality program production. A half-hour segment of a professionally produced educational television show may cost $30,000 or more. Film production costs generally run even higher than videotape. Unfortunately even low-quality production is likely to cost more and be less satisfactory than conventional methods of live instruction, where the give-and-take of the classroom provides the saving grace. Of all the forms of recorded instruction, by far the most inexpensive is audiocassettes. The student can buy his or her own for a few dollars, the tapes are mailable, and the cost per hour of reusable tape, exclusive of the instructor's time, will typically run about $180.00 for the master tape and $1.10 for the duplicate.

Production costs for motion picture film on the other hand are among the highest, if not the highest, of any form of recorded instruction. Film has the special advantage over video recording of greater mobility. Despite mobile television units, it is not practical to move from Afghanistan to Zimbabwe-Rhodesia with a millisecond transition except by motion picture film. Film is thus uniquely suited for dealing with ecology, geography, historic events, and sequences where time lapses are important.

Its use as an adjunct or aid to instruction is well-established, and public and private film libraries can supply a wide range of excellent films as a supplement to other forms of instruction. As a vehicle for carrying the full instructional burden, it is not widely used. Even institutions with excellent production facilities generally use it for special purposes only. For example, single-concept films of a few minutes duration may be an excellent aid to instruction when the topic is new technology, but few would be tempted to use film to teach an entire three-credit course.

VIDEOTAPE CASSETTES, VIDEO DISKS Videotape cassettes and video disks provide an independent and flexible medium for an individual to receive further education. Courses can be developed and shipped, then taken at a pace and a location convenient to the student. Videocassettes are becoming more popular because of their convenience. There seem to be fewer problems with cassettes than with tapes, and the cassettes are far easier to operate. Nevertheless, they are unlikely to serve a wide range of continuing education needs. Although convenient and, if well done, motivating and esthetically pleasing, cassettes do not permit interaction with the instructor or hands-on experience in three dimensions.

Another major barrier to the extensive use of video recordings is that broadcast quality recordings that take full advantage of the medium require the facilities of a studio and a technical staff. In a world of viewers conditioned to commercial television, the appeal of classroom quality tapes or cassettes is limited. Colorado State University has made video recordings of regular credit classes using only the necessary cameras and additional lighting. They have sent recordings to various locations within the state where students view the cassettes and discuss the material. In operation several years, this system has made credit courses accessible to students throughout the state at a reasonable cost. The extension of these courses to new markets is neither likely nor encouraged; the general public has developed a sense of production quality from commercial television, and significantly lower-quality production has little acceptance. It may work for highly-motivated credit-oriented students, but is unlikely to work in direct competition with other, more sophisticated or more personal alternatives. To develop commercial quality television tapes and study materials increases the cost tenfold. The cost for a one-semester three-credit course of commercial quality is likely to exceed a hundred thousand dollars and could easily cost three quarters of a million dollars.

Video disks offer a promising form of video replay with fewer technical problems and lower costs. However, they are just on the threshold of widespread use. The entire *Encyclopaedia Britannica* can be placed on one disk, and it is predicted that this revolution will make entire educational programs available in the home at a reasonable cost. Disk costs are dropping into a price range attractive to the home entertainment market. Once this equipment is in enough homes for entertainment, its use for education will also be possible. Software designed for the disks can ask the student to work a problem and then stop automatically. The student, when finished, can start the machine again and the disk will present the solution and continue on with new material. With its fantastic range of information storage it will probably replace the videocassette and tapes. It can also be coupled with two-way audio to provide give-and-take between instructor and students. Wise design of a video educational package would include development of a modular structure whereby those principles or educational modules remaining relatively stable could be packaged separately. Then other modules dealing with materials that change rapidly with time would be the only ones requiring modification for periodic update. Otherwise program obsolescence and updating become significant problems. Even the height of a speaker's hemline or the width of a speaker's necktie can date a program and reduce its credibility; hence, in addition to provision for flexibility in updating content, the producer needs to employ strategies for minimizing dating references. For example, a speaker in a laboratory coat is less likely to seem dated than a speaker in street dress, and illustrations from history will be more durable than those from today's newspaper.

AUDIOCASSETTES   As noted earlier, audiocassettes are inexpensive. They convey a sense of listening to a live person that the printed page does not. They can be used, of course, in conjunction with printed material, textbooks, assigned exercises, or even two-way communication. From the standpoint of efficient use of time, to be sure, a transcription can be digested at a fraction of the rate of a voice recording. The development of compressed speech has been used to reduce the time factor in audiocassette presentations, since a speech compressor can reduce the elapsed time by 40 percent without loss of intelligibility. This can be especially helpful if the cassette is being used for recitation as well as for presentation of material, because compressed speech reduces the listening time for the instructor.

Many professional, trade, and other organizations are making audiocassettes available with content varying from distinguished lectures to refreshers of basic course material. One potentially major audience is travelers who desire to use their time efficiently. Subjects such as conversational French lend themselves especially well to cassette recordings. The learner can use them on an automobile tape deck, during a solitary meal, or while doing routine chores. However, cassettes in most instances are used as supplements to more conventional methods. The increasing availability of cassettes from a variety of sources seems to attest to the growing popularity of the technique.

SLIDE-TAPE RECORDINGS   As an aid in classroom instruction or for occasional presentations, an alternative to audiocassette use is the slide-tape, one of the most economical to produce and most portable of audiovisual aids. Their adaptation to self-study or to use in learning centers has not been pursued to the extent of their potential. While they do not provide motion as do films and video recordings, they combine visual and auditory material, which if used with ingenuity can provide effective instruction at a fraction of the cost of other audiovisual materials. In the hands of a skilled producer they can almost create the illusion of motion. Inexpensive player-projection equipment can be provided to the user by loan or purchase and adapted to self-paced instruction. Fresno City College in California, for example, has a sophisticated learning center featuring slide-tapes. The center is opened to both the community and the student body and slide-tapes are an important part of the instructional library.

Computers

Much money has been spent on computer-aided instruction. The National Science Foundation has invested several million dollars in the Plato System, a centralized computer-based information retrieval system developed at the University of Illinois. Computer companies are spending many dollars in an attempt to more fully utilize computer instruction. Some outstanding packages have been developed and are particularly good for use in basic instruction. Portable computer terminals can be linked by telephone to a computer installation even in another city. Students sitting at the terminal can be instructed very simply on how to interface with the terminal. Once they have called for the proper program, they can easily work their way through to the conclusion. Students "talk" with the computer and have decisions evaluated and results fed back in seconds. There have been successful experiments at primary and secondary levels; however, the cost is still relatively high. The Center for Information Processing at California State University, Fresno, is one institution having a well-developed computer-assisted instruction program with course programs that were developed from all over the country.

Several excellent examples of case study and diagnosis are available at college level, and also in continuing education. Consider the actual case of a doctor asked to analyze the condition of a person walking into the emergency room with an apparent heart attack. The computer prints all pertinent information on the terminal, then asks the doctor which of fifteen listed items he would want more information on and whether enough information exists for making a diagnosis. If the doctor calls for the medical history or an electrocardiogram, the computer gives it. At some point the doctor must make the diagnosis. Once the diagnosis is made, the computer then tells the doctor if it is right, how many minutes or hours it might have taken to make this determination using normal emergency room and hospital standards, and the total cost of the diagnosis. Many computer games have also been developed. These are widely used in the classroom, especially in continuing education. Computer games allow people to make decisions under lifelike conditions without having to bear the real life consequences of error. The considerable number of computer-aided game simulations available today cover such diverse topics as industrial leasing and hospital management; the University of Nevada–Reno even developed a computer game on probability theory for serious gamblers.

The tremendous storage capacity and infinite branching opportunities can make learning by computer effective, provided the costly software development can be financed. The application of computers is especially useful for material that lends itself to a programmed learning format. The software development, however, can be in the tens of thousands of dollars for a limited educational program—say, five lessons of approximately one hour each in life cycle costing. As noted earlier in the chapter, the use of computers for grading correspondence lessons affords another promising teaching device. The computer can be programmed to "talk" with the student. If the student makes the correct choice of answers the computer may print out a complimentary remark or reinforce further by saying "Very good." If the student gives an incorrect answer, the computer can provide feedback on what led the student astray and where to find the correct answer. This variant on computer-based instruction lacks the immediate feedback that the student gets by sitting at the terminal but is far more effective than just knowing which answers are right and which are wrong. In the hands of a good programmer the responses can give the illusion of spontaneous dialogue.

Laboratories and Simulators

In addition to computer-based games, other forms of simulation exercises and hands-on experiments have been successfully adapted to the needs of the off-campus student. Instructional use of simulators received a major forward push during World War II with the military development of simulation equipment for gunners, pilots, and shiphandlers. Such equipment is expensive to produce but considerably less expensive to use than ammunition, airplanes, or convoys. The technique has been adapted more recently to such things as teaching police trainees to discriminate between "shoot" and "don't shoot" situations. Many other potential applications to situations that require a combination of judgment and skill deserve exploration.

Laboratory courses have been perceived as a major barrier to providing a full range of courses off campus, but the British Open University has been especially ingenious in devising laboratory exercises that can be carried out in the home kitchen or garage. It would seem that imaginative educators can overcome many of the barriers to off-campus learning. Another challenge to ingenuity is the educational adaptation of relatively inexpensive television attachments that now enable families to play games of skill using their television screen as a display terminal.

Telephonic Communication

TELEPHONE NETWORK The telephone network has been very successful in several places in providing an interactive system of education. As an example, the

University of Wisconsin has developed the Educational Telephone Network (ETN) for providing programs, both credit and noncredit, throughout the state of Wisconsin. Approximately 200 locations offer 224 courses and programs annually. In 1978 approximately 33,667 persons were served. This system has a series of dedicated telephone lines that can only be used for this purpose, thereby providing consistency of voice quality and full scheduling control. The network has often been compared to an overgrown party line, but with broadcast quality. A wide variety of courses are being offered, although the limitation of nonvisual presentation is apparent. In some cases, visual material is sent to each location. In this manner slides or transparencies can be coordinated with the lecture, laboratory experiments or demonstrations can be carried out, and classroom exercises conducted. Obviously this type of synchronization requires careful preplanning and adequate lead time, but the payoff is an instructional experience that comes close to the face-to-face experience in a well-run classroom.

One advantage of the telephone network is two-way communication between students and geographically-separated instructors. Instructors can be brought in telephonically from several locations so that geographically-separated staff can participate in presentation and in dialogue with each other as well as with the students. As a practical matter the distribution of materials and identification of students may limit the practical number of outlets to ten or twenty although the limitation on total number of students is little different than in a regular classroom. A great deal of flexibility and an increase in the feasible number of outlets can be accomplished by having at the point of origin a display board that records which outlets have questions or provides yes-no responses to questions. Such a display terminal, however, adds considerably to the startup cost and to line charges.

A course in financial management for resort operators illustrates the use of the network. Slides and worksheets were sent to each of fourteen locations where five or ten students were gathered. One member of each group acted as a teaching assistant, projecting the slides and distributing worksheets. Each student solved worksheet problems and answers were discussed with the two instructors, who team-taught the course even though they were in different locations two hundred miles apart. Now at least one national motel chain offers teleconferencing hookups, thus reducing the need for special on-campus facilities.

SLOW-SCAN TELEVISION   Two-way interactive voice programming can be supplemented by the use of slow-scan television using telephone lines for transmission. The cost of equipment and transmission varies with the speed of resolution of the picture. A moving image such as that obtained on broadcast or cable television is too costly for most types of instructional use. However, slow-scan, with an image resolution of about thirty-five seconds, gives a presentation rate that does not differ markedly from that of a live instructor using an overhead projector. The equipment may cost about $8000 per outlet and line charges for the voice and video combined may amount to forty dollars per hour for each outlet. The quality of transmission is sometimes a problem and a network that involves several independent telephone companies may involve further complications. Nevertheless the technology is steadily improving and offers opportunities to reach relatively small, geographically-dispersed groups at an acceptable cost provided that the level of use is sufficient to cover the initial outlay for equipment.

ELECTROWRITERS   To complement the telephone network, the University of Wisconsin also has developed the Statewide Extension Education Network (SEEN), which allows visual material to be presented by a device known technically as an electrowriter. There are twenty-three locations throughout the state, with approximately 85 percent of the state's population within a thirty-mile driving distance of some locations. In 1978, the system offered thirty-one course and served 1344 people.

Although technically not the same, the electrowriter network is often described as an electronic blackboard; a professor writes on a small electronic pad, and the written message is transmitted via telephone wires to each location, then projected on the screen for all participants to see. It has also been described as a poor man's closed circuit television, because expense is much less and display is limited as with the blackboard to numbers and figures. It will not transmit pictorial material. When electrowriter students evaluated their experience, however, only 6 percent said they would not take another course utilizing the SEEN system.

DIAL ACCESS   In an early trial for medical doctors, hundreds of procedures and medical messages were placed on tape, and doctors were able to dial in and select the tape for diagnostic purposes. This provided the early demonstration project for Dial-A-Tape. Now institutions in several states have Dial-A-Tape systems for gardening, continuing education for nurses, and other practical purposes.

The administrator, when faced with a responsibility to serve a large audience geographically dispersed, will first of all think of a delivery system. If the need is recurring, say that 300 to 1000 people will be using it daily, then fairly expensive systems such as television can be considered. If the number is smaller than that, however, then the electrowriter or educational telephone network may be a more reasonable investment. The administrator or instructor should not underestimate some of the motivational impacts of media mentioned in the open university experience with broadcast television. With the incorporation of study materials, media provide the pacing mechanism that improves completion rates beyond those of traditional self-study.

In all of these situations where media plays an important part, the faculty must understand their own limitations as well as those of the media. Training programs are extremely important, and much more can be done with them than first meets the eye. For instance, although one would assume that the Educational Telephone Network would not be suitable for a course in photography, it could be very effective if the faculty are properly trained and if mailings of the photographs go out on time. In fact, the discipline may cause the faculty to better prepare, and with this extra effort the course may be more successful than a course taught on closed circuit television or in a regular classroom.

SELECTING MEDIA AND METHODS

There are many ways of going about the selection process. One way is to list every combination of media and methods available for the course being planned and then to consider the selection criteria. Some of the criteria to be considered are:

convenience to the student or student groups (primary factor);

convenience to the instructor(s) (secondary factor);

comparative costs;

kinds and levels of motivation that exist;

nature and complexity of course or program content;

flexibility, or lack of it, for changing course content.

Consider, for example, a need for information about the state-of-the-art for microprocessors. Because subject matter is complex and content changes rapidly, there is little chance for correspondence, cassettes, film or self-study to be cost effective. The two-day institute, while being convenient for the program director but less convenient for the student, would be most cost effective. This method allows for good interaction between instructors and students, and easily accommodates several specialty speakers and workshop sessions on the state-of-the-art for microprocessors.

Costs

Relating costs to systems and methods is difficult because there are no common denominators. Nor are there accounting systems that include all appropriate expenses, particularly where student convenience is taken into account. The cost per student credit could be used for credit work as it can for continuing education units (CEU). The unit measure for continuing education, a CEU, is ten contact hours or the equivalent in time and effort. Few institutions are utilizing cost per CEU, which fails to take into account student convenience and material use. Some cost relationships, however, can be shown. Relating various methods to the percentage of student self-study, Figure 4.2 shows data taken from a single institution and clearly demonstrates that costs are lowered when self-study courses increase.

Figure 4.3 shows the relationship of cost to the number of students for three methods. Costs in relation to methods' effectiveness must be taken into account.

Motivational Factors

Everyone understands the difficulty in checking a textbook out of a library, then mastering the material; the amount of self-motivation necessary is overwhelming when considering other demands on time. Therefore, self-study methods require the very

Figure 4.2. *Comparison of unit costs (UNESCO, 1974)*

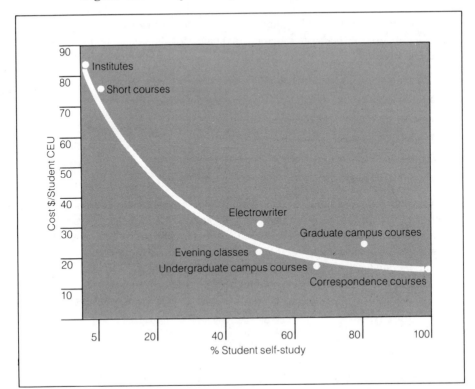

best efforts to improve readability, understandability, and enjoyment. Much of the subject matter in the Open University can be learned strictly from the study material, but over half of the investment is in television programming, which is considered a motivational technique and a pacing mechanism.

Problems of motivation may also be a factor in the dropout rate. While completion rates for correspondence courses may range from 30 to 70 percent or more, a 30 to 40 percent completion rate is probably most common. Dropouts from evening classes are seldom over 50 percent, and dropouts from two-day institutes or one-week short courses are seldom over 5 percent. The relationship between degree of self-study required and dropout rate may suggest that motivation is important in an equation of cost effectiveness.

In this chapter, instruction has been looked at from the standpoint of its design. Design deals with the form that programs take. Form exists as a vehicle for conveying a particular content to a particular clientele. It does not exist in a vacuum. The danger of an obsession with design is that content can be overwhelmed by an excess of gadgetry

Figure 4.3. *Relationship of cost to number of students (UNESCO, 1974)*

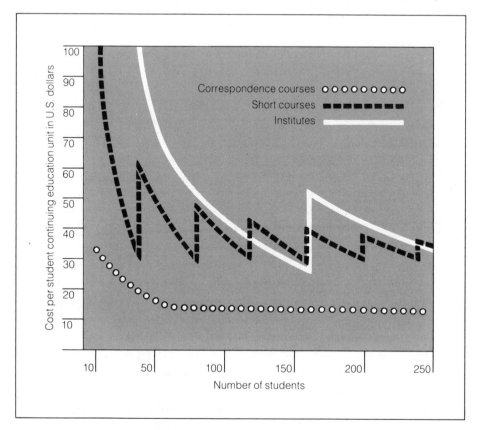

and gimmickry. Despite this threat, however, it is evident that educators are recognizing that their ancient love affair with the lecture platform must give way to the demands of an exploding content and a changing and expanding student body.

The process of adaptation can be viewed at the general systems level—design of a total delivery system. Total systems design, however, is composed of various media and methods. Some major ones have been described briefly and some of their advantages and limitations considered. We have passed over some familiar ones without comment—the blackboard, the flannel board, the flip chart, and the overhead projector, for instance—not because they are unimportant—indeed they are more widely used and valued than some we have discussed—but because they are so familiar that no discussion is needed. The newer technologies are discussed simply because they are not a part of every delivery system.

There is less novelty in the cataloging of methods, but here, too, the topics covered have been those that fall in the general methods category—classes but not the variants in the conduct of classes, such as buzz groups or directed discussion. The viewpoint has been that of the administrator and nothing has been said about what makes a good teacher. That is a topic that belongs in other books.

BIBLIOGRAPHY

Brudner, Harvey. "The Past, Present, and Future of Technology in Higher Education." *The Journal of Technological Horizons in Education* 4 (1977): 14–26.

Carnegie Commission on Higher Education. *The Fourth Revolution: Instructional Technology in Higher Education.* New York: McGraw-Hill, 1972.

Cornish, Thelma M. and William L. Carpenter. "Mass and Instructional Media." In *Serving Personal and Community Needs through Adult Education.* Edited by Edgar J. Boone et al. San Francisco: Jossey-Bass, 1980.

Dubin, Robert, and Thomas Taveggia. *The Teaching-Learning Paradox.* Eugene, Ore.: Center for the Advanced Study of Educational Administration, 1968.

Gibbons, J. F., W. R. Kincheloe, and K. S. Down. "Tutored Videotape Instruction: A New Use of Electronic Media in Education." *Science,* 195 (1977): 1139–46.

Goldstein, Irwin L. "Training in Work Organizations." *Annual Review of Psychology* 31 (1980): 229–72.

Houle, Cyril O. *Continuing Learning in the Professions.* San Francisco: Jossey-Bass, 1980.

International Institute for Educational Planning. *New Educational Media in Action: Case Studies for Planners—I, II, III.* Paris: Unesco, 1967.

Johnson, K. R. and R. S. Ruskin. *Behavioral Instruction: An Evaluative Review.* Washington, D.C.: American Psychological Association, 1977.

Parker, Lorne A. and Betsy Riccomini. *The Status of the Telephone in Education.* Madison, Wis.: Division of Educational Communications, University of Wisconsin–Extension, 1976.

———. *The Telephone in Education, Book II.* Madison, Wis.: Division of Educational Communications, University of Wisconsin–Extension, 1977.

Ryan, Bruce A. *Keller's Personalized System of Instruction: An Appraisal.* Washington, D.C.: American Psychological Association, 1974.

UNESCO. *Continuing Education for Engineers: A University Program.* Madison, Wis.: University of Wisconsin–Extension, 1974.

CHAPTER FIVE

DEFINING THE MARKET

Not *How* but *What*
Rifles and Blunderbusses
Marketing Strategies

EFFECTIVE SELLING TECHNIQUES

Creating Demand
Choosing the Approach

SELECTING MARKETING CHANNELS

Direct Mail
Newspaper and Magazine Advertising
News Releases
Telephone Sales
Word-of-Mouth
Sales Representatives
Inserts, Exhibits, and Handouts

MANAGING THE MARKETING FUNCTION

Organizational Alternatives
Promotion Effectiveness
Cost Control
Quality Control

PROGRAM PROMOTION

An old children's rhyme says:

> Smarty, smarty had a party
> But no one came to the party
> But Smarty

This was usually construed to mean that Smarty was not very popular; in modern advertising jargon, Smarty does not project a very good image. But other possible explanations do not reflect directly on Smarty's personality. Smarty's party may not have been very well planned. The refreshments may have been unappetizing, the planned events may have been dull, or perhaps someone simply forgot to mail the invitations. In previous chapters we have discussed finding out what the guests would like, how to plan an appealing menu, and how to set the table and prepare the food. But if the party is to be a success, the guests have to know about the party and want to come to it. Program promotion deals with the actions required to inform the right people that an event is to take place and to inform them in such a manner that they will want to participate. We will save the broader problem of Smarty's image for the chapter on public relations.

DEFINING THE MARKET

Let us leave Smarty and move directly into the problem of getting people to attend programs. We have used the term *program promotion* to describe this function, reserving the broader term *marketing* to include—in addition to the promotion of programs—the assessment of needs and the planning of programs to meet these needs. Thus program promotion is that aspect of the marketing function that deals with effective marketing communications. There are six essentials to this process.

1. The communication must reach the target group.

2. It must get their attention.

3. They must understand the message.

4. It must appeal to their needs.

5. It must persuade them that this is the preferred way of satisfying those needs.

6. It must be cost effective.

Not *How* But *What*

The foregoing six essentials are listed in the order in which they might be dealt with in planning the promotion. If they were listed in order of importance, however, the motto should be ''not how but what''; the culmination of the need assessment and program planning processes is a program designed to meet a need. The crux of program promotion is not how to reach a market but rather what we have to sell. So much of the marketing literature deals with products that students of marketing may tend to forget that we have graduated into a service economy and that the marketing of services differs in a number of respects from the marketing of products. Educational services are intangibles. They are not consumed. They generally serve higher order needs. They are not satiable in the same degree as most needs filled by consumer goods. The word *consumer* is in fact a misnomer for the user of educational services.

In a now classic article entitled ''Marketing Myopia,'' Theodore Levitt predicted trouble ahead for many companies because they are product- rather than customer-oriented. In promotional terms they see themselves as selling things rather than satisfying people's needs. Two examples from the transportation industry illustrate the point. The Baldwin Steam Locomotive Company, mentioned in Chapter 2, saw itself as selling steam locomotives. The Baldwin Steam Locomotive Company is no more. The Cunard Steamship Lines, on the other hand, decided to stop selling maritime transportation and start selling recreation afloat. Cunard thus became a leader in the cruise industry instead of competing with the airlines in the transportation industry. The service industry, including education, now consumes about 40 percent of the average family's spendable income. Yet typically the service industry spends less than half as much of its total income for marketing as is spent by manufacturers. The median expenditure as a percent of gross sales is a little over 4 percent for service firms and slightly over 9 percent for manufacturing firms. Marketing myopia? It could be.

The profit sector's growing interest in the educational market would suggest that the not-for-profit sector will be faced with increasing competition. This competition will concentrate on the segments of the market with the most favorable income to expense ratios, taking the cream and leaving the skim milk for those who continue to suffer from marketing myopia.

It is true that fads exist in education as in consumer goods; and markets do change with the times, but overall a great degree of rationality and stability is found in the educational marketplace. People select educational programs to enhance their understanding, enlarge their social and intellectual horizons, help them to advance, or maintain their competence. They are therefore more analytic and less responsive to simplistic sales pitches than are consumers of goods. They are concerned with getting evidence that what will be taught is what they need and evidence that the teacher is well-qualified to do the job. Academic institutions have an initial advantage in capturing or retaining educational markets. They have their own "Good Housekeeping Seal of Approval" as the result of accreditation procedures and long-standing acceptance of their credentials. But these advantages can be lost by continued underestimation of the importance of effective promotion.

Rifles and Blunderbusses

While the primary requirement for selling a program is that the content and the staffing are attractive to the potential audience, a promotional strategy must be tailored to considerations of price, geography, and the nature of the competition.

Price operates in complex ways. Too often programmers think only of what people are able to pay, forgetting that people must be both able and willing. The ability to pay is dependent on more than having money in the bank or in the pocket. People may be able to obtain credit, they may be able to get someone else to pay (employer, government, or other granting agency), or they may share costs with the government through the means of a tax deduction. Willingness is a still more variable quantity. As economists see it, the demand function varies from product to product. Demand is highly elastic and expands or contracts with variations in price for some items and is highly inelastic for others. It is probably more inelastic when a third party pays. If the program provides training for improving job skills, it is easier to price oneself out of the market if the potential student pays than if a large corporate employer pays. A high-priced program may require concentration on a relatively expensive personal selling effort, a different kind of brochure, or a different magazine or trade journal than a low-priced program.

Geography plays a significant role in the choice of promotional techniques. A three-day institute in a highly specialized, high salaried occupation may justify a national mailing. A similar one-day conference may justify only a regional mailing. A class that meets twice a week for two hours each evening is not likely to attract many students from more than a half-hour's commuting radius. Figure 5.1 gives a concrete example of how distance affected the attendance pattern of a credit course offered on weekends. Data of this sort can be used to determine a promotion strategy. As Figure 5.1 shows, the attendance pattern is clearly dependent on distance, whether for reasons of time or money, and the likelihood of a person's attending declines rapidly with the distance to be traveled. The implication is that, in this particular instance, the money spent on promotion beyond a 250-mile radius was wasted.

For comparison, two other programs—one two-day institute and one five-day—were studied. Both were in technical subjects. Both were promoted to a national audience. The median distance traveled for the two-day conference was 193 miles and

Figure 5.1. *Distance from classroom and its effect on participation in courses*

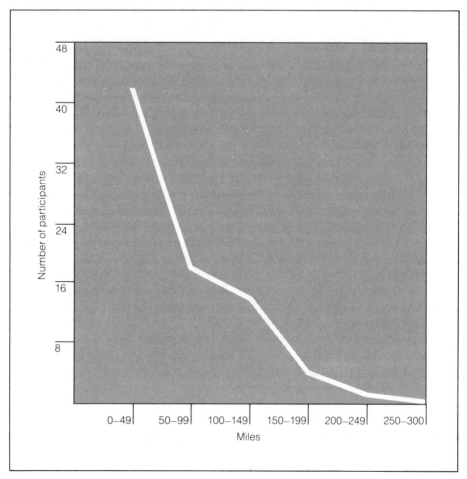

38 percent traveled 250 miles or more. The longest distance traveled by any participant was slightly over 900 miles. In the case of the five-day program the median distance travelled was 225 miles; 48 percent travelled more than 250 miles, six exceeded 900 miles, and two travelled about 1650 miles. While travel patterns depend on a variety of factors, two conclusions seem warranted. First, the distance people are likely to travel, and hence the area in which a program should be promoted, is in part a function of the way the program is packaged. Second, assuming that promotion costs are spread equally over all participants, the farther away a participant is, the more it costs to recruit that person. However, if enrollment limits are not imposed, the distant participants may be looked upon as the profit beyond the breakeven point and may thus be worth the additional promotional costs. It should be noted that the definition of a distant participant also varies with the way the program is packaged.

Competition plays a significant, if less direct role, in determining promotion strategies. The efficient marketer will recognize that it costs more to capture a share of the market in a competitive territory than in one without competition. It may be better in such circumstances to concentrate promotional efforts in home or neutral territory. If the decision is made to compete directly, it should be remembered that competing promotional efforts may cancel each other out if the market has a relatively low saturation point. It is therefore necessary to spend more for promotion when in competition, in order to capture any given share of the market. Assuming the competitors are equally effective, their margin of profit will be lower in the competitive area than in a noncompetitive one. Two alternatives, of course, are to divide the market by differential programming or by agreeing on territories. If, however, the market is numerically large, two or more agencies may operate in the same market without any disadvantage or even with mutually beneficial results. In this large market one agency's promotion tends to whet the appetite for many who cannot attend a course on that date; but when the next course is offered, possibly by a different agency, they are already committed.

Marketing Strategies

After a market has been identified and a program planned to meet the needs of that market, promotional strategy is concerned with getting the program information to the right people and presenting that information so that they will want to participate. Implementation of the strategy may be thought of as a three-step process.

1. Defining the market
2. Identifying the channels of communication
3. Designing the communications

We will discuss each of these within the framework of formulating a general strategy in this section and then deal with points two and three in more detail in succeeding sections.

DEFINING THE MARKET   The process of needs assessment should have accomplished part of the job of defining the market. However, needs assessment is concerned primarily with the general question of the existence of a market and may stop short of the specifics of scope of the market, locations, and total numbers. The process of needs assessment may also have considered only the primary market; further definition may be needed to define secondary markets. For example, a program designed primarily for health care financial managers may also appeal to administrators of nursing services, pharmacies, and laboratories. Mention was made earlier of another case—court reporters. The marketing strategy must be designed to reach both the free-lance group and those publicly employed and perhaps still another group, stenographers who occasionally take depositions or provide transcripts of quasi-judicial proceedings. Inquiry and imagination may be especially important in identifying these

105

significant secondary markets, and secondary markets may make the difference in reaching the breakeven point.

It is also sometimes important to decide not only who should be included but also who should be excluded. This raises the question of market segmentation. Do we want to appeal only to certain subgroups of a larger group? Do we, for example, want only secondary school mathematics teachers to attend and not teachers in postsecondary institutions? It frequently comes as a shock to a program coordinator to find that the wrong people are registering for a program. Good market definition and targeting are means of minimizing this possibility.

IDENTIFYING THE CHANNELS OF COMMUNICATION Although many means of promoting a program are available, old habit patterns sometimes get in the way of a full exploration of possibilities. The range goes from word-of-mouth promotion to paid television and full-page magazine ads or from direct mail to personal calls at homes and offices. The self-evident strategy is to reach the most potential enrollees in the most effective manner at the least cost. To approximate this goal five questions provide the point of departure.

1. What channels will reach our potential enrollees?

2. How many is each channel likely to reach?

3. What will the cost be in terms of dollars and cents per person reached, and obtaining the desired number of registrations from the target group?

4. In view of point three and the limits of our promotion budget, how can we best allocate our promotion dollars?

5. Beyond the general choice of channels, what specifics need to be considered: color vs. black-and-white ads, ten-second spots vs. thirty-second spots, the education supplement or the financial page, prime time vs. off-hours? Many of these decisions depend on knowing the habits of the target audience. Do they drive to work, at what time, what station do they listen to? An ad agency tries to have answers to these questions but in many instances the programmer, with or without agency assistance, may be the best judge of how and where to find the audience.

DESIGNING THE COMMUNICATIONS The general design strategy, like the two preceding steps, depends on a knowledge of the needs and perceptions of the audience. Whether the appeal should be to the achievement motive, the desire for knowledge, a sense of civic duty, or the desire to avoid harm, the promotion must first get attention, then appeal to a need, and finally persuade that this need will be met by participation in the program. Effective promotion must therefore talk to people in terms they will understand about how participation will benefit them, and it must be done in a context that conveys conviction and credibility. It cannot be something that is dashed off in a hurry and sent to the first outlet thought of. The programmer must plan promotional strategy with the same care that has been devoted to need assessment and program planning. Such planning requires not only all the expertise the programmer can muster, but also an opportunity to sit freed for a time from daily concerns that can so easily prevent development of a carefully considered strategy.

EFFECTIVE SELLING TECHNIQUES

For many people, selling is a dirty word. It conjures up images of fast-talking, unscrupulous purveyors of gadgets that break down as soon as the salesman is out of sight, or of remedies that are nothing more than colored water. On the positive side, selling is the lubricant that makes a complex society run smoothly. It brings together people who provide products or services and those who want these products or services, thus making possible the transactions that form the basis for our industrial society. The reluctance to describe the marketing of services as selling is widespread. The courts have only begun reluctantly to permit attorneys to advertise. Accountants, dentists, and physicians are sharply restricted in the ways they may publicize their availability. Education has tended to identify with the professions in this regard; the result has frequently been that people are not sufficiently informed about the options available to them and are therefore inadequately served by organizations designed to meet some of their most important needs. Surveys of would-be users of continuing education services show that frequently people fail to take advantage of an opportunity simply because they are not aware of its existence. There are four main reasons for communications failure.

1. *Insufficient information.* The traditional "five good serving men" should be expanded to six—who, what, where, when, how, and why. Most promotional materials do an adequate job with the where and when but many fail to do an adequate job with one or more of the other four. In the rush to go to press, instead of giving the names and qualifications of the program staff many program announcements fail to deal with the who, or worse yet, add insult to injury by stating that the speakers will be announced later. The what of program content is sometimes dealt with slightingly as though what will be covered and how it will be done are sufficiently conveyed by the program title alone. Equally important to many receivers of the communication are answers to queries of why this organization is offering this program and why this particular receiver should attend. Is this an area in which the organization has vast experience and expertise? Is it for the beginner or the experienced practitioner?

2. *Inadequate dissemination.* As mentioned in other contexts, the communication will be ineffective if it does not reach the intended receivers. Too small a mailing, poor choice of media for the intended audience, and chance events can render the communication useless. "I was out of town for a few days and didn't see the paper" or "I had a backlog of mail and only saw your announcement after the deadline for registration was past" are frequent enough comments to suggest that the communicator consider the advantages of repeat advertisements and repeat mailings, or the use of more than one medium to increase the likelihood that the intended receivers get the message.

3. *Misdirected information.* "Occupant" may be adequate identification for the users of soap, but mailings addressed simply to "Blank Corporation" will rarely reach the right person and mailings to the office frequently are not taken home to spouses. Bulk mailings may sit in the post office for a week or more during the Christmas season. Few small-businesspeople read education supplements. The academic question of whether a noise occurs when a tree falls in an uninhabited wilderness is not academic when applied to the act of communication; there must be a sender and a receiver as well as a message before a communication takes place. With the aid of directories, membership rosters, and similar sources, it is frequently possible to reach the intended receivers more effectively than by "to whom it may concern" mailings.

4. *Failure to get attention.* For most ordinary acts of communication, a basic rule is that one must get the intended receiver's attention. A good caption, an established logo, the right lead-in, a picture, color, a good design, or a celebrity's testimonial may do the job. Subtler problems also have to be contended with. The decision to use first-class rather than bulk mail may be crucial. Even the choice of a good commemorative stamp may help in tough cases. Sometimes, too, relevant information fails to get attention because it is buried. The use of large catalogs or two-page advertising spreads may get the attention of certain types of users but will fail to get the attention of potential users who are interested in only a particular type of event. For example a bulletin describing four hundred correspondence courses may prove to be an expensive and ineffective way of reaching a relatively small number of people with a specialized interest in interior design.

Creating Demand

Communication is a necessary condition if a sale is to take place, but there must first be a demand for the product. Demand is not always the result of a conscious need in search of a satisfier. Many needs, as noted in Chapter 2, exist below the level of consciousness, in conflict with other needs, or in a state of only partial arousal. The problem of the seller is to bring that need up to a level of strength that will result in a decision to act. In the broadest sense of the word, persuasion is required. The individual is the product of a set of genes and a set of circumstances that determine how he or she will react in any new situation. The effective persuader tailors each appeal so that it will result in the desired response. This presumes some knowledge, intuitive or otherwise, of the intellectual and emotional make-up of the target group. It also presumes some knowledge of the typical environment that this particular group inhabits. It would be easy to say that this is a matter of empathy—the ability to put oneself into the other person's shoes. This is the intuitive way to achieve this knowledge of the target audience, but a more reliable way is to develop a consumer profile on the basis of the best information available.

A consumer profile might include such information as the attitudes and values, type and level of education, motives, living conditions, age, income level, interests, and habits of typical members of the target group. Conversely, target groups may be better identified by constructing a consumer profile in answer to the question "What kinds of people are likely to be attracted to this kind of program?" For example, the profile of people likely to be interested in a course in estate planning would include some judgments about income level, type of employment, age, and so on, and would suggest that one potentially interested group would be self-employed people. Advertising could then be designed for and aimed at these people.

A good example of how demand can be created is a promotional approach used by New York University, which frequently has used the headlines "How to Get Out of a Job and into a Career" and "Give Us Nine Weeks and We'll Give You a New Career" to appeal to individuals who are looking for career changes.

Selling is always, in the final analysis, a personal thing: the potential buyer must conclude that he or she as an individual (or as a member of a group) wants something that the seller has, and is willing to pay the price. The price includes things other than money, including the expenditure of time and effort. The cost can be thought of in terms of other options competing for that amount of time, money, or effort. The decision may be further complicated by even the mere mechanics of commitment. If the decision to buy involves filling out a form or writing a check or checking with the boss or with the date book, the decision to buy may have time to decay into inaction or may give way to competing alternatives that arise a day later. Typically, of those who "write for further information," only a small percent finally enroll. It is important to minimize the barriers to a full commitment through the use of simple forms, reply coupons, telephone registration, charge card payment, and other devices that make the commitment procedure easier.

Choosing the Approach

Of the two basic approaches to selling, personal selling and advertising, personal selling is the ideal. It is the method that allows for a give-and-take between buyer and seller. It permits the seller to adapt the approach to the individual and to the situation. However it is only practical when the product is a Cadillac, a piece of real estate, or some other major expenditure. The cost of personal selling is high. It is a practical method only when there is either self-selection among potential buyers or when the field of potential buyers can be narrowed by some selection device such as prior inquiry, community of interest, or clearly-defined characteristics. This is less restrictive in the case of telephone sales, but even in this instance the telephone directory alone is a very inefficient guide to potential markets. Personal selling is also relatively efficient when appropriate interest groups become available—when, for example, the programmer is invited to speak at a convention where the entire group or a major portion thereof are potential buyers.

One-on-one situations where personal selling is worthwhile are sales where, for example, an officer of a corporation may be interested in sending a number of employees to one or more programs. In such cases sales calls by appointment may be well worth the time and effort, or a cold canvass may produce results. The cold canvass, wherein the caller arrives unscheduled and unexpected, may even be preferable to scheduled calls when the calls are part of a planned itinerary and when the caller has reason to believe that he or she will be able to see a high percent of those on the itinerary. A secondary advantage of gaining experience with personal selling is the value such experience has in giving the seller a feel for the market. This in turn may help in achieving better choice of media and better design of advertising appeals. Thus even when personal selling is impractical as a marketing tool, it may be worth the investment of time and effort because it increases familiarity with the market.

SELECTING MARKETING CHANNELS

The choice of marketing channels answers the question "How do I get my message to my prospective enrollees with the best combination of impact and cost?" The range of general options is fairly small, but each involves a large number of specific choices. For example the general decision to advertise in periodicals still leaves the programmer with the problem of choosing between a dozen or more periodicals aimed at that particular interest group. The final decision is not whether to use direct mail or paid advertisements. Rather, the decision requires comparing the expected effectiveness of a particular publication against the expected effectiveness of a particular mailing list.

Direct Mail

Direct mail is probably the most popular means of promoting continuing education courses in the United States. Millions, and possibly billions, of brochures promoting continuing education courses are sent out each year. Direct mail can be highly effective with a well-defined audience and a good mailing list. Exactly how effective can best be measured by the enrollment per thousand mailings, a figure that varies according to the geographical area being covered, the subject matter, and the intensity of need. One program director received thirty-seven enrollments on a mailing list of 200 people who had attended a program in the past, whereas another program director drew one enrollee per 3000 mailings from a list of professional societies and commercial mailing list companies.

RATES OF RETURN   High return rates come from the match between clientele and content. Equally critical is the timeliness of the topic. In the early seventies, "Environment, Industry, and the Law" as a course title would have drawn a larger audience than in the sixties; in the later seventies the course would probably have been canceled for lack of enrollment. Length of program will often affect the rate of return. That is, an advertised one-week short course is likely to draw one enrollee per thousand as opposed to three per thousand for a two-day institute. In direct mail on a state or national basis, ten per thousand return is considered excellent and one per thousand return marginal. These return rates must be considered in light of the cost per thousand for brochures, postage, labels and printing—generally about fifty dollars for a three-fold leaflet. The mailing list itself may cost fifty dollars or more per thousand when received from a commercial house.

The design of the communication is always a critical consideration. Should the promotion be incorporated in a catalog listing all the courses offered, or should each course be singly promoted to its own special audience? Annual or semi-annual catalogs are used by many companies and governmental agencies to plan training budgets and to begin processing advance approval forms. Functional catalogs covering a total set of courses are useful for such mailings to organizations but general catalogs may also be effective where good lists of potential individual participants can be obtained. For example, New York University has found that one large general catalog yields the greatest number of registrations, with past registrants from one program area subsequently registering in an entirely different program area. Their experience would indicate that past participants get the continuing education habit and tend to vary the program fare from one time to another.

DEVELOPING MAILING LISTS   Direct mail lists can either be purchased or, if enough programs are to be run, developed independently. Independently developed lists may be necessary but will seldom be more economical than purchased lists unless the list can be used for a dozen or more promotions. Even when more than a dozen programs are involved, the cost of an independent list is such that the alternative of purchase should not be discounted; a good cost analysis will help decide.

Sources of mailing lists include: (1) professional and trade associations, (2) publishing houses, (3) commercial mailing list vendors, (4) governmental lists, (5) previous enrollees, (6) special lists. If a professional society represents a clientele also targeted by the continuing education programmer, then the society's list may be the most effective. If a list is designed for a particular industry, Dunn and Bradstreet, National Business lists, and other lists having the Standard Industrial Code (SIC) may be most appropriate. If the course to be promoted is a recurring course, a list of previous enrollees is often the best source of future enrollees. Productive lists can often be developed through special means. One faculty member running a program on personal finance went to the county courthouse, obtained the names of everyone who had married in the last six months, and advertised the course to them. That list produced a high rate of return but, of course, required extra work and cost.

In designing a system to evolve a mailing list useful to a number of program directors, the programmer should give the potential enrollee an opportunity, when possible, to carefully select areas of interest, so that only the brochures for courses relevant to those areas turn up in his or her mail. Figure 5.2 illustrates how potential enrollees might make such a selection. Computerization is more than likely the answer if over a thousand names are on the list. For less than that, computerization would not be worth the cost. Clientele information is necessary. Knowing name, job title, and company name allows the program director to be selective in assuring the highest rate of return.

Figure 5.2. *Mailing list interest area card*

Department of Engineering and Applied Science

University of Wisconsin—Extension

Are you interested in future Bulletins and Flyers about some of our Engineering Programs?

If you want to be added to our current mailing list, please check your Interest Areas (not more than 7) and complete the Name and Address Section below.

Print (Block letters)

Last Name   Initials

Title or Position

Company

Address

City

State   Zip

Note: If you are attending a Program and receive this card, we automatically add your name to our mail list from the Program Roster in the Interest Area of that program.

If you have other Program Interest Areas, please check them also and be sure to print your name above.

Interest Areas (Do not check more than 7 total)

- ☐ Applied Statistics (incl. Operations Research)
- ☐ Architecture & Architectural Engineering
- ☐ Bioengineering (incl. Testing)
- ☐ Chemical Engineering
  Civil Engineering
  - ☐ Geotechnical
  - ☐ Municipal
  - ☐ Sanitary
  - ☐ Structural Analysis & Design
  - ☐ Survey
  - ☐ Transportation

- ☐ Computer Science (incl. Applications/ Information Handling)
  Construction
  - ☐ General Contracting
  - ☐ Heating/Ventilation/Air Conditioning
  - ☐ Electrical Contracting
  - ☐ Plumbing Contracting
  Electrical & Electronic Engineering
  - ☐ Networks/Systems
  - ☐ Digital Systems Design
  - ☐ Analog Systems Design
  - ☐ Instrumentation & Testing
  - ☐ Power Generation/Transmission/Conversion
  - ☐ Packaging—Circuits & Systems (incl. Mfg. Processes)
  Energy
  - ☐ Audits
  - ☐ Sources & Applications
- ☐ Engineering Mechanics
  Environmental Engineering
  - ☐ Air Resources
  - ☐ Hydraulics/Water Resources
  - ☐ Material Recycling/Disposal
  - ☐ Sanitary
- ☐ Food Technology
- ☐ Graphics
  Industrial Engineering
  - ☐ Health
  - ☐ Material Handling
  - ☐ Work Measurement & Methods
  Legal Aspects of Engineering
  - ☐ Environmental Law
  - ☐ Architectural/Engineering/Construction|Law
- ☐ Management (Methods & Skills)
  Material Science & Engineering
  - ☐ Assembling & Joining (incl. Bonding. Welding. Mech. Fastening)
  - ☐ Ceramics/Composites/Glass/Nonmetals
  - ☐ Metals & Metallurgy (incl. Coatings)
  - ☐ Plastics & Polymers
  - ☐ Wood & Paper (incl. Adhesives.|Coatings)
  Mechanical Engineering
  - ☐ Fluid Power & Fluidics
  - ☐ Heating/Ventilating/Air Conditioning
  - ☐ Machine & Product Design (incl. Noise Analysis/Control)
  - ☐ Manufacturing Processes & Production
  - ☐ Thermoscience
- ☐ Nuclear Engineering
- ☐ Optics. Industrial Photographics. Microscopy
- ☐ Package Engineering/Packaging
- ☐ Plant Engineering/Maintenance
- ☐ Product Safety/Liability
- ☐ Quality Control
- ☐ Safety/Health/Accident Prevention
- ☐ Technical Writing & Speaking
- ☐ Urban & Regional Planning
- ☐ Value Analysis/Engineering

UPDATING MAILING LISTS   The Direct Mail Advertising Association says that the annual rate of change in names and/or addresses is better than 20 percent. Individual mailing lists seldom change less than 10 percent and many change as much as 70 percent. It is important to establish a regular means for keeping a list updated.

The U.S. Postal Service provides regulations for costs and guidelines on their Address Correction Requested service. If the label side of a bulk mail piece is imprinted with Address Correction Requested, the post office will inform sender, within a one-year period, of any change in the address of a firm or an individual at home. Keeping track of names within a company is more difficult, although in-house mailing operations of large companies have the capability to check a list for current employees. Periodically the programmer should also survey those on his or her own list, both to make sure that those listed still want to receive announcements, and to see if perhaps their interests have changed.

AVOIDING DUPLICATION   When adding names or companies to a mailing list, the programmer should make a manual or a computer check to eliminate duplications. Checking services are also available for this task. Avoiding duplication is much harder when several different lists are used. Computerized lists can be cross-checked and duplications eliminated, but the process is expensive if the list combination will be used only once or twice.

Inevitably, duplications will occur. Some brochures anticipate them with the message, "If you receive more than one of these, please pass it along to a colleague." Preventing duplications is a struggle that can never succeed absolutely, but it is worthwhile to work hard at prevention. Ask the hapless program director whose mailing lists for a special Yoga course landed three identical flyers on the desk of a legislator just before budget time. What appears at first glance to be the most cost effective means of promoting may cost the institution dearly. It is good policy to expedite adjustments in response to specific complaints. Explanations of the cost effectiveness of multiple mailings seldom mollify the disgruntled recipient. However, if two lists are likely to contain duplications, spacing the mailings a week or so apart can reduce the appearance of waste and even increase enrollments.

Newspaper and Magazine Advertising

For general interest courses, advertisements in local newspapers are usually very effective. A course on insect control in home gardens could not be advertised effectively by direct mail, because no way exists for zeroing in on the audience. The size of ads should be determined with the advice of experts. Budget restrictions and other factors must be taken into account. A small ad on how to obtain loans for small businesses may be more effective in the business section than a large ad in another part of the newspaper. If 90 percent of the people who might be interested in that course read this section, reaching the remaining 10 percent may not be worth the additional expense.

The most common use of newspaper ads is for lists of courses being offered in a locality for a given semester. Full-page ads are often used, but may include a hundred or two hundred courses. Some of the large newspapers in urban areas have an education supplement in which universities can list, just before fall or spring terms, their course offerings for the general public.

Magazines present another opportunity for advertising, but have a more clearly-defined readership. A course on horse science should probably be advertised in the local horse owner's magazine or newsletter. For a larger geographical area—for example, for a national audience—a national magazine ad may be necessary. Advertisements must be submitted in advance due to the long lead times of magazines. Most magazines request the information between three and six months before the program, and it is well that the information appear at least one month before the program is announced.

Advertising rates vary considerably, depending upon type of publication; distribution of the ad—regionally or nationally; size and appearance of ad; and discounts available to education or service organizations. For example, a full-page ad in one major Chicago newspaper can cost from $12,000 to $18,000, but other options are available. In the same newspaper, a full-page ad in the tabloid-sized education supplement costs only $3515, or $46.06 per column-inch. If the educational ad is intended for placement on one of the standard newspaper pages, the full-page rate is $7656 or $52.50 per column-inch, still taking advantage of the educational discount. As newspaper ads are decreased in size, of course, the price per column-inch increases.

Magazine advertising involves more expense: a one-half column, one-time black-and-white ad insertion in a regional issue of *Time* magazine now costs over $3000, and an ad to receive national distribution in *Time* requires over $9000 for a one-half column, black-and-white, one-time insertion. Or, to place a one-time, one-half-page, black-and-white ad in a typical professional or trade journal a programmer may pay between $1200 and $1400, depending on the display.

These quoted 1980 prices will be affected by inflationary pressures, of course, but surprisingly the rates of increase for the type of advertisement described in the above publications ranged from only 7 to 10 percent. When the potential for distribution is assessed, newspaper and magazine advertising may well be one viable alternative for the programmer, even though initial advertising costs appear high. Interestingly, many schools offering national continuing education courses will not advertise in magazines. Most of the more prominent universities have balked at magazine ads, believing they would significantly increase the percent of their budget used for advertising.

News Releases

The news release remains one of the most effective means of promoting continuing education in public service programs. Editors of newspapers, magazines, and newsletters will carry continuing education releases as a public service if they are not patently an attempt to get free advertising. Such releases should emphasize the news value of the program. Stock releases saying "Siwash College takes pleasure in announcing . . . " are much less likely to be published than releases that have genuine news value. A famous name speaker, an unusual topic, or an interesting student body may make the feature page or even the front page. Routine releases may at least be used for filler on dull days.

Many trade magazines have a calendar of events section, which may list future meetings and continuing education courses. Key points to remember are: (1) send *only* appropriate course announcements, (2) provide enough lead time (three to six months), and (3) provide information in the format each magazine uses. News releases included in this section are extremely effective in promoting enrollments. In one course with a substantial fee, a short column in a national magazine brought eleven enrollments. With the necessary information and sufficient lead time, editors are often very cooperative. If the course treats a critical area of interest, or presents an interesting angle, an editor may even expand on the news release with a short article. If the information is incomplete, however, it will be likely to end in the wastebasket.

Telephone Sales

Commercial marketers have found the telephone effective in promoting products. Witness the number of companies trying to sell books through that medium. Although the person-to-person appeal to the public's desire for education seems a productive device (companies often stress the educational value of their products to make them sell better), telephone promotion is seldom used in nonprofit continuing education. Commercial correspondence schools use it, however, with apparent success.

Telephone contacts can be divided into two categories. The cold contact, using names picked more or less at random from a directory, is generally ineffective. Substantial success has been reported, however, in the other category, calls made to friends or previous course participants.

In the case of one program nearing its deadline with insufficient enrollment, twenty-five telephone calls to regular past participants produced an additional seven enrollments bringing the course safely over the breakeven point. However, this approach is effective only if used with care. If the additional enrollments are seen as payment for past favors or response to pressure tactics, a short-term gain may be a long-term loss. If, on the other hand, the calls are seen as a friendly followup, one's credit and credibility are not likely to be hurt.

Word-of-Mouth

Often the most effective and least expensive of all advertising forms is word-of-mouth; and the greatest word-of-mouth endorsements are generated by successful continuing education programs meeting individual needs. Word gets around when programs are effective, and people are anxious to participate.

Word-of-mouth promotion can be encouraged by establishing local advisory committees consisting of leaders in the community who have had significant positive contacts with the institution. Ideally, they are clientele or supervisors of clientele the institution has served in the past. By showing these individuals what is planned for the year, by asking what they think and what they might suggest for improving the plans, the programmer is likely to create good will in addition to garnering helpful comments. People who are thus involved then often become volunteer sales people with the advantage of greater credibility than insiders have.

Sales Representatives

Sales representatives are commonly used to promote commercial correspondence courses. Although often called by other names, such as counselor, the person fulfilling this function commonly signs a contract and receives a commission. The "sales rep" can answer specific questions, serve as a counselor during the learning period, and even be a positive force in insuring completions. Correspondence schools claim that sales reps follow up lessons that fail to come in, asking, basically, "Is there any problem we can help you with?" The sales rep encourages students to follow through. Unfortunately no evidence confirms that this is how things work since proprietary correspondence schools will not release their figures on completion rates. Because such sales reps are paid by commission, they may spend more time on sales and less on counseling.

Among colleges, two types of staff members perform a function comparable to that of sales representatives. Pennsylvania State University and Olympic College in the State of Washington, for example, have salaried area representatives who make contacts with individuals and groups to assess needs and assist in setting up programs. Kirkwood Community College in Iowa operates in a similar manner except that area coordinators, in addition to a base salary, are paid on a sliding scale based on the number of successful classes they develop.

Inserts, Exhibits, and Handouts

In promotion, as in almost all activities, a little imagination suggests a variety of opportunities beyond the obvious. Some of these may be primary channels, others will be secondary or incidental. Many organizations make regular mailings to employees or constituents. If such organizations see educational programs as a service to their members, they may be willing to include educational inserts in their regular mailings.

Opportunities to provide displays or exhibits are also more common than one might realize. There are many places where people with a little time on their hands will stop to pick up or read a promotional piece: a booth at the state fair, a poster and "take one" brochure holder on a bulletin board, a table outside a convention hall, a laundromat, a carwash waiting room, or a display at an airport. Handouts can also be placed in racks at the county extension office, the county courthouse, in stores or office foyers where their rate of disappearance gives some clue to the numbers reached. The value of such methods of distribution depends on the nature of the program, the location of the distribution point, and the effectiveness of the promotion piece itself.

Since these devices are most often an inexpensive, adjunct promotional activity, they probably should be used more often than they actually are.

MANAGING THE MARKETING FUNCTION

The management of the marketing function can be conveniently divided into two subfunctions, organization and control. Control in turn can be thought of as involving both a quantitative and a qualitative aspect: quantitative relating to cost and qualitative relating to questions of effectiveness, ethics, and good taste. This section will deal with some of the fundamentals that need to be kept in mind in dealing with organization, quality control, and cost control.

Organizational Alternatives

Many small continuing education operations will not have a subdivision identifiable as the marketing department. Even very large units will not have a marketing department that approaches the size of the marketing departments of large firms selling consumer goods. Nevertheless, marketing is a basic function of all units, large and small. Furthermore even if there is a separate identifiable marketing department, it remains true that the responsibility for effective marketing does not lie solely with the marketing department. In addition, for those units where public service programs are substantially subsidized by appropriations, contracts, gifts, and grants, the marketing function may not operate in the same way or to the same degree as in units largely dependent on program revenue. It is thus difficult to specify fixed amounts of money, or numbers of people who should have marketing as their primary responsibility.

If 15 percent of program revenue is assumed to be a fairly representative figure for marketing expenditures, and if 80 percent of this amount is assumed to be direct marketing expenditure (advertising, salaries of sales representatives, and the like), then the remaining 20 percent can be considered the cost of marketing management. How this management function is organized depends on a number of circumstances that tend to vary considerably from institution to institution. Four basic alternatives may be pursued separately or in combination: (1) an in-house marketing staff, (2) ad hoc or part-time staff, (3) access to staff within the institution but not within the continuing education unit, and (4) commercial advertising agencies.

IN-HOUSE MARKETING STAFF   In-house capability for program promotion is a possibility in both small and large units. The difference is that the head of the marketing function in small units may work half in programming and half in marketing or may be a part-time employee. Marketing may include both market research, which goes hand in hand with need assessment, and program promotion; or these functions may be kept separate but, necessarily, closely coordinated. In any event it is advisable not to leave everyone to his or her own devices in promoting programs, since equally effective programmers vary considerably in their skill at promotion.

AD HOC OR PART-TIME STAFF   When promotion is handled as a staff assignment within the smaller continuing education unit, it may not be easy to find someone with expertise in promotion and concomitant expertise in some other function to fill a dual assignment. Two other alternatives can be considered: a part-time promoter or a student project assistant who is majoring, for example, in advertising. In larger units, with revenues exceeding three million, it may be feasible to maintain one or more qualified full-time staff in promotion; although even at this level, graphics and other technical services may have to be farmed out and responsibility for writing copy may have to be shared with program staff.

SERVICE STAFF WITHIN THE INSTITUTION   Large multi-purpose institutions may have specialized staff serving the full spectrum of institutional needs for promotional services. These services may be paid for as internal sales—interdepartmental charges—or may be provided at no charge to the unit. The major problems with either of these arrangements are that the central staff may lack special expertise in the promotional requirements of continuing education, or continuing education promotion may have to take its place somewhere down the line in terms of general institutional priorities.

COMMERCIAL ADVERTISING AGENCIES   Generally the cost of using commercial agencies is high in terms of what the typical institution feels it can afford. Agencies that handle large industrial and commercial accounts are not always interested in smaller accounts. Furthermore, to an even greater extent than intrainstitutional service departments, they frequently lack special competence in the promotion of educational programs. Additionally, complications can occur, especially in public institutions, when working through a central purchasing department to contract for such services.

Given the right set of circumstances, however, there is certainly much to be gained by purchasing promotional services from an agency—knowledge about rates, circulation, audience, and so on as well as expertise in copywriting, layout, and other skills. Compared to the costs of developing in-house capability, the cost of an agency may be far less than it appears to be at first glance.

Promotion Effectiveness

Comparative cost studies of newspaper ads, magazine ads, and direct mail are necessary to determine the most effective advertising strategy. Further, cost comparisons between one magazine and another, one mailing list and another, refine the use of a given medium.

Information such as that in Table 5.1 helps identify effective lists, allows for more effective promotion, and avoids the annoyance from nonresponding lists. There cannot be hard and fast criteria for evaluating mailing lists. They vary too much in price, in expected return, size of fee, and other variables. But good records that afford

Table 5.1. *Comparison of in-house and purchased mailing lists*

List	Quantity mailed	No. of enrollees	Enrollments per 1000	Cost per enrollment
In-house	10,000	28	2.8	$60
Purchased	12,000	16	1.3	$95

comparisons can help in specific situations. A 2 percent response with an untried list is a reasonable expectation in most instances.

Cost Control

Clearly the measure of an efficient promotional piece is its ability to bring in the desired kind and number of participants at the lowest possible cost. The most cost effective method last year may not be the most cost effective method this year, and the habitual promotional preferences of programmers need periodic review. Cost analyses such as that illustrated in Table 5.2 suggest ways in which cost comparisons may be made.

The University of California–Los Angeles reports a 10 to 12 percent of total cost budget for advertising. Other public institutions report from 10 percent to as high as 36 percent for certain programs, with an estimated average of 15 percent or higher.

There is a constant battle with course directors who argue, "Why not spend another $200 on advertising if it returns $400 to the institution?" Although often sound on a single-course basis, the argument can lead to excessive promotion costs and administrative criticism.

Much can be learned from product marketing in industry. Robert Stone's *Successful Direct Marketing Methods,* for example, discusses the effectiveness of such methods as wording strategy of advertising copy. In some cases methods can be directly translated into educational marketing.

In a recent University of Wisconsin evaluation of advertising costs for correspondence courses, three means were studied—magazine ads, direct mail, and news releases. Table 5.2 shows the final results.

The magazine ads were small one-eighth-page ads in a national magazine with several hundred thousand readers. The mailing lists were a combination of in-house and purchased lists. The news releases were mailed to about 100 magazines. News releases had a low cost-to-enrollment ratio but unfortunately produced low enroll-

Table 5.2. *Evaluation of promotion for correspondence courses*

Method	Cost	Enrollments	Cost/enrollment
Magazine ads	$6000	108	$59
Direct mail	$3000	71	$42
News releases	$100	16	$6

ments; they should be regarded as only a partial answer. Therefore, direct mail was used with a higher degree of selectivity. The magazine ads were more costly under the present course cost structure than direct mail; but in circumstances where, for instance, sufficient enrollments cannot be obtained through direct mail and news releases alone, magazine ads might be used.

Advertising campaigns usually have secondary benefits not shown on summary tables such as Table 5.2. Some students enrolled in the courses after the six-month study and are thus not included in the statistics. Some students attracted by the advertising ultimately enrolled in other courses not encompassed in this study.

Quality Control

Promotion is a necessary part of good programming. Yet opportunities for abuse lurk always in the background. If ethical institutions begin acquiring some of the more objectionable commercial habits, all continuing education could be cast in a bad light. The Direct Mail/Marketing Association says in its first guideline for ethical business practice:

"Advertisers should make their offers clear and honest . . ." Other guidelines restrict the use of exaggerated claims, guarantees, use of the word *free,* and use of mail lists. Furthermore, sometimes misguided efforts to be cute or provocative are seen by the public as overstepping the bounds of good taste or propriety. Overly-enthusiastic promoters sometimes need to be reined in for the broader institutional benefit.

The first requirement in the successful promotion of continuing education programs is to have a quality product that meets a significant need. Given this essential prerequisite, the basic strategy is to expend the least amount of ammunition needed to get the promotional job done. This requires careful identification of the market, an appeal that speaks to market needs and selection of the best channels to carry the message. Channels that should be considered include direct mail, paid advertisements, and personal selling, usually in combination with word-of-mouth support, news releases, displays, and handouts as opportunity permits.

The institution must decide how to muster and organize its resources to carry out its promotions. For large units this may be by means of a professional in-house staff and in smaller units it may require a choice between hiring outside experts or having staff promotion as a part of their overall program responsibility. The right method is one that gets the job done at an acceptable cost and with a minimum of undesirable side effects. The right choice will vary from one institution to another. A flexible approach is needed.

BIBLIOGRAPHY

Buchanan, W. Wray, and H. G. Barksdale. "Marketing's Broadening Concept is Real in University Extension." *Adult Education* 25 (1974): 34–46.

Farlow, Helen. *Publicizing and Promoting Programs.* New York: McGraw-Hill, 1979.

Frandson, Phillip E. "The Great American Merger: Madison Avenue and Academia." *The NUEA Spectator,* June 1974, pp. 8–13.

Lamoureau, Marvin. "Threshold Pricing: A Strategy for the Marketing of Adult Education Courses." Paper presented at Adult Education Research Conference, April 1977, Minneapolis, Minn.

Levitt, Theodore. "Marketing Myopia." *Harvard Business Review* 38 (1960): 45–56.

Stone, Robert. *Successful Direct Marketing Methods.* Chicago, Ill.: Crain Books, 1975.

CHAPTER SIX

SOME USES OF EVALUATION

SETTING OBJECTIVES

Stating Objectives
Other Considerations

WHAT IS EVALUATED

The Instructors
Program Content
Instructional Materials
Arrangements

WHO EVALUATES

Self-Evaluation
Administrative Evaluation
Student Evaluations
Evaluation by Colleagues
Expert Opinion

THE DIMENSIONS OF PERFORMANCE

**DESIGNING AND CARRYING OUT
EVALUATION**

Design Strategies
Methods of Evaluation

EVALUATION IN ACTION

PROGRAM EVALUATION

Evaluation is a pervasive phenomenon. The conception and design of programs are based on evaluations—of the environment, of goals, and of alternatives. The desired results, in turn, are expressed as objectives. We are primarily concerned, in this chapter, with determining how well an established program accomplishes those objectives. It discusses the uses of evaluation, what is evaluated, who evaluates it, and how evaluation is done. Although this chapter concentrates on evaluation of curricular programs, as defined in Chapter 7, the principles discussed can also be applied, in a considerable degree, to evaluation of institutional programs (the academic program of the college) and of specific projects (the "Great Books" course).

SOME USES OF EVALUATION

"Why bother with evaluation?" the casual reader might ask. Or the smug but cynical individual might say, "I know that what I'm doing is good, and my formal evaluation is nothing more than an exercise designed to convince the administration to support me and my efforts." Most of us are neither casual, smug, nor completely cynical about the judgments that need to be made with respect to the results of our efforts. There are at least five important functions that can be served by an effective evaluation effort.

1. *Standards of accountability.* People behave responsibly in part because they know they will be held accountable for their behavior. In the simplest kind of example, the administrator holds staff responsible for a certain quantity of output—to teach twelve hours a week or to grade four hundred lessons a month. One function of management information systems, for instance, is to help account for the activities of staff. Too often, however, such systems call attention to sheer numbers rather than to more vital indicators of performance. Effective evaluation provides the programmer

with concrete evidence that his or her program has accomplished what was expected of it and, if necessary, a ready defense against critics.

2. *Feedback.* Feedback is important, since knowledge of results is both motivating and informative. If the instructor knows that the visuals were regarded as helpful but that the role-playing was perceived as a waste of time, she or he will make some adjustments accordingly in the next program. If it was hoped that 90 percent of the students would find a presentation very helpful and only 50 percent did, the instructor may, like Avis, try harder next time.

3. *Distribution of rewards.* Evaluation is an important tool for determining the distribution of rewards. There is an axiom in the field of work motivation that people will adjust their behavior to the reward system. If the reward system is geared to a set of desired outcomes, people are more likely to produce that set of outcomes. If we reward large enrollments, we may have to sacrifice effective teaching; if innovation is not rewarded, there will be less innovative programming. Beyond the effect on behavior, there is also the consideration of justice or fairness. Most administrators will sleep better if they feel that promotions, salary increases, and funds for programs go to the most deserving. Evaluations provide objective measures for identifying the most deserving. Furthermore, in the long run, the organization will be stronger if the rewards are commensurate with the contributions.

4. *Administrative decisions.* Good decisions about appointments, organizational development, staff training, and long-range planning can be made if useful information is obtained about the effectiveness of ongoing efforts. For example, an analysis of programs in one health care organization indicated that the separate professions—nursing, medicine, and pharmacy—were being served well but that interdisciplinary programs for health care consumers were neglected. A new organizational structure brought the health sciences together under one roof, resulting in less potential for duplication and a broader program scope.

5. *Justification of funding.* Evaluation is often necessary for choosing among alternative uses of resources. The most persuasive argument for funding future programs is likely to be the record of past accomplishment. If the program for people opening new businesses was a factor in the establishment of ten profitable new businesses, the case for next year's funding is considerably stronger than if the only evidence of success was the subjective judgment of the coordinator or a few student testimonials.

The cynic, then, was correct in assuming that evaluation would be useful for gaining support. But, as we have seen here, there are other important reasons for evaluating programs. Let us now consider how that evaluation is accomplished.

SETTING OBJECTIVES

Since objectives provide the standard against which outcomes are measured, some discussion of the quality of those objectives seems appropriate here. One might argue that a good objective is one that offers a 50 percent probability of success by fully-qualified and optimally motivated individuals. The modifier *optimally* is chosen advisedly and its significance should be kept in mind. An overly-motivated individual might pose long-run problems. The too-highly-motivated person may put too much emphasis on personal gain or immediate results. People who are zealously dedicated to their own programs are often blind to the fact that those programs may not benefit the organization as much as they think. They are also often blind to the fact that, although a program idea may be a good one, it should be carefully planned before it is implemented.

The criteria for and types of objectives were discussed in Chapter 3. Suffice it to say here that a good objective is a clearly-worded statement of purpose with a reasonable chance of success.

Stating Objectives

Unfortunately, not every programmer starts with a written statement of objectives. The evaluator may have to infer the objectives from other indicators or may have to articulate the objectives on the basis of what might reasonably be expected or demanded. For example, the arts and humanities division of a large continuing education operation may not have developed a statement of its own. Its program may consist of a large smorgasbord of offerings ranging from American literature to Zen Buddhism. Annual enrollments may be in the thousands and income may exceed expenses by a substantial margin. How well are they performing? By inference it would appear that their objectives are related to variety, numbers, and income. If that is true, then they are succeeding. However, a thoughtful, and perhaps hostile, evaluator might ask some disturbing questions: "Are you simply providing entertainment in the guise of culture?"; "What is the benefit to society?" or "Why couldn't this be done better by the private sector, which after all pays depreciation and taxes while you enjoy hidden subsidies at their expense?"

A clear statement of objectives, then, is desirable for several reasons. It defines the criteria on which the evaluation of the program will be based. It also forces the programmer to think in terms of the intended accomplishment, thus enhancing the chances for success, and it provides a justification for the activity.

Ideally, objectives should be results-oriented and measurable. The problem is that measures are often impossible or prohibitively expensive to obtain. The example of an arts and humanities program is a case in point. One objective, loosely stated, may be to stimulate intellectual growth or to enrich the lives of the participants. A good measure of intellectual growth may be conceivable but a competent job of measurement would probably be very expensive, and the enrichment-of-lives measurement may be nearly impossible. In some cases, those things that are most measurable may be several layers removed from the desired result and thus give only a partial measure of the desired outcome. One danger of concentrating on such partial measures of accomplishment is that they tend to become the dominant measures. Everyone agrees, for example, that end-of-course student evaluations of instructors are only one measure of instructor performance, but in the absence of any other quantitative measures, they come to be regarded as the only measure. Thus, although programmers may be fully justified in choosing objectives that are highly resistant to measurement, they must then resist the tendency to depend on partial or indirect measures for evaluating the desired final outcome.

To facilitate evaluation, objectives should be worded as simply and as concisely as possible. They should specifically state how the program will accomplish its goals. For example, "Professor Miles and a half-time project assistant will select and train twenty low-income people recruited from Central City to work as teaching aides in nursery schools and day care centers, using a combination of classroom instruction and supervised experience, and will place the graduates in paying jobs in nursery schools or day care centers."

Other Considerations

In addition to quality and quantity are some other aspects of programs that are important in evaluation, but are not explicitly stated and are difficult to measure. They are:

1. *innovation*—the extent to which future adaptability is assured by the introduction of an element of experimentation or creativity;

2. *stability*—the extent to which trends in retention rate, course attendance, enrollment, staff replacement, and so on, indicate that continuity of effort can be sustained; and

3. *noise* in the system—the extent of clashes between staff, complaints, gripes, mishaps, and other undesirable occurrences, which may not affect short-run outcomes but which reflect wear and tear on the system.

In a purely philosophical sense neither quantity nor quality are directly knowable. We get at them through indirect measures—subjective judgments, changes in student behavior, or patronage—all of which can be imperfect or misleading measures if their deficiencies are not kept in mind. Consider the familiar case of a highly entertaining but minimally educational program that nevertheless manages to attract a large registration, a very favorable student evaluation, and a strong repeat following. Should it be continued or is there a better way to use our resources?

Innovation, stability, and noise may be overlooked simply because they frequently do not have any immediately perceptible effect. Two units may generate nearly the same number of registrations, get almost equally good student evaluations, and produce an equal number of programs. Yet one unit may be clinging to a repertoire of *self-players* (programs that seem to bear almost indefinite repetition), may have a staff made up almost entirely of people nearing retirement with few prospective replacements, and may be frayed by internal squabbles and competition. Another unit may be allocating 10 percent of its resources to innovative programming and may have an orderly plan of staff development and a high level of cooperation among staff members. On the score of quantity and quality alone, the first unit may seem to be doing better than the second; but an evaluation system that overemphasizes quantity and quality may encourage behavior that in the long run can be quite destructive. Such units are in the same leaky boat as the manufacturing concern that, while attempting to achieve short-run profits, neglects research and development, staff training, and plant maintenance.

WHAT IS EVALUATED

The program is the means for achieving an objective. When we evaluate the program we are drawing conclusions about its effectiveness in obtaining that desired outcome. In this context the program can be thought of as comprising four components: teacher, content, materials, and arrangements. A completely effective program must be staffed well, cover the appropriate subject matter, make effective use of instructional tools, and take place under conditions conducive to learning.

The Instructors

A great deal has been written about the art of teaching and the qualities of an effective teacher. The fact of the matter, as programmers sometimes discover by trial and error, is that a teacher may be effective in one situation and not in another. The person who succeeds spectacularly in a small seminar of advanced students may fail miserably in presenting basic instruction to a large group, and the teacher who gave a virtuoso performance in dealing with a favorite topic may stumble badly outside of his or her field of interest and specialization.

There are, however, four general requirements of an effective instructor that evaluation will therefore consider. They are knowledge, methods, delivery, and preparation.

1. *Knowledge.* Although it may hardly seem necessary to say that effective teachers must know their subject, few of us have escaped involvement at one time or another with an instructor who had an inadequate grasp of the subject matter. The danger is greatest when a generalist is drafted into a specialized subdivision of the subject or when a specialist in one area cannot make the transition to another specialty. For example, consider the plight of a general practitioner teaching heart surgery or that of a heart surgeon teaching gynecology.

2. *Technique.* The effective teacher must choose the combination of methods best suited to convey the course content and must use the chosen methods with skill. Lecture alone is seldom the answer. Discussion, demonstrations, class exercises, role-playing, buzz groups, and a host of other techniques are available to carry the instructional message. The method must fit the content. An instructor may receive a standing ovation for a wise and witty lecture on the art of fly-tying, but the participants

are more likely to come away inspired to fish than competent to tie flies. If the objective was to teach them to tie flies, the program has not achieved its objective.

3. *Good delivery.* The essence of good delivery is the ability to communicate. This includes qualities such as clarity of expression, organization of material, contact and rapport with the students, freedom from distracting mannerisms, tempo, emphasis, and enthusiasm for the subject.

4. *Preparation.* While there are a few highly gifted instructors who can come to an institute or conference, belatedly look at the classroom, ask a few questions about the make-up of the student body, and improvise a half-day's presentation, there are more who think they can, but fail. Preparation, for most effective instructors, involves learning all they can about their prospective audience, knowing the surroundings in which they will operate, organizing or adapting their presentation to the situation at hand, and reviewing their material beforehand. One embarrassment that an instructor will likely encounter is being caught off-guard by a student's inquiry regarding a recent development in the subject area.

Program Content

It is not easy to separate the instructor from the content of the program, especially if the instructor bears the burden of responsibility for course content. In the field of continuing education, however, the instructor is frequently chosen after the course content has been determined. Thus, whether the instructor is responsible or not, it is useful to consider content as a separate object for evaluation. This approach takes into account such instances as a course that fails to achieve its objectives, despite the right choice of the instructor, because the wrong content is chosen. For example, a course on "job burnout" was planned and offered to a group of government employees by a team of thoroughly competent instructors dealing with a subject matter that had been well-received in other settings. The program was a dismal failure principally because the students had an entirely different conception than their instructors of what the content of such a program should be.

Instructional Materials

The choice of instructional materials also tends to be judged separately from the performance of the instructors. Texts, visuals, handouts, and class exercises may help to redeem an otherwise weak instructional effort. Indeed, if the objective of the program is mastery of a substantial amount of subject matter, students may learn quite well in spite of poor instruction if the text or other materials are adequate. Most studies of end-of-course achievement measures show low correlations with end-of-course evaluations of the instructor. Presumably, if the material is available, students will learn, almost in spite of, rather than because of the instructor.

Arrangements

As a general rule, in a well-run program, the arrangements surrounding the program tend to have low visibility for the participants. It is usually when arrangements get in the way that they are noticed. Room temperature is unlikely to be noticed if it is within the range of seventy-two to seventy-six degrees. Room accommodations and food service are taken for granted if they fall within some acceptable range. The quiet of the classroom, the lighting, clear lines of vision, and the timing of breaks are noted only when they intrude on the presentation. But let the temperature rise to eighty-five degrees, let the guaranteed room reservation be sold out, let an air hammer run all day in the adjacent street, let the breaks come so far apart that half the class is on the move sometime during the presentation, and an otherwise well-planned program will lose much of its effectiveness.

WHO EVALUATES

Of the five sources of evaluation two are inevitable: self-evaluation and administrative evaluation. The other three possibilities are evaluation by students, by peers, or by outside experts. Each has its advantages and disadvantages. A combination approach, coupled with an awareness of the limits of each can bring the process closest to the ideal of balance, equity, and comprehensiveness in the final assessment.

Self-Evaluation

Self-evaluation is inevitable because all of us are gifted with the capacity for introspection. No coordinator or instructor can complete a program without having some idea of how well it went. An objective and perceptive judgment about one's performance is the best possible feedback because of its immediacy and built-in credibility. The problem is that people differ widely in their capacity for objective and perceptive self-evaluation. There are four major limitations on self-evaluation. First, people differ in their level of self-esteem. Some very able people have poor opinions of themselves and some not so able people have an exaggerated notion of their own abilities. The result in these instances is a systematic under- or overestimation of their degree of success. Second, since self-evaluation, like other forms of evaluation, often needs to be communicated to others, its value depends in part on the accuracy of its communication. But people have other ambitions besides improving their performance. Despite reservations about how well they may have done, individuals may consciously or unconsciously overstate their success in order to get a promotion, more recognition, or a salary increase. Third, perception is a selective process. We hear what we expect to hear. We see what we expect to see. The insecure individual perceives the two whisperers as critics. The egotist hears the compliment and misconstrues the criticism. Self-evaluation is more prone to this kind of error than are the evaluations of most outside reviewers. Fourth and finally, self-evaluation (in common, it is true, with other forms) is based on incomplete information. The compliments are often paid face-to-face; the complaints are often unstated or expressed only in the corridors. Instructors who have worked with certain groups of international students are likely to have faced a situation in which the audience was most attentive, smiling and nodding, applauding warmly, and being free in their expressions of appreciation, only for the instructor to find (or fail to realize) that there has been very little actual communication because of cultural and language barriers.

Administrative Evaluation

Administrative evaluation is unavoidable because the administrator makes the final judgments about assignment of tasks, promotion, retention, and salary increases. Administrative judgments, however, are most often based on secondary sources of information. The average administrator is responsible for too many people to have adequate first-hand knowledge about each of them. Furthermore, in many academic situations, direct observation by administrators is resisted more than almost any other form of evaluation. Direct administrative evaluation generally relies on the data generated by some form of management information system in addition to whatever secondary sources are available. The tendency is for management information systems to be weighted on the input and instrumental sides—a topic that will be dealt with in more detail in the section on the dimensions of performance. It suffices to say at this juncture that administrators need constantly to press themselves and their providers of data to keep outputs in the forefront of their thinking in order to avoid substituting an assessment of time spent for the assessment of results obtained.

Student Evaluations

Evaluation by students tends, whenever it is used, to dominate formal evaluation systems. There is considerable logic to this in continuing education as contrasted with residential degree credit programs, since continuing education students are less a captive audience than their residential counterparts. They more often vote by dropping out or by staying away from programs, whereas the residential student embarked on a course of study is more likely to endure islands of poor instruction and what are perceived as arbitrary or meaningless requirements. Two principal problems arise with the use of student evaluations. First, because they are readily generated in numerical form, they often become a substitute for other equally valid forms of evaluation. Second, they too often reflect what is popular rather than what is educationally sound. Clearly, student evaluations are important, but educationally sound decisions are more likely when student evaluations are weighed in combination with other evidence.

End-of-course evaluations in particular may be unduly influenced by minor flaws in the program or may undervalue courses with no obvious short-term benefit. Energy management programs, for example, tended to be undervalued in the early days of the energy crisis but have since become a flourishing program area.

Evaluation by Colleagues

Colleague evaluation, or peer review as it is sometimes called, is a major form of evaluation in many institutions, especially with respect to decisions about tenure, promotion, and salary. Who can argue about the constitutional right to be tried by a jury of one's peers? Indeed, there is considerable justification for giving weight to the judgments of a person's coworkers—people with similar kinds of expertise performing similar tasks. Peer judgments, however, are subject to their own peculiar biases. Because most members of a working group in an educational setting are working somewhat independently of other members of that group, much of their information about one another's programs is based on hearsay or observation of isolated incidents. Furthermore, all of them know that there is an interaction between their evaluations of the outputs of others and their own final standing in the distribution of rewards. There is an inevitable element of competition in the evaluation of a colleague's activities. Finally, and in organizational settings most importantly, peer review can inhibit organizational change by powerfully reinforcing the prevailing values of the group. This problem is familiar to administrators who are trying to increase the emphasis on continuing education in an organization where this function is combined with the functions of residential teaching and research. Frequently the majority of staff in such a setting have a strong commitment to research; the colleague who stints research in order to do more continuing education may find that the budget reflects the values of the dominant majority.

Expert Opinion

Outside experts can provide a significant, though limited, form of evaluation—limited because of the cost in dollars and in the time-demands that can be made on outsiders. Outside review can have two principal benefits. First, the outsider can bring a greater degree of objectivity to the process. Second, the outsider may have expertise that is not available within the organization. This type of review is sometimes abused by being used for political purposes, when, for example, the administrator wishes to convince those at higher levels of control to agree to a proposal. The review is therefore designed to support a foregone conclusion. Such pseudoreview may serve a purpose, but that form of review belongs in the chapter on public relations rather than in this one.

The selective use of outside experts, generally reserved for major personnel or program decisions, may range procedurally from informal telephone conversations through solicited letters to site-visits by a review panel. The reviewers may be other practitioners, professional consultants, or scholars in the field. A number of institutions have concluded that it is desirable to have outside reviews of major program areas either periodically, for example at five-year intervals, or when any major reorganization is under consideration. As any wise administrator knows well, the chief caution to keep in mind is that such outside reviews must be regarded as a supplement to, and not a substitute for, the administrator's own professional judgment.

THE DIMENSIONS OF PERFORMANCE

One method of measuring performance is to express it as the ratio of cost to benefit compared to an acceptable standard. Cost lends itself reasonably well to measurement, whereas benefits resist assessment and standards are often arbitrary or far-fetched. It may be relatively easy to compare the cost of a children's theater workshop with the cost of a program on the great books for older adults—most of the input dimensions can be converted to dollars with some degree of logic. Then what? If one views programs solely as economic enterprises, income comes immediately to mind. Yet, few educators would accept this easy escape. Indeed, few educators view programs as economic enterprises. They are, after all, primarily educational enterprises. But, like astronomers, we have to get along as well as we can with the instrumentation available. This section deals with the problem of identifying the dimensions of performance, and the following section considers the problem of measurement.

Measurability has been an underlying theme in this chapter. The human inputs of time, effort, and ability, and the material inputs of capital, equipment, supply, and expense should be readily available from the record of operations. Although even these data can be deceptive or misleading, they are more easily verified than the claims of programmers or administrators with respect to their accomplishments. Identification and measurement of outputs, then, are at the heart of the problem. The search for good measures of output begins with an identification of the possibilities.

Outputs can be divided into two main types: instrumental and ends-oriented. Instrumental outputs are those that further the achievement of an educational objective but that are intermediate to the attainment of some end results. Attendance at a conference, attrition in correspondence study, fee income, repeat business, and student satisfaction are examples. None of these give any direct indication that an educational objective is being accomplished and yet they may be necessary preconditions to that accomplishment. As such they are legitimate but incomplete measures of end results. In some instances they may be the only ones readily available, but they can be misleading. We may use a standardized test of musical judgment to measure the changes that have taken place as a result of a course in music appreciation, but we may leave unanswered the question of whether the participants subsequently increase their involvement in musical activities, which would provide a truer picture of whether their appreciation of music had increased. On the other hand, there are popular and profitable courses that nonetheless fail to realize their stated objectives.

To the extent possible, it is desirable to go beyond the instrumental outputs and to use the best ends-oriented outputs that are available. We have used the term *ends-oriented outputs* rather than *results,* because the term suggests that our efforts are attempts to reach some ideal (the objective). The best measurements of ends-oriented outputs can tell us how close we came to achieving it.

Educational objectives may be thought of as falling into one of three categories: (1) acquisition of new knowledge or understanding; (2) changes in behavior; or (3) situational change. The course in music appreciation could fit any or all of these categories. Thus the ends-oriented measure of understanding might be the standardized test referred to. The change in behavior might be patterns of attendance at musical events. The situational change, probably as the result of a major program emphasis rather than of a single course, might be an increase in community support of musical activities.

Once the dimensions of input and output have been identified and measured, we are still faced with the problem of finding a standard of comparison. Such familiar ratios as cost per student contact hour or conference days per full-time-equivalent staff member yield numbers that can be compared with similar numbers generated in comparable situations. If obtainable and when interpreted with caution, they can be useful guides.

The foregoing implies three limitations on ratios: first, many situations simply do not lend themselves to the computation of ratios; second, ratios can mislead; and third, valid comparison ratios are not always available.

It would be difficult, for example, to come up with a meaningful ratio to measure the effectiveness of a weekly newspaper column for home gardeners. Furthermore, far-fetched ratios can create a false sense of objectivity that greatly exceeds their validity. Even the difference in cost per student contact hour from one pharmacy program to another may reflect major differences in the content and format offered just as the difference in cost between a course in accounting and one in nuclear engineering reflects inherent differences in the subject matter and teaching methodology. Perhaps the best way to think of ratios is as a means of asking questions rather than as a way of getting answers to questions. They can, in short, play a role in evaluation, but at best they are only part of the picture.

DESIGNING AND CARRYING OUT EVALUATION

This section deals with the two questions that are the basis of the evaluation process: how are evaluation studies designed and what methods can be used to carry out the design. In the case of the CPA review example that will be developed in the next subsection, the design problem is one of developing a logical structure from which inferences can be made; the methods problem is to develop one or more measuring instruments that will yield the numbers or other values to fill in the blocks in the design. We say numbers or other values because the blocks can be filled in with three different kinds of values, each requiring a somewhat different set of analytic tools. These three different kinds of values are: ordinal numbers, cardinal numbers, and nonparametric data. Ordinal numbers deal with ranks: of our three children, only one was born first, one second, and one third (even if they were triplets). On the other hand the body weights of a random sample of one hundred college students of the same sex will approximate the normal distribution curve, with almost infinitesimal differences between some members of the group and others. In still other cases, we deal with either-or kinds of differences: male-female, yes-no, living-dead, and so on. We can also, for purposes of analysis, "force" normally distributed data into a nonparametric form: pass-fail, for example, doing violence to meaning. This overview of the alternative ways of generating data serves simply to remind the evaluator that more than one kind of data can be used in planning the design and methodology of an evaluation study. But unless one intends to settle for only the simplest kind of analysis, it is well to consult experts before choosing to measure outcomes in any one of the foregoing ways.

Design Strategies

Without pretense of dealing with the complexities of methodology, this section provides a brief overview of some of the basic design strategies figuring in educational evaluation research. These strategies range from the simple to the complex. Because the more sophisticated the design the more costly the evaluation in terms of time and effort, the working administrator and the programmer must settle most of the time for relatively simple methods. Only occasionally can they enjoy the luxury of a major evaluation study. Most often such major efforts arise either when an externally-funded program incorporates an evaluation component, when a cooperative effort is undertaken with research workers, or when the staff have both program and research responsibilities. These more elaborate evaluations can be useful in their own right and are often helpful in validating the simpler day-to-day procedures.

Whether simple or complex, these designs have two things in common: first, they are meaningful only to the extent that they make comparisons possible; and second, they operate within some time constraint. Comparisons are essential whether the evaluation is as simple as a yes or no answer to the question, "Did you find this program helpful?" or as complicated as a longitudinal, double-blind multivariate experimental analysis (of which we will say more later in this section). For a simple illustration of the preceding statement, consider the case of the one-question, yes-or-no evaluation. The fact that 60 percent answered yes and 40 percent answered no has very little significance unless this response is compared with the responses in comparable situations. Basing a judgment of our performance on this response alone may lead us to think that we had done quite well. But if we know that in a comparable situation someone else got an 80-20 response, we will know that we did not do as well as we could have.

Comparisons of this type may seem unnecessary since it could be argued that we need only compare our accomplishment to the objective itself.

> . . . and each in his separate star,
> Shall draw the thing as he sees it
> For the God of things as they are.

So says Kipling's view of eternity and so we might say about the works of an Einstein or a Galileo, but for most earthly mortals comparisons are the measures of our worth.

We may be judged inadequate because our objectives are of a low order as compared with the similar objectives of others, or we may be judged inadequate because of our failure to achieve our objectives as well as others achieve their similar objectives. There is something to be said for evaluation based on idealism. And it is true that comparisons can reinforce a cycle of mediocrity. But it is also true that judgments about performance are based on a frame of reference that grows out of experience and depends on comparisons.

As to the part that time plays, any evaluation, simple or complex, takes place at some point or points in time. We may evaluate during the program, at the end of the program, or at some time afterward, or we may take a series of readings at various points in time. Both students and teachers recognize that time influences their evaluations. The laborious presentation that rated so low in the end-of-course evaluation may conceivably pay spectacular dividends in some succeeding time. Ideally, longitudinal studies, which make assessments at intervals over some considerable time period, are preferable to cross-sectional studies, which make their assessment at any one point in time. Deferred assessments are preferable to end-of-course assessments if a cross-sectional evaluation is done. We have qualified these statements about timing because the ideal is rarely possible. Longitudinal or deferred evaluations are costly and are likely to be plagued by a low rate of response. Students get lost, change jobs, leave town, or simply cannot be bothered, and the evaluator is left to speculate as to whether the nonrespondents are a major source of bias in the data.

Given that a time factor applies to both simple and complex designs, the main difference between the simplest design and the most complex is the degree to which strict logic can be applied to the conclusions drawn. The simplest kind of evaluation is that in which some numerical value, a percent or a composite score on a questionnaire, provides the basis for comparison with the percents or scores generated by other courses or other instructors. Such gross comparisons have value but must be used with caution. For example, when two programs are compared on the basis of a student evaluation form that employs a 0.00 to 4.00 scale, and when the difference between program A and program B is 0.10 on the average, we are faced with the question as to whether that difference is due to chance alone or whether it is indeed a real difference. A simple statistical formula and a few minutes of computer time can answer the question.

Comparison groups can sometimes also be found in standard sources. For example, standardized achievement tests are available for many academic subjects and comparison data (test norms) are provided by the testing service. Other comparative data can be obtained from governmental agencies such as the United States Department of Labor and the United States Department of Agriculture statistical publications. Comparisons such as these must be viewed with some caution, since there is no assurance that the two groups are comparable in all significant respects nor do the results permit a clear separation of cause and effect.

A more rigorous approach is the use of quasi-experimental designs wherein the achievement of participants in a particular program can be measured against the achievement of some group that serves as an outside control—one not under the control of the evaluator. For example, a group who completed a review course for the

Certified Public Accountant examination might be compared on their pass rate with a randomly selected group who had not taken the review course. Again the comparison is more meaningful if some statistical test of the significance of the difference is incorporated in the study, but since the evaluator has had no substantial degree of control over the characteristics of the comparison group, inferences must be made with considerable caution.

A far more rigorous design would match an experimental group with two control groups, one which receives no experimental treatment and another which serves, in the terminology of medical research, as a placebo group—that is, one which is subjected to some relatively meaningless manipulation that appears superficially to be relevant to the study goal. For still better results, the study could be double blind—that is, neither the subjects nor the experimenters would know which people were which group. The statistical technique could be analysis of variance in which variance due to the experimental manipulation could be separated from the placebo effect and the no-treatment effect.

This basic design concept can be elaborated still further by multivariate design techniques whereby a number of variables are manipulated simultaneously. The analysis technique makes it possible to estimate the effect due to each of the experimental variables. One does not need to be a statistician to conceive such designs. For a start, it is only necessary to think very logically, but the help of a good statistician is needed before plans are set. In the Certified Public Accountant review case, for example, a large enough sample—say several hundred students—would make possible an evaluation design that could deal simultaneously with all of the following variables: the effect of visual aids, the frequency of feedback, the amount of live versus mediated instruction, the spacing of practice intervals, and the meaningfulness of program content. Such designs are not easy to implement and substantial expertise is needed to carry them out.

As noted earlier in this section, the more elaborate and rigorous the evaluation design the more costly it is in terms of time and effort. In return, the complex design that is well-conceived and well-executed will yield substantial results. The solid middle ground is to use simple designs for day-to-day purposes, being fully aware of their limitations, but to use more elaborate designs as checks whenever the opportunity presents itself through external funding or the interests of some research expert.

Methods of Evaluation

Almost all evaluation methods are designed to compare outcomes of a given program with one or more external criteria of effectiveness. The criteria, and therefore the method, will vary with type of program to be evaluated. The assessment of a multifaceted community development effort will require a different approach than that of a ten-minute single-concept film on the proper maintenance of chain saws. Some methods will yield objective data and other methods will rely on subjective arguments. The choice of methods depends on the desired balance between the total cost of the method weighed against the value of the information the method will produce.

In this section, we examine six methods of evaluation with respect to their application and usefulness: (1) attitude scales, (2) achievement tests, (3) behavioral change, (4) indirect indicators (e.g., completion rates for correspondence study), (5) direct indicators (e.g., increased productivity following a job training program), and (6) case studies.

ATTITUDE SCALES   The literature on attitude measurement is extensive, going back more than half a century to the pioneering work of L. L. Thurstone in the twenties. Attitudes are expressions of subjective judgments, revealing how a person feels about something or what a person might do under certain hypothetical conditions. Often a fine line separates the expression of an attitude and the respondent's statement about a matter of fact. For example, a yes answer to the question ''Did you have a good time at the party?'' is better understood as a statement of attitude than as a statement of fact—a recognition that people often give a socially acceptable response in preference to a factual one. Similarly, the answer to the question ''Do you plan to attend any of our future programs?'' is at best an expression of an attitude. If the question is asked by the instructor in the presence of a group of students, a yes answer may be no more than a conventionally polite response. Attitudes are of use only to the extent that they are either predictive of future behavior or truly informative about the conduct and content of the program.

A number of different methods for measuring attitudes are available, ranging in simplicity from a yes or a no answer to a single question, to elaborate and sometimes cumbersome scaling techniques. The elaborate methods are not necessarily better than the simple ones. Any good scale must meet three interacting requirements: (1) sensitivity—the extent to which it differentiates among degrees of response, (2) reliability—the extent to which it produces consistent results, and (3) validity—the extent to which the expression of attitude reflects the true state of affairs. The simple yes or no response to a single question lacks sensitivity because it does not allow the respondent to distinguish between a merely adequate program and one that is outstanding. Ambiguous questions or statements will give unreliable results because people with any given attitude may be about as likely to respond in one way as in another and the wrong questions or statements will give invalid results in that they do not adequately relate to what one is trying to assess. For a course on death and dying, the question, ''How did you enjoy the program?'' could lead to results that are both unreliable (''What do they mean 'enjoy'?'') and invalid, because enjoyment bears no relation to the program's objectives.

A relatively simple measure of attitudes will serve most purposes. There are two types of scales in general use, both accomplishing essentially the same thing. These are graphic scales in which the individual records an attitude by placing a check or an x at a point on a line, or an adjectival scale in which the attitude is indicated by checking one of a series of adjectives arranged in order of desirability. The resulting marks are then usually converted to some numerical value for comparison with other programs or people.

In both types of scales respondents are asked to react to more than one question or statement. The effectiveness of the scale depends essentially on whether the right questions are asked and how well they are stated. In each of the scales the intention is to focus on the significant aspects of overall effectiveness and to do so in such a way that the respondents will make a serious effort to give meaningful responses. Because a composite score indicative of overall merit is desired, care must be taken not to load the composite score with more questions about any one aspect of the program than the importance of that aspect would merit.

No matter how carefully attitudinal measures are done, they tend to be heavily loaded with a simple satisfaction factor. Satisfaction is, to be sure, an important variable in its own right; unfortunately, some people make a dangerous extrapolation from numerical ratings of student satisfaction to numerical ratings of instruction quality. Student reaction is affected by many variables, some of which have little to do with course content or instruction. For instance, one department found that short courses of the one-week variety have higher average ratings than two-day institutes or seminars; specific subject matter courses have a higher overall rating than general subject matter; noncontroversial courses rate higher than controversial courses. In addition, not all students have the ability to measure the importance of content or to tell whether the content is actually valuable or only seemingly so because of a skillful presentation.

That the average participant in a continuing education course is less than adequately able to separate presentation skills from content skills was brought out by the notorious Dr. Fox experiment. "Doctor" Fox was an actor, untrained in the subject matter, who lectured to a group of psychiatrists, social workers, educators, and administrators, using a smattering of technical jargon, some common sense, and an impressive delivery. Even though he knew almost nothing about the topic, he received favorable ratings from the attendees.

ACHIEVEMENT TESTS The total body of knowledge on the design of achievement tests is probably as voluminous as that dealing with attitude measurement. The problems of sensitivity, reliability, and validity are similar. The main difference is that users of attitude scales are more likely to be aware of the limitations of the method than are users of achievement tests. Nevertheless, achievement tests play a significant role in course evaluation, especially so if the course deals with a fairly standardized body of knowledge, which is the case with such areas as accountancy, mathematics, navigation, or with subjects that involve a significant amount of rote memorization—the vocabulary of a foreign language, for instance. Specifically they measure what has been committed to memory; they have not proved to be of much use in measuring the comparative effectiveness of different instructors, the effects of class size, or the differences among most methods of instruction.

This paradoxical state of affairs gives rise to two perplexing questions: first, if good teaching does not necessarily result in good learning, what then does result in good learning?; second, if judgments about the quality of instruction are not predictive of the quality of learning, what does good instruction mean? The answers to these two questions are more important in continuing education than in residential degree programs since, as has been pointed out before, the audiences for continuing education are less captive due to the minimal compulsion or social pressure of continuing education.

The answer to the first question dealing with the relation between teaching and learning seems to be that students will learn if they know what is to be learned, if they want to learn it, and if the necessary material is available. Apparently, if the instructor makes the necessary contribution in these respects the students will manage fairly well whether or not they found the presentation pleasing. The answer to the second question as to the effect of good instruction seems to be that most efforts to measure instructor performance or quality of the course are primarily indicative of student satisfaction rather than of student accomplishment. As such the attitudinal measures have a great deal to do with whether students will come back another time or whether they will encourage others to attend. Achievement tests, on the other hand, are of use for program evelation primarily to signal gross defects in program concept and execution. These tests tell very little about how satisfied people are with the course or with the instructor.

BEHAVIORAL CHANGE   Most continuing education activities have as their ultimate objective some kind of behavioral change. Many such changes cannot be measured by achievement tests at all. A sensitivity training course or a community action program is not designed to impart formal knowledge or to develop specific skills. Such programs are designed to change complex social behavior. Furthermore, even those programs with a considerable element of formal learning usually see it as a means to an end. A course in art history that necessitates learning a great many facts—names, dates, and terminology—still has as its overriding goal some kind of behavioral outcome implied in such words as understanding, appreciation, or awareness.

There are two ways of getting at changes in behavior: direct observation and inquiry. Each has its difficulties. Direct observation is time consuming, and often the process of observation causes different behavior than might occur when people are not under observation. Inquiry, on the other hand, is subject to distortion through memory error, the desire to make a good impression, and perceptual bias. But carefully gathered behavioral data probably comes closer to that unknowable reality than any other method can. From a practical standpoint, however, few situations lend themselves readily to behavioral evaluation. For one thing, in many situations behavioral change requires a time lapse. It is difficult enough to interview, and even more difficult to observe the members of a group after they have scattered and returned to their home communities and jobs. Furthermore, measurable changes in behavior are less likely to result from a single short-term experience than are measurable changes of attitude or knowledge.

Behavioral observation can produce some of its most useful results in situations involving the learning of a skill. For example, a course in interview skills for personnel managers or for social workers can utilize videoplayback to document and evaluate progress. Direct observation is also used for interior design courses in which each student is assigned a final project or in which there is follow-up on an on-the-job project.

Interviews, on the other hand, can obtain statements about behavior far more readily than the behavior itself can be observed and, if done by skilled interviewers, may yield a reasonably accurate picture of the actual behavior. An example of utilizing an interview to get at behavioral change was an evaluation study of an executive development program. The program consisted of two three-day sessions spaced several weeks apart. The control group was a second group of managers from the same company. Managers were assigned at random to the two groups. The interviews were conducted several months after the training sessions; members of the control group were interviewed during the same time interval. The interview method used the critical incident technique, asking each interviewee to describe critical incidents that occurred during the last few months and to indicate how they handled these incidents. The interviews were then analyzed as to the content of incidents reported and as to the way in which they were handled. The two groups were compared regarding what they perceived as critical incidents and how they dealt with these incidents. The investigators found several differences between the trained and the untrained group and, because the method concentrated on job behavior rather than on opinions about training outcomes, there is presumably good reason to believe that the effects found were genuine.

Another example of this type of evaluation comes from a Working Drawing Institute (two days). A survey, sent to over 370 individuals who had participated in the course during a period of three years, sought to determine (1) how much money was saved as a result of their participation, and (2) how much time was saved. Of the 146 respondents who sent back the questionnaire, 76 said yes, they had saved money, but only 46 were able to make estimates of the savings. These 46 estimated their savings at an average of $451,000. In addition, 57 of the respondents suggested that it would take three years of experience to gain what they had learned in this two-day program.

INDIRECT INDICATORS   Dealing with the side effects of programs rather than with direct outcomes, indirect indicators are informative because they focus on measurable outcomes rather than on how people say they will behave. Completion rates, repeat registrations, and enrollment growth tell us nothing about what people have learned, but they are decisive factors in the survival of programs. One example of the use of indirect indicators is found in a 1979 report on evaluation of Adult Basic Education programs, where dropout rates were used to compare the effectiveness of several alternative programs. The principal danger of drawing conclusions from such indirect indicators is that they may be substantially affected by a number of uncontrolled factors that have no relationship to the program itself—changes in the economy, fuel shortages, and regional or seasonal variations, to name a few.

DIRECT INDICATORS   These indicators frequently deal with group or population data rather than with changes in the achievement, attitudes, or behavior of individuals. They thus have in common with indirect indicators the threat of being influenced by uncontrolled external factors. Indeed their validity depends on the extent to which these external factors can be identified and controlled. In the case of the Adult Basic Education evaluations mentioned above, comparisons of direct indicators for completers, noncompleters, and nonparticipants are subject to conflicting interpretations. If completers have higher incomes, less unemployment, and better jobs one year later, is it because of program content or because they were more highly motivated in the first place?

A number of direct indicators are possible, such as grievances and turnover in supervisory training programs, morbidity data for community health programs, productivity in agricultural programs, and library circulation data for cultural programs. Since most of these changes are not of a dramatic order of magnitude, fairly large samples are needed in order to do any meaningful statistical evaluation. Again, considerable caution is required in order to avoid overlooking possible confounding effects.

CASE STUDY   Case studies are useful in evaluation as a source of supporting data. They are helpful in identifying cause and effect relationships and in highlighting some of the complex interactions that statistical studies fail to deal with. They also bring a human interest dimension to evaluation studies that may be particularly useful in arousing the interest and support of funding agencies. A study conducted by the Adult Education Resource Center at Worcester State College, in cooperation with six New England adult learning centers, used case studies as a supplement to achievement tests, interviews, and surveys, to illustrate how participation in an Adult Basic Education program had changed the lives of a number of its participants.

Evaluators can use the tools of evaluation to deceive others, they can be deceived themselves, or they can use evaluation methods to inform and be informed. Often a fine line separates one use from another. Unfortunately, for most purposes the programmer can only afford to use some of the simpler methods. Nevertheless, simple methods, tempered with an awareness of their limitations, can be informative.

EVALUATION IN ACTION

It is with some trepidation that we attempt to illustrate a working model of continuing education program evaluation: trepidation because no one model will suit everyone. It is not intended as a model for the research worker but rather for the working administrator. As such it is far more oriented toward the practical than toward the ideal. An affluent or strongly research-oriented organization may judge that this example is inadequate; a production-oriented organization may feel that it cannot afford the cost or interference with daily operations that even this basic effort requires.

Any continuing managerial or professional education program area of almost any size can be considered for this example. To make the example concrete, we consider real estate as a program area. The objective is to provide continuing education for real estate professionals, including preparation for licensing and upgrading of practitioners. Comparisons are drawn with other program units within the same organization and with base data on prior offerings of the same programs as well as with similar programs in other organizations.

On the input side, financial data on most expense items are available from the business office. Two cautions need to be exercised in the use of these data: first, all cost allocations must be comparable; second, indirect costs must be taken into consideration. To illustrate the first of these points, postage costs may not be allocated by program unit but should be compared, since two units may differ considerably with respect to their postage expenditures. In regard to the second point, one unit may hold a number of its programs out in the field where some rental charges must be paid, whereas another unit may hold most of its programs on campus and therefore show no cost for this space. Incidentally, sometimes the seeming cost advantage of the non-profit over the for-profit sector evaporates when such indirect costs are taken into consideration.

On the output side the most elemental measure—and often one of the most misleading—is income and its logical extension, the income to expense ratio. It can be misleading because as noted earlier, there are sometimes inherent differences in program costs that are not fully offset by what can be charged to the students, but the ratio provides one convenient benchmark. The other measures of quantity of output are the number of programs run, the number of students enrolled, net revenues, and the number of student contact hours generated. Any of these can be put on a cost basis (e.g., cost per student contact hour) or on a workload basis (e.g., student contact hours per full-time-equivalent staff member). The figures for both are easily obtainable; both may be desirable because differences in the number of higher salaried senior staff may run cost figures up even though workloads are similar to those of comparison groups.

Quality measures are somewhat more elusive. End-of-course student evaluations may be taken as a given. A deferred evaluation in the form of results-oriented questionnaires can be given six months later. These serve the dual purpose of determining lasting changes in attitudes and behavior attributable to participation and of providing material for future promotional efforts. Additional inputs bearing on quality are obtained by administrative review of the program, the variety and types of clientele served, and evidence corroborating good planning and preparation. Finally, and in appropriate instances, most decisive is the comparison of success rates in passing qualifying examinations in such areas as appraisal and brokerage.

Administrative and advisory committee review should also assess innovation: is the program changing as needs and requirements change? As noted earlier, innovation is often the key to the continuing vitality of a program. A review of personnel records gives a basic indication of stability and noise as does review of the nature of any complaints or grievances, inquiries into the nature and cause of any staff turnover, and occasionally use of a staff survey instrument such as an organizational climate scale.

As is evident from the foregoing account, a number of these evaluation procedures involve subjective judgment. Others involve objective data that must be interpreted with considerable care. Perhaps discussion with other administrators and with those being evaluated is the best safeguard against the pitfalls of this approach to evaluation. This will provide as broad a perspective as possible not only with respect to the significance of each indicator but also with respect to the weight given each in arriving at some sort of conclusion about the overall performance of the unit.

Although evaluation cannot be reduced to a deterministic set of formulae, we have counseled in this chapter against yielding to despair. Like any other art, evaluation works to advantage when it is applied with order and with skill. Two independent, equally competent evaluators may differ, but the crux of the matter is that informed and intelligent observers will differ considerably less than will less well-prepared observers. Hence, sound evaluation procedures carried out by competent evaluators will provide useful feedback and relevant reinforcement. Evaluation will then have accomplished its purpose.

BIBLIOGRAPHY

Alford, Harold J. "Assessment and Evaluation in Continuing Education." *Adult Leadership,* April 1974, pp. 324–26.

Anderson, Scarvia B., et al. *Encyclopedia of Educational Evaluation.* San Francisco: Jossey-Bass, 1975.

Astin, A. W., and R. J. Panos. "The Evaluation of Educational Programs." In *Educational Measurement.* 2d ed. Edited by R. L. Thorndike. Washington, D.C.: American Council on Education, 1971.

Bennett, Claude. "Up the Hierarchy." *Journal of Extension* 13 (1975): 7–12.

Greenwood, Gordon and Richard Renner. "Student Ratings of College Teaching: Their Validity and Use in Administrative Decision-Making." *Science Education* 54 (1975): 493–98.

Harbison, Frederick. *Educational Planning and Human Resource Development.* Paris: UNESCO, International Institute for Educational Planning, 1967.

Klus, John, and Judy Jones. *Engineers Involved in Continuing Education.* Washington, D.C.: American Society for Engineering Education, 1975.

Knox, Alan B., ed. *Assessing the Impact of Continuing Education.* San Francisco: Jossey-Bass, 1979.

Knox, Alan B. "Continuous Program Evaluation." In *Administration of Continuing Education.* Edited by Nathan C. Shaw. Washington, D.C.: National Association for Public School Adult Education, 1969.

Long, Huey B., Roger Hiemstra, et al. *Changing Approaches to Studying Adult Education.* San Francisco: Jossey-Bass, 1980.

Popham, W. James. *Educational Evaluation.* Englewood Cliffs, N.J.: Prentice-Hall, 1975.

CHAPTER SEVEN

**CURRICULUM IN CONTINUING
EDUCATION: A PERSPECTIVE**

Certificates, Degrees, and Diplomas
Internal and External Degrees
The Audience for Degrees and Certificates

TYPES OF OFFERINGS

Nondegree Curricula
Standard Degree Curricula
Continuing Education Degrees

MODES OF EARNING CREDITS

Credit by Examination
Tutorials
Self-Paced Learning
Transfer Credits
Competency-Based Learning
Experiential Learning
Learning Contracts

CURRICULUM DEVELOPMENT

Planning the Overall Program
Sequencing Courses
Admissions and Credits
Accreditation and Quality Control

SPECIAL PROBLEMS

Control of Attrition
Logistics
Cost Effectiveness

CURRICULAR PROGRAMMING

Continuing education programs are generally either self-contained courses or programs of comparatively short duration, state-of-the-art courses that may be repeated periodically, or a sequence of courses leading to some kind of formal recognition upon successful completion. We are using the term *curricular programs* to describe sequences that usually result in some form of certificate, distinguishing them from the single short-duration programs that are the mainstay of most continuing education operations.

Curricular programs have been increasing in number since the early sixties as a consequence of both a greater concern for occupational credentials and a favorable response to nontraditional degree programs. While skeptics may tend to view this trend as simply another academic fad or fashion, many serious observers see it as meeting a growing demand for alternatives to traditional forms of education. From the standpoint of the administrator of continuing education programs it can be viewed as a logical movement toward continuing education in depth.

This chapter begins with a clarification of terminology and then examines the patterns of growth with particular reference to external degrees and their utility in meeting educational needs. It then describes some emerging patterns in curricular programs, discusses some of the problems and imperatives of curriculum development, and concludes with some thoughts on the requirements for successfully launching and operating curricular programs.

CURRICULUM IN CONTINUING EDUCATION: A PERSPECTIVE

From the viewpoint of the student, a study curriculum is a roadmap to an educational objective. It may be a straight and narrow road or it may be one with a number of alternate routes and side trips, but in any form it describes a study plan that goes beyond single courses or a sequence of courses. The objective may be civic, cultural, or vocational. The culmination—the attainment of some kind of educational goal—is usually symbolized by some sort of formal recognition. There is nothing new about such curricular offerings. They have been the stock in trade of traditional residential instruction since the Middle Ages. The relatively novel feature is the growing acceptance of the idea that part-time students can accomplish long-term educational objectives in somewhat the same manner that traditionalists have long reserved for full-time students.

Certificates, Degrees, and Diplomas

Three terms are most commonly used to describe the formal recognition received by those who complete an organized program of study: *certificate, degree,* and *diploma. Certificate* is the least precise of the three terms since certificates may be awarded for anything from a one-day conference to several years of study. They may at one extreme certify mere attendance and at the other extreme a high level of attainment. They are awarded by manufacturers of beauty aids and cookware and by the graduate faculties of accredited colleges and universities.

Fortunately, professional associations and regulatory and licensing boards, as well as academic institutions, exercise some control over what can be certified to and under what conditions. Furthermore, the acceptance of certificates for practical purposes usually depends on knowledge of what is certified to and on the subsequent performance of the holder of the certificate. For purposes of this discussion, we will reserve the term for those planned programs of study that involve completion of several courses over some period of time and that require some evidence of attainment beyond mere attendance.

Common usage has generally limited the term *degree* to levels ranging from the equivalent of two years of full-time postsecondary study for associate degrees, to the equivalent of six or more years for doctoral degrees. In most states there are few legal restrictions on who can offer degrees as long as outright fraud is not involved, but the distinction between a bachelor's degree from State University and the Bachelor of Psychic Wisdom from Ectoplasmic University is fairly clear.

Diploma is used rarely to describe a specific academic award. Rather, it is principally a generic term referring to the piece of paper or sheepskin on which the award of a degree is recorded. It can also be used to describe a professional credential awarded for a combination of examination and experience, as is the American Psychological Association's diploma in clinical psychology. Such diplomas usually presuppose academic qualifications and completion of an examination but are not linked to any further required coursework. The diploma is sometimes used as an alternate to degrees and certificates. The Energy Manager Diploma, awarded at one university for the completion of four weeks of study and eight hours of examination, was used to avoid confusion with state and federal certification requirements. Also, New York University offers eighteen-credit diploma sequences in several occupational areas, including publishing, real estate, appraisal, and financial management. Students usually possess a bachelor's degree. And the University of California–Los Angeles has, in addition to certificate programs, sequential programs leading to professional designations and awards in a variety of occupational specialties.

Other terms may be used to apply to recognition of a course of study completed either under the auspices of a trade or professional association or a licensing board— for instance, Chartered Life Underwriter, Licensed Security Dealer, or Fellow of the Health Financial Management Association. These also provide a possible opportunity for curriculum development by colleges and universities, with the difference that the award is made by the association or board alone or in cooperation with the college or university. The academic institution usually has very little latitude in planning the curriculum for this type of program since the course of study is determined by the requirements of the granting agency.

Internal and External Degrees

Both full-time and part-time students study for degrees and certificates. Until recently the principal differences between full-time and part-time study programs were in the duration and scheduling of the courses. Since the early sixties, however, a process of divergent evolution has taken place with increasing differentiation of content and methodology. Cyril Houle describes the evolution of the part-time student degree in his book, *The External Degree,* and we have borrowed his terminology for the purposes of this discussion. Table 7.1 takes his distinction between extension, adult, and assessment degrees as its point of departure, and treats the various degree programs in terms of a typology. Actual programs tend to resist typologies since they usually mix elements from more than one category. Nonetheless, the typology does describe the predominant mode of most programs.

Houle uses the term *extension degree* to describe those part-time student degree programs that follow the same requirements as the traditional full-time student degree. Typically the courses are taught in the same format by the same faculty (often at a higher fee to the student and a lower rate of pay to the faculty). This was the prevailing pattern in the evening college in the fifties and earlier, and is still the pattern that serves the largest number of students nationally.

The *adult degree* gained prominence in the sixties when the University of Oklahoma introduced its Bachelor of Liberal Studies. The requirements were different, the traditional courses were replaced by broad areas of knowledge, and the degree awarded had a different name. Nevertheless, it resembled the traditional residential degree in several significant respects. Everyone took the same course of study, the reading list was prescribed, periods of on-campus residence were required, and most of the teaching was done by the regular faculty.

In a way, the still newer *assessment degree* reached back over a hundred years to borrow from London University's external degree, which was a system of examination only, with virtually no teaching programs offered. Essentially, the assessment degree is

Table 7.1. *Typology of degree programs*

Type of degree	Curriculum	Courses	Credits	Admission	Residence	Faculty	Grading
Internal							
Prescriptive	Lockstep; few electives; traditional degree	Highly standardized, e.g., "English composition"	Tied to set number of student contact hours	At beginning of term, high school diploma and H.S. prep.	Four years of full-time study as a rule	Full-time, Ph.D. as terminal degree	Numerical or letter grades, occasional pass-fail
Flexible	Many electives, wide choice of majors; usually a traditional degree	Nontraditional or idiosyncratic e.g., "communication skills"	Tutorial; independent study, individualized learning permitted	May have open-ended entry; flexible or open admission requirements	Work study, junior year abroad, and other options	Uses tutors, preceptors, proctors, and practitioners as well as Ph.D. faculty	Competency, credit for experience, learning contracts
External							
Extension	Parallels internal degree	Same as for internal degree	Same as for internal degree	Generally follows internal degree	Same number of instructional contact hours but no full-time residence requirement	Generally similar to internal degree; may use more part-time instructors	Same as for internal degree
Adult	May be fully prescribed or tailor-made; usually a special "adult" degree	Courses are nontraditional in format or content or both	Generally credit for broad areas of competence; evidence by various means	Somewhat selective but giving weight to experience	Short periods of residence with extended periods of part-time study	Tending to rely on full-time faculty	Leaning away from traditional grading
Assessment	Defined in terms of compentencies; frequently defined jointly by a mentor and student as a learning contract	Dispenses with courses as such	Generally regards the means as irrelevant; no credit hour requirements	Frequently waives high school diploma or accepts "equivalent experience"	No residence requirement	May be practitioners	Generally attainment of an acceptable level of competence; a "pass" requirement

based on the belief that it makes no difference how one learns something and that what one learns should be a matter of student as well as faculty initiative. New York's Empire State College is one of the most flexible with respect to the assessment procedures used. A student may earn credit by taking conventional courses at any kind of institution, by working in a group with other students, by a variety of independent learning formats, and by direct experience. Empire State does not offer any courses of its own but requires at least three months of study for the associate degree and six months for the bachelor's. Minnesota's Metropolitan State University goes even further in putting full responsibility on the student to plan and carry out his or her degree contract. The only constraint is that the plan must insure competence in five general areas: basic learning skills, civic skills, cultural-recreational competencies, vocational competencies, and personal and social awareness. In Metropolitan State, as in Empire State, competence can be demonstrated in a variety of ways.

Community college commissions have also been developed around the external program concept. One such program began in 1974 when the New Jersey State Legislature made it possible for counties to establish community college commissions. The Community College Commission in Hudson County (HCCC), for instance, is funded like a community college. It enters into contracts with existing educational institutions in order to provide services for its students, and as well provides some direct services such as its evening college program and academic and financial aid counseling. Either a diploma, a certificate, or a degree is awarded, depending upon the specific plan developed between the student and the commission. Essentially then, the community college commission provides interviewing, career counseling, testing, program planning, and related services to meet the needs and interests of students, and develops a program for a student that uses the resources of the contracting institutions to meet student goals.

The Audience for Degrees and Certificates

Although most surveys have indicated that degrees and certificates do not rank high as motivators for continuing education, analyses by Houle, the Carnegie Commission, and the Newman Commission put the potential high. This potential can be observed in the population projections from the Census Bureau, which estimate that for persons twenty-five years old and over the number who have completed one to three years of college totals over 16 million. By 1990 they will number over 22 million. Another 58 million will have completed only high school. Although the standards for earning high school diplomas vary considerably, it seems a safe assumption that a majority of this number would meet the admission requirements of some colleges and universities. These figures suggest that by 1990 the pool of potential associate or baccalaureate degree candidates who are not being served by the traditional systems could number 80 million. If this 1990 group bears any resemblance to the 1972 group surveyed by the Commission on Non-Traditional Study, around 10 percent might be expected to have some interest in working on a degree. The Commission also determined that nearly 16 million people were interested in some kind of occupational certification. That brings the total number of potential participants—people who presumably would be unlikely to participate in present-day formats—up to 24 million by 1990.

These figures, of course, describe the maximum possible. Realistically, there are many factors tempering potential future enrollments. For one thing, it is a diverse market. It would take many different programs to serve the entire range of potential participants. It would also take a massive effort to achieve even a modest 10 percent penetration of the potential market. Projections must also take into account the fact that it takes four or five part-time student enrollments to generate the same number of student contact hours (or any other measure of output) generated by one full-time student. But still, there are good reasons to believe that the unrealized potential could add 5 to 10 percent more participation in higher education than can be achieved by traditional programs alone. While not enough to offset the projected enrollment declines of the 1980s and early 1990s, it could be a significant buffer against what may otherwise be a serious adjustment problem in the years just ahead.

TYPES OF OFFERINGS

The range of curricular choices and instructional methods is extremely varied. On the far outer fringe are mail-order degrees that are conferred for a price. At the other extreme are the degrees that exceed traditional criteria in terms of procedures, requirements, and standards. Some are nonnegotiable pieces of paper, while others have been accepted as a basis for admission to graduate and professional schools. Outside of the traditional boundaries of higher education, professional associations such as the American Management Association, private firms such as Arthur D. Little in Massachusetts, and government agencies such as the United States Department of Agriculture are deeply involved in the development of curricular offerings and the granting of degrees.

One useful way of ordering the various curricular programs is to classify them under three main headings: nondegree curricula, standard degree curricula, and continuing education degree curricula. As noted in the preceding section, the common feature is a sequence of courses taken over some span of time, usually on a part-time study basis.

Nondegree Curricula

Nondegree curricula award some kind of formal recognition of completion other than a degree. The most usual form is a certificate of completion, which may or may not have value as a credential. Apart from any value as a credential many of these programs have gained recognition as a measure of vocational competence.

Nondegree curricula frequently employ either a short-course format or a part-time study format. The short-course format is one of the earliest forms of nondegree curricula, having begun in the 1880s with the Farm Short Course. Courses were planned so that the working farmer could participate between growing seasons. Some measure of their significance can be seen in the fact that they were typically mentioned in the farmer's obituary along with church affiliation and offices held in the Farm Bureau or the Grange. The executive development programs at such institutions as Harvard and the Massachusetts Institute of Technology follow a similar pattern and have achieved much the same level of credibility among their constituencies.

A short-course program usually requires full-time residency for ten to twenty weeks, during which time a variety of subjects are taught. Typically it is a ''living-in'' experience, featuring interaction with fellow students, homework assignments, and extracurricular activities. Somewhat less structured arrangements were the summer programs of the Chautauqua Society at Chautauqua Lake, New York, in the late nineteenth century and, in a much shorter version, the recent Elderhostel movement.

Sequential programs based entirely on part-time study are more widespread than the foregoing short course residential programs. The majority of part-time student programs are built around an evening class program that offers students the option of taking either single courses for personal development or a specified combination of courses to qualify for a certificate. In some instances candidates for a certificate take the same courses as candidates for a degree. In other cases there are separate not-for-credit courses for which some type of unit credits are awarded—either continuing education units or something similar. The most common pattern for occupational and professional certificates is to require anywhere from four to twelve courses, each involving sixteen to forty-eight contact hours. The total number of contact hours is likely to range from 150 to 400, with a mean of approximately 250. An outside study requirement is a part of most of these courses.

For example, the qualifying sequences for a real estate broker's license from the University of California–Los Angeles and for the Health Care Financial Management certificate from the University of Wisconsin–Madison, require between 200 and 250 contact hours; UCLA's Attorney Assistant certificate requires five months of full-time study and Wisconsin's Energy Manager Diploma requires 120 contact hours. Since the traditional baccalaureate degree entails around 1600 contact hours and the typical associate degree around 800, there is little overlap between the typical certificate program and degree programs in terms of contact hours.

There is very little standardization in the bases for awarding certificates except where the programs are linked to the licensing requirements of a government agency or trade association. Number of courses, contact hours per course, outside study, and nomenclature vary not only between institutions but also within institutions. The acceptance of certificates as a symbol of academic accomplishment, therefore, varies with the credibility of the institution, the acceptance by students and their employers, the perception of a need, and, in the long-run, the experience of participants.

Standard Degree Curricula

Standard degree curricula are programs that offer traditional degrees— associate, bachelor's, master's and doctor's—but are designed for part-time students.

They differ in some respects from the typical residential degree, as in the case of the Bachelor of Liberal Studies at the University of Oklahoma, but they nonetheless follow the same sequence from associate to bachelor's to master's to doctorate. The associate degree is the one most often offered. This partly reflects the influence of the two-year community colleges, which are generally much more oriented toward the needs of part-time students than are the majority of four-year and graduate institutions. In most cases these are what Houle calls extension degrees, differing from their residential counterpart only by the time of offering and their special orientation, if any, toward the part-time student. The Regents External Degree programs in New York are among the relatively few exceptions to this generalization, since their Associate Degrees in Arts and in Nursing are actually assessment degrees.

Adult and assessment degrees are most prevalent among baccalaureate programs, but even here the extension degree is clearly the general rule. This is probably even more the case with master's degrees since master's programs in business and in education dominate the field, and the demands of accrediting agencies and of graduate deans sharply limit any impulses toward innovation. There is some hope that this may change, however. The University of South Carolina offers a master's degree program in health care financial management. The first of its kind to have substantial periods of intensive off- and on-campus study, combined with independent research under the supervision of a faculty advisor, it qualifies as an adult degree in Houle's typology.

The 1973 listing of the National University Extension Association (NUEA) included only six doctoral degree programs for part-time students. Few graduate school deans have been sympathetic to part-time study for the doctorate. While many doctoral candidates are part-time students for a portion of their careers, nearly all are required to spend some period, usually a minimum of one year, in full-time residence. History provides one notable exception. Illinois Wesleyan granted a Ph.D. by correspondence study before abandoning such study early in this century. A recent innovative approach has been Walden University's Ph.D. program, offered on the basis of four weeks of required residence at one of several centers and independent research and study under the supervision of a largely part-time faculty.

Continuing Education Degrees

A degree based on an entirely different course of study and an entirely different credit base than the standard degrees has been gaining acceptance in continuing education circles. This type of degree is literally a degree in continuing education.

For instance, in 1970 the University of Wisconsin developed the Professional Development Degree in Engineering. The PD degree is a formal postbaccalaureate degree for those who want to combine the latest technical aspects of their jobs with broader responsibilities. Designed for part-time study by the working engineer, the degree requires 120 continuing education units (CEU).

Because of the wide divergence of job descriptions and responsibilities in practice, standard degrees are limited in their extent of orientation toward a specific job. In contrast, the PD degree was developed in the belief that engineers needed to have more say in the development of their continuing education. Faculty advisors work closely with each PD degree candidate, tailoring study to individual educational needs within the candidate's field. Even within the same field—electrical engineering, for example—no two programs are the same. This kind of flexibility is possible in large part because of the variety of study formats offered at Wisconsin. PD degree candidates can choose from several hundred institutes, seminars, short courses, correspondence courses, evening classes, and independent study. If the candidate cannot attend the University of Wisconsin in person, at least half of his or her PD degree credits can be earned in classes at a local university and the rest can be obtained through University of Wisconsin correspondence and independent study courses.

Perhaps the PD degree's greatest advantage is that it is directed toward a particular career goal rather than toward a particular field of knowledge. The plant engineer, for example, must have a broad understanding of the manufacturing operation, not only in the different technical realms but also in terms of economics, business, planning, and personnel management. Yet plant engineers most often come to the job from a single field of knowledge—civil, mechanical, or electrical engineering, for instance— and are, therefore, poorly trained for their position. They need the broadening that the PD degree can supply.

Broadening is a theme that inevitably recurs in speaking of the PD degree. Where traditional advanced degrees such as the master's take the student into ever narrower channels of expertise, the PD degree works in the opposite direction by broadening his or her background for a specific purpose. It often serves as an educational transition between past and future careers.

Professional development degrees are becoming more widespread. About six other schools are offering PD degrees in engineering and several other schools have expanded the PD degree concept into science and education. Other schools have developed a Master's of Professional Development, which follows similar requirements but exists predominantly in education.

MODES OF EARNING CREDITS

The part-time learner faces obstacles that are unknown to the average full-time student: conflicts with the demands of a job, transfers, promotions, family obligations, and lack of social reinforcement by association with a community of students. These and other obstacles operate within a time frame that may seem interminable.

If degree programs for part-time students are to thrive, they must reconcile the conflict between time and academic quality. The end-of-course examination is a part of most part-time student degree programs, but there are a variety of alternatives intended to speed progress without diluting quality. We know that older adults have continued to learn after leaving school and that some of what they have learned warrants academic credit. Several bases have gained acceptance for granting the appropriate advanced standing or for combining academic instruction and life experience.

Credit by Examination

For the part-time, adult student, credit by examination is one way of accelerating progress toward a degree. Standardized tests as a basis for advanced standing came into widespread use after World War II. Both the General Educational Development (GED) tests and the further refined College Level Examination Program (CLEP) have the potential for establishing two years of college equivalency.

The other principal avenue for establishing credit by examination is through the use of instructor-made examinations. Such examinations are either those used in regular courses or examinations constructed specifically for part-time students. For example, the University of the State of New York not only accepts credit based on standardized examinations, but also allows for the development of specific examinations where existing examinations are not adequate. Special examinations may measure the results of an individual's personal learning efforts. They may be used also to validate the results of instruction outside the boundaries of routine transfer credits. A course in accountancy taken at a nonaccredited school, for example, might warrant a special test. In some cases, "cram courses" that capitalize on a combination of on-the-job and classroom learning and that are oriented toward a special examination may be provided to speed the student's progress.

Tutorials

A common problem in granting credit for nonacademic learning is the lack of a one-to-one correspondence with the content of a college course. A manager with ten years of job experience and well-developed reading habits may have learned much of what would be covered in a course on the management process, but may not have learned it in exactly the same context. If this manager is weak in certain areas, tutorial instruction of relatively short duration may be all that is needed to adequately prepare him or her to pass an examination. What may take the continuing undergraduate forty-eight hours of classroom instruction to master may thus take the experienced manager only ten or twelve hours of guided learning. The student would then be granted the appropriate number of credits for the course or could take a special examination to determine the number of credits to be granted.

Self-Paced Learning

Similar in rationale to credit by examination, self-paced learning modules using mastery examinations may allow the older adult to move rapidly through those areas where learning is buttressed by experience, while allowing as well, time for more extended study in those areas where a background of experience is lacking. The Keller Personalized System of Instruction, which is discussed in Chapter 4, lends itself well to this approach.

Transfer Credits

Nearly all institutions accept transfer credits from other accredited institutions. Most set some limit on the number of such credits they will accept. External degree programs have generally been more liberal than residential degree programs. The Regents External Degree of the State of New York sets no limit at all on the number of units of accomplishment that may be satisfied by transfer credits. Conceivably, a student who had taken work at a great number of institutions but had never stayed long enough to satisfy any one institution's residency requirement could present enough assorted credits to satisfy all of the requirements for the Regents Degree.

New York State has also done pioneering work in another aspect of credit transfer — the granting of credit for nonacademic course work. In cooperation with The American Council on Education in 1976 they published a guide to credit for noncollegiate programs. Since that time the American Council on Education has extended this program to a national program with its 1980 publication of *National Guide to Educational Credit for Training Programs,* which contains recommendations for credit for courses taught by such diverse sponsors as the American Institute of Banking-Buffalo Chapter, the New York City Police Department, and the Xerox Corporation. As discussed further in Chapter 11, this publication and annual supplements make credit recommendations for a large number of noncollegiate programs.

Competency-Based Learning

Competency-based learning, as it applies to part-time student curricula, focuses on the assessment of the achievement of behavioral objectives. This is accomplished by observing the student in situations that are designed to assure a predetermined level of competence. A simple example is the common practical test for driving, where the driver is evaluated behind the wheel rather than in a pencil-and-paper test. In the case of a manager learning about management, instead of a pencil-and-paper test, the manager's actual on-the-job performance would be judged in terms of a predetermined set of behavioral objectives.

One curriculum utilizing the competency-based learning concept is the innovative external degree program of the Community College of Vermont (CCV). CCV produces sets of guidelines showing the clusters of competencies that must be met in order to qualify for the degree. There are three general competence areas: social, physical, and intellectual. Goals are defined in a learning contract, which includes a list of learning experiences and the documentation to confirm that the learning did occur. Thus CCV's curriculum focus is on the learning outcomes rather than on the teaching input.

Experiential Learning

Credit for experience has been the center of considerable controversy. In concept it is not very different from competency-based learning in that both base achievement of an educational goal on some assessment of behavior or performance. One difference is that competency-based learning is prospective, setting objectives and then planning the learning around these objectives; experiential learning is often retrospective, evaluating the results of past experience. An older student seeking a degree through the Regents External Degree may receive substantial advanced standing based on evaluation of past experience. Past experience may be evaluated by documentation: a military service school record; an on-the-job project; an article or a painting that the person has produced; written reports, interviews, or testimonials; or any other credible evidence.

Critics are quick to point out that everyone has experiences from the moment of birth. Credit, they say, should be earned in an academic setting under suitably controlled conditions and subject to validation by some end-of-course evaluation. Certainly, even the most enthusiastic proponent of experiential learning would be quick to agree that not all experience merits academic credit. The two criteria that are applied without exception are that the experience must be relevant to an educational objective and that hard evidence must substantiate that the experience resulted in an amount and a quality of achievement deserving of credit.

Learning Contracts

Although learning contracts are not assessment techniques in themselves, they are frequently combined with competency-based learning and experiential learning to implement the quest for an external degree. In essence, they involve a negotiated statement of educational objectives whereby the student and the institution agree that a degree will be awarded when the conditions of the contract are met. The institution commits itself in turn to provide aid and support and to monitor progress toward the fulfillment of the contract. The modes of earning credit may include credit for experience, demonstrations of competency, completion of courses, and independent study. Typically, the learning contract involves great flexibility in the permissible methods of learning and in the selection of learning content to fit the abilities, interests, and needs of the student. The crux of the matter is agreement as to what constitutes a legitimate set of educational objectives that, when achieved, would justify the granting of a degree.

CURRICULUM DEVELOPMENT

A curriculum is, after all, a coordinated sequence of learning activities. What was said in Chapter 3 about single-course development is equally applicable to the combination of activities that make up a curriculum. This discussion of curriculum development will therefore deal only with the process of putting courses together into some kind of curricular offering.

Planning the Overall Program

Any institution about to embark on a curricular program faces some general decisions during the early stages of development. The first decision may be whether to offer a degree or a certificate. This choice is usually easily resolved by measuring time requirements against the objectives of the program. If simple licensure by a state board is the major objective, the inclusion of general or theoretical courses may be self-defeating. People seeking a real estate broker's license may simply choose the shortest route to that objective, however much they may concede the desirability of a broader educational base. On the other hand, if the necessary program length is almost enough to justify a degree, the additional inducement of credit toward a degree may increase the attractiveness of the program.

A middle-of-the-road approach may be to put together a package that includes a certificate as a milepost for some and as an end point for others. Thus the best of all possible worlds is presented to two different groups of potential enrollees. This may be an especially practical alternative in the case of some postbaccalaureate programs in which much of the program content may be of value to many who either do not want a graduate degree or who may not meet the requirements for admission to the graduate school. Such students may, as one alternative, be admitted to courses on a pass-fail basis or be granted continuing education units for work completed. While these students receive a certificate as the end result, the degree candidates are given credits toward the degree and are graded on an A through F scale.

If the curriculum is to lead to a degree, then the choice between a special degree and adaptation of an established degree may be the next step. It is sometimes easier, politically, to opt for a special degree. The orthodox critics of nontraditional programs may feel less compromised if the new degree does not bear the name of the old one. From the standpoint of the development of the new program this may have the added advantage of allowing greater latitude in deciding what is to be included and how it is to be taught. On the other hand, the innovative degree may lack credibility and may be discounted by those who see degrees as the currency of academia.

Sequencing Courses

Once the broad outlines are determined, a number of specific decisions have to be made. One of the most comprehensive is the choice between a lockstep program and one with flexible entry. A lockstep program is one in which all enrollees in a given cycle enter at the same time and finish at the same time. New cycles may begin at intervals ranging from twice a year to every several years, but the expectation is that the members of any one class begin and end the program at the same time. A flexible entry program will offer all of its courses on a recurring basis, and the students in any given course may be in their first year or in their last year. Prerequisites are held to a minimum so that a continuing influx of students occurs.

The lockstep program has the advantage of building courses firmly on the foundation of the preceding courses. Members of the class have more of a feeling of community and of a shared experience. A disadvantage of the lockstep program is that substantial attrition can take place, both because some programs may extend over a period of years and because the lack of choice in courses and times may be unacceptable to some. Thus a program that is a financial success in its first year may be a financial disaster in its final year. A number of schools having such programs, however, claim that student retention is surprisingly good when careful screening of applicants takes place before admission and when some kind of contractual understanding is a precondition for admission. Another possible disadvantage of the lockstep program is that the integrity of the institution may be at stake when there is a commitment to complete the program cycle but insufficient enrollment to support continuation. With flexible entry, continuing recruitment can usually offset the effects of normal attrition.

Adequate planning is essential to either program. Perhaps the greatest pitfall in planning is a failure to anticipate the cumulative effects of maintaining a continuing program. If ten courses are required for completion of a master's degree, for example, the first-year offering might be only one course each term for a total of two in the first year. In the second year, two more courses will have to be added, and so on through the cycle. Quite clearly, it may be necessary to offer ten courses in year five, which may be beyond the capability of the institution. The point to be understood is that both the institution and the students need to project their programs through their entire life cycle. In that way the student who plans carefully will not end up with no course to take in any one term. Similarly, the institution will not offer some of its courses so frequently that low enrollments or staff resources become a problem. A long-range plan is needed before the first student is enrolled, and each student, in turn, needs to use this as a basis for personal planning.

Admissions and Credits

Evidence indicates (Cagiano et al., 1978) that the grade point average of returning students improves in direct proportion to the length of time they have been out. Whether this is due to improved performance or to grade inflation is not entirely clear. In any case, most institutions, even the more tradition-bound, tend to relax admission requirements for students who have been away from academia for some interval of time. In such cases aptitude test scores may be given additional weight or, in graduate and professional programs, successful job experience may be a basis for deviating from a strict adherence to grade point requirements. In addition, there may be a more liberal policy with respect to probationary or conditional admissions for returning students. The amount of justifiable flexibility will depend on the nature of the program and on the relevance of alternative bases for admission. Business experience may be a good basis for waiving admission requirements in a business degree program and a doubtful basis for waiving requirements in a technical program or in a general liberal arts program.

The problem of granting advanced standing for work taken some time ago also needs to be looked at in a specific context. A course in Shakespeare taken twenty years ago may have the same content as one taken today, and retention may be good because of subsequent reinforcement. On the other hand, a computer science course taken twenty years ago may be of doubtful significance when technological change or lack of retention has nullified its value.

The use of achievement tests to validate prior learning offers one solution to the problem. It is a limited solution, however, given the way such tests are often designed. If the course content is highly standardized, as it usually is in mathematics or accounting courses, a test may be a good measure of learning. If course content differs considerably from one instructor to another or from one institution to another, however, the use of a regular end-of-course test may be a poor indicator of achievement. Special tests that emphasize concepts rather than course minutiae may be necessary.

Accreditation and Quality Control

There are two particular dangers in the establishment of nontraditional curricula. The first is that it may be difficult to distinguish poor programs from good ones. The second danger is that good programs may be downgraded by accrediting agencies or by the public simply because they do not fit established molds. To offset these hazards, both the student and the institution offering the program need to take special care to document course content and requirements. The more unorthodox the curriculum, the more important it is that a student document the work done. Documentation becomes especially important when a student wants to change institutions or needs to use a degree or a certificate as a job credential or to gain admission to a graduate or professional school. The growth in acceptance of nontraditional methods of learning and their assessment is indicated by the 1976 finding that 78 percent of graduates of the New York State Regents External Degree program had been admitted to graduate work in collegiate institutions and thirty-eight state boards of nursing accept the Regents degrees in nursing. The University of Oklahoma's Bachelor of Liberal Studies also gained a high acceptance as preparation for graduate or professional study.

SPECIAL PROBLEMS

Three special problems need to be noted in connection with the administration of curricular sequences: control of attrition, logistics, and cost effectiveness. Each of these is dealt with in other contexts elsewhere in this book, but their special bearing on curriculum development requires some additional comment here.

Control of Attrition

It seems a truism to say that the longer the road, the more the people who fall by the wayside. Obviously, as a general rule, more people will drop out from a course of one year's duration than from a one-day conference. Curricular sequences, which by their very nature continue over long periods of time, require careful attention to attrition control especially when independent learning formats are used. Control begins when the student applies for admission. The student should be fully informed about what participation entails and should be reminded of the competition from job, family, and social life. High pressure selling and understatement of the expected difficulties will increase attrition. Learning contracts can be used to communicate expectations and to foster a sense of commitment. While these are not contracts in a legally enforceable sense, they nevertheless cause the student to pause and examine the degree of his or her commitment. From such examination, the student either draws back or begins with a stronger resolve to complete.

Reinforcement through study groups can also be used, to overcome the sense of isolation experienced by the independent learner and the part-time student. In one program that enrolls students only in groups of two or more, group members alternate with one another as proctors for mastery examinations and provide direct and immediate feedback to each other during weekly meetings. Instruction is also given a human touch through weekly telephone contacts with the instructor. Audiocassettes can give an added sense of contact, and in some courses, a photograph of the instructor is provided, along with the audio and visual aids, to remind students that a human being is behind all the syllabi and study guides.

Student mobility poses a special problem in long-term learning situations, but courses can be designed to increase portability of credits. Such, measures include reciprocity agreements with other institutions, more liberal credit transfer policies, and availability of alternative routes to course completion.

Logistics

Logistics poses a special challenge in long-term study programs, especially when a variety of study methods is used to accommodate different types of subject matter. Access to library services can be a serious problem when students are located in remote areas, since copyright restrictions on photocopying limit the distribution of materials. For students living at a distance from campus, periodic stints of intensive study (the long weekend, the week away from home) in the campus community can partially substitute for daily access to a library. Regarding another type of service, access to a computer, portable terminals, and telephone connections can help to overcome the barriers of time and distance. In the case of the British Open University ingenious adaptation of laboratory exercises to the home kitchen have introduced additional instructional flexibility. In short, imaginative programmers have been able to compensate in a variety of ways for the difficulties imposed by time and space.

Cost Effectiveness

A number of nontraditional programs have been born of a union between institutional ingenuity and external funding. Some of these programs have enjoyed a healthy infancy only to die in early childhood from malnutrition. High startup costs have been covered by gift and grant funds, but once the external funds are gone the cost of continuing has exceeded institutional capacity. Expensive program software has required expensive maintenance and updating. The problem has been especially severe for those continuing education programs that must recover 100 percent of costs through fees. Introductory courses with high enrollments and the resultant lower cost per student have not always been able to carry advanced courses with higher unit costs.

Programmers must resist the temptation of high-cost methods when lower-cost methods can be used effectively. Radio can often be used instead of television, audiocassettes instead of videocassettes, and teaching assistants rather than full professors. Modern word-processing methods and loose-leaf study guides can hold down the costs of course revision and updating, since the revision of individual modules does not require a whole new press run and the accompanying costs of collation and binding. And finally, instead of each institution going its solitary way, more extensive sharing of educational software can help spread some of the fixed costs of course production over a wider base. The midwestern Committee on Institutional Cooperation is doing this with correspondence study guides, just as the University of Mid-America does with televised instruction.

Curricular programming is riskier, in general, than short-term programming, both because of the higher startup costs and because of the uncertainties inherent in any form of long-range planning. It is also an area in which success begets imitation. Thus, in spite of the potential numbers cited early in this chapter, the threats of market saturation and of preemption by residential institutions and by the private sector are very real.

If programmers succeed in overcoming the risks and threats, however, it may well be that by the turn of the century, the boundary between traditional and nontraditional curricula will be so blurred as to be indistinguishable. If so, it will not be the first time in history that the children of the iconoclasts have become the leaders of the establishment.

BIBLIOGRAPHY

American Council on Education. *National Guide to Educational Credit for Training Programs*. Washington, D.C.: American Council on Education, 1980.

Cagiano, A. M., M. Geisler, and L. Wilcox. "The Academic Performance of Returning Adult Students." *College Board Review*, Winter, 1978, pp. 13–16.

Dubin, Robert, and Thomas Taveggia. *The Teaching Learning Paradox*. Eugene, Oregon: Center for the Advanced Study of Educational Administration, University of Oregon, 1968.

Houle, Cyril O. *The External Degree*. San Francisco: Jossey-Bass, 1973.

Keeton, Morris T., et al. *Experiential Learning*. San Francisco: Jossey-Bass, 1976.

Klus, J. P. "A Professional Development Degree for Engineers." *Professional Engineer*, November 1970, pp. 32–35.

Perry, Walter. *The Open University*. San Francisco: Jossey-Bass, 1977.

Pitchell, Robert J., ed. *A Directory of U.S. College and University Degrees for Part-Time Students*. Washington, D.C.: National University Extension Association, 1973.

Project on Noncollegiate Sponsored Instruction. *A Guide to Educational Programs in Noncollegiate Organizations*. Washington, D.C.: American Council on Education, 1976; and Albany: The University of the State of New York, 1976.

Trivett, David A. *Academic Credit for Prior Off-Campus Learning*. Washington, D.C.: American Association for Higher Education, 1975.

CHAPTER EIGHT

**HOW ORGANIZATIONS ARE PUT
TOGETHER**

Structure and Function
Problems of Organization
Criteria for an Effective Continuing Education
Organization

**ALTERNATIVE ORGANIZATIONAL
STRUCTURES**

Program Control
Workable Compromises
Geographic Decentralization of Field Staff
Community College Organization

BASES OF DEPARTMENTATION

Departmentation by Discipline
Departmentation by Format
Problem-Centered Departmentation
Departmentation by Clientele
Task Force Organization
Matrix Organization

INTERAGENCY ORGANIZATIONS

Program Coordination
Community Relations

ORGANIZATION

Continuing education and extension operations have certain functions in common. All must plan, produce, and finance their operations. However, these common functions can be carried out by units that differ greatly in their organizational structure. The differences often depend on the size of the work group and on the nature of the work. The director of a one-person operation, for instance, cannot delegate the work to others. Departments and their relationships to one another have little or no meaning in a very small operation where division of labor is simply the allocation of personal time, and not the assignment of responsibility to members of a staff. This chapter, therefore, concentrates on units that are large enough to require formal divisions of authority and responsibility. Experts disagree on the point where size becomes critical. However, some degree of formal structure emerges when the unit reaches six to twelve members. Hence organization is relevant even in comparatively small operations.

Organizational differences also depend on differences in missions and circumstances. Geographic decentralization may be important in a state university and of little concern in a private urban university. Academic rank and tenure are of no concern to a large-scale operation based in a metropolitan YMCA. In a large community college, part-time student programs may blend imperceptibly into the full-time student programs. There may be universal principles of organization, but there are certainly enormous differences in their application.

This chapter will deal mostly with large-scale organization in academic settings. Such organizations embody most of the problems of other continuing education operations plus a few that are peculiar to colleges and universities. We will begin with some of the basic requirements of effective organization and then will consider alternative kinds of organizational structures. Because specialization of function is essential to large-scale organization, we will also consider the various ways of setting up operating departments. Our examination of organization will conclude with a look at structures for handling interinstitutional relations.

HOW ORGANIZATIONS ARE PUT TOGETHER

Structure and Function

At a national symposium on university public service, C. Brice Ratchford, then president of the University of Missouri, began his speech with the optimistic note that "good people who have a common understanding of the goals to be achieved will produce excellent results regardless of the administrative arrangements." As he progressed into his speech, he soon qualified his statement by stating that the traditional organizational structure in universities for residence teaching and research is ill-suited to the extension function.

The concept of continuing education and extension puts the resources of higher education to work outside the traditional classroom, wherever the resource base of the institution is relevant and potentially useful. This often involves situations that refuse to be confined by disciplinary boundaries, and thus require a different kind of organizational structure. If knowledge is to be translated into early action in a complex social environment, the institutional structure must be problem-centered and results-oriented. It is a more complex and demanding function than the delivery of knowledge in the traditional classroom setting.

Problems of Organization

We referred earlier to the universal problems of organization. This section will briefly review the most pertinent of these problems. Of course, there are no universal solutions. But, since those responsible for the structure and operation of any organization will have to face these problems, it makes sense to be 'aware of how they may affect the operation of the organization.

BASES OF AUTHORITY　Most people who direct the activities of others assume that their orders will be followed; that is, they do so until something goes wrong. There are three reasons why people fail to follow directions: they do not understand them, they are incapable of complying, or they are unwilling to comply. The last of these three is related to the problem of authority. There are a number of sources of administrative authority. Two of these, moral and technical authority, pertain to the personal qualities of the administrator. They are, therefore, not directly related to the formal organizational plan. Moral authority refers to that quality in the administrator that inspires a high level of commitment. It is sometimes referred to as leadership, charisma, or normative authority. Technical authority is based on recognized competence or expertise. An engineer, an accountant, or an attorney may be called upon to give directions because of his or her recognized professional competence, even though that individual has no formal authority in the organization.

Four other bases for authority are pertinent to organization-building. We will define each and explain briefly why they need to be considered in planning an organization.

1. *Economic authority.* In the broadest use of the term this refers to the ability of the administrator to control the distribution of rewards. If, for example, salary increases are distributed across-the-board, and if promotions are on a strict seniority basis, then the administrator has little economic authority.

2. *Legal authority.* Originally, legal authority was based primarily on ownership of property and of the means of production, and there were few, if any, restrictions on what an employer could do. Over the years, legal authority has become far more complex. The right to hire and fire has been restricted by law in a number of respects. Courts have opened personnel files, modified retirement policies, and have restricted the forms of disciplinary action. Nevertheless, in spite of lamentations about the erosion of administrative rights, administrators do still have some legal authority. Unfortunately, they sometimes hesitate to use it because of their fear of causing confrontations with unions, regulatory agencies, or the courts.

3. *Contractual authority.* Legal authority and contractual authority converge when formal contracts are involved, as, for example, when collective bargaining agreements are in effect. But there is another area in which employment contracts are more the result of mutual understanding. In effect, these unwritten contracts are the result of clear communications between administrators and staff whereby both commit themselves to a beneficial exchange of obligations and benefits. This relationship is dealt with in some detail in Edgar Schein's *Organizational Psychology*, where it is called the psychological contract.

4. *Collegial authority.* In many organizations, particularly academic ones, some degree of authority resides in the staff itself. It may be the authority of a senate or a tenured faculty or it may be that of a full faculty or an elected committee. Usually it is authority to act in certain defined areas such as curriculum or promotion. Such authority may, in theory or in practice, be subject to administrative review or to review by the board of control. It may be subject to both, and may even be subject to appeal to the courts.

With respect to the four kinds of formal authority we have described, the following generalizations might be made.

1. Perceived administrative control over the reward system is a significant source of support for administrative authority.

2. A clear understanding of the limits of legal authority is important for the intelligent exercise of administrative discretion.

3. A clear mutual understanding and acceptance of a staff's privileges and obligations will strengthen the position of the administrator and increase the commitment of the staff.

4. Collegial authority should operate within carefully defined limits. It should be delegated in areas where the staff has special competence, but limited so that its exercise does not endanger the health or survival of the organization. For example, an external degree program might appropriately be a collegial decision but subject to administrative review of its budgetary impact.

TALL AND FLAT ORGANIZATIONAL STRUCTURES   The structure of organizations can vary along two dimensions—the number of people reporting to each supervisor, commonly called the span of control, and the number of levels in the chain of command. A wide span of control characterizes organizations with a small number of levels, and a narrow span of control results in a tall structure with a greater number of levels.

For many years management theorists have debated the question of optimum span, but generally agree that there is a practical limit to the number of people any one person can supervise, which will vary with the amount and kind of supervision required. If the span is too narrow, people are likely to receive too much supervision and lose their sense of autonomy, especially in the case of professionals who are trained to operate with a high degree of independence. Furthermore, with a narrow span of control and the concomitant increase in the number of levels, the lines of communication are longer, making more likely a breakdown of communications and a sense of separation from the sources of top level decision making. Of course a similar sense of isolation can develop if the span is too wide and the immediate supervisor is supervising so many people that access is excessively limited. Another danger of an excessively wide span of control is the tendency to create personal staff positions—"assistants to" and the like—to avoid stretching the supervisor too thin. The result can be a proliferation of functionaries who purport to speak for and act as a conduit to the supervisor who can thus become isolated from the operating staff. There are no magic formulas for resolving these problems, but an awareness of the need for balance and a sensitivity to the danger signs can be a significant help in organizational planning.

DEPARTMENTATION   Any complex organization must have some kind of division of labor to be reasonably efficient. In a business enterprise, departments are frequently based on the function performed: finance, marketing, production, and personnel. Other bases in business and industry are product, customer, geography, and process, each of which has a possible counterpart in education. The corresponding bases might be format (departments of correspondence study, evening classes, and institutes and conferences), clientele (professional groups, for example), geography (geographic departmentation), and function (the correspondence study unit may be divided into such units as receiving, grading, records, and mailing). These illustrations suggest that several kinds of departmentation, based on some criterion of best use of resources, may exist within the same organization. In addition, another option exists in continuing education and extension operations: task-centered departmentation. Task-centered departments may be temporary units designed to deal with a specific problem, as in the case of the Pico-Union project cited in Chapter 1, or they may be more or less permanent units dealing with issues such as energy conservation or community health. Later in this chapter under "Bases for Departmentation," we will discuss some of the specific considerations governing departmentation in continuing education and extension operations.

LINE AND STAFF   In the overall division of labor in any large organization there are two kinds of people: those who do the principal work of the organization (the line) and those who perform some kind of supporting function (the staff). The line organization is generally responsible for planning and executing the basic programs of the organization. The staff provide support in the form of either advice or services. Legal counsel is an example of the former and data processing an example of the latter. In some instances staff people have limited authority in their own right as in the case of building security staff. In this context line and staff are differentiated on the basis of the function performed. In other contexts *line* is used to describe the channels through which authority flows—who gives orders or direction to whom—and *staff* is used as a generic term for all personnel. The distinction is usually clear from the context.

It is important to insure that line and staff relationships are synchronized since conflict is likely. The business office is frequently seen as interfering with the work of the line organization by demanding more paperwork or by turning back requests for funds. Service departments are perceived as controlling operating decisions by setting unreasonable deadlines, failing to deliver a service at the desired time, or dictating procedures (''I'm sorry but the computer won't allow you to do it that way''). There is a growing movement in large-scale industrial organizations to minimize or eliminate the distinction between line and staff by greater use of functional teams or task groups in organizational design. These approaches will be discussed in the later sections on matrix and task force organizations.

DECENTRALIZATION OF CONTROL   Centralization of control is a matter of degree. In a highly centralized organization all major operating decisions are made at the top. In a highly decentralized organization most major operating decisions are made at lower points in the organizational hierarchy. Decentralization may be either functional or geographic. Functional decentralization occurs when operating decisions are made by a subject matter or problem-centered department. Geographic decentralization occurs when operating decisions are made by field units.

Both forms of decentralization can stimulate initiative and increase the sense of responsibility of the people on the firing line. Since these are the people closest to the clientele, they can be expected to have a more intimate knowledge of what will work and what will not. On the other hand, decentralization, by definition, implies some loss of central control. It also frequently leads to jurisdictional problems when two departments program in overlapping subject or clientele areas or when territorial lines are crossed. If lines of communication are good and if the staff are optimally motivated and well-qualified, decentralization can produce excellent results. But we will see in the section on Program Control Structures that there are some problems with decentralization in continuing education that set it apart from other enterprises.

Criteria for an Effective Continuing Education Organization

Apart from the various organizational arrangements that may be employed, there are certain requisites for an effective continuing education delivery system. In the previously mentioned national conference on university public service, President Ratchford outlined six such criteria. Although these criteria are not equally applicable to nonacademic continuing education and extension operations such as trade and professional associations, and public accounting firms, they are generally indicative of some of the pitfalls to be avoided.

1. *Institutional commitment.* Although the principal administrators and faculty of a college or university may be inspired to develop or to give some support to the continuing education and extension function, the commitment is all too often only nominal and grudging, resulting in an ineffective or marginal program. A truly effective commitment requires both understanding and active leadership by key faculty members and administrators. Without such a commitment, the administrator in charge of continuing education activities is well-advised to keep his or her goals modest.

2. *Budgetary identity.* The role of the budget in influencing the activities of the faculty can never be underestimated. An effective extension operation requires continuity of funding and budgetary separation. When extension is funded on a project-by-project basis, the programs rarely develop the continuity or the impact made possible in residential instruction and research programs by sustained funding. Furthermore, the comingling of research, residential instruction, and extension funds results in the stinting of that function which has the lowest priority (usually extension), whereas a clear separation of funds is perhaps the best guarantee of adequate attention and continuity.

3. *Administrative responsibility.* Someone should be given clear responsibility for the administration and maintenance of the extension function. The principal extension administrator should be placed on a par with other chief administrators, either with the title of dean, or some other suitable title, which insures direct access by that administrator to the chief administrative officer of the institution.

4. *Integration with the total institution.* Integration with the total institution implies two things: first of all, that those people who fill the continuing education and extension role for the college have full academic citizenship, including salary, perquisites, titles, and privileges comparable to those of all other staff; and second, that they have a close relationship to their counterparts in residence teaching and research.

5. *Mission definition.* There is a danger in an institution of attempting to be too many things to too many people. It is obvious, for example, that a university lacking a medical school should approach the area of health care delivery with considerable reserve and caution. Equally unfortunate, on the other hand, is the university structure that permits some schools and colleges to stand apart from outreach and others to be deeply involved. It is not uncommon to find a land-grant university with an extensive and active agricultural extension service but with minimal extension operations in other equally large and well-developed faculties within the university. Thus, it is important that the public service goals and functions be carefully thought out and defined so that the program does not develop willy-nilly, reflecting simply the passing interests of individual faculty members.

6. *Geographic decentralization.* It is almost axiomatic that an effective continuing education system within a large institution needs some degree of decentraliza-

tion of staff. This can be the type of decentralization found in most U.S. Cooperative Extension Services, which have community-based staff many of whom are based far from the campus, or it may be the kind of approach more characteristic of earlier extension operations, in which itinerant staff moved from the campus into the community and back again. It may also involve the utilization of off-campus centers that provide a locus for either temporary or permanent staff in branch campuses or in rented or shared facilities. These various alternatives for geographic decentralization will be discussed in more detail in a subsequent section of this chapter. The point at this stage is simply to establish that some kind of geographic decentralization is required for any extension operation purporting to serve any but a very small geographic area. Even a strictly local institution in a small- to medium-sized community can benefit from operating off-campus as well as on if transportation, ethnicity, or parochialism keep people off the campus.

ALTERNATIVE ORGANIZATIONAL STRUCTURES

Program Control

When control of operations is centralized, the administrative head reports directly to the president, with a title that places him or her on an equal footing with all other principal administrators of schools, colleges, and other major functions. The centralized model has its own separate budget and staff for programming with authority to make academic appointments and to grant rank, tenure and titles to staff members. In short, the degree of control and the separation of functions in extension is as great as it is in residential schools and colleges. Figure 8.1 portrays this model.

At the other extreme, the fully decentralized model either has no overall extension administrator reporting directly to the president or chancellor or else the chief extension administrative position is a staff, as opposed to a line, function. Continuing education and extension program authority is vested in the separate residential teaching and research units. All program staff report directly to the dean or director of the school, college, or other subdivision of the institution. Rank, tenure, title, the power of appointment, and budget are all vested in the separate residential schools and colleges. Figure 8.2 represents one such model.

The fully centralized model has several advantages. First of all, it makes possible the recruitment and development of a fully committed, professional staff whose primary responsibility is to the extension function. It is often true that a good research worker or undergraduate or graduate teacher is less well-qualified for the extension role. Of course, the reverse may also be true. Where staff are recruited and held accountable for a specific function, it is possible to develop a higher level of staff competence. A second advantage is that budget control rests with the extension administrator. It is possible to reallocate funds as priorities change, to penalize nonproductive units, and to give additional support to productive units. This kind of flexibility is rarely possible when funds are budgeted directly to departments, schools,

Figure 8.1. *Centralized model, University of California–Berkeley (after Gordon, 1974, by permission)*

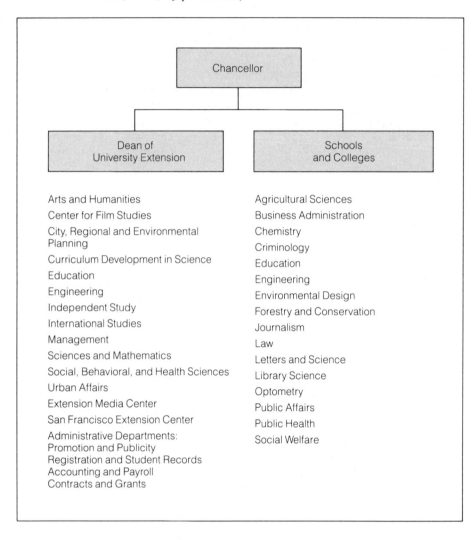

or colleges. Third, it makes possible the maintenance of a mission-oriented, problem-centered, cross-disciplinary kind of operation. It is considerably more difficult to get this kind of cross-disciplinary focus from faculty members who are accountable for professing a particular subject. Fourth, it tends to increase the willingness and ability to develop innovative and experimental kinds of programming. The very nature of extension and continuing education necessitates more experimental and innovative programming than is required in a residential operation. Separation of the two functions increases the flexibility that is typical of the most successful extension operations. As

Figure 8.2. *Decentralized extension, The University of Michigan–Ann Arbor (after Gordon, 1974, by permission)*

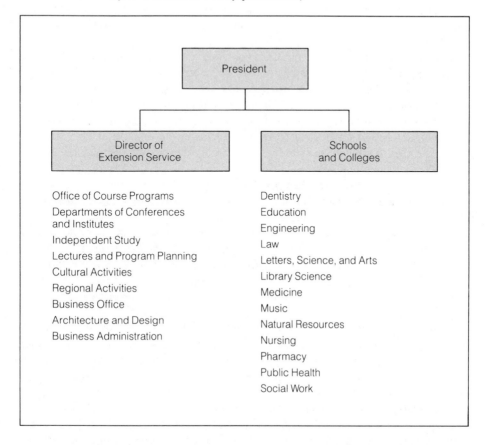

Bernard James and Robert Fagaly wryly comment in an article entitled "Organizational Marginality and Opportunity in University Outreach Education," "The promising thing about outreach education is that its out-of-sight and out-of-mind marginality is also an organizational advantage because it provides the freedom needed for invention and innovation. It also might provide opportunity for testing new models of education aimed at increasing university 'relevance.' It may yet prove one of the more promising sides to university life in the coming decade."

One disadvantage of centralization is that the separation of extension from residence teaching and research tends to create a separate institution within the institution, and to nullify or minimize the advantage that an academically based extension operation has over continuing education programs operated by nonacademic agencies. A separate extension with its own staff and budget is less able to tap the full resources of the total institution and limits the ability of faculty members to work across disciplinary lines.

173

In a decentralized operation, where extension is integrated into the total academic unit, there is freedom, and under ideal circumstances at least, there are incentives for all faculty to participate. Thus, the full resources of each school or college, rather than only the talents of a few segregated specialists, are more readily brought to bear on problems.

On the other hand, a decentralized operation tends to have narrower, uncoordinated program focuses that are not fully responsive to the problems of the larger society. Professional schools, for instance, may serve only the members of the profession rather than the total community. In the field of health care an extension operation entirely located within the medical school is more likely to concentrate on providing continuing education for physicians than to focus on the broad problems of health delivery in the community. In short, extension operations often reflect faculty interests rather than community needs.

There are also budgetary and personnel problems associated with a fully decentralized operation. The extension function is often considered less valid or meritorious than residential functions, an attitude which is evidenced by differences in salary, promotion, and the granting of tenure. Discrimination between extension and residential faculty may either reflect actual differences or simply the perception by the dominant faculty group of what is meritorious. Whatever the basis for discrimination is, however, the extension operation may suffer. Extension funds may be diverted to research and residential teaching, or the extension unit may be forced to accept marginal faculty.

Fortunately, the decision is not an either-or choice; there are several middle-of-the-road possibilities. One of these is to have a strong staff position in the top administration with a title such as vice president or vice chancellor, with control over budget allocations but without direct control over staff or program. Under this type of arrangement, while budget control and access to the chief administrator are vested in a vice president, the extension has no faculty of its own and all part-time teachers require the approval of the academic department head or the dean. Also, all courses and curricula have to be approved by the separate schools and colleges. In effect, the vice president for extension gets his or her authority from control over the budget. In practice, however, access to faculty resources often depends upon the lower levels in a complicated and often unresponsive chain of command. Availability of faculty tends to depend on the lack of other commitments for the faculty at any point in time rather than upon the specific kinds of skills and talents that faculty members may have. It becomes thus a program based on targets of opportunity or use of excess capacity rather than a program directly responsive to priorities originating in the total community. Figure 8.3 illustrates the staff function approach.

Workable Compromises

On two points there is almost unanimous agreement: first, a truly effective outreach operation requires a top-ranked administrative officer who reports directly to the chief administrative officer of the total institution; second, this extension adminis-

Figure 8.3. *Staff function model*

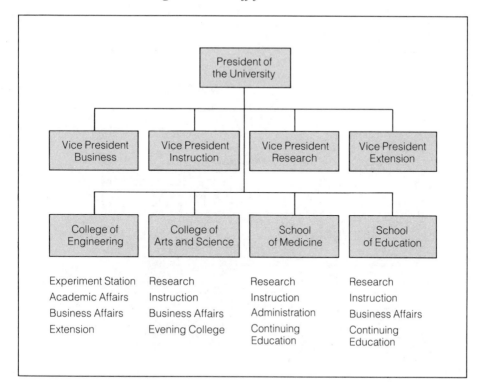

President of the University			
Vice President Business	Vice President Instruction	Vice President Research	Vice President Extension
College of Engineering	College of Arts and Science	School of Medicine	School of Education
Experiment Station	Research	Research	Research
Academic Affairs	Instruction	Instruction	Instruction
Business Affairs	Business Affairs	Administration	Business Affairs
Extension	Evening College	Continuing Education	Continuing Education

trator must have a significant degree of control over allocation of budgetary resources for the extension function. Beyond these two conditions, the arrangements may vary considerably from one institution to another, depending on the specific circumstances of the institution.

THE INTEGRATED DEPARTMENT More workable kinds of centralized-decentralized operations may be those in which a unit extension administrator reports directly to the chief administrator of the college and has a separate budget and direct administrative control over the extension program. Such administrative control includes being able to exact accountability from faculty for that portion of their time budgeted to the extension function and, most important, being able to control the program planning process. Under this arrangement, however, the extension staff may still be fully integrated with its residential counterpart, differing, however, in having another line for program and budgetary accountability. Faculty assignments may vary from time to time between residence teaching, research, and extension; reallocations of budget can be made occasionally as individual staff members' talents are required for a particular program.

Figure 8.4 is an example of such a structure. This type of organization utilizes

175

Figure 8.4. *Integrated department structure, matrix organization*

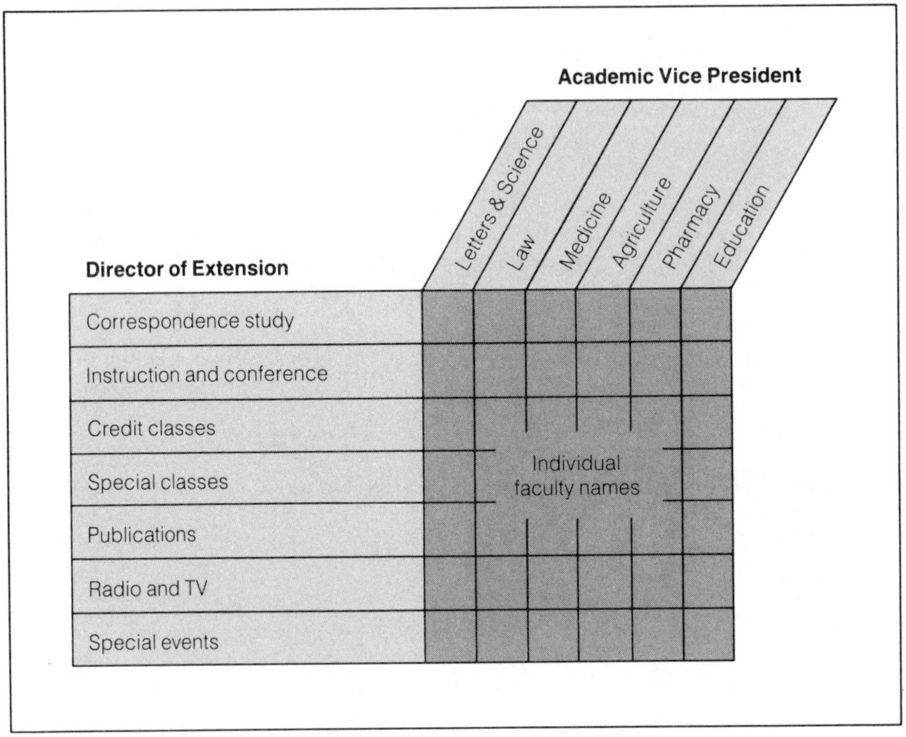

what has come to be recognized in management literature as the matrix form of organization. It breaks with some of the principles of classic organization theory: unity of command, continuity of office and position, and hierarchy of control.

There are disadvantages to this arrangement. The dual accountability of the faculty members under such an arrangement may create additional red tape, double record keeping, double accountability. Often, even routine decisions regarding how to charge travel or telephone or secretarial help may become a bone of contention between the head of the extension operation and the chief administrative officer of the residential school or college. It also does not eliminate the possibility of a double standard between faculty members who have a primary extension responsibility and those who have other, more traditional, kinds of responsibility. Conflicts with respect to academic standards for purposes of salary, promotion, and qualifications for appointments may create difficulties as well.

SEPARATE FIELD BUT INTEGRATED CAMPUS STAFF   In some partially decentralized operations, direct accountability for campus-based faculty may lie with the dean of the residential school or college, but field operations may be controlled directly by the chief extension administrative officer. Thus, the extension administrator has direct control of field staff and indirect budgetary control of campus-based staff. The University of Missouri follows this plan.

JOINT APPOINTMENTS   Another variant of the mixed approach is the type of organization in which an extension may have its own separate faculty and the power to appoint and promote but, at the same time, seeks to have and to support a limited number of joint appointments with the residential operation. These joint appointments then become the bridge between the two operations, although a number of faculty have only extension responsibility.

Extension administrators disagree as to which of these arrangements is preferable. The most experienced generally favor a limited degree of decentralization. The decision may depend upon how responsive faculty members are to the needs of nontraditional students. A more decentralized operation may be effective where there is a disposition to cooperate on interdisciplinary matters, and a responsiveness to the local community such as has been traditionally found in colleges of agriculture. On the other hand, for many universities the highly decentralized type of operation is ineffective, and leads only to a token type of extension program or to one in which involvement varies greatly from one department to another. If this is the case, then a greater degree of centralization is needed to produce institutional involvement.

Geographic Decentralization of Field Staff

The issues of geographic decentralization are only indirectly related to the issues of decentralization of program responsibility on the campus. Nevertheless, the two present somewhat parallel problems. Decentralization involves increased responsibility on the part of field staff. A well-organized and well-trained field staff can perform a number of important functions that would otherwise be controlled by headquarters staff. The first is problem identification. The field staff can identify and shape program priorities through direct contact with the local community. The second is programming. Field staff can plan and execute local teaching and technical assistance projects, thus reducing the need for bringing staff from the central campus into the community. Third, the field staff perform a brokerage function, acting as liaison with the campus to match needs in the community with resources on the campus.

The field staff can relate to the campus-based staff in one of three basic ways. First, the field staff may be organized on a geographic basis. Administrative control over field staff then is exercised by some sort of district officer who performs essentially the same functions that a department chairman performs in a residential unit. In this type of organization the tendency is for the field staff to be generalists with little in the way of specialization of their own. Second, field staff can be specialists located in strategic areas. Area specialization has not been tried on a large scale except in Cooperative Extension, in part at least because other types of extension have not had a comparable level of federal funding. Area specialization in Indiana has gained excellent support from state and local government by a judicious blend of responsiveness to local needs and responsiveness to program leadership at the state level.

Area specialization requires a dual type of accountability in which the area specialist reports to a program head for subject matter functions and to a district director for administrative arrangements. This type of separation of functions has had mixed success in extension operations, partly because it has been launched in some cases without prior preparation. In particular, where local communities have had "their extension person" the move toward area specialization has led them to fear that they will be deprived of services or that the service will become less personal. Outside observers have speculated that this type of specialization might result in erosion of local support. However, after more than a decade of area specialization, Indiana continues to remain among the top states of the nation in percent of support by county governments. Their success seems to hinge on careful advanced preparation and local participation in the change, with clear accountability demonstrating that each county is getting its fair share of service, maintenance of the local identity of the extension office, and improved service to the local communities. Figure 8.5 is a representation of this type of structure.

One other type of field staff has only been mentioned in passing thus far. Looking for an alternative to the community-based staff or staff located in area centers, some institutions have made use of itinerant staff or "circuit riders," who are based on the

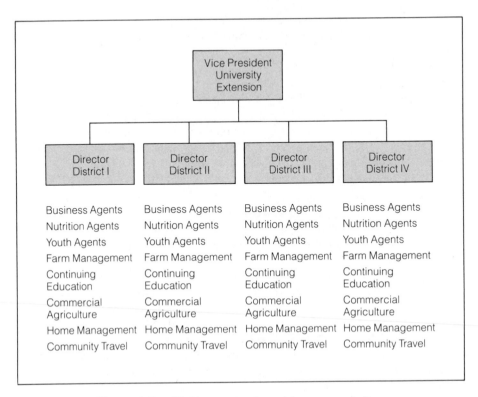

Figure 8.5. *Field organization with area specialists*

central campus but who follow a regular itinerary out into the regions served. Such itinerant staff may or may not be specialists; because they are controlled to a degree by the itinerary, they are less able to respond to on-the-spot problems in a timely manner. They tend to function more like the traveling salesman or the visiting nurse rather than as a programmer.

Community College Organization

The structure for administering continuing education in community colleges is usually less complex than that of four-year state colleges and universities for two reasons: first, because community colleges are on the average smaller than their four-year and graduate counterparts, and, second, because they frequently serve a smaller geographic area. Also, there is sometimes confusion about the organization of community college programming because of variations in terminology. Under the Higher Education Act of 1965 and subsequent amendments the term *community services* appears in the heading of Title I, linked to *continuing education*. This title applies to two- and four-year postsecondary institutions. Community colleges are dealt with separately under Title X. But in community college usage the term *community services* is used to refer rather specifically to that aspect of community college activity that is called *continuing education* or *extension* in most other postsecondary institutions.

Despite differences in the average size of institutions and service areas, there is considerable diversity in the organizational forms for community service among community colleges. Four basic structures have been developed.

1. *Integrated structures.* There is no sharp distinction between the full-time student program and the continuing education program. In community colleges with this type of structure, day and evening courses, credit and noncredit are not administratively differentiated.

2. *Dual structures.* Community service programs, essentially composed of noncredit continuing education, are administratively distinct from the credit programs that primarily serve the full-time student group.

3. *Consortia arrangements.* A group of institutions pool resources through a central ''brokerage''—for example, John Wood Community College in Illinois or Hudson County Community College Commission in New Jersey.

4. *Decentralized operations.* These have no central campus but use community facilities throughout the service area—for example, WOR–WIC Community College in Maryland or Pioneer Community College in Kansas City, Missouri.

The choice of organizational structures depends on population, size of the service area, funding patterns, and student mix. In states such as Wisconsin it also depends on the legislative mandate, which has created a system of two-year colleges as part of the University of Wisconsin system and another system of postsecondary vocational and adult education institutes serving a comprehensive statewide network of vocational school districts. Both offer associate degrees and both offer noncredit continuing education.

BASES OF DEPARTMENTATION

In addition to decisions on the locus of program authority and patterns of geographic dispersal, a further essential consideration for organization is that of the kinds of functions to be performed and how they should be reflected in the organizational structure. As used in this context, the term *function* refers to academic disciplines, program format, problem areas, and clientele groups. One or a combination of these becomes pivotal in determining the organizational structure of the operation.

Departmentation by Discipline

Departmentation by discipline is the form of departmentation in which faculty are grouped administratively within traditional subject matter areas. This option prevails in those institutions where continuing education is fully integrated with residence instruction. It is also found as a partial basis for departmentation in some centralized operations such as the University of California–Berkeley model illustrated in Figure 8.1.

Departmentation by Format

On the other hand, in the Michigan model illustrated in Figure 8.2, the organization of extension is based on format. The departments within the extension service include an office of course programs, a department of conferences and institutes, an independent study department, a lectures and program planning department, a cultural activities department, and a regional activities department. Thus, the structure is built around the ways in which material is delivered rather than around the material itself. Staffing and subject matter decisions are controlled to a significant degree by the residence departments. One difficulty with this arrangement is that the lines of formal organization and communication between people with related program interests go through a unit head who is concerned primarily with the packaging of programs. Thus, the programmatic question that is raised tends to be, "What kinds of programs should we mount within this format-oriented unit?" rather than, "What kinds of formats do we need for programs dealing with certain problems or clientele?"

Problem-Centered Departmentation

In the problem-oriented type of extension organization, such as the University of Wisconsin, the administrative units tend to reflect the problem areas that extension and the university as a whole deal with. One difficulty with this type of arrangement is the likelihood that a number of more or less ad hoc institutes and centers will be created, thus making the programmatic capabilities of the university extremely diffuse. This need not be the case, however. In some units that use the problem basis for organization, the problem areas are defined broadly enough to have a considerable continuity and to maintain optimum size. The program development example in Chapter 10 illustrates this type of broad problem orientation. However, problem-centered budgeting does not necessarily imply that departmentation need be on a problem basis. Program planning and budgeting systems are a device for interdisciplinary programming, using budget as the tool for getting across disciplinary barriers.

Departmentation by Clientele

Departmentation based on clientele tends to be characteristic of highly specialized types of operations, in particular, those based in professional schools. The resulting structure is similar to a highly decentralized extension where departmentation is based on disciplines and extension has no separate existence. In fact, the major distinction between the two lies principally in the narrower focus of the clientele-oriented organization and in its concept of the mission. The pharmacy program is specifically for the training of pharmacists, the legal program specifically for the continuing education of lawyers, and so on.

Task Force Organization

In the problem-oriented organization, programs generally serve several clientele groups—community action groups and individual users of the services, for example, as well as practitioners.

Another approach to the problem basis for organization is one that has come to be known in industrial circles as task force management, or, as Peter Drucker in his book entitled *Management: Tasks, Responsibilities, Practices*, calls it, task-focused design. As he points out, this type of design has been used most effectively in areas where innovation was at a premium—in industries where new product development was given a high priority. The basic concept is one of creating essentially ad hoc structures by drawing from a pool of manpower; the intent is that these ad hoc groups would disperse after they have served their function. From a practical standpoint, this is not a highly efficient use of manpower. It presumes a rather large pool from which the task-focused designers can draw. It assumes that the group can then be usefully redeployed upon the dissolution of the task force. As an organizational principle, it tends to be an addition to, rather than a replacement for, more stable types of organizational structure.

In one continuing education operation, as an example, the administrator wanted to explore the potential for using cable television for programming. A task force was created; members included representatives from five of the most likely program units plus a staff member with expertise in television production and a staff member from program promotion. The task group was given a budget, released time, and some general guidelines with respect to product objectives, time constraints, and sources of help. They were also asked to provide periodic progress reports. Other than this general

181

framework they were given freedom to proceed without further administrative interference. From appointment to project completion the project lasted six months and became the basis for the future planning of cable television programming.

Matrix Organization

In a matrix type of structure, a tridimensional or multidimensional kind of organization may develop. The most typical form taken by this type of organization structure is one in which there are second-level administrators for both format and problem or discipline. Staff at the program production level—those directly responsible for program—are held accountable to two types of administrators, one dealing primarily with format and the other primarily with the problem or clientele. Alternatively, program production itself is seen as a team concept. One illustration of this is in the design team concept. In this type of program development, several campus-based and field staff may work together in developing and identifying a clientele need and in collectively determining what the program content should be. Involving people with special expertise in packaging programs, they then jointly make the decision as to what method or methods can best be used to convey this particular content to this particular clientele in order to produce a particular set of results.

The matrix type of structure differs from the task force approach to organization, primarily, in that the members of a matrix organization retain more or less permanent relationships to organizational units and may be involved in several program projects at the same time. Their situation is comparable to that of some field staff organizations in that they are accountable for different functions to different administrators: for example, one for subject matter and one for method. Those who have studied traditional textbooks on organization will recognize that this violates one of the classic management principles: each person shall report to one and only one supervisor. Adherents to this traditional point of view are fond of pointing out that Frederick W. Taylor's concept of functional foremen was tried and rejected. Different times create different necessities, however, and the traditional two-dimensional concept of organization that worked in a simple straight-line type of organization is increasingly less suitable for the more complex kinds of operations that are evolving today. In particular, organizations that make extensive use of costly media, such as television or moving picture films, require a closer wedding of content and media in order to assure the best possible blend of cost control and program impact. The integrated department structure illustrated in Figure 8.4 is an example of a matrix structure.

None of these bases for organizations are mutually exclusive categories. Within any given operation one may find combinations or instances of several. Furthermore, as indicated previously, it is not uncommon to find one basis for organization operating at one level of the structure and another basis operating at a lower level. However, the type of structure at the top will be the principal determinant of the programmatic and operational focus of the organization.

INTERAGENCY ORGANIZATIONS

Program Coordination

Because of the threat of wasteful duplication and the need for better citizen access to existing programs, the problem of coordination with other agencies for more efficient use of resources remains a central issue. Unlike Cooperative Extension, which in most states operates from a single institutional base, other extension programs originate in different educational and nonacademic institutions as more and more move into the public service area. Problems are compounded by institutional loyalties and empire-building tendencies, but the basic problem is to develop lines of communication between the various agencies to insure the optimum use of resources. There tends to be wasteful duplication and overlap when more than one agency responds to the same problems at the same time and when agencies compete for the same clientele. This will have its most adverse effect on units that pay for low-fee programs with the proceeds from high-fee programs: for example, a program for inner-city small businesspeople cannot run because an executive development program was cancelled, because of lack of enrollment caused by competition with another agency's similar program.

In some areas external coordinating agencies have met with limited success. Pressure is now being applied by the federal government for creation of such external commissions under federal legislation—the so-called 1202 commissions; in addition, some federal grants are made with the proviso that they must have the sanction of the governor's office or of the 1202 commission. As is likely to be the case with an externally imposed control, these commissions are frequently viewed with suspicion. They are often staffed by people with little or no experience in the kind of operations that they are supposed to coordinate—people remote from the constituencies that are to be served. The regulated institution is more inclined to work at dodging these regulatory efforts rather than cooperating in them. However, almost any publicly supported institution recognizes that accusations or evidence of duplication and overlap are damaging. Voluntary cooperation in their mutual self-interest is a more powerful incentive than pressure from external agencies.

One of the most common methods for organizing coordination, particularly if externally imposed, is to attempt to coordinate by defining spheres of influence. Such spheres of influence may be with respect to clientele, subject matter, or geographic territories. Spheres of influence may be reasonably effective where lines of demarcation are clear, when, for example, one institution has a course in diesel mechanics and another has a course in electric motor repair. However, in problem-oriented extension operations, it is rarely the case that any one institution has all the resources needed to deal effectively with any major social problem. Here the use of multiple resources is highly desirable and spheres of influence become a barrier to cooperation.

One helpful device has been an interlocking directorate, established at the top level of the agencies involved or at some lower level. Such voluntary coordinating bodies may develop guidelines to minimize overlap or they may function as a clearinghouse and adjudication body for determining program priorities where agencies are in apparent competition. However, probably the most effective kind of coordination, if a climate of cooperation exists, is that which results from joint need assessment, program planning, and division of labor based on institutional interests and capabilities. Such voluntary planning is most effective where there is a high degree of interinstitutional trust and good lines of communication. However, voluntary coordination between institutions can be very time consuming, although perhaps little more so than coordination within many large institutions. Under the worst of conditions individuals may be torn apart by two organizations going in contrary directions. Under the best of conditions, joint efforts, when administered with understanding by both agencies, contribute much to interagency cooperation.

Joint planning is the easiest step toward cooperation. Joint implementation is more difficult. While interinstitutional consortia may program jointly, using each other's facilities, sharing staff, and jointly funding projects, it becomes more difficult if done on a larger scale. The art of cost accounting is imperfect at best and agreement on money matters is even more of a problem between organizations than it is within. The leadership of organizations become uneasy if they feel that an unfair share of credit is going to one of the parties. Consortia arrangements are thus more likely to succeed as ad hoc arrangements than as broad-purpose continuing bodies. In the long run, continuing formal arrangements between organizations succeed only if the individuals involved work hard to make them succeed.

Community Relations

Coordination of the services of units with similar programmatic objectives is quite different from coordination with local leaders and local governments who are the recipients of such services. It is axiomatic that successful extension programs must be responsive to the needs of the users and the ultimate users are groups of clientele, either political or geographic communities, or communities of interest such as various occupational groups. For many years the most highly evolved example of effective community participation was the model developed by the Cooperative Extension Service. In theory and, to a great degree, in fact, it was what the name implied—a cooperative programming effort between the federal government, the land-grant university, and the local community. In the Cooperative Extension model, the community or county extension office relates directly to a local board or committee of county government. In addition, other committees deal with special functions such as home economics and 4-H programs.

This close relationship between postsecondary education and the local community has more recently enjoyed its greatest growth through the rapid expansion of community colleges in the post–World War II era. In addition, regional or statewide citizen boards help coordinate the activities of potentially competitive organizations. The advisory committees under Title I of the Higher Education Act are one such group.

Such groups have two possible advantages over interagency staff consortia or commit- tees: first, they provide an outside point of view in program planning, and, second, they can claim a degree of disinterestedness that a group of insiders cannot. Of the three forms of interagency organization—externally imposed boards, voluntarily created staff groups, and voluntarily created citizen groups—the latter is probably least often used and deserves more consideration. These are not mutually exclusive choices. Use of the two kinds of voluntary groups may itself be a good method to keep an externally imposed regulatory agency from getting out of hand.

Whatever options are chosen, the premise with which we began this chapter applies. That is, no form of organization guarantees success, and, conversely, rela- tively poor organizational plans will work reasonably well if run by people with ability and enthusiasm. Nevertheless, good people will work better when a sound organiza- tional structure buttresses their efforts. The organizing job of the administrator is to know the options available and to select those most suited to the situation. One final cautionary note: there is a tendency to see reorganization as a cure-all for whatever ails an organization. The result can be a constant state of flux at the cost of output. The organization becomes a kind of institutional hypochondriac moving from one nostrum to another or the weight of structure becomes a burden. Function, not structure, is the ultimate measure of organizational effectiveness and, as with all complex organisms, disease is more often a condition of the cells than of the gross anatomy.

BIBLIOGRAPHY

Drucker, Peter. *Management: Tasks, Responsibilities, Practices*. New York: Harper & Row, 1974.

Frandson, Phillip E. "Centralization: The Educational Perspective." *Continuum* 41(1977): 8–11.

Gordon, Morton. "The Management of Continuing Education." In *Power and Con- flict in Continuing Education*. Edited by Harold J. Alford. Belmont, Calif.: Wadsworth, 1980.

Gordon, Morton. "The Organization of Continuing Education in Colleges and Univer- sities." *NUEA Spectator* 37 (1974): 20–27.

James, Bernard J., and Robert D. Fagaly. "Organizational Marginality and Opportu- nity in University Outreach Education." *Journal of Higher Education* 43 (1972): 646–54.

Knox, Alan. "New Realities—The Administration of Continuing Higher Education." *NUEA Spectator* 39 (1975): 6–9.

Lowe, John. *Adult Education and Nation-Building*. Edinburgh, Scotland: Edinburgh University Press, 1970.

Ratchford, C. Brice. "Organizing to Accomplish the Public Service Objective." In Proceedings, *National Conference on Public Service and Extension in Institutions of Higher Education*. Athens, Ga.: University of Georgia, Center for Continuing Education, 1974, pp. 79–83.

Schein, Edgar H. *Organizational Psychology*. Englewood Cliffs, N.J.: Prentice-Hall, 1972.

University of Missouri Cooperative Extension Service. *University of Missouri Extension Councils*. Columbia, Mo.: University of Missouri Cooperative Extension Service, 1961.

CHAPTER NINE

MEETING STAFFING NEEDS

Basic Strategies
Full-Time Faculty
Supplementary Faculty
Qualifications of the Continuing
Education Professional

STAFFING STRUCTURES

Workload Planning
Job Descriptions

THE PERSONNEL FUNCTIONS

Recruitment and Selection
Induction and Orientation
The Reward System

INCREASING STAFF EFFECTIVENESS

Evaluation Techniques
Staff Development
Legal Issues in Staffing

DEVELOPING
FACULTY AND
ADMINISTRATIVE STAFF

The basic functions of management are planning, organizing, staffing, directing, and controlling. Clearly, staffing is a logical outgrowth of planning and organizing. Staff requirements are dictated by the unit's program plans and the organizational structure. Insuring that staff are fully informed, motivated, and trained then becomes a matter of administrative direction and control.

Particular situations play a major role in determining the basic staffing strategy. If a strong residence faculty has only minimal interest in part-time students, for instance, additional faculty with nontraditional experience may have to be hired. On the other hand, a faculty with a clear and strong commitment to part-time students can concentrate on filling gaps in subject matter specialties. In this chapter, *staff* will include both line positions and staff positions.

Sources of financial support are also important in determining the staffing pattern. In an earlier stage of development, the Cooperative Extension Service staffing patterns were to some degree dictated by the federally approved project areas. Likewise, in an institution in which most of the support comes from clientele fees, the basic strategies for staffing will be dictated by the actual or expected sources of income. For example, if supervisory training is growing and is self-supporting, staff may be added to meet the continuing education demand even though it plays no part in the full-time student program.

Staff are needed to perform four essential functions: (1) general administration—chancellors, deans, directors, and their immediate subordinates; (2) program administration—planning and implementing programs; (3) teaching; (4) support—covering a wide range of responsibilities from business management and registration to custodial services. In a small-scale operation, one person may perform all of these functions. In a large-scale operation there will be a high degree of specialization. In this chapter we are primarily concerned with program administration and teaching. We will refer to the people who carry out these functions as the academic staff.

This chapter will thus cover alternative strategies for meeting academic staffing requirements and for planning and describing academic positions; it will then proceed to examine the basic faculty personnel management functions of recruitment, selection, training, and compensation and will conclude with a brief look at the legal climate in which personnel management finds itself today.

MEETING STAFFING NEEDS

Basic Strategies

Most institutions employ a variety of staffing strategies. However, there are basically four approaches.

1. The first of these is the maintenance of a separate extension unit. This strategy is characteristic of the universities of Wisconsin and Chicago.

2. A second basic strategy integrates continuing education into the residence schools and departments. The University of Michigan uses this type of strategy. In this type of staffing pattern, the continuing education program unit maintains its own program planners and coordinators and relies heavily on the residence units for instructional staff and academic content.

3. In the third approach, a relatively small continuing education faculty plan and coordinate the programs, and ad hoc instructors drawn mostly from outside sources teach them. New York University is an example of this staffing structure.

4. The fourth type of approach is characteristic of those Cooperative Extension Services where extension is an integral part of the academic departments although separately budgeted. In this form of staffing, faculty are often responsible for more than one function, moving between residence teaching, extension, and research. Because of conflicting scheduling demands of extension education and residence teaching, extension and residence instruction are less frequently combined than extension and research.

The foregoing choices apply primarily to four-year colleges and universities. Community colleges usually have integrated structures because there is no great distinction between full-time and part-time students, and because their faculty are seldom judged on the basis of research output. Thus, the degree of specialization of function common in large universities has not troubled the community colleges. Generally, they have also minimized the invidious distinction common in four-year and graduate institutions between liberal and vocational education—a distinction that has tended to increase the separation between extension and residence faculty.

Advocates of the separate extension staff argue that in integrated units, extension staff tend to become second-class citizens, primarily viewed as a source of additional income, public relations, or student recruitment rather than as part of the basic mission of the institution. Thus, so the argument runs, one needs to hire full-time professionals with a primary commitment to continuing education and extension rather than relying on the dubious good will of residence departments to devote significant effort to this purpose.

The counter-argument says that the purpose of continuing education and extension is to extend the resources of the university. To create a separate unit for this purpose, is to, in effect, deny residence faculty the opportunity and the obligation to contribute to university outreach. The trend today, based on the experience of many units, seems to be toward an eclectic approach, in which the extension and continuing education unit maintains a staff of specialists in program format and an increasing number of instructors budgeted entirely to extension, but can still make liberal use of both residence faculty and qualified ad hoc instructors.

The optimum mix will vary with the mission of the unit, the organizational structure, and the particular situation. However it is increasingly clear that two considerations are essential. First, the integrity of the continuing education function needs to be maintained by a separate budget. Second, close ties between the subject matter departments and extension help to insure a broader base of operations for both. It might also be added that having some highly qualified faculty budgeted primarily to extension, helps to keep the commitment in the forefront of overall operations.

Full-Time Faculty

Only a department with a high degree of program specialization could afford to lock itself into a primary emphasis on full-time staff to meet both its program administration and teaching needs. But, if there are enough courses requiring a given specialty, hiring full-time teaching faculty probably provides the best instruction. Certainly there are fewer administrative problems in hiring one person to teach four courses than in hiring four people part-time. Also, full-time faculty can provide teaching continuity in addition to such functions as needs assessment, program planning, and student advising, which part-time staff are less able to provide. On the other hand, full-time staff commitments can lead to inflexibility, where the program is planned around staff rather than the other way around. On a project-by-project basis full-time staff may also cost more than part-time staff when base salary, fringe benefits, and general support are all considered.

Supplementary Faculty

No matter what the strategy, most institutions find it necessary to supplement their basic staff in one of several ways. Among the ways commonly used are: (1) ad hoc and adjunct faculty, (2) overload payments to residence faculty and time purchase arrangements, (3) joint appointments, and (4) volunteers. Each has advantages and disadvantages, and in most instances a mixture of all the types will serve the institution best.

191

AD HOC AND ADJUNCT FACULTY   Ad hoc faculty are staff paid on a program-by-program basis. Adjunct faculty are appointed on the basis of a continuing part-time commitment. In most instances, there are indirect economies in terms of the absence of any requirement for fringe benefits. On the other hand, ad hoc and adjunct faculty can create additional burden on full-time staff with regard to committee assignments and general administration. They usually also generate more paperwork per unit of instruction. When, in addition, they require the special approval of the residence unit offering the program, they add another complication to the appointment procedure.

Ad hoc faculty are appointed for a specific program. Adjunct staff, on the other hand, may be appointed as clinical professors are in schools of medicine; that is, on the basis of a continuing commitment. Thus, the necessity of program-by-program approval is eliminated. An additional advantage of adjunct staff is that by building up and maintaining a continuous commitment to the unit, these people are proven performers for future programs. Adjunct staff may be granted rank in the same manner as full-time staff such that the distinction is made between adjunct instructors, assistant, associate and full professors and progression proceeds along regular academic lines, but without tenure implications. The use of adjunct staff is especially attractive in large metropolitan areas, where a number of people with expertise in various areas, who enjoy teaching occasionally and who do it well, are available. For example, the best tax attorney in the city may value teaching as a change of pace and a way to order his or her thoughts. There may also be some personal advantage in the contact with potential clients. In many cases, people in this category welcome and enjoy the academic contact and may be available at considerably less cost than full-time staff members performing essentially the same functions.

The use of ad hoc and adjunct faculty has proven especially valuable in community colleges where, on the average, well over half of course staffing uses part-time instructors. As a number of observers have indicated, the greatest weakness in the widespread use of part-time instructors is the tendency to take them for granted—the failure to develop sound personnel procedures and to integrate them fully into the total educational program.

OVERLOAD AND TIME PURCHASE ARRANGEMENTS   Overload is additional salary or stipend paid to full-time staff members—normally those attached to residence units. From the standpoint of meeting programmatic needs, two factors argue strongly in favor of overload payments. One is the changing pattern of needs, which permits one, through overload, to obtain a specific set of talents without making a permanent commitment; the other factor is that overload payments are normally on a scale that is somewhat less than the scale of pay for full-time staff duties. It is paradoxical that institutions permitting extensive outside consulting relationships and writing for pay, nevertheless, often disapprove of overload payments within the institution and set very low dollar limits on the amount of overload they will permit. While it is not unreasonable to limit the amount of overload payment a staff member may receive, the practice of doing this in constant dollar amounts tends to bar senior faculty or to create a lower commitment for senior faculty than for lower-salaried junior faculty. A better method of administering overload payments is to set a limit, if one is necessary, on the basis of a percent of total academic year or annual salary. Furthermore, such limits should be based upon a judgment of the discretionary time that a staff member might reasonably allocate without detracting from the basic full-time assignment. Professional development considerations provide another justification for overload payments. An instructor working with part-time student groups frequently brings back to the classroom examples and insights gained from contacts with older, more experienced students.

Time purchase arrangements offer an alternative to overload payments whereby the continuing education unit agrees to "buy" a percent of a faculty member's time for a particular project. If a person with a special competence can be brought into a program in this manner, it can add strength to the program. Unfortunately, often the most desirable people are the least available and there is a need to avoid getting trapped into picking up less-qualified faculty.

Two variations on overload and time purchase can be useful on occasion: off-time payments and deferred compensation. Off-time payments involve timing programs so that a full-time faculty member is scheduled for the continuing education program at a time when he or she has no other assigned responsibilities—during recesses or between terms. Deferred compensation involves a commitment to pay a person later for work done now—for example, payment during a summer session for a course taught during the spring term. Both off-time and deferred payments are subject to institutional policy restrictions but, under some circumstances, may be useful to avoid the problems created by overload and time purchase arrangements.

JOINT APPOINTMENTS   In a joint appointment, a staff member is budgeted to extension for a fixed percentage of time and to residence for another percentage. This arrangement has the advantage of building staff relationships into the residence department and the extension operation so that staff members function as an integral part of both units. Joint appointments have the additional advantage of making possible the selection of staff members who have a specific interest in and commitment to both. However, obligations to two units are often difficult to reconcile for the individual staff member and are frequently perceived as the source of conflicting demands on one's time. In addition, joint appointments tend to be inflexible: the demands in residence and extension may conflict and budget adjustments may be difficult. Furthermore, when the extension activity is off campus and the residence activity is on campus, it may be difficult to reconcile schedules. Also, there is some danger of using extension as a depository for residence staff who have proven to be ill-fitted to the requirements of the residence unit but who are as much or more ill-fitted to extension.

A more flexible strategy that may accomplish some of the purposes of joint appointments is the time purchase arrangement, either on an ad hoc or a continuing basis. Continuing time-purchase arrangements may, in effect, commit the extension unit to investing a predetermined amount of money into the purchase of the time of any residence staff members for specific extension purposes, without tying extension to any one staff member. Allocations of time can be negotiated as the need arises, but the continuing arrangement with the residence unit is built into the basic budget and negotiation determines which staff members will be released for what length of time.

VOLUNTEERS   The use of volunteers is a relatively untapped staff resource. In 1970 Cyril Houle estimated that over one million volunteers were working for the Cooperative Extension Service. Volunteer lecturers, teaching aides, and resource people can enrich and expand program capabilities. A number of people see volunteer work as a community service; the pool of talent thus made available can be substantial. In some off-campus programs, volunteer preceptors assume a major teaching role, comparable to that of on-campus teaching assistants. Volunteer advisers, coordinators, and area representatives can vastly expand the range of outreach.

A study cited by Houle indicates that volunteers as a group differ from the average citizen. They are better educated, more often work in a vocation that requires a high level of education, and are in the higher income brackets. For example, women who have passed the stage in which child care is an integral part of their family responsibility frequently look for volunteer opportunities and can be a significant supplement to the basic staff requirements of an institution. Volunteers can be effectively utilized in direct programming and as members of advisory committees as well as other program planning and support functions. For example, a course in environmental education called "Prairie Grasses and Plants" at one institution was substantially handled by volunteers. The volunteers served on the advisory committee, promoted the program, instructed, and were tour guides in the field.

Qualifications of the Continuing Education Professional

There comes a time in the development of any skilled and demanding occupation when its practitioners take a somewhat self-conscious look at themselves and ask, "Is our occupation a profession?" In some instances an affirmative answer to this question leads to certification or licensure; in all instances it relates to the standards for qualification and performance.

As in most professions today, the time has passed when the well-meaning amateur can meet the performance standards expected in continuing education, but unlike many professions, there is no single career path into continuing education. Administrators are therefore faced with the problem of identifying the promise of professional calibre performance from a diverse field of candidates. The line between the professional and the technician introduces a further complication. The difference between the physician and the medical technician or between the architect and the electrician lies very largely in the scope of the job. Professional educators should not be confused with educational technicians.

Every administrator who has hired and promoted any number of staff has known the disappointment that comes from making bad choices. It is, therefore, with some trepidation that we suggest some selection criteria to consider in evaluating candidates with the potential for turning in a truly professional level of performance. The implication, of course, is that continuing education is a profession when its practitioners meet certain performance standards. We suggest six criteria that merit consideration.

1. *An inquiring mind.* Scholarship takes a variety of forms. For the technician it can involve a profound knowledge of a very small slice of reality. For the professional it involves a wider range of intellectual curiosity. In technical jargon it involves divergent rather than convergent thinking—the ability to see relationships rather than the ability to proceed by strict logical analysis.

2. *Rapport.* In a clinical sense, rapport is the ability to relate to the patient or the client. In continuing education, it is the ability to relate to groups of students, to make them perceive the relevance of their own experience to the concepts that are being developed in the classroom or through the media, and to translate their perceptions into future action.

3. *Technique.* Because the continuing learner is a unique kind of learner, and because continuing education settings vary, the continuing education professional needs to be conscious of technique, knowledgeable about methods, and skillful in putting various methods to use. At the same time, the mature professional does not let technique intrude on content. Skill in choosing and using methods is an art that conceals art.

4. *Enthusiasm.* As Emerson said, "Nothing great was achieved without enthusiasm." It is a contagious quality and especially important in dealing with noncaptive audiences. Enthusiasm is a major factor in maintaining a critical level of student involvement, especially in continuing education, because the will to learn must compete with the demands of family, job, and social life. For example, breathing life into an evening class peopled by students who have already completed an eight-hour working day presents a challenge that is quite different from that presented by a group for whom classroom and study *is* the working day.

5. *Action-orientation.* As noted elsewhere in this book, to a large degree, a traditional student's learning is intended to provide deferred economic or psychic benefits. The credits earned are to be converted into coin of the realm at some future date. The continuing education student wants a more immediate payoff. His or her teacher must therefore be especially concerned with utilitarian values. This tends to be true whether the learning experience deals with job skills or enjoyment of the liberal arts.

6. *Creativity.* Closely related to the capacity for divergent thinking, creativity is an especially desirable quality in the type of education that is most closely tied to the economic and social marketplace. Job requirements are changing more rapidly than ever before, new social issues and problems are emerging, and the technology of teaching is changing. Creativity is important in identifying content, choosing methods, and promoting programs. It follows that the continuing education professional must have a positive attitude toward innovation with its attendant risk and uncertainty. Those who are averse to risk will have a happier life and greater success in the more structured environment of the conventional classroom.

Quite obviously, the foregoing qualities do not leap out at the administrator in the typical resumé or interview. Nevertheless, they are qualities that individuals possess in varying degrees and it is the belief of these writers not only that they are important indicators of future success in continuing education, but also that they can be assessed to a reasonable degree through observation, interview, and inquiry.

STAFFING STRUCTURES

Workload Planning

Staff loads can only be determined by a variety of considerations that are specific to the mission and the situation of a particular operation; therefore, general rules of thumb are at best rough approximations. For example, a typical ratio of clerical staff to professional staff in institute and conference programs is one to three. However, that ratio will vary widely, depending on the operating patterns of each institution. Allowance also has to be made for what production managers call a *learning curve,* which is to say that output per unit of time will increase up to some maximum as staff gain proficiency. For example, the first study guide that a new staff member prepares can be expected to take appreciably longer than subsequent ones of equal complexity. Furthermore, a faculty member's output will vary with the amount and kind of support staff available. If professional staff have to do much of their own clerical and technical work, they will have less time for course preparation or classroom teaching.

Job Descriptions

Specific but brief job descriptions should be developed for all major positions. This serves, over time, to provide organizational continuity. It provides a rational basis for determining levels of compensation; and by focusing attention on the duties of the job, it proves valuable in both evaluating performance and recruiting and selecting personnel. The initial job description should be prepared by the incumbent or, if the position is new or vacant, by the person most familiar with the desired requirements. The description should then be reviewed by the person who will have supervisory responsibility over the job in question, and finally, approved by a representative of the top administrative level. Overall administrative review is important in order to maintain an alignment of jobs within the total organizational structure.

Once job descriptions have been prepared, salary structures can be developed, based upon the job descriptions. If a job classification structure already exists, as within public institutions in the state of California, salary structures are determined largely by relating them to existing structures in the classified service. In instances where a classification system does not exist, surveys of comparable jobs in similar organizations or in the private sector can be used to establish reasonable rates. The detailed preparation of the salary structure is a major undertaking; fortunately for the peace of mind of most administrators, the structure exists. The task is one of fitting positions into that structure. In the area of faculty salaries, annual reports by the American Association of University Professors and survey data that are regularly published in the *Chronicle of Higher Education* can be helpful.

THE PERSONNEL FUNCTIONS

Recruitment and Selection

The methods of recruiting and selecting staff differ considerably between support staff and academic staff. Clerical and technical personnel are commonly recruited locally; academic staff are usually part of a national market, but in both instances "walk-ins" and unsolicited applications should be viewed as incidental sources. Excessive reliance on passive recruitment and selection procedures is ill-advised. Highly desirable employees are often satisfied with their present positions and must be attracted by aggressive recruiting, including paid advertisements, identification of people through employment services, and active contacts with other institutions. Furthermore, some present employers encourage outside opportunity for qualified employees who lack opportunity for advancement and will recommend them for more responsible jobs.

For the recruitment of academic staff, interinstitutional contacts through professional meetings and direct inquiries, particularly in the case of people completing advanced degrees, become a valuable source of information. Other common sources are advertisements in such periodicals as the *Chronicle of Higher Education* or *Science* or placement services offered by many professional associations.

Business, industry, and government are fruitful recruiting grounds for institutions programming in continuing education for professionals. In spite of the fairly high salaries in business, industry, or government, many people are interested in changing to what they perceive as a more rewarding form of work. They may be interested in accepting jobs at lower salaries because of some unfulfilled interest in teaching. It is often possible to provide on-the-job try-outs for such people by starting with ad hoc appointments. Many times, people who have enjoyed this type of experience are legitimate and promising candidates for full-time staff positions. In addition to being a known quantity based on performance in ad hoc appointments, these individuals bring a wealth of on-the-job experience from their previous occupations.

The purpose of recruitment is to produce a slate of qualified candidates from which a selection can be made. Selection is a twofold process. The employing institution must first identify the most desirable candidate, and then it must persuade that candidate to accept an offer. The problem of selection has become increasingly complex in recent years: restrictions have been placed on freedom of information and access to personnel files, and court decisions and legislation have limited the use of psychological tests. With respect to matters that are irrelevant to qualifications, the employer must exercise considerable care not to violate restrictions by asking questions that imply some kind of discriminatory action. The use of tests that are specifically and clearly job-related remains completely appropriate. Testing the typing speed of a prospective typist or gauging the ability of a keypunch operator are useful and sometimes practically necessary activities. Tests of this sort, specifically job-related, are not restricted by any existing legislation and are not likely to come under restriction in the foreseeable future. However, appropriate tests for professional staff are not common and general aptitude tests are likely to be found to be discriminatory.

Application forms that avoid questions carrying any implication of discrimination are still in order and should focus specifically on job-related qualifications. The use of resumés and application forms, both of which serve essentially the same purpose, should be regarded as more than a *pro forma* requirement. It is extremely important, for example, to verify the claimed employment history and attainments of the individual. Verification through telephone calls, the solicitation of documentary support, and other safeguards are necessary in order to avoid serious mistakes in the hiring of personnel. The value of letters of reference has been considerably reduced by present requirements for open personnel files; however, letters of reference never were particularly useful as a means of assessing the qualifications of individuals. A far more effective means of getting useful information is by telephone contact with people who know the prospective employee or who are in a position to get first-hand information, especially if the inquirer knows these contacts personally.

Interviews and visits to the campus by prospective employees are highly desirable—not so much because of the effectiveness of the interview as a means of assessing competence, but rather because the interview becomes a useful means of informing prospective employees about the job. It gives them some insight into the nature of the work, and makes them fully aware of both the advantages and the disadvantages of the job. A number of studies have shown that staff turnover can be reduced by insuring that prospective employees are fully informed about the nature of the jobs prior to undertaking them. In addition, interviews can help clarify and verify information contained in resumés and application forms.

With respect to resumés and application forms, often, significant data can be inferred from omissions. It is not uncommon for omissions in the history of the individual to reflect periods of employment that the applicant would rather leave unexplored. A serious study of resumés and application forms is in order if they are to be of value. Furthermore, particularly in the case of professional employees, samples of their work can be a valuable and meaningful addition. There is a tendency for individuals completing resumés and applications to inflate the complexity and level of responsibility of past employment. A sampling of the work done, and verification of the level by former employers provides a safeguard against such misleading information.

Induction and Orientation

There are three basic requirements for the induction of a new employee. The first of these is to fully inform the individual about the rights, responsibilities, and privileges of the job. The second is to provide some degree of familiarization with the total organization. The third step involves adequate job instruction. These requirements are important whether the employee is working at a relatively routine job or at the highest professional level. Too often, these steps are left largely to chance and the employee falls short of expectations or is dissatisified.

A sound induction procedure is a sequence of events that assure adequate orientation. The first step is usually an interview in which the new staff member is informed of the privileges and responsibilities of the job. This kind of an interview can best be conducted by the immediate supervisor, or by a person handling personnel matters, if a more specialized kind of expertise is desired. It is helpful to follow up the induction interview within thirty to sixty days by a second interview in which elements of the first interview are reiterated and feedback is sought from the employee with respect to observation and experiences on the job. Most organizations provide the staff with an employee handbook presenting detailed, written material regarding hospitalization, retirement, payroll deduction, and other administrative matters to supplement the interview and to provide a continuing reference. If the number of hires in a three or four month time period is large enough to justify one or more orientation sessions, much of the orientation can be done in small groups rather than on an individual basis. During such organized instruction, there should be a general orientation toward the entire organization and a more specific orientation toward the department and the specific job. In addition, many organizations have found it good practice to assign a new employee to some more experienced employee as an "understudy." This may involve the new employee in observing the more experienced employee for a period of time as a means of familiarizing the understudy with the job and the organizational setting, or it may simply provide the new employee with a "big brother" or "big sister" who can be contacted for further information, reassurance, or whatever other needs may arise in the course of the initial on-the-job experience. Also, a checklist of contacts that will need to be made over the first month or two of employment is useful both as a reminder and as an assurance that the individual undergoing orientation has had a thorough familiarization tour and an introduction to the people with whom he or she will be dealing in the future.

Unfortunately, in many instances induction procedures of the foregoing type are imposed from above and only perfunctorily carried out by the immediate supervisor. In order for these procedures to be effective, there must be some degree of preparation and follow-up to insure that the staff know what is expected of them and are given the time and the recognition to insure that a good job is done.

The Reward System

Community colleges, because of their primary community service mission, have little trouble evaluating the continuing education activities of their faculty. But most four-year institutions have experienced considerable difficulty in integrating nontraditional types of academic staff into the rank, tenure, and salary structure of the institution. Institutional practice in dealing with this problem varies. Some institutions have no formal rank structure for extension and continuing education personnel; others follow essentially the same ranking procedures as exist in residence units. A third practice is to provide some kind of parallel rank structure, using different titles. Larry Bramblett and W. C. Flewellen (1976) reported that approximately one-half of all institutions surveyed give academic rank to extension faculty. However, in many instances not all of the extension faculty receive this rank.

Some kind of ranking exists in almost every organization, whether or not it is formally expressed in salary structures, chain of command, lines of promotion, tenure, or job security arrangements. Although terminology varies considerably, the three major subdivisions among staff in most institutions are:

1.   faculty-staff with primary teaching and research responsibilities;

2.   technical-professional staff specializing in programmatic activities that directly support the faculty's teaching and research—for example, audiovisual specialists; and

3.   support staff—clerical and custodial.

There is great ambiguity in the distinction between faculty and technical-professional staff as reflected in the division of labor and decisions regarding granting professorial rank. For example, in some Cooperative Extension Services, people budgeted entirely in extension are not given professorial rank; in other states, campus-based specialists are given professorial rank, whereas county- or area-based staff are not; in still other states, both on- and off-campus staff receive professorial rank. An alternative system is to have parallel rank structures for technical staff such as scientist, associate scientist, and senior scientist. Where tenure is an issue, technical staff may be given some other form of job security such as *continuing employment status.*

Although some of these distinctions may seem overfine, the fact remains that grievance machinery, bumping rights, discharge and layoff proceedings, and, broadly, the whole range of issues relating to fairness under the law, require that personnel administration be handled systematically. The growth of faculty unions has increased this need. All things considered, the best strategy (with some exceptions for special problems) is probably a combination of traditional professorial ranks for subject matter staff and a parallel rank structure for those who specialize in the various kinds of continuing education and extension delivery systems. This is not too different from the strategy used in some institutions with a heavy research commitment: in those institutions, faculty with independent teaching and research responsibility hold professorial rank, and other staff members with responsibilities in a research laboratory or other support operations may be given ranks such as assistant scientist, scientist, senior scientist, or other designations. Having staff members on these parallel ladders may add flexibility in setting compensation rates and developing promotion criteria for some staff categories.

When establishing criteria for the distribution of rewards for continuing education personnel who hold professorial rank, it is generally easier to establish the parallel between residential and continuing education staff who perform a teaching function. The more difficult problem is determining the weight given to research. In institutions with a heavy research commitment, publication in refereed journals is usually a requirement for promotion, but continuing education teaching staff are not likely to build strong research records, either because of lack of opportunity or inclination or both. One solution is for administrators to establish more flexible criteria as to what constitutes evidence of scholarly activity and to establish the principle that the optimum mix of research, teaching, and public service can and should vary from staff member to staff member, depending on the nature of their job assignment.

In a number of institutions continuing education is under pressure to achieve a 100 percent cost recovery, or more. However, once the decision is made to place extension academic staff on the professorial track, the institution incurs an obligation to provide opportunity and incentive for continuing education faculty to meet the prerequisites for promotion. One way of solving the problem is to seek outside research grants for these faculty members. Another solution is to emphasize joint appointments with residence, so that for periods of time or for a portion of their time, extension faculty are able to function in the same manner as residence colleagues. Third, service-related research opportunities can be developed, whereby the staff member can at least occasionally generate income in the process of carrying out research. This is possible where staff members are dealing with the problems of business and industry, or, on some occasions with the government, which can provide research funds in return for services rendered. It is not often feasible in most liberal arts subject areas.

When the number of professorial staff is small and a large proportion of the staff are not in the professorial rank structure, a last-resort strategy may be to provide some limited degree of staff support out of programmatic "profits." This may at least encourage a limited amount of research activity on the part of a relatively small number of staff members.

INCREASING STAFF EFFECTIVENESS

Evaluation Techniques

Most institutions of higher education evaluate staff performance on the basis of administrative or peer review or a combination of both. Decisions as to retention, promotion, salary adjustments, and the granting of tenure are based on criteria of varying explicitness. Probably a smaller number of institutions provide some kind of planned feedback in the form of periodic—usually annual—performance reviews. Evaluation used either in the determination of rewards or as a technique for staff development is often poorly received by staff and inadequately administered. The effort to introduce a systematic approach through the use of rating scales produces disappointing results in all too many instances. Performance-based scales have the apparent advantage of focusing attention on what the person does or does not do, but such scales suffer from the same problems of reliability and validity that accompany other forms. Nevertheless, almost any form of systematic evaluation is better than purely subjective judgments; both evaluator and evaluatee are forced to deal with something explicit and therefore less shrouded in mystery.

Under a variety of names, management by objectives or results management is the most widely used system. It focuses on a set of well-defined and measurable objectives worked out jointly by the employee and his or her supervisor. Performance is then measured against goal attainment, usually on an annual basis. The extension division of the University of Iowa began a program of management by objectives in 1974 and has reported very satisfactory results during the period this program has been in operation. Each staff member, having set goals for the year's operation, sits down at year's end to discuss with a senior staff member the quantity and quality of goal attainment. Decisions are then made regarding merit increases, promotion, self-development needs, and ways of improving performance in the next period. The William Rainey Harper College in Palatine, Illinois, has also built its staff evaluation and development on similar principles.

Management by objectives should not, however, be considered the sole basis of evaluation, because it necessarily concentrates on a manageable number of concrete goals. Less tangible aspects of performance, such as relations with fellow employees or contributions to general organizational goals, must also be considered.

Staff Development

While management by objectives directs attention to a set of annual goals, it does not directly confront the long-term issues of keeping current in one's field or of preparing for greater responsibility. However, self-development plans can be a logical outgrowth of performance evaluation. In large operations many of the staff development needs can be provided by the organization itself. New program opportunities, advances in educational technology and in the subject matter, and changes in the clientele can be dealt with in part through in-service training activities. In smaller organizations these needs are usually met primarily through external sources, such as attendance at regional or national conferences.

In both large and small organizations a significant amount of staff development must come from professional association meetings, periodicals, books, and regional or national conferences. Policy that permits staff to take advantage of opportunities both within and outside the organization needs to be established. Some common policy considerations include reimbursement of expenses for a specified number of meetings or dollar amount, provision of significant books and periodicals, released time for developmental activities, traineeships, and sabbatical leaves.

Legal Issues in Staffing

In recent years academic appointments in public institutions have been increasingly subject to legislative control and judicial review. The relationship between the individual and the institution is recognized as a contractual relationship even though the usual appointment procedures do not in themselves constitute a formal contract. Administrators may be held personally liable as well as institutions. In both public and private institutions this liability extends upward through the board of control. Many boards are now covered by personal liability insurance.

Review of academic due process has been carried to the United States Supreme Court in two landmark decisions. In *Board of Regents* v. *Roth*, the Court has held that the institution is not necessarily compelled to give reasons for nonrenewal of a non-tenured appointment. However, once justification is initiated either through precedent or through response to an inquiry, an obligation probably exists to carry through with some form of due process. In a second decision, *Perry* v. *Sindermann,* the Court has further held that in the absence of any formal action granting job security, the institution may incur an obligation by creating, even inadvertently, ''an expectation of continuing employment.'' Although these complicated issues extend beyond the scope of this general treatment of staffing, the point to be grasped is that administrators must be aware of the extent to which personnel actions, discipline, terminations, possible discriminatory actions, and appointments are subject to review beyond institutional walls. In addition, the implications for the individual administrator and for the institution must be recognized. Administrative rules and procedures regarding personnel matters should be standardized and reviewed by competent counsel. The day of casual actions and gentlemen's agreements is over.

Equal employment opportunity issues can bring other complications to the administrator's doorstep. These take two forms: inadequate efforts to hire women or minorities; and discriminatory practices in salary, promotion, and occasionally terminations. Both federal and state laws play a part, and the administrator needs to keep abreast of changes in the law and administrative rules. In recruitment and selection, the administrator is faced with the expectation that women and minorities will be represented on staffs in proportion to their numbers in the qualified population. Frequently, the desired representation cannot be achieved by the customary methods of recruitment and selection, and new recruitment channels and selection techniques need to be explored. For example, paid advertisements in general circulation publications may be less effective in reaching certain minorities than advertisements in the ethnic press.

Apparent discrimination also may occur in salaries and job responsibilities. If an underbudgeted position happens to be filled by a woman or a member of a minority, it may seem to be a case of discrimination. In short, an organization may find itself in difficulty in spite of good intentions. The best protection is a combination of awareness of requirements and good faith effort to meet them.

In addition to specific relations with individuals, a growing number of institutions are becoming involved in collective bargaining. In the long-range view, the organization may be making a choice between collegiality—the governance of the organization by its members—or collective bargaining, which views faculty as employees. Some academic organizations have tried to maintain both: collegiality in program matters and collective bargaining in matters of salary, fringe benefits, and job security. The continuation of collegiality, while limiting collective bargaining to economic matters, depends on a high degree of trust between administrators and staff. The 1980 Supreme Court decision on faculty governance at Yeshiva University has introduced another dimension by removing the faculties of private colleges and universities from the jurisdiction of the National Labor Relations Board if it appears that they function to a significant degree as part of institutional governance. Both state and federal laws may be involved, and a huge number of administrative board and court decisions set precedents. Thus, in the area of collective bargaining, as in the areas of academic due process, administrators should seek legal counsel and observe considerable restraint in order to insure the legality of their staffing decisions.

BIBLIOGRAPHY

Bramblett, Larry, and W. C. Flewellen, Jr. "Evaluation and Reward Systems for Continuing Education and Extension Professionals: A National Review." *NUEA Spectator* 40 (1976): 9–12.

Bruch, Glen. *Challenge to the University: An Inquiry into the University's Responsibility for Adult Education*. Notes and Essays Series. Chicago: Center for the Study of Liberal Education for Adults, 1961, p. 79.

Florell, Robert J., Richard P. Lorah, and Laren R. Robinson. "Joint Appointments—Pros and Cons." *Journal of Extension* 10 (1972): 39–43.

Gordon, Morton. "The Organization of Continuing Education in Colleges and Universities." *NUEA Spectator* 37 (1974): 20–27.

Hackmann, J. Richard, Edward E. Lawler III, and Lyman W. Porter, eds. *Perspectives on Behavior in Organizations*. New York: McGraw-Hill, 1977.

Hinschowitz, Ralph F. "The Development of Staff for Institutional Change." *Adult Leadership* 23 (1975): 211–13.

Kolb, David A. "On Management and the Learning Process." In *Organizational Psychology*. 2d ed. Edited by D. Kolb, et al. Englewood Cliffs, N.J.: Prentice-Hall, 1974.

Langerman, Philip D., and Douglas H. Smith. *Managing Adult and Continuing Education Programs and Staff*. Washington, D.C.: National Association for Public Continuing and Adult Education, 1979.

Livingstone, J. Sterling. "Myth of the Well-Educated Manager." *Harvard Business Review,* Jan-Feb 1971, pp. 79–89.

Strother, George B. "Qualities of a Professional." *Journal of Extension,* Jan-Feb 1977, pp. 5–10.

CHAPTER TEN

BUDGETING FUNDAMENTALS

Functions of the Budget
Types of Budgets

**PROGRAM PLANNING AND BUDGETING
SYSTEMS**

Elements of Program Budgeting
Program Categories
Program Structure and Program Objectives

DEVELOPING THE BUDGET

Costing: The Expense Budget
Funding: The Income Budget
Funding Patterns

FUND MANAGEMENT

Use of Funds
The Time Factor
Fine Tuning: Administrative Control

BUDGET DEFENSE

Preparing for the Presentation
Procedures for Budget Presentation
Evaluation and Budget Review

BUDGETS
AND FINANCE

This chapter looks at the budget process from the viewpoint of nonfinancial administrators. It does not attempt to deal with the technical aspects of accounting but seeks to build a bridge between the technicians who handle finances and those who put on programs. It deals with the functions performed by budgets and with the types of budgets used to carry out these functions. Considerable attention is given to the concept of program budgeting as a means of bringing program management and financial management together in an integrated statement of intentions, methods, and costs. The income side of the financial statement is looked at in terms of the kinds of funding needed to achieve program objectives. The chapter closes with a look at budget presentation and justification.

BUDGETING FUNDAMENTALS

Of all the forms of internal warfare between various breeds of administrators, none is more debilitating than the budget strife between program managers and financial managers. All too often program managers see the budget as a kind of strait jacket. Financial managers, on the other hand, often get their major satisfaction from catching program administrators in the act of overspending or making unauthorized shifts from one account to another. A good budget, however, results from close cooperation between program administrators and financial administrators.

A budget is basically a process for translating intended activities into dollars and cents. But intended activities do not always turn out as expected, and budgets are not cast in bronze or engraved on granite. Budgeting must be a continuing activity, not something that is simply done annually or biennially. Ideally, planning for the next period starts when the budget for the current period goes into effect and the current budget must be fine tuned or even radically recast as events unfold. Admittedly, having the flexibility to do this may not be possible always, especially in the public sector.

Functions of the Budget

Those who live with budgets on a daily basis may be surprised to find that the term itself is of comparatively recent origin. The first written usage of this word in its modern sense occurred somewhere around 1733 in Great Britain. As an adaptation of the French word *bougette*, meaning a bag, it was applied to the custom whereby the Chancellor of the Exchequer brought his financial plan to the Parliament in a bag or valise. Apart from this special use of the term, it does not appear to have gained wide usage until the early 1920s, thus leading critics to wonder whether, since we got along without budgets for so long, we should not return to that earlier state of blessedness. We hope to show that this nostalgic view of the good old days is about as valid as a proposal to reduce air pollution by going back to the horse and buggy. Budgets have become an essential tool of management in any modern complex organization. They may, like any other tool, be used badly or well; badly used, they may do more harm than good. The purpose of this chapter is to provide some help in using them well.

We define a budget as a document outlining a set of intended activities to be accomplished in a given period of time while relating these activities to their expected cost and the way in which those costs will be met. This document serves five important purposes for any organization.

1. *Planning*. As a statement of intended activities it is the outcome of a close look at problems and opportunities and an evaluation of alternative ways of dealing with them; it involves forecasting future developments and shaping the future by the actions that we take.

2. *Delegation*. By setting goals and allocating resources for their accomplishment, higher levels of administration can assign authority for execution of elements of the overall plan to lower levels of the organization, with less need for close monitoring than would be necessary if the plan existed only in the minds of higher level administrators.

3. *Coordination*. Since the plan describes a set of interrelated activities, it frees the various participants to carry on their part of the plan without excessive checking with those responsible for other parts of the plan; like a good set of blueprints, it enables the various specialized functions to be carried out without having to change plans or improvise because the plumbers, electricians, and heating engineers all want to run their conduits between the same two studs.

4. *Control*. Because of human error and unforeseen events the best laid plans can go wrong; the budget sets financial standards of performance so that deviations from the plan can be detected and timely corrective action taken.

5. *Performance review*. As a record of intentions the budget provides a basis for evaluating the degree to which the intended activities were successfully carried out;

it helps identify the strong and weak spots in a plan, providing a foundation for future improvements, and the elimination of sources of trouble.

Types of Budgets

A number of types of budgets are in current use. In most organizations two or more types may be in use simultaneously, each serving a different purpose. We begin with an outline of the types that are in common use in academic institutions; each is described briefly before attention is given to program budgeting as the one that specifically serves the needs of the program administrator. The main types that we discuss are as follows.

A. By type of funding request
    1. Incremental
        a. Open ended: *no restrictions* on requested increases
        b. Quota: a specified *limit* on all requests
        c. Alternative level: two or more allowed *increments*
    2. Zero base: the *entire budget* must be justified
B. By expenditure category
    1. Program: budgets built around *intended activities*
    2. Line item: budgets built around *specific costs*
C. By general purpose classification: budgets based on the *reason* for the expenditure

TYPE OF FUNDING REQUEST   In the foregoing outline we have listed three kinds of incremental budget requests. These types of requests can also be applied to zero base budgets. They are included here because they originated and are most commonly used in the context of incremental budgets. In open ended budgets, requests for increases can be submitted without any limit on the amount. One problem with such requests is that budget developers vie with each other to present the largest and most appealing proposals on the assumption, often based on past experience, that new funds will be allocated on a percentage share basis, with some advantage going to those with the largest requests.

To prevent this kind of budget inflation the top policy-makers may either set a quota, limiting all requests to some absolute amount or to a fixed percent of base, or they may set two or more alternative levels for requests. For example, a policy directive might say, ''We anticipate that next year's funding will be somewhere between 5 and 15 percent above current levels; in order to facilitate budget adjustments when the funding level is established, each department should request new funds at three levels: 5 percent, 10 percent, and 15 percent.'' In periods of economic decline, of course, the normal procedure might just as well be that of asking budget managers to provide alternate budgets reflecting 5 percent, 10 percent, and 15 percent cuts in allocations. One problem with both quota and alternative level limitations is the implicit assumption that all departments should be subject to, or can equally well justify the same increments.

The zero base budget, on the other hand, assumes that no budget level, current or intended, should be taken for granted. As a practical matter, zero base review can be made manageable if departments or other budgetary units can be scheduled for it on a rotating basis, with each unit coming up for full review every three to five years. Likewise, quota or alternative level limits can be used to establish priorities within departments, while avoiding the pitfall of automatic across-the-board authorizations, if program content is examined on its merits. This strategy can be carried one step further by requiring each unit to identify a certain number of low priority programs that could be eliminated if necessary. In other words quotas or alternative levels can be set for program reductions or elimination as well as for increases.

Traditionally, budget requests have been for additional funds for the coming budget period; continued funding at the current level was assumed. Justification for budget increases has been typically to expand existing programs, cover increased costs, or add new programs. The concept of zero base budgeting came into national prominence when it was announced as federal policy by the Carter administration, although it was in earlier use in business, notably in Texas Instrument Company, which claims to be the home of zero base budgeting. The term *base budget* describes the current budget level, with new budget requests described as increments over this base. With its assumption that the entire budget, including current funding and all increments, is subject to review and rejustification, the zero base budgeting approach has considerable appeal in principle; but the cost in time and effort often makes zero base budgeting merely a perfunctory exercise.

EXPENDITURE CATEGORY   In any large organization, authority to spend and accountability for funds has to be delegated to subdivisions. In manufacturing concerns these subdivisions are often called cost or profit centers. They are the control points at which problems are identified and corrective action takes place. Their budgets may be further subdivided internally into such components as utilities, travel, personnel, supplies and equipment, but the cost center is the lowest level at which overall operating responsibility for budget control is assigned. In academia the department is usually the comparable unit. A workable line item budget provides for discretion within the department in reallocating funds between, for example, the supply and the travel budget; it normally sets rather strict limits on the amount of permissible reallocation between accounts. Other limitations are also imposed so that, for example, all travel reimbursement must be at the tourist rate or so that equipment purchases of over $3,000 require bids. The line item budget is thus the basis for most fiscal controls.

Modern cost accounting deals fairly comfortably with tangible products, the cost of their production, and their market value. Hence, manufacturing concerns handle these budget items with comparative ease. However, the cost center concept is less readily applied in the rendering of services, especially in nonprofit institutions. A lake renewal project, for instance, may require inputs from chemists, plant pathologists, marine biologists, hydraulic engineers, soil scientists, geologists, and a half dozen other kinds of experts. Inputs with respect to a particular project cut across departmental boundaries. Thus, the concept of program budgeting has evolved with special reference to public service programs. We deal with program budgeting in more detail in the following section. For the present purpose of outlining basic approaches it will be dealt with only briefly.

Program budgeting does not replace line item budgeting. After programs are developed and cost projections are made, line item budgets are needed in order to allocate and control costs. Historically, line item budgets were the only budgets. The principal difference with respect to program budgeting is that it begins with the planning of programs regardless of the departmental boundaries. It proceeds from program development to program costing and only then allocates costs to units within the organization. It is thus only in the final stage of program budget development that the line item budget is established as an offshoot of the program budget.

GENERAL PURPOSE CLASSIFICATION   The principal function of a general purpose classification budget is, as the term implies, to classify expenditures according to their general purpose. Like any other approach to budgeting, this type of budget will begin with a review of the previous period of operation. It will then usually deal with five classifications:

1.   *low priority activities:* those that would most readily be eliminated if reductions or reallocations were to be made;

2.   *costs to continue:* expenditures necessary to maintain current levels of service; for example, increased cost of debt service, funding of negotiated commitments for increases in salary and fringe benefits, inflationary increases in supply and utility costs;

3.   *new and changed services:* cost of new programs or those that are to be substantially altered;

4.   *workload increase:* cost necessary to meet the increased demand for existing services; more people are to be served or a greater amount of service is to be provided to present clientele; and

5.   *transfers:* funds to be moved from one account to another; these may be no more than minor adjustments in the books or they may be major reallocations of resources as old programs are phased out and new ones begun with the same base dollars.

Unlike the other types of budgets discussed in this section, a general purpose classification budget is primarily for external use. It enables those who control funding, a board or a legislature, to identify the way in which money is to be spent. It provides a basis for setting priorities. If resources are limited, the increases needed to maintain present levels of service take precedence over increases to support an additional workload, and an addition to workload is likely to be viewed as more important than adding new programs. One notable exception to the foregoing generalization is in the area of gift and grant funds: new programs are apt to be more attractive to a foundation or federal agency than is the support of already existing activities.

While each of the types of budgets described above can serve a useful purpose,

211

the administrator directly concerned with programming will find the program planning and budgeting approach the most relevant; hence it is dealt with separately in the following section.

PROGRAM PLANNING AND BUDGETING SYSTEMS

Program budgeting has probably existed for as long as thoughtful administrators have tried to balance program goals and available resources, but it has been recognized as a specific technique only recently. Under such titles as Planning-Programming-Budgeting Systems (PPBS), Program Budgeting, and Budget Program Analysis, a variety of technical articles, books, and monographs have been published to develop or debunk the idea. The basic premise, that budget should be an outgrowth of program, is hardly debatable. How this translates into action and what it has resulted in has provoked mixed reactions. The point of departure is the question as to what constitutes a program. Operationally, this may be any major group of related activities such as continuing education for the professions or agricultural production and markéting. Major program clusters are then broken down into a manageable number of sub-programs. For example, continuing professional education might be broken down into such subprograms as engineering, law, nursing, and so on, or agricultural marketing and production broken into animal husbandry, horticulture, farm safety, and the like.

Elements of Program Budgeting

The basic elements of program budgeting are:

1. definition of the needs the program is to meet, stated as program categories,

2. statement of program objectives and how they will be met,

3. identification of the resources needed for the program,

4. specification of the costs of the resources, and

5. evaluation of the intended results as outcomes and in comparison with alternative expenditures.

In the next section the first two elements—needs and objectives—will be examined. Manners of funding, costs, and evaluation will be considered later in the chapter.

The process of program budgeting does not necessarily follow these five elements as sequential steps; the elements overlap and often have to be reviewed or redone. But at some point program budget planning should answer five questions.

1. What do we want to do?

2. Why do we want to do it?

3. How will we do it?

4. What do we need in order to do it?

5. How will we know whether we have succeeded?

Program Categories

Need assessment is dealt with in Chapter 2. As noted there, specific needs are numerous and become manageable only when dealt with as clusters or categories. Program categories, once set, remain fairly stable. But within each category the subprograms may change as the division of labor or content of the programs shift to meet specific needs. Thus, while a program to improve environmental quality or to maintain the health of farm animals may represent a continuing need, a subprogram for improved solid waste disposal or for the control of brucellosis may accomplish its goal and be phased out to make way for new subprograms. Categories will, of course, differ with region, the institution, and its relationship to other institutions and government agencies. In smaller institutions with fewer resources, the categories may be more specific. In a larger institution, it may be necessary to divide program categories into subprograms and projects within subprograms to describe the total program. How a program is subdivided depends on how the subprograms will be mounted or how they will be marketed. If continuing education programmers in business or engineering are specialized by industry or by function, then it may be best to break subprograms in the same way. On the other hand, it may be more appropriate to organize subprograms by size, process (for example, mass production, job shop, etc.), or market (consumer nondurables, consumer durables, etc.), depending upon the structure of the economy served, technology, raw material base, or other criteria. The particular breakdown should reflect the objectives, the clientele characteristics, or whatever else would be most relevant in terms of program content and delivery. General interest programs may be organized by subjects such as arts, humanities, and social sciences.

Program Structure and Program Objectives

Objectives play a significant role in programming at several stages. They have been discussed in Chapters 3 and 6. Here they will be discussed in a somewhat different context—that of their role in budget development and presentation.

Specific program objectives should form a hierarchy that contributes to overall program objectives. If, for example, the geographic area served is predominantly a resort area, one subprogram for improving market practices might be directed toward retail establishments, while another for providing off-season attractions for conferences and conventions might be directed toward hotel managers. The objectives of the subprograms (better merchandising and a longer operating season) are thus logically derived from the broader objective of promoting regional economic development. Such emphasis on the interdependence and hierarchical nature of program objectives increases the chance of success, because the elements within the total program structure

213

complement and support each other. In the foregoing example, a longer season for the resorts means a longer season also for the retail merchants. Better merchandising may attract more people. Thus the retail practices and resort operations may work together to produce the desired improvement in the local economy.

The complementary and interdependent nature of program structure and program objectives in strengthening program outcomes is equally advantageous from the standpoint of obtaining budgetary support. The legislator with a special interest in the tourist industry is likely to support a budget request for providing management services for retail merchants, once the benefits of such a program to the tourist industry have been made clear. Program structure—how the various subprograms are organized and articulated with one another—provides the organizational foundation for the accomplishment of objectives, and objectives are what sell programs.

Objectives are initially statements of intention conditional upon funding. Objectives developed during the budget proposal stage will have to be restated (or eliminated) at the end of the budget decision-making process if they are not funded. A saleable objective is a specific description of an activity to be undertaken with a certain end result in mind. Such a statement of objective includes a specific description of (1) the needs to be met, (2) the clientele affected, (3) the methods to be used, and (4) the expected outcomes. Since proposals will be reviewed at higher administrative levels where numerous other proposals for programs converge, they should be written clearly and concisely to convey that essential information.

After program objectives are developed, the search for alternative ways of accomplishing the objectives begins. For example, if the objective is to make the arts more readily available in the inner city, a variety of alternatives may be possible. To a degree, the likelihood of coming up with an imaginative solution is dependent upon the number of alternatives considered. Should we form a local arts council? Should we rent an unused store and hold exhibits? Should we work with the area schools? Brainstorming, nominal groups, and the Delphi method, which are described in Chapter 2, are simply techniques for getting people to think up more and better ways of attacking a problem. They play a major part in budget development because they apply to cost effectiveness as well as to content and methodology. It would be difficult to overemphasize the importance of this stage of budget development. Much research on problem solving has shown that the quality of solutions is closely related to the amount of time spent searching for alternative approaches to the problem.

The process of evaluation and selection of alternatives follows the search phase. In budgetary terms this is the stage of cost-benefit analysis, which will be examined in more detail later in this chapter. The question that is asked with respect to each alternative is, ''What is the probable cost of this alternative and what are the expected benefits?'' To the extent that a satisfactory answer can be found, alternatives can be directly compared and the selection of alternatives made on the basis of which provides the most benefit for the most realistic cost. Unfortunately, in providing human services it is often difficult either to assign a monetary value to outcomes or to predict the amount of benefit that may result. Thus estimates of expected service benefits are apt to be highly subjective and the likelihood of disagreement among decision-makers is considerable. In the relatively simple case of choosing between two arts programs for young people—say a youth symphony orchestra and a young people's theatre—the estimate of benefit is apt to vary according to the biases of those doing the estimating. Nevertheless decisions must be made and they are made best when a deliberate evaluation process weighs the comparative value of each alternative.

The outline below is an example of a decision item narrative for a project designed to improve the quality of prenatal care in a low-income community.

A. *Need.* The Pocono district of Soday City, with its 4000 inhabitants, has a birth rate 1.5 times higher than the rest of the city and a median family income of approximately one-fourth the average of the entire city. Health care facilities are minimal and 75 percent of all expectant mothers are not seen by any health care professional until the time of delivery, if then. Maternal mortality is two and one-half times as high as for the city as a whole, and the percentage of abnormal births (stillbirths, birth injuries, early postnatal mortality, etc.) is more than three times the city average. Many of these problems can be alleviated by better education of Pocono district families in the basic elements of prenatal care.

B. *Clientele.* This program is designed:
  1. to provide direct contact with fifty families each year
  2. to provide general information designed to reach a majority of the remaining families of childbearing age.

C. *Methods*
  1. For direct contact with families, one health care professional (midwife, nurse, or technician) will be trained in basic principles of prenatal care—nutrition, hygiene, recognition of danger signs, sources of professional assistance—and will make monthly visits to fifty selected homes.
  2. For the larger community, twenty-five to thirty presentations will be made at churches, neighborhood centers, or other locations, intended to present in as interesting a manner as possible basic information about pregnancy, birth, and prenatal care, reaching at least 500 people. One or more presentations will also be made to smaller groups of ten to fifteen people, thus permitting substantial interaction with the groups.
  3. Through short articles in neighborhood or locally distributed news media and bulletins, through attention-getting posters and displays, and through radio spot announcements, an effort will also be made to create a heightened community awareness and understanding of the importance of good prenatal care.

D. *Intended Results.* In the fifty families, the goal is to reduce the incidence of pathology by 30 percent the first year, and by an additional 20 percent by the end of the third year.

The total community effort is not likely to produce measurable results in the first year. It will require some time for the program to take effect. The intention is that, by the end of the third year, the district morbidity rate will be reduced by one-third.

The outline illustrates the end result of a decision-making process. The final form the subprogram took was arrived at after a variety of alternatives had been weighed. For example, the preparation and distribution of extensive printed material was considered and rejected because of the high incidence of illiteracy in the district. Television was considered and rejected because of high costs relative to the size of the target audience. Such considerations need to be part of the armament of those who present the budget at the level where funding decisions are made. Thoughtful budget reviewers ask searching questions, and there is nothing that can weaken a presentation more than having to say, "We didn't think of that."

DEVELOPING THE BUDGET

Any separation of a complex process into a series of steps is likely to be somewhat arbitrary. Budgeting is no exception. As administrative review of the budget progresses, budgets are frequently sent back for revision. The case of a public university budget is illustrative. Its budget may be sent back for revision after review by the academic vice president, by the Board of Regents, by the state department of administration, by the legislature, or even by all of these. A similar process applies in a community college network as the timetable in Table 10.1 illustrates. Usually the required adjustments are downward but may involve transfers, further justification or, rarely, additions. Thus discussions of planning, development, and funding need to be thought of in the additional context of replanning, redevelopment, and refunding.

Subsequent discussion in this section will focus on two important aspects of budget development: the income budget and the expense budget. Costing is the refinement and detailing of cost estimates initially made during the planning stage. Funding involves identifying where the money will come from. Presentation is concerned with the justification of program proposals during administrative review.

Costing: The Expense Budget

The continuing education and extension budget is part of a total institutional budget, and the format for presentation is usually dictated by higher levels of administration. This can pose problems since the general institutional budget is likely to reflect traditional academic formats that are not directly comparable to those employed in the extension budget. As a preliminary to budget development, it may be necessary to work with the general institutional administration to add categories that will adequately describe functions peculiar to extension. The outline below lists categories that include both the traditional functions and several that may be unique.

A. Primary program categories
    1. Degree credit instruction
        a. Evening classes

Table 10.1. *State Center Community College District, Budget cycle, 1980–1981 (by permission)*

Target Date On or Before	Responsibility	Sequence Ref. No.	Action Needed
1/28/80	District Office	1	Prepare budget assumptions.
2/5/80	Board of Trustees (Board Finance Committee)	2	Consider and approve budget assumptions and income projections. Approve budget calendar.
2/6/80	Chancellor's Cabinet	3	Consider budget assumptions, budget calendar.
2/13/80	Colleges	4	Complete full time equivalent projections for individual instructional units. Determine certificated staffing needs for 1980–81.
3/3/80	District Office	5	Complete distribution of budget request material to all divisions and departments.
3/4/80	Board of Trustees	6	Consider and approve certificated staffing for 1980–81.
3/24/80	Colleges	7	Submit budget requests to district business office.
4/1/80	Colleges	8	Submit requests and justification for additional classified staff.
4/16/80	District Office	9	Business office review of budget requests and compilation of preliminary budget document.
4/23/80	Chancellor's Cabinet	10	Review preliminary budget and requests for additional classified staff.
5/6/80	Board of Trustees	11	Preliminary budget, additional classified staff requests and proposed new programs and services to Board of Trustees for review.
6/18/80	Colleges Chancellor's Cabinet District Office Board of Trustees	12	Revise preliminary budget and develop tentative budget.
6/19/80	Board of Trustees	13	Approve tentative budget.
6/20/80	District Office	14	Submit tentative budget to County Superintendent of Schools for review.
7/11/80	District Office	15	Tentative budget returned by County Superintendent of Schools with any comments. Change if needed.
7/15/80	Board of Trustees	16	Approve budget for publication.
7/18/80	District Office	17	Submit publication budget to County Superintendent for publishing in newspaper.
7/28/80	District Office	18	Revise publication budget if necessary.
8/5/80	Board of Trustees	19	Public hearing and budget adoption for 1980–1981.

      b. Off-campus classes

      c. Correspondence study

      d. Other: weekend, tutorial, contract, etc.

  2. Research and information services

      a. Problem-oriented studies

      b. Publications

      c. Reprints

      d. Dial access

  3. Informal (credit-free) instruction

      a. Evening classes

      b. Off-campus classes

      c. Certificate programs

      d. Correspondence study

      e. Short courses

      f. Institutes and conferences

  4. Advisory services

      a. Technical assistance

      b. Community development

      c. Laboratory testing

  5. Special events

      a. Lectures and concerts

      b. Clinics

      c. Exhibits and displays

B. Support Services

  1. Media

      a. Broadcast

      b. Telephone

      c. Films

      d. Cassettes

  2. Libraries

  3. Student service

  4. Auxiliary enterprises

      a. Conference center operations

      b. Duplication

      c. Bulk mailing

  5. Physical plant and utilities

  6. General administration

Each of the functions listed involves certain common expense items: personnel, supplies, equipment, travel, and so on, but the mix varies with the type of program. The amount of detailed breakdown of these items that will be required varies with the purpose served and the level of review. The top management or board may want only a three- or four-item breakdown; the departmental administration may want a number of items. For purposes of budget development a fairly detailed breakdown is desirable internally if for no other reason than to insure that all major costs are covered in the budget request.

The most general breakdown of costs is into direct and indirect costs. Direct costs are out-of-pocket expense items such as salaries and supplies. Indirect costs include space, maintenance, utilities, and general administrative overhead. In the past, fringe benefits were sometimes included in the indirect costs, but now these are more commonly treated as part of direct cost. As a general rule, indirect costs are set somewhere between 30 percent and 60 percent of salaries, with most audits placing them somewhere in the upper end of this range. Fringe benefits tend to vary from 12 percent to 25 percent of salaries. Obviously these costs, although not directly related to productivity, are still a substantial part of the total cost of doing business. From the standpoint of the program administrator they are also a source of frustration in that they are not controlled at the program level. Further frustration arises when dealing with support services that are charged to the user at a rate that is determined by the provider, for example, duplicating or audiovisual services. Support services may be budgeted by the program unit as internal sales or may be budgeted by support units and carried by the support unit as part of their budget. Internal sales are essentially transfers from one account to another within the same organization in return for services rendered. Thus when support services are handled as internal sales they must be shown in the program budget as a direct cost just as external sales are. The separation of internal and external sales at the program level mainly serves the purpose of helping in the preparation of a consolidated budget at higher administrative levels. On the other hand, if support services are simply carried in another unit budget, it is necessary to communicate to the support unit the amount and kind of support that will be required so that these costs can be incorporated into their budget request.

In program budgeting, costs may be carried in the budget request as program costs, but at some point in the budget process a transition is made from the program budget to the line item budget. The program budget frequently cuts across departmental lines, but the line item budget details expenses by department. For example, a program budget dealing with environmental problems might include activities in departments of agriculture, business, and engineering, each unit taking responsibility for a complementary share of the total program. Costs must then be allocated to each of the units so that during implementation each can be held responsible for managing its own expenditures.

If funding of a proposed program requires anything other than state appropriations in a public institution or allocation of general funds in a private institution, the next stage in development of the budget is to prepare data on funding, which is the subject of the next section.

Funding: The Income Budget

This section will deal with sources of income and the part they play in balancing the budget. The sources and amounts of income will vary considerably from one organization to another, especially between public and private institutions. However, only the first category dealt with below is peculiar to the public sector and all of the remaining categories apply in some degree to both.

TAX REVENUE   Most public postsecondary institutions receive state or local tax revenues to cover a part of their operating budget, in a few fortunate cases, as much as 80 or 90 percent. Continuing education generally receives less than do full-time degree programs. Tax revenue usually comes in the form of appropriations from the general revenue fund of the government agency or as a part of the property tax levy. In some jurisdictions the source of revenue may be the property tax and the mill rate may be set by the institution's board of control. In this type of situation income may rise automatically as a result of property reassessment or expansion of the tax base.

The property tax base may be more predictable than general revenue appropriations since the latter may fluctuate more with the mood of the electorate. In fact, voters in some states—Washington and Oregon, for instance—are able to vote directly on community college and school budgets. If a budget proposal in Oregon is defeated, the voters keep returning to the polls until a proposal is passed. But in almost any situation where the income budget depends largely on tax revenue, income projection is an annual agony. Fee income, on the other hand, is a continuing agony.

TUITION AND FEES   The distinction between tuition and fees varies among institutions. Commonly, tuition refers to a basic instructional charge for credit courses. It may differ from one school or college to another. It may be different for residents than it is for nonresidents, but it is designed to cover some fraction of the basic cost of instruction. Fees, on the other hand, are charges made for special purposes. Full-time students may be charged a student activity fee, for example, from which part-time students may be exempted because they receive no benefit from it. Other fees may be assessed to cover library use, laboratory supplies, instructional materials, or paper-handling tasks such as transcript and class add/drop procedures. The term *fee* is also usually applied to charges for credit-free instruction. Some institutions, in times of budgetary stress, may pursue a strategy of keeping tuition down by adding or increasing fees. This strategy may have appeal on two grounds: first, in public institutions tuition may be controlled by legislative action and fees may be subject to less scrutiny; and second, tuition increases are more visible and therefore more likely to affect enrollment, whereas fees are to some degree a hidden cost for the student—hidden, that is, until time for payment.

The projection of income from tuition and fees is related directly to enrollment projections and rates charged. Enrollment projections are usually the result of forecasts at both the program unit and higher levels. Rates charged may be set at a higher level—board or legislature, for example, and hence be beyond the direct control of the continuing education unit. This is likely to be the case for degree credit instruction. It is less likely to be the case for credit-free courses. To the extent that the extension unit has control over the charges to students, it must consider the interactive effects of charges, registrations, and income. This usually involves a review of past experience and an estimate of the elasticity of demand: will enrollments drop significantly as charges are increased? For example, if the practice has been to increase charges every other year and the size of increases has varied from time to time, there is a historic base for judging the extent to which an increase will affect enrollments, and thus a basis for estimating the effect on income. The combination of known charges times expected enrollments then provides the entry for the tuition and fees section of the operating budget.

In some public institutions the problem of estimating fee income is compounded by the fact that tuition and fee income go back into the government's general fund and must then be offset by an appropriation in order to be used by the continuing education unit. This is most often the case when workload funds are a combination of receipts and tax revenues. In such instances, receipts from increased enrollments do not automatically become part of the income budget and, if retained, may not generate matching appropriations.

GRANTS AND CONTRACTS   Every not-for-profit institution can qualify for some form of grant and contract income. All are eligible, for example, for funds from one or more of the following: Title 1 of the Higher Education Act, the Fund for the Improvement of Postsecondary Education (FIPSE), the National Endowment for the Arts, or the National Endowment for the Humanities. There are many other possibilities. Some are earmarked for particular types of institutions and others, like the four above, are a potential source of funding for almost any institution. Such funds introduce complications into the budget process. For one thing they require the establishment of restricted accounts that are subject to audit by an outside agency. For another thing, the funding cycle seldom coincides with the institutional budget cycle, and phasing people and resources in and out of such activities requires additional fine tuning. In addition, there are some basic disadvantages to such external funding. Most such funds are regarded as ''seed money'' by the granting agency. The expectation is that once the project has been launched the institution will absorb it into its ongoing program on a self-sustaining basis. Often the institution is not able to do this without a budget increase or reallocation of funds.

External funding can have several attractive benefits. It can provide an opportunity for the institution to do something that it wanted very much to do but could not afford; or to do something that it was going to do anyway, thereby freeing up funds for some other purpose. External funding can be used as the experimental edge of an institution. A particular project may be replicable in the regular curriculum once it has been tested with external funds. And often, from the standpoint of the unit administrator, such funds may provide an opportunity to demonstrate what can be accomplished and thus provide leverage for sustaining funds after the grant expires.

An unofficial or extralegal benefit may come from the added flexibility that external funds bring to the budget process. For example, most federal grants and contracts allow for overhead charges up to 60 percent of salaries. While these overhead funds represent a justifiable cost allocation, they do not create a direct increase in out-of-pocket expense and may therefore be used, at least in the short run, to relieve pressure at some other point in the system, thus serving somewhat the same purpose as discretionary funds.

AUXILIARY ENTERPRISES AND SALES   Many continuing education operations provide food service, overnight accommodations, information services, textbooks, or publications for their clientele. Such operations are usually expected to cover their own cost at a minimum and may be expected to show a profit—an amount in excess of both direct and indirect costs. Sale of course materials such as study guides may also provide additional income. Although course materials to students may be included in the tuition or registration fee, sales to other institutions can be a helpful addition to income. When print materials are involved their sale even ''at cost'' can be profitable, since the cost of additional increments is considerably lower than the average unit cost.

GIFTS   Many organizations realize a significant portion of their operating expenses from gifts. Public radio and television, for example, are heavily supported in many areas by gifts from citizens and from corporations. Benefits and telethons, direct mail campaigns, and donor clubs are used to provide general operating funds or to support specific activities. Continuing education operations in private institutions may also receive an allocation of gift funds from the general operating budget of the institution. Whereas an educational television station may realize 20 to 25 percent of its operating budget from unrestricted gift funds, such funds are seldom a significant part of the general operating budget for instruction. Restricted gifts, such as those designated by the donor for a specific project, like grant and contract funds, provide only limited help toward the costs of general operations or may even add to operating costs.

MISCELLANEOUS SOURCES   Other miscellaneous sources should be kept in mind in planning the income budget. In some instances, such as the federal matching funds for Cooperative Extension, the ''other source'' may provide half of the total operating budget. Other sources may include endowment income, royalties, contributed and in-kind services, and student aids. Although for most organizations these amount to only a small part of the budget, they should not be overlooked. Royalties, for example, have a potential for making a substantial contribution to some continuing education operations.

In the final analysis, the income budget defines what the unit will be able to do and what it will not be able to do. In a few instances a unit may be able to borrow venture capital from the parent institution, but in most operations deficit financing and borrowing are not possible. The administrator who ends the year in the red is likely to find his or her actions severely restricted in the future, if he or she is permitted to continue administering at all. Unfortunately, from the standpoint of administrative peace of mind the income budget can vary considerably during the operating year. A smooth-running operation depends greatly on the accuracy of the income forecast. If the administrator is too cautious the budget will be too restrictive; if the administrator is overconfident, there may be a budget crisis. The income forecast should be made account by account and should represent the collective judgments of those who are best informed. The administrator may have to adjust the estimates of various staff members upward or downward, depending on whatever additional evidence the central staff may have, and on knowledge of the tendencies of specific program staff to over- or under-estimate.

Funding Patterns

Continuing education and extension can be grouped into three categories: degree credit programs, informal (credit-free) instruction, and public service and technical assistance programs. Funding sources and strategies vary with the type of program. In general, the tendency is for public service programs to be funded largely from public or foundation funds, for informal instruction programs to be funded by registration fees, and for degree credit programs to be funded by a combination of tuition and general purpose revenue. The variations are great. Paradoxically, for example, whereas on-campus degree programs for full-time students in public colleges and universities may receive public funds for as much as 100 percent of cost and may average around 75 percent, a very high proportion of degree credit work for part-time and off-campus students in the same institutions may recover 100 percent or more of direct cost in tuition charges. In other words, the cost recovery through tuition for the same course varies with location, time of day, and student status.

Degree credit charges in extension can be compared directly with on-campus charges but there is usually no similar reference point for informal instruction programs, which are generally peculiar to the extension division. Community service programs likewise differ in form and objectives from on-campus programs and are frequently the function of an administratively and budgetarily separate staff.

Although patterns of funding differ by the type of program, the tendency is for the general revenue funding level in extension to be well below that of the residential full-time student operation. The problem of discriminatory funding is international in scope. John Lowe (1970), writing with reference to developing nations, says, "adult education receives far less support from external aid than any other branch of education but would probably yield exceptionally advantageous returns." Likewise, in the United States, the report of the American Council on Education's Committee on the Financing of Part-time Students (1974) found that "part-time students on the whole are massively discriminated against." That report makes a strong argument for ending the discriminatory pricing of education in degree credit instruction. The report points out that the assumption that the part-time student is better able to pay a large share of cost is at least questionable and at most totally unwarranted. Likewise, the assumption that further education for full-time students is more in the public interest is made arbitrarily.

In all fairness, the distribution of support should rest on the mix of interests. Many university extension programs mainly serve the public interest and should be publicly supported. Other programs, while serving the self-interest of the individual, also serve a public interest. For example, a program to improve citizen participation in community planning is almost entirely in the public interest, whereas a program to train ambulance attendants in cardiopulmonary resuscitation serves both an occupational need and the public interest. The question of how to allocate support should depend on the mix and on the ability and willingness of the clientele to pay. For instance, while continuing education for physicians may enhance their earning power it also serves the public interest by supporting a higher quality health care for the consumer. However, despite a high average ability to pay, most physicians, like other self-employed professionals, tend to look at the opportunity cost of continuing education. By attending a continuing education conference, they incur not only the cost of tuition and often room, board, and travel, but also must consider the loss of income while away from the job. As long as continuing education is on a voluntary basis it may make sense for the public to support programs even for people able to pay, as long as it is in the public interest to have greater participation in these programs and if willingness to participate is influenced by program fees.

FUND MANAGEMENT

Educational organizations rarely know at the beginning of a budget cycle exactly how much they will have to spend. The first budget developed is usually an asking budget. Once the budget review is completed then the operating budget can be developed. The operating budget is in turn only an approximation of what the actual income and expense will be. Cost overruns, enrollment shortfalls, and income windfalls require continuous monitoring and periodic adjustments.

Fund accounting is the job of the business office, but in the final analysis, the management of funds is the responsibility of the administrator. The business office can provide invaluable help, but unless there is good communication between it and the administrator, the administrator will fail to make the best use of the budget as an instrument of policy. In this section we will highlight some elements of fund management that require top administration attention.

Use of Funds

The use of funds can be unrestricted, restricted, and discretionary. The last of these will not appear in the standard lexicon of accountants but its utility will be evident from the following discussion. Unrestricted accounts or general purpose revenue, as they are sometimes called, are funds that may be used for any programmatic purpose within the boundaries set by policy, law, or administrative rules. Appropriated funds and program income fall into this category in many institutions. However, in some institutions, and especially in the public sector, this may not be the case. Appropriations may be line item appropriations and fee income may revert to the general fund. In these institutions the only administrative flexibility comes from the way funds are accounted for. Since cost accounting is something less than an exact science, cooperation between the business office and program administrators can still achieve a reasonable degree of flexibility through the mechanism of judicious cost allocation.

Restricted accounts include, in addition to line item appropriations, fund accounts resulting from gifts, bequests, grants, and contracts. These accounts must be kept separate from the general purpose revenue account. The proper use of gift and bequest accounts depends primarily on good faith, although occasionally allegations of misuse may end up in the courts. In the case of grant and contract funds either an outside audit or report is required. When federal funds are involved, the institution will be held liable for misuse of funds, sometimes to its considerable fiscal embarrassment.

The third category, discretionary funds, has been listed to call attention to the fact that it is frequently possible to establish one or more accounts that are not subject to the standard restrictions on use. This is especially desirable in public institutions where some outside government agency sets unduly restrictive rules. Such discretionary funds, sometimes referred to pejoratively as "slush funds," are usually established by gifts that can be placed in an account not subject to governmental audit—an alumni foundation or a separate bank account, for example. Such accounts are usually frowned on by officialdom and are certainly vulnerable to misuse, especially when program revenue is diverted into such accounts in some extralegal manner. Nevertheless, from the viewpoint of the administrator a discretionary account can be a valuable source of flexibility. It may, for example, cover entertainment expenses that cannot be covered by other funds or it may permit a more expeditious response to a problem than is possible under standard operating procedures.

The Time Factor

In addition to use restrictions, fund accounts differ with respect to a time constraint. In most public institutions, appropriated funds lapse at the end of the fiscal year. The problem faced by the administrator, therefore, is to insure that such funds are not lost through inadvertence or bad management. Politically there is a double threat in allowing funds to lapse—not only that the funds are lost but also that the next year's budget may be reduced by the amount of the unexpended funds. Insofar as the general good is involved it is, of course, quite fitting that unneeded funds should be allowed to lapse. However, the administrator should be aware of the possible consequences. If it is desirable to prevent lapsing, there are several strategies. As noted earlier, cost allocations are, to a degree, a matter of judgment; cost allocations may be made to lapsing funds in preference to nonlapsing. Frequently, billings also can be delayed or purchasing needs anticipated so that accounts end in balance. Furthermore, there is usually some latitude as to when and how the books are closed at the end of a fiscal year.

Nonlapsing funds are generally of two kinds: revolving funds and certain restricted accounts. A revolving account is usually an income account that is maintained separately from general operating funds. Gift accounts usually carry over from year to year. Some grant and contract funds are nonlapsing but are usually subject to some kind of time constraint imposed by the funding agency. Revolving accounts are desirable from an administrative point of view because they permit longer range planning and the accumulation of funds for major expenditures that do not occur annually—for example, the publication of a biennial catalog. Such funds can also provide the administrator with a source of risk capital—funds that can be used to support experimental undertakings or response to targets of opportunity that are not provided for in the regular budget or that require a longer time horizon than the fiscal year.

Fine Tuning: Administrative Control

Another opportunity for administrative flexibility offers itself in the management of the budgetary equivalent of what banks call *float*. If every unit is fully budgeted there will be budgetary slippage because position vacancies are not filled instantaneously or because program cancellations unexpectedly occur, income exceeds expectations, or costs run below projections. Some of this float may be needed to cover unexpected expenses or cost overruns in other departments, but in most institutions that have good budget control the float can amount to 5 percent or more of the budget. One way to reduce float is to allow each unit to overbudget by a certain amount. The flaw in this approach is that float will vary considerably from one subdivision to another, and a license to overspend can easily backfire. The safer administrative policy is to hold units to firm budget limits and to capture the float for administrative allocation. It thus becomes another source for providing venture capital. This capture can be accomplished in two ways: one by close monitoring of expenditures and the other by imposing a level of required savings on the subunits. The latter strategy may be workable when the subunits are large, but in small units it will have the same adverse impact on budgetary responsibility in the subunits that overbudgeting will have.

Finally, with respect to fund management, the administrator who operates under any other kind of an income budget than one based almost entirely on appropriations must view the budget process as a commitment to variable or flexible budgeting. Response to changes in income and expense must be made continuously through readjustments to the budget. Monthly income and expense reports need to be reviewed and adjustments made before they reach crisis proportions. In addition, major reviews and readjustments need to be made at least quarterly with something like the care and consultation that has gone into the initial building of the annual budget itself. To do so requires that the business office provide timely information. When it takes six weeks to complete the monthly reports of financial operations, the system is out of control. The turnaround should be two weeks or less. It is important also that these monthly reports provide comparative data on the preceding year's operations so that the administrator has not one but two yardsticks to measure performance.

BUDGET DEFENSE

Once an asking budget has been prepared, the transition to an operating budget is a long and sometimes arduous road. Six or eight months may separate the two. Indeed the interval in public institutions may be much longer in those, fortunately rare, instances when governor and legislature or the two houses of a legislature disagree. When a stalemate develops, the public institution may operate under a continuing resolution whereby expenditures are limited to last year's level or, in still rarer cases, whereby payments have to be deferred. Happily, in most instances the unit is funded before the beginning of its fiscal year. This interval between the asking budget and the operating budget is the period of budgetary defense.

An asking budget is usually a mixture of politics and rationality. Ideally it is composed entirely of activities that the unit would like to do and could do well, but it is usually developed with the knowledge that, however reasonable its requests, total funding is unlikely. Some purely political aspects of budget defense are discussed in the chapter on public relations, but the basic defense is internal. In most instances the defense outside of the institution is carried on by the top institutional administrators. In fact, continuing education unit administrators who take an advocacy role outside of their own institution, without direction from above, usually do so at their peril. Thus this section concentrates on the internal defense although its applicability may be extended with due caution to the external defense.

Preparing for the Presentation

This section considers budget primarily from the standpoint of a general purpose classification budget, since this is the form that the defense most often takes. In such a defense, the base budget may or may not be the major problem. During periods of belt-tightening the base budget may be under attack, and the unit administrator is well-advised not to take the base budget for granted if there is any doubt about the political climate.

There are two lines of defense with respect to the base budget: first and foremost is the general support of ongoing programs, and second is the strategy for dealing with the identification of low-priority problems. The general defense is seldom a detailed justification of the total program. We have already noted the impracticality of an all-out zero base budgeting approach. Thus the base defense tends to be a selective defense with an emphasis on the more successful programs and a judicious anticipation of programs that may be singled out for attack by one or more of the reviewers.

A somewhat different strategy is usually applied to low-priority programs. The most common strategy is to identify as low priority certain programs that are indeed dispensable but that have supporters among the reviewers. For example, a Suzuki violin course may reach relatively few people and may make at best a modest contribution to the general welfare. Nevertheless among its happy registrants it may include the daughter of the chairman of the board. The logic of this strategy is that, if one or more of the key reviewers recognizes the merits of the program and supports it, the unit's low-priority programs are worth retaining. Therefore, it follows that programs with a higher priority must have as much or more merit.

Costs to continue are among the most readily documented and therefore the most likely to survive. The reviewers' own utility bills have just gone up 10 percent and thus the reviewers know that it will take 10 percent more to heat the conference center. Workload increases also tend to fare well if it can be demonstrated that past projections of increase have materialized. Line graphs or bar charts are helpful in making this point. The principal problem with the justification of workload increases, if they are well-documented, is to muster evidence that the unit should accommodate itself to the anticipated increase. Evidence of support from users is helpful. Evidence of tangible benefits to the community will make a still stronger case. If, for example, the florists of the community testify that they are hiring graduates of the flower arranging course and are willing to hire still more, the case will be stronger than if one argues somewhat vaguely that the course is enriching the lives of countless individuals—even if enrollees are being turned away.

Usually that budget portion showing new and changed services is the most difficult. First of all, it is seen as an obvious addition; second, its benefits tend to be speculative. Thus, the demonstration of need and community benefit must be as firmly grounded as possible. Furthermore, more than any other part of the budget it needs to reflect the interests of an influential constituency. In short, it is usually the most political part of the budget. For example, if the president of the board is a retail merchant in an area with a tight labor supply, a new program to train retail clerks may get support whereas a program to train union leaders in the retail trades may receive short shrift. While this type of defense may seem Machiavellian, the fact remains that there is very little to gain by supporting sure losers, and indeed the expanded base in one area may provide maneuvering room to do other things with less political appeal but greater moral justification.

Finally, in most institutions pay increases are dealt with as a separate category. Generally the continuing education unit is simply a beneficiary of whatever general pay increase is finally authorized. This final authorization may be complicated by collective bargaining as contrasted with a unilateral determination by the administration, board, and legislature. In rare instances the continuing education unit may have special needs: for example, an increase for fee graders in correspondence courses or better pay for adjunct instructors. One choice is to include these in the cost to continue request. The other is to make this request an adjunct to the pay increase package. Since it is basically a part of the expense budget, the former may be the preferred strategy.

Procedures for Budget Presentation

How can an administrator assemble the description of need, clientele, methods, and objectives and the information on costs into a budget presentation? Because the extension budget is part of a larger institutional budget, it may require forms and procedures beyond the public service administrator's control. However, most budget presentations follow a general outline of procedures like those we discuss here.

BASE BUDGET REVIEW   First, the base budget review should be separated from the request for increases. The base review, if it is to be tied clearly to the new budget request, must be completed before the new budget is finished, and the new budget request must in turn be prepared some time before the beginning of the operating period (e.g., fiscal year or biennium). The base review therefore necessarily deals with an incomplete period of activity (the budget cycle) and must rely partially on estimates of outcomes. However, estimates of outcomes of ongoing activities are generally more accurate than estimates of outcomes of future activities and can therefore provide a useful point of departure.

Base review can usually be done effectively with less detail than is needed to justify new expenditures. A single review outline will probably cover an entire program whereas requests for new and changed services or workload may need to be broken down by subprogram or separate elements. The following is an outline of what might be included in the base budget review of a major program activity.

A. Cost data
   1. Personnel numbers and expense
      a. Professional staff
      b. Support staff
   2. Supplies and expense
   3. Travel
   4. Miscellaneous
   5. Capital expenditures
B. Funding
   1. Income from fees and tuition
   2. General purpose revenue
   3. Other
C. Program description
   1. Need
   2. Objectives
   3. Clientele
   4. Methods
D. Program evaluations
   1. Numbers reached: clientele contact hours or quantitative measures
   2. Results obtained: financial benefits, behavioral changes, other indications of program effectiveness
   3. Cost-benefit analysis: cost per clientele contact hours or other appropriate measure weighed against measured results
E. Recommendations: increase, reduce, maintain, restructure, or discontinue program; justification for recommendation

The categories outlined are not as simple as may appear at first glance. Even so simple a statistic as clientele contact hours, which is readily available for traditional instructional programs, resists quantification, for example, in programs that rely on the use of mass media. Also, programs that have general educational value, such as programs in the arts, do not lend themselves as readily to cost-benefit analysis as do programs having an economic payoff, such as programs for accountants. Nevertheless, a systematic review of the base budget based on the best evidence available is preferable to the traditional tendency to take the base for granted. When the base review is complete, the administrator has laid the foundation for documenting requests for additional funds. The procedures will be similar to those for base budget review.

COST-BENEFIT ANALYSIS   Cost-benefit analysis is important in budgeting. However, the theory is difficult to apply. Many program objectives do not have an economic payoff; for many other programs the economic payoff is only part of the total expected benefit, or calculation of the economic payoff is highly speculative. Still, a serious effort to describe tangible outcomes citing numbers or success stories is sure to be more persuasive than glittering generalities.

Cost-benefit analysis is necessary before the final step in budget development—setting priorities. Budgets seldom survive the review process intact. It is therefore necessary to establish priorities in response to the almost inevitable question: "How would you propose to reduce this request?" In the context of a complete set of program requests, the question is often answered in the least rational matter: by pro rata reductions of all requests.

Indeed, many cost-benefit analyses make assumptions that will not stand up under strict logical scrutiny. They rest often only on subjective probabilities. Yet in ordering alternatives, if the choice is between establishing priorities by lot or on a political basis rather than by weighing costs against expected benefits, even subjective probabilities are preferable to wishful thinking. For example, the students in a program designed to rehabilitate prisoners are estimated to have a recidivism rate of 25 percent as compared to a 50 percent overall rate. If the cost of the program is $25,000 and the cost of trial, arrest, and reincarceration of each recidivist is $15,000, some approximation of cost-benefit can be made, even if several debatable assumptions are part of the argument.

As we move from reform of prisoners to the even less tangible benefits of an arts program, for example, estimates of benefits become even more subjective. However, since the program is presumably offered on the basis of expected benefits, these expectations should be stated as explicitly as possible. To what extent do arts programs make the community a more attractive place to live? How one ranks arts programs in a priority list that includes economic development programs and programs to rehabilitate prisoners depends on value judgments, desired program balance, judgments about the respective probabilities for success, and the proposer's judgment as to salability at various stages in the review process.

Evaluation and Budget Review

Public and private institutions alike are facing increasing scrutiny from their supporters. The competition for scarce resources grows more intense as costs rise. The comparatively small investment in public service programs puts a still greater burden of accountability on such programs if they are to maintain or improve their share of future funds. The problem is compounded by the tendency of funding sources to accept the values of traditional forms of educational activity as a given, but to regard public service as the frosting on the cake. A continuing program of evaluation is thus necessary not only as a part of good management but also as justification for higher priority for these less well-established functions.

We have devoted Chapter 6 to program evaluation. The focus there was more on internal review and quality assurance. However, evaluation plays a role in budget review also. It becomes the foundation on which future requests for funding are based. Thus this section will take a second look at evaluation with respect to its role in the budget process.

It is reasonable to expect that intentions and results will not be the same. To the extent that truly innovative experimental programs have been undertaken, a certain number of programs will have failed completely. Others will be partial failures. But credibility of budgets also requires that some programs should have succeeded beyond expectation. Success, in this context, can be defined in three principal ways: quantity, cost, and quality.

QUANTITY   Quantitative data, which provide the most basic yardstick, can be obtained for most types of activities, although comparisons between one activity and another can be misleading. And the difficulties of developing elementary quantitative data increase with the range of activities.

Diverse activities can be quantified to some extent, but direct comparisons between them is often forced, to say the least. It is better to avoid direct comparisons based on highly arbitrary assumptions or artificial common denominators and simply to build a record over time that at least provides a basis for assessing the effects of program adjustments. To determine quantity of activity, management information systems are increasingly used. Providing a numerical accounting for program activity, these systems furnish a basis for costing program elements; they generally yield a useful data base and aid in a variety of management decisions. Comprehensive management information systems for extension and continuing education have been implemented by a number of institutions, one notable case being the University of Georgia.

COSTS   Progression from numerical output measures, such as numbers enrolled, to cost measures introduces still another difficulty: the inherent differences in cost for various types of programs. It is a well-established fact in residential instruction that costs vary by level of instruction (e.g., first degree vs. advanced degree programs) and by discipline (e.g., history vs. physiology). Similar differences can be expected in continuing education. In addition, since community service and several varieties of nontraditional instruction are also involved, accountability becomes even more complex.

Not all program costs or benefits can be stated in economic terms, and efforts to force them into an unsuitable economic mold can be misleading and unconvincing. Still, viewed in a broader context of social value, any program should be held answerable for demonstrating benefit beyond the production of income or numbers of participants, and cost-benefit analysis need not be restricted to economic effects only.

QUALITY   The problem of coping with numbers is minor compared with the problems of qualitative evaluation. What results can be attributed, for example, to a program designed to enable citizens to better understand the workings of local government? Or what are the results of an educational program to increase highway safety? In many instances, the number reached is too small a portion of the total population to warrant any statistically significant conclusions, or, apparently significant conclusions are suspect because the groups worked with were not representative.

Too often, budgets are looked at as ends in themselves or as something that is the concern principally of the business office. We have tried in this chapter to present budgets and finance as management tools. In this viewpoint, financial accounting and control are seen as means to aid in achieving the best possible use of resources to accomplish program objectives. It would help if every program administrator had a degree in financial accounting in addition to his or her other qualifications. On the other hand, expertise in financial accounting would be counterproductive if the administrator became preoccupied with financial operations at the expense of program development. Perhaps in the best of all worlds, the administrator needs to have a good understanding of the budgetary process, a general knowledge of budgetary strategy and tactics, and the ability to communicate effectively with technically qualified staff in the business office.

BIBLIOGRAPHY

American Council on Education, Committee on the Financing of Part-Time Students. *Financing Part-time Students: The New Majority in Postsecondary Education.* Washington, D.C.: American Council on Education, 1974.

Austin, L. A., and L. M. Cheek. *Zero Base Budgeting: A Decision Package Manual.* New York: American Management Association, 1979.

Coles, E. T. *Adult Education in Developing Countries.* Oxford, England: Pergamon Press, 1969.

Ingram, R. W., ed. *Accounting in the Public Sector: The Changing Environment.* Salt Lake City: Brighton, 1980.

Knox, Alan B., and James A. Farmer, Jr. *Alternative Patterns for Strengthening Community Service Programs in Institutions of Higher Education.* Champaign, Ill.: University of Illinois at Urbana, 1977.

Loring, Rosalind K. "Dollars and Decisions: The Realities of Financing Continuing Education." In *Power and Conflict in Continuing Education.* Edited by Harold J. Alford. Belmont, Calif.: Wadsworth, 1980.

Lowe, John. *Adult Education and Nation Building*. Edinburgh, Scotland: The Edinburgh University Press, 1970.

Lyden, F. J., and E. G. Miller. *Public Budgeting: Program Planning and Evaluation*. Chicago: Rand McNally, 1978.

Merewitz, L. P., and S. H. Sosnick. *The Budget's New Clothes*. Chicago, Ill.: Markham, 1971.

Ohio Board of Regents, Management Improvement Program. *Program Budgeting/ Two-Year Colleges*. Columbus, Ohio: Ohio Board of Regents, 1974.

Patillo, J. W. *Zero-Base Budgeting: A Planning, Resource Allocation and Control Tool*. New York: National Association of Accountants, 1977.

Steele, Sara M. *Cost-Benefit Analysis and the Adult Educator*. Syracuse, N.Y.: ERIC Clearinghouse in Adult Education, 1971.

Steiner, George. *Top Management Planning*. London: Macmillan, 1969.

White, V. P. *Grants: How to Find Out About Them and What To Do Next*. New York: Plenum Press, 1975.

Wildavsky, A. B. *The Politics of the Budgetary Process*. 3rd ed. Boston: Little, Brown, 1979.

Woodhall, M. *Cost-Benefit Analysis in Educational Planning*. Paris: UNESCO– International Institute for Educational Planning, 1970.

CHAPTER ELEVEN

ESTABLISHMENT OF ESSENTIAL SERVICES

Differentiating Services: Essential and Auxiliary
The Student Body

ADMISSIONS SERVICES: GETTING THEM IN

Nontraditional Credit for a Degree
CEU Credit for Continuing Education
The Graduate Admissions Paradox
Performance Evaluation

OTHER ESSENTIALS: FACILITATING THEIR LEARNING

Student Financial Aids
Counseling and Advising
Housing and Food Services
Library Services

STUDENT
SERVICES

Student services have too often been neglected in the world of the part-time students. This chapter primarily discusses the student services needed by part-time students; attention is given to some special problems confronted by this group and by those who serve them. The problems of financial aid for part-time students are reviewed and counseling and advising services are discussed. The logistics of housing, food and library services are considered with special reference to the difficulties encountered in smaller institutions and in off-campus programming. The basic assumption underlying these discussions is that, while the services needed by part-time students are different from those needed by full-time students, their need for services is as great.

ESTABLISHMENT OF ESSENTIAL SERVICES

The full-time candidate for a college degree leads a well-programmed existence. The fortunate student will enroll in the most convenient sections of the desired courses. On Tuesdays and Thursdays, he or she sleeps in or spends a leisurely hour with coffee and a morning paper before starting the day with a ten o'clock class. On Mondays, Wednesdays, and Fridays, he or she arrives slightly groggy and more than slightly late for an eight o'clock class. A well-engineered class schedule brings the day to an end at two, or perhaps leaves the middle of the day open for study, with classes ending at four or five. A cut or two on Friday makes possible a long weekend. Many will look back on this time as a happy interlude before being forced out into the real world.

University operations and services have evolved to accommodate the full-time student. The curriculum is fairly well outlined in the catalog, advisers are reasonably accessible, and fellow students trade authoritative information about which courses and instructors to seek and which to avoid. The student health service provides everything from contraceptive pills to psychiatric treatment, and the academic counseling service provides vocational guidance, aptitude tests, and help with learning disabilities. There is a financial aids office, an employment service, a student newspaper, and a variety of organized student activities that support in varying degrees one's academic, social, and vocational objectives. The working full-time student may not be able to use all of these advantages, but they are available for all who can use them.

For the part-time student, who studies on or off the campus, much of this is an unknown world. The fringe benefits are not available, registration is often at the end of the registration period after classes are picked over, and there is not time between the 5:00 P.M. close of the working day and the 6:30 P.M. class to do more than grab a sandwich and get to class. After class ends at 9:30 P.M. the counseling center is closed, and even the instructor is reluctant to linger long to give advice or to help with special problems.

To a great degree, the problems of the part-time student are the consequences of systems that were initially designed to serve residential students. This situation is compounded by the common assumption that the part-time student, usually older and more mature, is fully employed or in charge of a household, and can manage without all of the support services that are routinely provided for the regulars. Some institutions serve the needs of part-time students well; but generally, part-time students receive fewer and poorer services than full-time students, even though their needs may be just as great.

Consider the needs of part-time students. They are often in midcareer or starting a new career. In many cases, they are proceeding at greater risk than are the full-time students. Risk, of course, describes both a subjective and objective state. The subjective state involves anxiety and uncertainty. The objective state often includes the burning of bridges that have provided income and job security. In some cases, it involves a new life following the death of, or divorce from, a spouse. In others, it involves a search for fulfillment that a previous occupation has failed to afford, and a gamble that greater success will follow an investment in further self-development. In almost all instances it involves a sacrifice of time that was previously devoted to recreation or service to others. The effects on social and family life may be considerable. These adjustments come at a time when the total work life expectancy has decreased, when some of the buoyancy and adaptability of youth are gone and when family demands and fixed obligations are on the increase. Furthermore, all of these pressures are borne without the full social reinforcement of a community of fellow students, and all too frequently, as noted before, without the institutional resources available to the full-time student.

It is true that many part-time students have their tuition paid by employers. It is also true that many full-time students who commute to a large urban campus while working twenty or more hours a week have similar problems with access to campus resources, and lack the social reinforcement of campus life. Nevertheless, institutional resources are, as a rule, much more available to full-time students. On the average, part-time students are more likely to be stinted in terms of support services.

236

Differentiating Services: Essential and Auxiliary

The needs of the part-time student include essentially the same areas of service that are needed by the full-time student, but with important differences in content and approach. Essential student services are:

1. admissions, registration, and records;
2. financial aids;
3. information—bulletins, handbooks, staff contacts;
4. counseling and advising (including orientation);
5. logistic support—food, lodging, parking, etc.; and
6. library services (including tutorial and audiovisual services).

Auxiliary services, often denied to part-timers, are:

1. health services,
2. extracurricular activities,
3. student activity regulation, and
4. placement.

The basic student services are needed by all students. The auxiliary services listed are those which, for one reason or another, are needed by fewer of the part-time student body. They may nevertheless be important for a few. A brief consideration of these auxiliary services is given here, to be followed with an effort to identify the student body and to see how the essential services can best be adapted to the needs of the part-time student.

Health services for the full-time student may include health insurance, an out-patient clinic, infirmary and hospital care. These things are frequently taken care of in other ways by the part-time student. At the very least, however, some provision needs to be made for possible medical emergencies when substantial numbers of part-time students are involved—a large group spending several days at a conference center, for example. If a conferee who knows no one else at the conference and is a thousand miles from home has a heart attack, some procedure for providing emergency medical service becomes an obvious necessity.

Extracurricular activity services—social organizations, recreational activities, special events, and student groups of all sorts—may play a relatively minor or nonexistent role in the world of the part-time student, but perhaps there is a too ready disposition to assume that extracurricular activities are unimportant for part-timers. In fact, the comparative isolation of part-time students probably has much to do with their high dropout rate. Thus, such services may be desirable under some circumstances, as when a group of part-time students working toward an external degree can develop a sense of community and draw mutual support from an occasional social event. Valencia Community College of Orlando, Florida, is one institution that promotes such support services within its women's re-entry programs, just as the LaGuardia Community College of the City University of New York does in its extensive program for displaced homemakers.

As to student activity regulation, certainly one of the rewards of teaching part-time students is that most of the usual campus discipline problems are absent. Among part-time students, there are virtually no *in loco parentis* problems and few in-class problems. Cheating on examinations and use of ghost writers are two of the few concerns, and these only in some circumstances.

Placement services are likely to be neglected in part-time student programs. For one thing, many are permanently employed. For another, where employers pay a significant amount of support for students, they view placement services with disfavor. Finally, and probably most important, the existing placement services do not fit part-time student needs. Only in a few special purpose programs where training is aimed at preparation for new jobs—a training program for legal aides, for example—are placement services developed with concern for the requirements of the part-timer.

Apart from establishing a specialized placement service for part-time students, which may be too costly for the number of people served, two other approaches deserve consideration: (1) closer liaison with the existing institutional placement service, and (2) liaison with private employment services. Many of the latter charge the employer rather than the student, thus avoiding a possible conflict of interest in referring students.

The Student Body

The potential audience for collegiate part-time public service programs may be virtually the entire population of the United States exclusive of the 7 million who are full-time college students. A look at the variety of programs indicates that age is no barrier. Neonatal care, Headstart, children's theater, and education programs for the elderly are but a few examples of how many people are the targets of programs originating in postsecondary institutions. Many collegiate institutions believe their extension role means extending all their academic resources to the limits of their financial resources. Since the range of such resources spans the full spectrum of knowledge, virtually nothing is excluded *a priori*, and virtually everything has been tried somewhere at some time, it would seem.

The reasonably reliable national figures that are available give an impressive picture of this student body. For instance, data from the National Center for Education Statistics show that total registrations in noncredit adult and continuing education activities at colleges and universities grew from 5.6 million in 1967–1968 to 8.8 million in 1975–1976 to 10.2 million in 1977–1978. Total part-time degree credit registrations in institutions of higher education had grown by 1977 to approximately 4.5 million, which is about 41 percent of the total full- and part-time registrations for credit. Because of differences in the way institutions do student headcounts and because of the ways in which data are compiled, these figures almost certainly understate part-time student participation. The 106 community colleges of the state of California alone enroll over 600,000 part-time students. Certainly the growth rate in numbers of part-time students has been rapid, in contrast to the full-time student growth rate, which is destined to hover about the zero point during the early 1980s and to decline by 15 percent or more by 1990.

Federal Extension Service reports listed almost 104 million direct contacts during 1979; this represents the best estimate of students served by means other than organized classes—the people-to-people or public service types of activities that are traditional approaches of the Cooperative Extension Service. These approaches are being used more and more for other types of programs where nationwide data are not available: technical assistance in fields such as urban development, health care delivery, and business management. In addition, mass media are being used extensively to reach people who have never set foot on a campus or had face-to-face contact with a college faculty member. Some examples of such use of media are: the county extension agent's weekly column in the local newspaper, the radio and television broadcasts by college faculty and staff, the leaflets and brochures available at sports shows and fairs, sale of publications, and the growing use of dial access.

Stated in commercial terms, each institution must determine its own product-market strategy based on its capabilities and on the definition of its mission. It is quite likely, to judge from the varied data available, that in many states postsecondary outreach programs directly touch the lives of nearly one-fourth of the population each year.

Although the student body, broadly defined, is so diverse as to defy categorization, discussion in the remainder of this chapter concentrates principally on services for part-time students participating in organized instruction—whether they are going to school for credit toward a degree or for nondegree-oriented self-development. It thus deals with the counterpart functions serving full-time students in the areas of admissions, financial aids, and counseling. In other areas such as community service and person-to-person activities, the student services are generally integrated into the program.

ADMISSIONS SERVICES: GETTING THEM IN

In Chapter 7 we discussed some of the various modes by which adult students can earn credit and thereby progress toward a degree, a diploma, or a certificate. In this section we examine how student services can facilitate a part-time student's admission into those various curricular programs. The admissions service is a basic, necessary student service, whatever the student body. To be of value to part-time students, however, this service must take into account the special needs and interests of its part-time clientele.

Nontraditional Credit for a Degree

Until recently, credits for part-time degrees have been earned in essentially the same way as full-time student credits. Credit for experience and credit by examination, while for some time given limited recognition in college and university catalogs, were largely confined in the immediate post-World War II era to the General Educational Development (GED) examinations, which recommended granting high school equivalency and up to twenty-four college credits.

Through subsequent development and extended use of the College Level Examination Program (CLEP), varying degrees of advanced standing have been granted for learning in nontraditional settings. There is a great variation, but a number of institutions will grant up to sixty credits for the five general examinations or for the subject matter examinations or a combination of the two.

Nontraditional credits have become more acceptable both in institutions that anchor credits to the full-time student program and in those institutions that have separate external degree programs. Pioneering examples are the Bachelor of Liberal Studies degree at the University of Oklahoma, the Regents degree program of the University of the State of New York, the Metropolitan State University program in Minnesota, and the Coastline Community College in California, the latter being a college without walls that enrolls more than 40 thousand students.

The main problem now is that clear bases for evaluating such credits are lacking, especially in a transfer between institutions. The same problem arises in meeting prerequisites and in defining equivalency of courses. Mention has been made in Chapter 7 of the American Council on Education's guide to credit for noncollegiate programs. Evaluations of programs are conducted by review teams of educators who recommend level, amounts of credit, and course equivalencies. These recommendations can be accepted by institutions for waivers of requirements or for transfer credits. ACE publishes an annual update on programs reviewed since the publication of the 1980 guide. As of the 1981 supplement nearly 1500 courses in 124 corporations have been recommended for credit. Recommendations are made at four levels: vocational certificate, lower division, upper division, and graduate. The Office on Educational Credit also publishes a *Guide to the Evaluation of Educational Experiences in the Armed Services,* formulates recommendations for credit for the College Level Examination Program, and administers the General Educational Development Testing Service.

Individual institutions have also set up procedures for evaluating experience gained in other settings. Organizations such as Minnesota's Metropolitan State University and the University Without Walls may grant recognition for work experience and self-study, based on the evaluation of faculty advisers. Such programs differ in two major respects from the more traditional means of granting high school equivalency or advanced standings. First, acceptance of credits is almost entirely based on the discretion of the individual institution. One institution may grant CLEP credit for a fiftieth percentile algebra score and another may require the ninetieth percentile. Institutions may accept anywhere from sixty CLEP credits to none. Second, the number of independent correspondence study courses that may be counted toward the degree is sharply restricted in most institutions; few institutions recognize any graduate credit by this means. There seems to be a trend toward reducing or even removing such restrictions. The undergraduate credit policy relating to extension courses in the University of Wisconsin System is one of the more liberal, stating that, since Extension courses for degree credit in every instance have departmental approval for both the course and the instructor, there should be no distinction between that course when offered on or off the campus, by regular class, media, or independent study. Such courses should be accepted in transfer on the same basis as the equivalent course taken on campus at normal hours of instruction.

Often the more liberal policies are indirectly undermined by requirements for some minimum amount of full-time study toward the degree—a year or more for the baccalaureate, for example, or the requirement that the last sixteen credits must be taken in residence. In the less traditional degree programs these requirements can usually be eliminated or replaced by short-term periods of residence, as was described in more detail in Chapter 7. To illustrate: it is at least theoretically possible for a person with only eight grades of schooling to become a candidate for the baccalaureate degree at Metropolitan State University, based on high school equivalency examinations. By successfully completing the CLEP examinations he or she can win sixty credits of advanced standing. By completing all upper division requirements through a variety of nontraditional means, that same individual can then receive a degree without ever having been in a traditional classroom.

At the other extreme, the part-time student seeking a traditional degree may be allowed very few credits from outside the traditional curriculum. Today, however, virtually all institutions will accept high school equivalency established by examination. Most institutions will accept credits from independent correspondence study, the number of credits varying with institution, field of study, and numerous other factors making generalizations difficult. Also, a maximum of about ninety part-time semester credits is typically accepted by institutions.

CEU Credit for Continuing Education

Degree credits, semester or quarter, have been a long-established way of recording accomplishment by students. But only in recent years has there been any effort to standardize the recording of continuing education credits. Use of the continuing education unit as a measure of accomplishment in nondegree areas began in 1974, when a national committee published a manual establishing criteria for granting continuing education units. *The Continuing Education Unit* is available from the National University Continuing Education Association at One DuPont Circle in Washington, D.C. Use of the CEU has now been recognized by the Southern Regional Accrediting Association in their rules for member institutions under Standard 9 of that association's policy statement.

Continuing education units are coming into extensive use in a number of professional groups as a means of satisfying requirements for recertification or relicensure. As noted in Chapter 7, they have also been used to measure progress toward the professional development degree, a continuing education degree that is being offered by the Board of Regents of the University of Wisconsin System and by several other institutions. The continuing education unit also is useful for a variety of certificate programs that require a sequence of courses.

The continuing education unit is defined as ten contact hours of organized instruction or an equivalent thereof. *The Continuing Education Unit* cautions against establishing any criteria for interchangeability between the continuing education unit and traditional degree credit, but in some cases it seems unavoidable. For example, whereas continuing education units are sometimes used as a measurement toward recertification and relicensure, some students may elect to take credit courses. The equivalency must then be recognized. It is generally presumed that one semester hour of undergraduate credit represents one hour of lecture and two hours of outside study a week for fifteen or sixteen weeks. This equals 48 hours of work or 4.8 continuing education units for undergraduates. At the graduate level, we might assume that a credit costs 64 hours of effort, the equivalent of 6.4 continuing education units. This conversion cannot be presumed reversible. There is no evidence of any trend toward accepting continuing education units as equivalent to degree credit work. However, the recommendations of the prestigious American Council on Education in its guide suggest that the future will bring a relaxation of the distinction between degree credit and continuing education courses.

The Graduate Admissions Paradox

The problem of admission becomes even more complicated when graduate work is involved. Almost without exception, graduate schools require a higher grade point average for both admission and for continuation. This poses something of a paradox. The implicit assumption that degree-oriented postbaccalaureate education is only relevant for those with higher grade point averages makes very little sense if the purpose of the postbaccalaureate degree is related to on-the-job performance. The paradox is even stronger when the applicant has a solid record of on-the-job performance in increasingly responsible positions over an extended period of time. Exclusions solely on the basis of the academic record make some sense when that is the only record. When applied to the individual with a record of three or more years of postbaccalaureate experience, the presumption of experiential learning and changes in motivation needs to be given weight.

The admission of older students to graduate study raises questions about

1. the predictive efficiency of test scores for grades;

2. the predictive value of earlier grades to later grades, especially when there are substantial discontinuities of both time and content;

3. the predictive efficiency of course grades with respect to job performance;

4. the predictive efficiency of test scores with respect to job performance.

The answer to all of these questions is that the correlations are low enough to inspire a search for better predictors. The poor predictive value of grades with respect to job performance offers an example of how the grade point elite paradox might be resolved. The reliability of the testing procedures may be at fault, or the course content may itself be less appropriate than the instructor believes it to be. Better performance predictors may come from better achievement measures in the classroom, more relevant course content, or both. The competency-based learning movement represents such an effort. There are other alternatives. Either in combination with or distinct from admission based on experience, various types of restricted or conditional admission provisions may be used. The student may be admitted as a nondegree candidate (special student) or on probationary status.

A different kind of problem is sometimes posed by the frequent lack of admission qualifications in nondegree programs. Without some control, there is no way to insure that the student has adequate background for the material to be presented or to insure that there will be an exchange of information among students with a common set of qualifications and expectations. Explicit requirements may also be important in handling complaints and inquiries by people who are excluded or denied admission. In an era of equal opportunity and open meetings, it is obvious that one cannot exclude people arbitrarily. Yet, it is equally obvious that continuing education programs often need to be built on some common background among participants if the work is not to prove repetitious for some and beyond the comprehension of others.

In view of the detail with which prerequisites for degree credit courses are specified, admission requirements for nondegree programs seem to be a neglected area. Lack of control over admissions may be at the bottom of the dissatisfaction some students express about course results.

Performance Evaluation

Now that traditional classroom grading practices are being supplemented by assessments of accomplishment other than the usual pencil and paper tests of course content, the specific issue of performance evaluation can be raised. Nontraditional assessments usually take place in a flexible timeframe rather than in the fixed limits of a semester or a quarter. Such assessment methods typically incorporate those modes for earning credit that were discussed in Chapter 7 such as credit for experience, competency-based education, special examinations, and learning contracts.

To accept or to assign credits arising from nontraditional learning experiences requires, as we have already suggested, that equivalencies be established; and this implies that the standards of performance are to be in some degree comparable to those measured by more traditional means. The best solution would be to have this evaluation done by individuals who have extensive experience in the more traditional methods and who possess the confidence of their colleagues. While these nontraditional methods of evaluation have not yet gained widespread acceptance, their basic rationale differs very little from that of the doctor of philosophy degree as described in the *1977–78 Graduate School of Management Catalog* of Northwestern University.

> Every effort is made to provide each candidate with maximum opportunity for freedom and initiative in his or her progress toward the degree. Each student's program is unique in some way, because it is planned to incorporate the individual's interests and background. For example, prior graduate work may be acceptable for credit in some course areas, while competence in other areas may be measured by examination.

In just this parallel, however, one major difficulty becomes evident. The granting of credit for accomplishment both in doctoral and in nontraditional programs can be far more costly than the more standardized procedures in traditional classrooms.

Traditional credit transfer procedures are based on judgments of equivalency that can be made by well-trained clerical staff; judgments of performance in nontraditional experiences must be made by people with special expertise. Furthermore it takes considerably more time for these more expensive personnel to evaluate several pages of documentation than it does to determine that "English 345" at Podunk is the same course as "Literature 734" at Siwash.

In addition to granting advanced standing credits toward a degree, several other kinds of problems are on the rise as part-time student programs grow in number and variety. Some kinds of letter grades are given frequently in nondegree certificate programs—often the usual A,B,C,D,F system—and in some cases reimbursement by an employer may be based on an employer-imposed criterion of satisfactory completion. Reimbursement may even be graduated on the basis of grade received. Thus, in addition to the problem of determining a comparable performance standard, there is the further problem of placing too much emphasis on grades, which may cause trouble for the student who is really interested in self-development. Grades are often more appropriate for degree-oriented programs than for continuing education. Grades need not be a problem always: some nondegree-oriented courses as well as some degree credit courses may be graded on a pass-fail or satisfactory-unsatisfactory basis.

A different concept, however, that seems extremely logical is the concept of mastery learning, which is built into most courses using the Personalized System of Instruction described in Chapter 4. Here, the concept is that one proceeds to the next unit only after having demonstrated mastery of the preceding units. Thus course accomplishment tends to become an all-or-none outcome; one either knows the content or the unit or one does not. Under this philosophy degrees of attainment are sometimes distinguished on the basis of additional optional units elected. Thus, in one version every student who masters the basic twelve units has earned a C; students may elect additional units to raise their grade to a B or to an A. Evaluating performance in such courses should pose fewer problems.

Because the work of part-time students is spread over a longer timespan and because of job changes as well, the need for credit portability and for flexible assessment and admissions procedures is gaining greater recognition. Such changes in the traditional ways of evaluating and admitting students have long been overdue. Continued demand by part-time students for this service should insure that this aspect of student services will be considered by administrators in all areas of postsecondary education.

OTHER ESSENTIALS: FACILITATING THEIR LEARNING

At the beginning of this chapter we noted that while the services needed by part-time students are different from those needed by full-time students, their need for a broad range of services is as great. Indeed the learning experience can be enhanced greatly by administrators who pay adequate attention to the basic services discussed in this section.

Student Financial Aids

As noted in Chapter 10, in 1974 the American Council on Education published the report of its committee on the financing of higher education for adults. That group concluded that "part-time students on the whole are massively discriminated against in federal and state student institutional aid programs, Social Security Survivor's Benefits, institutional tuition rates and financial aid programs, and the income tax requirements." The report documents a pattern of higher fees, lower public support, and limited availability of financial aids for part-time students. The report indicates that 54.6 percent of part-time students pay for their educational work through personal finances and 25.9 percent receive help from employers. Only 18 percent receive any financial assistance from public funds.

Employer reimbursements are available in most instances only if the study is directly job-related. Those who want to educate themselves for a new job, a different job, or general self-development must rely on their own resources or on the limited availability of state and federal funds. For certain special educational goals, foundations and other organizations provide some exceptions to this rule, but only a few. Of the twenty-eight states that set up state aid programs for postsecondary students in 1974, only four made any provision for part-time students. On the federal side, basic educational opportunity grants have been available only to full-time students. Social security education benefits for children of retired or disabled persons are restricted to full-time students between the ages of eighteen and twenty-two. Part-time students have received no more than supplemental opportunity grants. The Guaranteed Student Loan Program is one such opening. About 14 percent of the guaranteed student loans in 1972 were made to part-time students. The National Direct Student Loan program in 1972 gave part-time students about 22.5 percent of its grants. The GI Bill of Rights, which is of declining importance as the number of eligible veterans has decreased, provided about 50 percent of its support to part-time students. In addition, there are many institutions today that provide financial aid to students over sixty who may be able to participate in a wide variety of programs on a no-fee or reduced-fee basis.

Most of these sources of financial aid, with the exception of employer reimbursement, are restricted to degree credit programs. Eligibility seems based on the demand that a vocational objective must be involved and on the assumption that only degree-oriented programs have a vocational focus in colleges and universities. Still, noncredit programs of proprietary schools may qualify for some kinds of aid, veterans' benefits for example.

A number of proposals have been advanced to eliminate financial aid restrictions on part-time education. Widely discussed has been the idea of a life-time drawing account that would finance the educational equivalent of up to four years of full-time college, but there seems little evidence that implementation is imminent, although other voucher plans continue to surface.

Recently, some institutions have established credit card methods of payment for part-time students. The institution gains the dual advantage of providing ready financial credit to the student while avoiding, for the institution, the problems of collection. The principal value of the credit card arrangement is for short-term credit. Interest rates charged for longer-term credit are substantially higher than for the established student aid programs. Extended credit under a credit card account has traditionally cost 1.5 percent for the first five hundred dollars, and beyond that, cost 1.0 percent per month. With rising interest rates and tightened credit, this form of financing is becoming less attractive. Bank charges to the institution for such credit appear to be negotiable. Sometimes banks provide low discount rates or even waive charges as a public service. In other cases, full rates are charged. The institution going into the business of credit cards has commonly had to pay between 5 and 6 percent; under present unstable economic conditions, a decision on credit card use must be based on careful assessment of this changing situation. Some institutions prefer to handle their own credit arrangement rather than paying such a discount, but very few institutions are in a position to grant long-term credit without having loan funds, and these are rarely available to part-time students.

Almost every session of Congress brings national change to student financing. The offices that specialize in serving the part-time student must keep up with those changes in order to take full advantage of the opportunities, however limited. And of course, the cost of administering financial aid under the highly complex federal system will be a consideration in extending services to part-time students.

Counseling and Advising

GENERAL SERVICES   Four principal motives have emerged from studies probing the motivations of part-time and older students. The first is self-development—the desire to know. Second is the effort to prepare for work, in either a new job or present employment. The third most common motive is to make recreational use of leisure time. The fourth motive, ranking substantially lower than the rest, is to discharge social responsibilities.

Data from such studies suggest that those who involve themselves in continuing education programs in order to become better informed are generally satisfied with the outcome. Those learning for the sake of their present jobs feel similarly rewarded. The record is not nearly so impressive for those who aim at new employment. Those who have taken courses for the sake of new employment have often characterized the education as less effective.

It thus appears that one of the more pressing needs of the part-time student—to develop new kinds of marketable skills—is one which is being least effectively met. While part of this failure may be attributed to the courses, a more likely cause is lack of good educational guidance. The full-time student has traditionally been able to obtain counseling and guidance of considerable quality. But it only recently has been recognized that the guidance needs of part-time students are at least as great as those of full-time students. There is also growing recognition that these needs may be quite different from those of the full-time student, and that mere access to traditional services is not enough.

The six kinds of counseling services that appear to be most desired by adult and part-time students and the probable order of their importance is as follows:

1. Assessment
2. Information about careers
3. Help with developing learning skills
4. Evaluation of individual's motivation
5. Counseling on personal matters
6. Advice on procedures and requirements

Reading between the lines, we can see that people returning to education lack confidence in their own capabilities. They rank the need to evaluate their capabilities, aptitudes, and interest very high. They are concerned about their ability to learn. They are uncertain about their own motivation and they frequently need occupational and career information that would enable them to look at alternatives to their present employment. Their needs suggest that basic counseling and guidance services can be classified under three major headings: information services, evaluation of potential, and attitudinal problems.

1. *Information services.* One of the dominant needs is for better information about career opportunities, kinds of jobs one might prepare for, the job market, and the requirements and advantages of various kinds of employment. This includes information about the availability of courses, admission requirements, prerequisites, and other factual data that are part of the standard routine of full-time student advising.

2. *Evaluative services.* These include evaluation of learning ability, aptitudes, and interests for various kinds of activities, as well as advice about ways and means of pursuing goals. Aptitude and achievement test services are needed as an integral part of this type of counseling. Such services were widely available to veterans after World War II but have not been so readily available to as many in more recent years.

3. *Attitudinal counseling.* Many adult learners need assurance. They often lack confidence and wonder if they can re-enter the classroom. Often they are unsure of their own feelings about returning to school. Frequently, contact may be initiated through a request for information. As the counseling process goes forward, it only then becomes apparent that the individual also has to deal with anxieties and attitudes before simple facts or technical advice can be useful.

Evaluative and attitudinal counseling should be undertaken with caution by any other than trained counselors with at least a master's degree, although from time to time a less well-trained counselor of special sensitivity may be helpful, provided that the paraprofessional counselor recognizes his or her limitations. Information counseling is less demanding and can usually be handled by a person who has a wide grasp of the necessary facts and who can articulate a clear relationship between opportunities and individual needs.

SPECIAL SERVICES   As extension educators become more aware of the problems of ethnic and other groups that have been poorly served in the past, the need for special kinds of counseling services becomes increasingly evident. More women are entering the labor force, for example. Many are doing so after being away from gainful work for a number of years, or deciding to make their first foray into full-time employment. They seek a satisfying and rewarding career. But they are considerably older on the average than full-time college students who are entering the labor market, and consequently they often have doubts about their ability to learn. They are not sure what goals they should pursue and are ambivalent about undertaking a new career after perhaps a decade or more of homemaking. Members of minority groups are also likely to have problems that differ from those of the dominant majority. Both ethnic and racial minorities are likely to have experienced discrimination in entering the labor force or advancing on the job. They frequently have some past educational disadvantage. When a large number of minority students must be served, it is especially helpful to use counselors who are themselves members of the minority. It is absolutely essential that counselors working with individuals from diverse racial and ethnic backgrounds at least have understanding of and sensitivity to the groups they serve.

A different kind of problem is presented by working with professional and managerial groups. In these cases, the counselor is dealing with people who have already begun the ascent on their career ladders; their problems are those of meeting requirements for upgrading in their chosen line of work or changing direction. Mandatory requirements are being developed for many professions in many states, particularly as a result of increasing pressures for recertification and relicensure. As mentioned earlier, in a number of states, physicians, nurses, accountants, and attorneys are required to take a certain number of continuing education hours over established periods of time. Counselors working with these groups need a thorough background in the requirements of the profession, a clear picture of the individual's experience, and the foresight to help them in their plans. For example, now in use are profiles that break down a physician's practice into the number and kinds of conditions dealt with. One physician's practice may involve a high frequency of trauma cases, another's may involve large numbers of cases of coronary disease. These profiles are then compared with the knowledge base that the physicians have, and recommendations for continuing education are based upon the gaps identified between the demands of the practice and the physician's professional knowledge. A similar diagnostic approach is needed in such occupations as engineering and business management, where significant qualitative changes take place in the nature of the job as individuals move up on the career ladder. While early and midcareer engineers need to specialize in technical interests, their subsequent rise in responsibilities may call for greater management, administrative, and executive skills.

ALTERNATIVES   Since educational counseling services on most campuses are not designed for the part-time student, two alternatives should be considered: to increase the availability of existing resources, or to develop a separate capability to serve the continuing education student. The latter option, by avoiding the conflict between service for full-time students and service for part-timers, appears to be preferable if it can be adequately funded.

Patterns of resource allocation for student counseling suggest that a continuing education office dealing with as many as 10,000 registrations a year will have to provide at least fifteen minutes of counseling for over 20 percent of them. Assuming that these 2000 clientele contacts are of minimal or moderate complexity, two counselors are probably adequate to give them a passive type of service, in which clientele come to the counseling facility. Some of the larger continuing education operations have developed specialized centers to work with particular clientele needs. For example, New York University has a comprehensive, fee-supported Career Counseling Center and Adult Learning Center, as well as an Adult Transition program in preparation for degree work. In addition, NYU has free preregistration advisement for noncredit courses. In such operations as this, it can be expected that many of the clients will arrive as referrals from less specialized counseling organizations.

A similar specialized approach may be found in offices dealing specifically with older people or professional groups. Specialized centers are highly desirable where there are clientele requiring unique expertise. In addition to counseling, specialized staff may have responsibilities in teaching, program development, and other activities. This dual arrangement is particularly useful in dealing with the continuing education needs of a professional group. For example, such external degree programs as that of Minnesota's Metropolitan State University sponsor a close relationship between faculty mentors and individual students to combine academic advising with the more general counseling needs of the students. Such relationships are intended to be continuing relationships throughout the student's study program.

Intensive counseling is especially effective where counselors have access to an assessment center, which in its most highly evolved form offers a broad range of services. Clients are frequently subjected to as much as three days of interviewing, testing, and exercises in job simulation and decision making. The result is an extensive evaluation of the individual's interests, abilities, and special needs. While the entire field of psychological testing has become more controversial in recent years, psychological tests still appear justified as a supporting tool in vocational and educational counseling, if for no other reason than as a means of stimulating discussion and thought. When coupled with the more varied techniques of an assessment center, they can be still more helpful.

Most economical in those instances where clientele are widely dispersed, is an itinerant counseling service of part-time paraprofessionals. The University of Wisconsin has developed this service extensively with a particular emphasis on employing and training paraprofessionals from the interest groups to be served—minorities, women, and so on. Under the supervision of a trained counselor, these paraprofessionals are available in libraries, community centers, and other locations where they can help interested people. Newspaper advertisements, public service radio announcements, posters, bulletins, and contacts with various groups have turned up substantial numbers of clientele that would otherwise not be served. Since the service is meant primarily to help people approach their own educational goals, it is not simply one of selling programs. The purpose is to provide information about services of both the sponsoring institution and other community organizations. The service is a highly cost-effective way of reaching people on a person-to-person basis. It has also proven effective in reaching people who would not come to a campus or other permanent facility for counseling. The staff of twenty-two counselors average eighteen to twenty hours of counseling time each week, serving about 12,000 clients per year in a combination of person-to-person and small group counseling sessions.

One problem in providing a geographically dispersed service is that it is necessarily a less specialized service. The ideal arrangement may be to combine a geographically dispersed service with backup service of a more specialized nature. Where resources are limited, however, one or the other may be chosen, depending largely on clientele and their needs.

One method of combining specialized service with geographic mobility is to take advantage of the growing number of learning resource centers in different states. A learning resource center is designed primarily to provide students with specialized facilities such as videocassettes, but it can also serve as a locus for a mobile counseling service. A less frequently employed method is to house an office in a trailer and move it from community to community on a rotating schedule. The cost of such an operation is high, considering the number of contacts, but pays off in moving visual displays and other equipment that would otherwise not be available.

A variant of the itinerant counseling service is the type of mobile van service in use at Los Angeles City College and at Cuesta College in San Luis Obispo. In these instances a fully equipped van moves counselors and their paraphernalia to shopping centers, high schools, and senior citizen centers throughout the service area.

Group counseling programs are another cost effective counseling approach. Some have been organized as regular courses with a career or an educational planning theme. For example, Metropolitan State University requires all students to begin their study programs with registration in a six-week orientation course, having as principal objectives, active exploration of the student's capabilities, interests, and needs, and the custom tailoring of a study plan to fit them. This not only serves an information function but, where an educational plan is one of the course outcomes, also deals effectively with individual advising and planning. Perhaps even more importantly, the group experience is therapeutic. Older women entering or re-entering the labor force, for example, gain reassurance through the discovery that others have the same problems and anxieties. Confidence in their ability to learn is strengthened by group support, and their motivation is likely to be greater as a result.

Housing and Food Services

In the larger institutions, housing and food services become an integral part of continuing education operations. Many have built special facilities such as short-course dormitories and continuing education centers. The centers, in many instances, combine conference facilities with food services and living facilities. Management of these installations is a profession in its own right, and is beyond the scope of this brief treatment of student services. However, for institutions contemplating entry into this field, several considerations should be weighed. First of all, some institutions have overbuilt in terms of their program commitment. The institutional criterion of sponsoring programs that fit the mission of the institution, tends to break down in such instances, and a conference center becomes a general purpose convention facility. Several problems are thus engendered. First, competition with the private sector often creates public relations difficulties. Second, people are attracted with interests and concerns entirely unrelated to the interests and concerns of the institution. The alternative of dropping below a 65 to 70 percent occupancy rate makes it hard to charge reasonable rates and still survive economically, and full cost recovery becomes difficult.

A more appealing alternative for institutions with good full-time student services and regular student dormitories is to schedule programs that require on-site residence during a ''down-time,'' when it is possible to use surplus dormitory and food service facilities without competing with the regular student programs. A second alternative for the smaller institution is to use commerical facilities. These are often available at a reasonable rate. In many instances where students are housed in commercial facilities, conference spaces are made available at no additional charge, or at a nominal charge. Commercial facilities are usually reasonably well-equipped, offering much the same advantages as facilities in a large full-time college or university conference center. Blocks of rooms can be reserved well in advance and held until a reasonable deadline of a week or two before the program so that conferees can be assured of housing.

When small institutions stage programs where only meal services are required, catered food service can be advantageous. In many small communities, church and civic groups are happy to supply these services as a means of raising funds, and larger communities have commercial catering services. Thus, a smaller continuing education operation need not try to set up housing and food services like those of their larger counterparts. Further, commercial facilities give greater mobility to the small continuing education operation. Programs can be brought to the clientele, making it more likely that they will attend.

As to providing one's own living facilities, 65 to 70 percent occupancy is a reasonable breakeven point only if it can be reached without excessive promotional costs. Even a center that is built entirely with appropriated or contributed funds can be a drain on institutional resources without enough programs. The program must generate enough funds to hire professional staff and pay for such hidden costs as parking, equipment procurement and maintenance, and user services. In most institutions, the temptation to build self-amortising living accommodations should be assessed with great care and realism.

Library Services

There are two main choices for providing adequate library services for the part-time student: (1) access to on-campus services, and (2) provision of off-campus services. Under on-campus services, in turn, two principal difficulties can be identified: (1) off-campus students often need these services outside library hours, and (2) getting to the library can be difficult when one lives some distance from the campus. A telling example involves courses offered on weekends—all day Saturday and a half-day on Sunday, for example—to students who came from as far as several hundred miles away. There is little time for library work before or after class sessions. Furthermore, twelve class hours in two days is a grueling pace, especially after a full work week. Students can hardly be expected to have enough reserve time or energy to either precede or follow up this session with several hours in the library. They need flexibility in library access.

Consider also the problem of the evening class taught three hundred miles from the campus. For one thing, even with nearby learning centers it is not possible to duplicate the resources of a major library. For another, students at off-campus locations often commute a considerable distance to the off-campus location and thus have a problem similar to, though less severe than, that of the student who travels some distance to the campus. The problem is compounded for those who learn by independent correspondence study or through broadcast media. Graduate schools in particular see the library problem as a principal reason for putting restrictions on graduate study by nontraditional means.

The library problem may, however, be exaggerated. For one thing, faculty may have an inflated notion of how much time students spend studying in libraries. There is no doubt, however, that library study is important in many courses. Provisions need to be made, and there are several ways of doing so.

1. *Use of supplemental texts.* Additional texts consisting often entirely of readings reduce the need for a library, but textbook costs are a formidable barrier.

2. *Photocopy reproduction of readings.* Many materials can be available through reproduction services, though this too is fairly costly, and use is complicated by copyright laws.

3. *Learning centers*—off-campus centers supplied with materials appropriate to the courses being offered.

4. *Reciprocal arrangements with other libraries,* both public and private.

5. *On-campus study periods* as part of the course.

6. *Audiocassettes and other types of mailable materials.* The Open University has used this method effectively in some kinds of laboratory work; it has some value as a substitute for on-campus resources.

7. *Reprints.* Many periodicals offer reprints at a nominal cost, which can be passed on to students for less than the cost of a supplemental text. The principal drawback is the lead time required to select, purchase, and assemble reprints in the desired numbers.

8. *Microfiche and microfilm.* Most libraries have the capability of providing reproductions of some materials on a cost recovery basis. These require special equipment for readout at the off-campus location.

9. *Telecopy.* Some off-campus locations have the capability for reproducing material via telephone lines. Unless leased lines are available, this method is too costly for general use.

10. *Computerized transmission.* Although not yet widely available, the capability for "reading" and transmitting material is in limited use and will become more generally available in the near future.

In the final analysis, it is clear that deliberate effort must be made to offset the disadvantage of limited library access for the part-time student. While the importance of library access may be exaggerated, there is nevertheless a problem, and deliberate planning must insure that problem is minimized.

In this chapter, we have tried to emphasize the importance of adequate support services for part-time students. These services differ from those for full-time students in the particular combination that is considered optimum, but they are no less important. To some degree, the high dissatisfaction among part-time students results from inadequacies in counseling and other educational support services. To some degree, failure to deal intelligently with these inadequacies probably contributes to the low esteem with which many faculty view part-time education. On the other hand, however, the evidence is impressive that as a group, part-time students, including independent learners, when working under optimum conditions, do as well as their full-time counterparts. Better services can insure that the optimum is maintained for existing courses while expanding the variety of learning opportunities as well.

BIBLIOGRAPHY

Bartholomy, J. M., and J. Harcourt. "The Service Function: An Opportunity for Improving University Teaching." *Continuum* 41 (1977): 16.

Bostaph, Charles F., and Marti Moore. "Strategies for Advising Adult Students." *Continuum* 42 (1977): 24–25.

College of Continuing Education. *Ways and Means of Strengthening Information and Counseling Services for Adult Learners.* Los Angeles, Calif.: College of Continuing Education, 1978.

Farmer, Martha L. *Counseling Services for Adults in Higher Education.* Metuchen, N.J.: Scarecrow Press, 1971.

Frandson, Phillip E. "Territorial Imperative: The Part-Time Student." *The NUEA Spectator,* June 1976, pp. 43–45.

Grabowski, Stanley M. "Educational Counseling of Adults." *Adult Leadership,* March 1976, pp. 225–27.

Hall, G. E., and H. L. Jones. *Competency-Based Education: A Process for the Improvement of Education.* Englewood Clitfs, N.J.: Prentice-Hall, 1976.

Hartwig, John. "A Competency-Based Approach to Adult Counseling and Guidance." *Counselor, Education and Supervision,* September 1975, pp. 12–20.

Scaggs, William F., and Curtis Ulmer. *Guide to Adult Education Counseling.* Englewood Cliffs, N.J.: Prentice-Hall, 1972.

Williams, G. D., et al. "Urgency and Types of Adult Counseling Needs among Continuing Education Students." *Journal of College Student Personnel* 14 (1973): 501–06.

Wishnoff, R. "Student Personnel Services in the University Without Walls." *Personnel and Guidance Journal* 53 (1975): 507–11.

CHAPTER TWELVE

THE SCOPE OF PUBLIC RELATIONS

Specialists and Generalists
Relation to Promotion and Marketing
Goals: Creating a Support Base

**IDENTIFYING AND RELATING TO
SIGNIFICANT PUBLICS**

Staff
The Parent Organization
Other Institutions
Organized Influence Groups
Government Agencies
The General Public
Clientele and Suppliers

PUBLIC RELATIONS STRATEGY

Knowing the Constituencies
Planning Communications
Getting the Message Across
Coordinating and Controlling

CHANNELS OF COMMUNICATION

Personal Communications
Mass Media
In-House Publications
Other Channels
Choosing the Channels

PUBLIC RELATIONS

Just as every living creature must relate effectively to its environment in order to flourish, so must every organization. Adapting is more than simply obtaining resources in exchange for providing goods or services. It is the complex process of establishing a niche, of maintaining dominance or harmony with other organizations, of anticipating future needs, and of being able to alter the environment to make it more favorable. The exchange of goods or services for resources is a necessary but not a sufficient condition for organizational health. These exchanges take place in an economic, political, and social environment, and the web of relations in which the transactions are embedded—the context surrounding the primary functions of production and marketing—is the concern of public relations in its broadest sense.

This chapter will focus on the organization's task of relating to its total environment. It will begin with a look at public relations as a job, dealing with the question of whose job it is, how it differs from other related jobs, what it seeks to accomplish, and by what means. We then go on to define the various publics and to consider how they can be dealt with, and what some of the general strategies can be. The chapter closes with a consideration of some of the specific channels of communication that can serve our purpose.

THE SCOPE OF PUBLIC RELATIONS

Specialists and Generalists

Public relations is too often seen as the function of creating a favorable image for the organization. Based on this narrow view there is a tendency for other members of the organization to assume that public relations will be taken care of by the specialist.

Certainly the public relations office, by whatever name it may be called, provides a valuable kind of expertise. Even more important than the art of writing a good news release, is the know-how required to insure that it will appear in the right paper, in the right section, at the right time. Likewise, it takes special skill to insure that the organization's interests are adequately communicated when legislation is needed, when pending legislation requires modification, when actions of the organization are under fire, or when groundwork needs to be laid for a change. Public relations in its fullest sense, however, is a responsibility of every member of the organization. The typist in an inner office, the keypunch operator, the building service worker, all have lives outside the organization and in that outside life they communicate their attitudes—from enthusiastic to antagonistic—and information or misinformation to people outside the organization. This does not imply some elaborate program of indoctrination by the administration, but simply that everyone in the organization should have some degree of understanding of the organization's objectives and general operations and some concomitant degree of pride in being identified as a member of the organization.

In terms of continuing education programs, public relations thus broadly construed relates to the ability of the organizational unit to promote understanding and gain support from its own members and all those relevant others in other units of the larger organization as well as in external units that interact with extension.

Relation to Promotion and Marketing

The lines between functions, which seem so sharp and clear on organization charts, in reality run together. Those responsible for organization-to-environment relationships may be selling the organization's services, the organization itself, or, as is more likely, a combination of the two. It is therefore largely a matter of convenience that public relations is separated from program promotion and marketing. Although marketing is that aspect of public relations dealing specifically with potential participants in programs, it also has implications for the larger public beyond the target audience. For example, during a legislative budget session, a university extension worker offered a program in winemaking. The program sold out—a success. That is, it was a success until the voices of the critics were heard. The vociferous misuse-of-public-funds group included an editorial writer on one large daily paper, who devoted several column inches to this abuse of the public trust. At least one legislator took public notice and commented on the budgetary implications. The fact that the program more than paid its own way was largely overlooked.

A timid and, consequently, ineffective organization may run for cover whenever anything even remotely controversial comes into view; but peace is bought at a price, for controversy may have very positive effects. Certainly any healthy organization will find itself involved in controversy from time to time. But one should not blunder into controversy. The staff should be aware of the fact that activities in the public arena can have unintended as well as intended consequences. A skilled public relations specialist may be of value in anticipating the effects of various activities that an organization may be proposing to undertake. In the final analysis, however, effective public relations involves the sensitivity of all decision-makers in the organization, and, in the most successful organizations, the collective ability to decide whether any given undertaking is likely to produce undesirable and unintended side effects. The role of the public relations specialist then is like the role of any other staff specialist: to provide expert advice and supporting skills in furthering the objectives of the organization as a whole and of its separate line subunits.

Goals: Creating a Support Base

The general goal of public relations is to create and maintain a favorable environment in which the unit is free to realize its fullest potential. To accomplish this, good public relations must concentrate on several more specific goals. CAMEL provides a mnemonic device for five important goals:

Cooperation

Acceptance

Money matters

Entry

Legal climate

Let's consider each one briefly.

COOPERATION   The folk saying, "You scratch my back, I'll scratch yours," takes on a special meaning in organizational settings. Organizations or units within an organization may work together or at cross-purposes. Frequently the difference between a yes or no answer to a request is a matter of the direction one leans. It may be a simple thing such as trading classrooms or moving a rush duplicating job to the head of the queue, or it may be a major decision between two organizations to do complementary rather than competitive programming.

ACCEPTANCE   The credibility and creditability of an organization—whether its claims and credentials are accepted at face value—is a matter of confidence, and confidence depends on more than the quality of the product. It depends on what the organization communicates to others about itself. Whether, for example, an employer will approve an employee's attendance at a program may depend as much on how the employer feels about the organization as it does about the content of the specific program. Grades in courses taken at another institution are counted or discounted on the basis of reputation. The credentials of an individual are weighed on the basis of the source. In all of these examples, how people feel about the organization influences their judgments about its merits.

MONEY   Nearly all continuing education units rely on three sources of funding: fees, contributions, and grants. Fee income depends directly on what the unit offers the individual client and how well it markets the offering, but it also depends on the potential client's perception of the organization. Contributions are gifts given without expectation of a return. The contribution may be space provided by the parent organization without charge to the unit, or it may be a building given by a foundation, or even a bequest by someone who has never had direct contact with the organization. Grants—and here we disregard the federal government's rather fine distinction between grants and contracts—are sums given by the grantor (a foundation or government agency) for service provided to a third party: the scientific community, the disadvantaged, the profession, or the general welfare. Contributions and grants more so than fees, are general expressions of confidence or good will, which in turn are as much the result of the organization's image or repute as they are of its specific capabilities. Thus an organization's contributions and grants are significantly affected by its public relations.

ENTRY   It is not always easy to gain access to the decision-makers and opinion-makers of one's world. Most people in the higher levels of large organizations have buffers between them and the many who want some of their time. An effective public relations program should help to open doors. It should build contacts where they are likely to be needed—in government, in business, and in the not-for-profit world of foundations, professional associations, and educational institutions. This includes the people within one's own parent institution: the president, the chancellor, the vice presidents, deans, and department heads.

LEGAL CLIMATE   Long ago the United States Supreme Court held that the power to tax was the power to destroy. This assertion of the power of government has been expanded slowly but inexorably to the point where most of our plans and expectations can be aided or thwarted by acts of government—not only by legislative bodies but by administrative rules and acts of government agencies. Thus organizations must concern themselves with the legal climate in which they operate. The range of problems and opportunities is broad. It includes, for instance, agency definitions of eligibility to apply for certain grants, appropriations under a variety of legislative acts, affirmative action requirements, and the requirements of regulatory and licensing agencies.

The extent and manner in which any given continuing education unit involves itself in these matters will depend on its size, its staff resources, and the restraints imposed by its parent organization. But no unit is so small or so detached from its environment that it can view these goals as of no concern. Good public relations are no more the result of chance than are good continuing education programs. The administrator must provide leadership in this area, as in all other areas of administration. Furthermore the good will that results from good public relations cannot be built on a crash basis in times of crisis. It must be banked with regularity and the account must be drawn on with restraint.

IDENTIFYING AND RELATING TO
SIGNIFICANT PUBLICS

Modern complex organizations have been commonly described in terms of an open systems concept. They have an identity and continuity in time. They have a bureaucratic or corporate character that defines structure and boundaries; organizations therefore can be described in personal terms. They can also be thought of as organisms dependent on a reasonably steady-state internal environment maintaining some kind of equilibrium with an external environment. This equilibrium depends on internal and external sensing mechanisms, and on a set of responses to the information provided by the sensors. If the sensing is defective or if the responses are inappropriate or in-adequate, disequilibrium results, in extreme cases, in disintegration and death.

Public relations is an integral part of this sensing and responding mechanism, and is essential in maintaining a favorable environment. To be fully effective, it requires that the significant publics be identified, monitored, and responded to. Figure 12.1 is a visual representation of these significant publics. It shows the unit interacting with its internal and external publics. The internal public is the unit's employees. The ex-ternal publics, if we think of the extension and continuing education unit as a separate

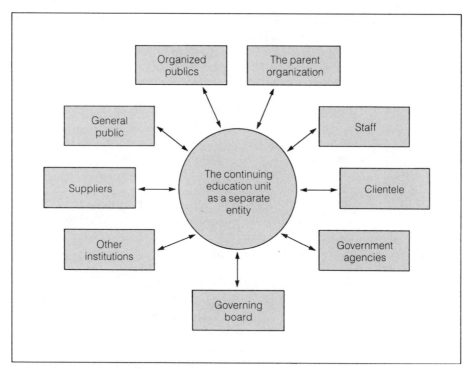

Figure 12.1. *The organization and its publics*

entity, can be divided into seven main groups existing in varying degrees of intimacy to the unit:

1. the parent organization—the college, university, or other institution of which the unit is a formal part, and the "owners"—usually a governing board;

2. other institutions or units with similar mission;

3. organized publics—groups of people operating in concert usually through not-for-profit corporate bodies such as trade associations, special interest groups, and the like;

4. government agencies—local, state, and national;

5. the general public—members of the community operating as individuals;

6. clientele—the customers who use the unit's services;

7. suppliers—providers of goods and services that keep the organization operating.

The situation is somewhat complicated by the fact that individuals in each of these categories may also be in one or more additional categories and may even behave somewhat differently when acting in one role than in another: the legislator who liked the course he took may still vote to reduce your budget.

The mission of public relations is to motivate these publics to contribute to the health of the organization. In the following sections, we will suggest some ways for dealing with each of these publics effectively.

Staff

Staff can be considered either as individuals or as a collectivity of individuals. Collectivities of staff may be a part of organizational governance, members of a collective bargaining unit, or a combination of the two. For example, the professional staff may vote on matters of curriculum, and support staff may bargain on wages. Since such collectivities usually operate under a broader authorization than the continuing education unit's, we will not deal with them here.

Relations with staff as individuals, however, are a part of the job of the unit administrator. These relations tend to take somewhat different form when they involve two classes of staff: the professional staff and the support staff. Professional staff are involved directly in program planning and implementation. They have different career ladders than support staff and they usually identify with other members of the same profession as well as with the employing organization. Support staff—clerical, custodial, and technical workers—usually operate under different work rules and have a more narrowly defined role in the organization. There are legal distinctions as well. Yet both groups can vary in their relationship to the organization from an attitude of serious alienation to one of enthusiastic identification.

From the perspective of public relations, the principal concern here is with internal communications: the amount and kind of information that staff receive about their organization and its relevant subdivisions. These communications take place in three ways: via media, in meetings, and person-to-person.

COMMUNICATIONS MEDIA   In this context, media include bulletin boards, public address systems, and printed communications. Imaginative use of these media can add significantly to staff relations efforts. The bulletin board tends to be self-defeating when it is poorly managed. A cluttered bulletin board that is rarely cleared of dated information will quickly lose its attention-getting value. Also a bulletin board with a wide range of miscellany will discourage readership. Several bulletin boards, each of which is confined to a well-defined function, will serve better. For example, in a large organization one functional bulletin board may deal with job opportunities, thereby implementing a policy of promotion from within. Another might be a place to display the gleanings of a clipping service.

Also useful are the public address system, which can combine music and spot announcements of general interest, and the staff newsletter, which can carry a variety of items of personal and organizational news. Of these various media, the staff newsletter is the most widely used. Indeed a public relations specialty has grown up around the newsletter or house organ, and a well-edited, well-produced newsletter can be a major vehicle in improving staff communications. In a small organization periodic informational memoranda may serve the same purpose at a lower unit cost.

MEETINGS AS A COMMUNICATIONS DEVICE   Periodic staff meetings, preferably in small groups with an opportunity for give and take, have two advantages over media—they are more personal and they provide an opportunity for immediate feedback. They can be used to offset the adverse effects of the communications grapevine and they can foster a feeling of involvement in decision making. On the negative side, if they are perceived as simple "show and tell" or selling, they can quickly lose their effectiveness.

PERSONAL COMMUNICATIONS   While most personal communications, whether oral or written, deal with the business of the organization, they may also be used in strengthening staff relations. Their use may vary from the casual visit over coffee or at lunch to the annual notice to each individual as to the amount paid into his or her account for health insurance, group life, and retirement benefits. The administrator who leaves the office to make personal contact with staff, even just to ask how things are going, is keeping the lines open and helping to strengthen identification with the organization and its administrators. A personal note on the occasion of a promotion, a sentence or two on a greeting card, or a telephone call about a matter of common concern can do much to reduce the feeling of impersonality that can develop even in small organizations.

Communications by media, in meetings, and individually serve one important purpose. They increase understanding and acceptance of the goals of the organization and, as a result, bring about a more intelligent commitment to the organization. Singling out specific individuals for special recognition or awards as part of this process can further highlight and reinforce the kinds of behavior that are regarded as desirable.

The Parent Organization

Internal institutional public relations is the subject of the most frequent complaints in extension and continuing education operations. Complaints center around two principal points: the low priority that many institutions assign to public service and the low esteem that other staff afford it when evaluating the performance of their colleagues. Many institutions perceive continuing education as being only a public relations function in the narrowest sense of the term. It is valued if it serves influential constituencies, attracts students, or generates income in excess of expenses. The problem in many institutions is that the public service and extension staff accept their colleagues' valuation. The long-range remedy is the development of a highly qualified staff who believe in their unit's mission. In the shorter run, this is an area in which personal contacts are the best means for stimulating change.

Planned contacts need to be cultivated with members of the board of control, top administrators, and colleagues. They may include briefing sessions, planned involvement in programs, or simply opportunities to exercise gentle persuasion. Tying public service programs to research interests and opportunities may stimulate desirable interaction. Even providing opportunities for residential colleagues to earn supplemental income may serve as a means of first gaining interest and then converting. Judicious inclusion of board members on appropriate mailing lists provides another channel. But it may be even more important to insure that a selected number of influential board members are especially well-informed and that they have open lines of communication, preferably on a first name basis, with key members of the unit who are able to present the case for the unit's interests. This may be accomplished either by identifying pre-existing contacts and using these lines effectively or by building bridges from scratch for this purpose. One avenue that might be explored is to have the dean, working with the president of the board, identify two or three members (who would constitute a miniboard) whose knowledge of continuing education could be cultivated. Such a miniboard could serve as a liaison and support group to the larger group.

Administrators at the top institutional level may not look kindly upon communication outside the official chain of command. It is naive to assume, however, that such contacts will not take place, or that only official communications play a role in shaping people's judgment. Tickets to lectures and concerts, intimate dinner parties, and spouses who play in the same bridge club may shape destinies in ways undreamt of by some writers of white papers and budget narratives. Needless to say, there are ethical and sometimes legal limits on the ways that can be employed.

Since direct efforts to communicate with a governing board may alienate the top administration, whose support is equally important, indirect channels should not be overlooked. Sometimes a person who does not warrant a box in the organizational chart—the secretary to the president or a budget analyst in the vice president's office, for instance—may exercise considerable power, as sociologist David Mechanic has pointed out in his classic paper, "The Sources of Power of Lower Participants in Complex Organizations." A cocktail at a nearby bar, a small box of Valentine candy as thanks for past favors, a pleasant chat in the corridor, or an invitation to sit in on a program may result in a significant form of communication via unofficial channels.

On a more formal basis, effective communication with top administrators must steer a fine line between informational overkill and some minimal level. Written communications have limited value at best and an excess of written communications to a busy administrator may result in functional blindness. Likewise, communication at scheduled staff conferences can serve only limited purposes. In the communication of critical concerns, contact with one or two administrators at a time is more effective. Although such contacts need to be made with reasonable frequency, they are more effective if made on a somewhat random basis as issues are identified rather than on a regularly scheduled basis.

A common error is to view such sessions as occasions to make a hard sell. This approach may be effective for encyclopedias and hearing aids, but a more effective approach for the selling of services is to seek the guidance of the top-level administrator or to engage in a genuine exchange of views. To be perceived as one whose appearance guarantees a sales pitch is to subvert any chance of communication. The best form of support is one that grows out of a joint effort to achieve shared goals.

As in the case of board members, selective invitations to welcome groups or to address sessions may provide the administrator from the parent organization with both information and visibility. If it be at the opening dinner or the graduation banquet, seating the right person by the administrator may result in further useful exchanges of information and viewpoints.

Internal relations, then, must be especially cultivated through a combination of informational activities and direct interaction. A systematic effort needs to be made to get involvement through person-to-person contacts, joint program development efforts, and use of residence instruction and research staffs in appropriate programming.

Increased recognition of the continuing education function requires positive objectives such as an internal emphasis on increased scholarly activities in the public service arm—research support, for example—and an increased sense of worth on the part of staff who themselves encourage negative attitudes by devaluing their function. In the competition for institutional resources, the status of the unit and of those associated with it have a great deal to do with who gets how much. Often, time and effort spent on these internal relations will have a greater payoff than the same amount of time spent outside the organization. A $50,000 grant may be spent in a year or two, but one new position in the base budget may last for years.

Other Institutions

Relations with other institutions have become much more important in recent years. In part the result of the greater availability of mass media and rapid transportation, territorial boundaries have become harder to define or defend. Pressures at federal and state levels to create or to strengthen coordinating councils or 1202 commissions have also brought interinstitutional relations to the forefront. In addition more and more institutions are increasing the level of public service activity. This includes many organizations other than institutions of higher education, but these are the units among which competition is most direct and pressures for coordination greatest.

While these instances involve program as well as public relations, they serve to point up the fact that interinstitutional relations, having become a significant concern in the external relations of most institutions, require planning and skill in cooperation and negotiation. They are part of the public relations responsibility of administrators rather than of the public relations specialists. More than anything else, they require institutions not only to cooperate but to present a common front to the public. Once the public press or politicians have started talking about wasteful duplication of effort, institutions are put on the defensive. Joint programming, coordination of program activities, and a united front to the public can forestall external intervention if potentially competitive institutions will recognize that their common interest exceeds any advantage to be gained by competition and confrontation.

Organized Influence Groups

While public relations efforts directed toward the general public have some value, professional public relations staff tend to concentrate too much on them. The general public may be important in winning elections but they are not likely to be a source of aid and comfort in the competition for scarce resources. Specific interest groups are more likely to expend time and effort in support of a continuing education unit's goals. Many such groups also have both the experience and the resources to lobby in behalf of programs they value. A unit, for example, that is working closely with organized labor or with the federation of cooperatives can usually receive active and competent support from one of these constituencies when the welfare of their program is at stake. Depending on the program mix of the unit, some potentially important constituencies are discussed below.

REGULATORY AND LICENSING BOARDS With the increase in emphasis on continuing education in the professions, these groups can be valuable aids in identifying program needs, promoting programs, and providing recognition for programs that may play a role in certification or recertification. For example, cooperation with the licensing board for real estate brokers resulted, in one state, in a profitable correspondence study course designed to prepare would-be brokers to take the licensing examination.

PROFESSIONAL AND TRADE ASSOCIATIONS Many business and professional groups may play a role similar to regulatory and licensing agencies; in some professions, such as law, the professional association may also play a central role in regulation and licensing. One example of the benefit of ties with an association is the following: a state hospital association, which makes regular mailings to member hospitals, is willing to include appropriate items in its newsletter and in its regular mailings. For a nominal charge they also provide address labels covering their membership.

SPECIAL INTEREST GROUPS   Many voluntary organizations that serve a particular cluster of interests—farm organizations, chambers of commerce, industrial development groups, or associations of cooperatives, for example—may have convergent interests. Such groups may regard it as a desirable member service to carry news items or editorial material supportive of other organizations that serve their members. They also will actively support legislation that is in their members' interests, including money for a conference center or operating funds to serve their programmatic needs.

ALUMNI   Regular participants in programs constitute an audience that may be cultivated by a newsletter or other informational mailings. Such an audience may constitute a key group when support is needed.

FOUNDATIONS   Foundations are in the business of supporting programs related to their missions; they are also more specifically in the business, under legal mandates, of giving away money. While competition for their resources is considerable, the fact remains that the resources are available. Listings such as *The Foundation Directory* or the *Annual Register of Grant Support* will identify foundations that may be helpful. Smaller foundations are valuable sources of support. Unlike the giants with assets in the millions, these smaller foundations may deal in grants of hundreds or thousands. Regular contact, however, may lead to significant help. In some cases, too, their advice alone may be of value and their advice, well-taken, may also lead to future, more tangible help. The Foundation Center in New York City is a major depository of information about foundations and is open to the public. They have also established a regional center that is housed in the Marquette University's Memorial Library in Milwaukee. These collections provide more recent and detailed information than the published directories.

Since the business of educational and charitable foundations is to give away money for deserving causes, they tend to be accessible to aspiring donees. The submission of unsolicited proposals is, however, generally the least effective means of gaining entry. It is important to identify the interests of the foundation, since many are limited by their charter as to geographic area, type of project, or other restrictions. Others specialize as a matter of policy, and specialties may change from time to time.

A call on the executive director may be effective either with or without a project in mind. Still more effective, especially in small foundations, may be a contact mediated by one of the foundation directors. Names of the directors are usually readily obtainable; in the smaller local foundations a channel to one of them can often be found within one's own organization.

Informational literature about one's organization may be sent periodically to the foundation having related interests. Invitations to appropriate functions may help to kindle the interest of the management or directors of the foundation. The pinnacle is reached when the foundation solicits you to make a proposal or to take on a project.

ASSOCIATIONS   Most continuing education units or their parent organizations will have membership in one or more national associations that will assist in a variety of public relations activities, especially those that relate to the federal government. Among these are the American Association of State Colleges and Universities, the American Association of Community and Junior Colleges, the National University Continuing Education Association, and the National Association of State Universities and Land Grant Colleges. All of these maintain offices in Washington, D.C., and have staff with expertise in public relations, particularly in influencing the outcome of pending legislation.

Maintaining relationships with key organizations on the local, state, and national scenes must, of course, be done selectively. In a small operation, three or four key contacts may be all that the unit can afford. In a large organization, the number of key contacts may be considerable. In one large operation, a "partial listing" of organizations and associations with which the unit has "continuing relationships" includes fifty-five interest groups such as the League of Women Voters, fifty-three trade and professional associations, twenty-four state agencies, seventeen federal agencies, and six institutional associations for a total of 155 associations and agencies.

Government Agencies

Following some years of rapid growth in public sector employment and a concomitant increase in the scope of government, government relations have come to occupy one of the most essential roles in most continuing education and extension units, especially those that are themselves public. These relations include lobbying for favorable legislation, seeking grants and contracts, and educational services to individuals and agencies.

As noted in the preceding section, lobbying is generally accomplished at the federal level through national associations. Special staff in the central institutional administration tend to perform this function at state and local government levels. However, considerable benefit can come from maintaining direct contact with appropriate agencies at all levels of government. The benefit may be in public employee participation in continuing education, in fund raising, in influencing the development and application of laws and administrative rules, and in having access to sources of information.

Many organizations fail to realize the ease with which direct contact can be established with appropriate agency personnel or the amount of help that can be obtained from elected representatives in establishing contacts. These contacts become especially effective if one can establish a mutually supportive relationship. For example, individual legislators at all levels are often in need of information that can be obtained from a higher educational institution. In some of the larger institutions, liaison with specific state or federal agencies can be delegated to the most appropriate staff members, who are then responsible for the flow of information to and from such agencies. As in the case of all interrelationships, the ideal situation is one where these relationships can be developed on an informal, first-name basis.

Such relationships develop quite naturally where there is a statutory or other formal basis as exists between the Federal Extension Service and the state Cooperative Extension Services or between the latter and county governments. Highly developed patterns of cooperation exist in these instances. The potential for similar development has been too often neglected by other units. Several days spent visiting informally with agency personnel in Washington, D.C., or in the state capital can be informative at the least and highly productive at best. Congressional or state representatives' offices can be helpful, too, in setting up initial contacts. Most members of Congress have offices in their home district as well as in the capitol. Since these public agencies exist to serve the public, they are in most cases more accessible and cordial than the uninitiated might imagine.

With respect to state or local government, where these are important sources of funding, one effective way of building support is by providing services to government on a regular basis. The county agent in the Cooperative Extension Service commonly does this for county government. The Urban Observatory, a federally-sponsored project for city-university cooperation, was a somewhat similar concept for municipal government. Some federal funds have been available through the National Science Foundation to provide limited services to state governments. The idea deserves more extensive development. A capitol county agent who can provide continuing contact with state government, arranging credit and continuing education courses and providing access to research and information sources within a university, can build a reservoir of good will that is at least as valuable as the patently institution-serving efforts of a lobbyist or legislative liaison person. In fact, the two can complement each other.

Two cautions need to be considered. First, such a service is not likely to succeed as a purely passive service. An office, a name, and a telephone number are not enough. Such a person must seek out the potential users of information—legislators and their staffs, and government officials—to identify needs and to follow up requests on a continuing basis. Second, the service function is best kept separate, up to a point, from lobbying activities. Services provided must not be based on an obviously expected return. Nevertheless, while such a service should stand on its merits as a programmatic activity, it can also serve a significant public relations function. Any good program will do so in some degree, but some such as this have more public relations potential than others.

Since they hold memberships in a number of national organizations, there is a tendency for most educational institutions to feel that governmental relationships will be taken care of by these national offices. This belief is dangerous. To a great degree, there has been a shift of power to the states, a shift that began with revenue sharing in the Nixon administration and that has been accelerated by the increasing voice of independent voters as the pivotal group, by the one man—one vote ruling of the Supreme Court, and by the establishment of a variety of locally based boards, regional offices, and commissions that control the flow of federal funds. Furthermore, in the last two decades the number of important state and local agencies has expanded geometrically. The number of bills introduced into state legislatures has doubled or tripled. At the same time, state legislative turnover has increased. Biennial turnovers of

25 percent to 40 percent are not uncommon, and the newcomers include greater numbers of youths, women, and inner-city representatives. There is more need for person-to-person contacts, more bills to be monitored, more hearings to attend.

All of this may seem remote from running programs for personal and community uplift—until one gets out of the swimming hole only to discover that someone has walked off with one's clothes. For example, a $25,000 continuing education item was inadvertently left out of a budget bill in one state. The university administration, with a great many important issues on its agenda, was unwilling to expend ammunition on this small restoration. A telephone call from one continuing education staff member to a friendly legislator was all it took to have the item restored in committee—mission accomplished quietly behind the scenes. On a larger scale, the legislative hearing can be important. A staff member may simply appear in the capacity of an interested citizen, or several of the staff may sit in the audience having registered as opposing or supporting a given bill. Sometimes an appearance or two may tip the scales or at least prevent an end run by opposing forces. For example, a legislative hearing was held in one state to consider whether a university's educational broadcasting license should be transferred to another state agency. The university made arrangements for representatives of several influential groups to appear in support of the university's position and the license was retained. Failure to muster support at this hearing would in all probability have resulted in transfer of the license.

Timing in such appearances is important, as are personal contacts. There is a point in prolonged legislative hearings when the committee's eyes glaze over and temporary absences become epidemic. A word to a friendly committee chairperson can improve the timing of a crucial appearance. Furthermore, if press coverage is important, a seemingly off-the-cuff statement buttressed with a press handout can combine to carry conviction in the oral presentation and in coverage from the press.

Since most legislators at the local, state, and national levels are strongly influenced by the views reflected in their mail, mail campaigns in which sympathetic constituents bombard their legislative representatives in a spontaneous outpouring of support can influence political outcomes. The word *spontaneous* in this context implies that stereotyped responses are less effective than those that appear to be individual expressions of opinion. The principal danger lies in obvious manipulation and overkill. More than one administrator has had to seek new employment as a result of heavy-handed politicking. The best way to strike just the right note is to follow the advice of a friendly, pragmatic, and seasoned politician.

Much more could be said about state government relationships. Many of the same things can be applied to county and municipal governments. If one has access to experts, to lobbyists for friendly organizations, or to qualified members of one's central administration, the job is simpler for the administrator. Often, however, the experts are overworked or otherwise occupied. This is no reason to leave important issues to chance. The important points to remember are that power has shifted to state and local government, that the composition of government is changing, and that comparatively small numbers of organized and knowledgeable people can make a difference.

The General Public

In the larger theater of community relations, there are two broad constituencies: the one that might be called the general public, and the organized groups who have or who potentially might have some direct interaction with the public service arm of the institution. There is no sharp line between these two in institutions with an interest in a full spectrum of public service activities. Almost anyone might be viewed as a potential student or as a constituent. Nevertheless there are differences in approach to the general public and to the special publics.

The general public is not likely to rise up in support of an endangered institution. However, a general awareness of the institution and some appreciation of the value of its services can have utility in creating a favorable operating climate. The right kind of press releases, feature stories, public service announcements, and community involvement may have considerable indirect effect. There remains the question of priorities, however. To what extent should resources be spent on general public relations and to what extent should effort be concentrated on specific constituencies? There is no simple answer, for it is not in fact a simple question. Image-building activities directed toward the general public may have more lasting value than the self-serving releases designed to promote a specific program. On the other hand, in times of crisis, organized groups are the best means to rally support. The general public itself is an elusive target but institutionally sponsored support groups that purport to represent the general public can be quite effective.

Most broad range extension units rely in some degree on such special groups to assist in program planning and promotion and also to provide support for institutional objectives. The Cooperative Extension Service in particular has long worked with citizen groups at local, state, and national levels. The most effective of these groups have some clearly recognized common interest such as youth work, homemaking, recreation, or the dairy industry. Public broadcasting stations have also done a generally effective job of mobilizing support groups drawn from the general public as have community colleges.

In recent years there has been a growing interest in the use of broader based groups for overall advice and support. The extension councils in the state of Missouri are an example of such groups. Missouri's extension councils, established by legislative enactment in each county of the state, are composed of a combination of elected and appointed members. Qualified voters may elect members in much the same manner as any other public officials are elected. There is thus a considerable potential for generating public interest in and awareness of the extension function among citizens in general. In addition, members are appointed by designated groups that have a special interest in various aspects of extension. Council members serve without pay although they may receive reimbursement for some expenses.

The councils have both advisory and administrative responsibilities, which are spelled out by the statutes. In a broader sense, the councils provide a bridge between the general and special publics of extension and the professional and administrative staff. The threat of an insulated bureaucracy serving itself or a small number of

271

special clientele groups is reduced by the electoral process and by the broad base of representation.

Clientele and Suppliers

Clientele have been dealt with in some detail in Chapter 5. Suppliers, on the other hand, tend to be taken for granted because, under most circumstances, the burden of relating falls largely upon them. During periods of scarcity, as during wartime, the tables may be turned and suppliers may be the wooed rather than the wooers. Even in times of plenty, however, the good will of suppliers can make a difference in expediting services, assisting with special orders, or in cutting red tape. They should not be taken for granted.

PUBLIC RELATIONS STRATEGY

General public relations strategy consists of identifying the key segments of the public that are important to the attainment of one's objectives, setting priorities, and developing the major strategic concepts. Execution of the general plan then becomes a matter of specific tactics. From the viewpoint of tactics, the development of an effective public relations plan requires four things:

1. knowing the constituencies,
2. planning communications,
3. getting the message across,
4. coordinating and controlling.

Knowing the Constituencies

These simple steps imply a great amount of effort in planning and implementation. Julius Caesar, a consummate strategist, started his account of the Gallic Wars with a description of Gaul. In the same manner, one who intends to have an effective public relations program must know the territory that is to be occupied. Basically, this involves identifying those constituencies that are the most important, ranking them in order of relative importance, and knowing what matters to them. If, for example, organized labor is a significant power in the state legislature and if organized labor is primarily interested in issues regarding wages and fringe benefits, then a public relations effort based on services affecting the economic betterment of the worker should be directed toward organized labor.

Planning Communications

In terms of what one communicates and how, clearly one communicates about those things that have motivational value for the target constituency, and one utilizes the channels that will most effectively reach that constituency. To take an extreme example, one does not use a print medium to reach people who do little reading, just as one does not try to reach low-income workers in a magazine read almost entirely by upper middle-class homemakers. Studies have shown, for example, that small-business people do not, as a general rule, learn new skills by reading books and magazine articles. Also, in general, they do not travel considerable distances in order to learn new techniques. Therefore, if the intent is to reach this group, oral or audiovisual presentations in geographically dispersed locations will be more effective than the use of written materials or presentations at central locations.

Getting the Message Across

Once the content and audience have been identified, the process of implementation requires that the right people be chosen to do the job. One does not send a representative of the American Bankers Association to gain the support of the local Credit Union League. Beyond finding the right people for any given job, in any complex effort it is essential that a division of labor is made so that each of the component operations in a campaign is identified, and responsibility for accomplishment of each component clearly assigned. In a campaign to influence the outcome of a particular piece of legislation relating to the status of women, for example, one person may have responsibility for reaching housewives, another for working mothers, another for professional women, and another for the elderly.

Once responsibility has been assigned, a major job of the administrator is to delegate the necessary authority. This goes beyond merely delegating the power to decide. It also includes providing the necessary means to carry out the assignment. If money is needed, or supporting staff, or access to information, no one can be held responsible unless given the authority to command these resources. Provision of these means is an essential obligation of the administrator if responsible performance is expected.

Coordinating and Controlling

In any large-scale effort, the activities of those responsible for the various component operations must be coordinated centrally. Such coordination is necessary when, for instance, the timing of an effort to head off a budget cut in the legislature must be coordinated with the efforts to reach the legislators at home during recess and at the capital during the session. Further, activities in the capital and on the home front must be synchronized. Clipping services, newsletters, attitude surveys, periodic activity reports, and informal contacts can help achieve the needed followup. "Fan mail" and records of such things as attendance, complaints received, and telephone calls may be used as before-and-after measures. For example, complaints about mailing lists are a common irritant and one that relates to the organization's public image. The effectiveness of a plan for reducing duplicate and inappropriate mailing can be measured by reduction in complaints and returns, but only if good records have been maintained.

In the political realm, coordination and control may mean knowing when hearings are scheduled, what the timing on a letter-writing campaign should be, who needs to be alerted and briefed to testify, and who should contact whom and when. In dealing with influence groups, contact persons need to be identified, timing of contacts determined, and contact persons provided with whatever ammunition they need. It is important to know what information any opposition may have, who will be acting in their behalf, and what their tactics are likely to be.

Finally, the ongoing effort must be constantly monitored so that adjustments can be made as the situation changes. If a printers' strike prevents the timely mailing of an information piece, then a shift to a broadcast medium may have to be made. If an informational meeting designed to influence an outcome is poorly attended, a supplemental effort utilizing a different approach may have to be tried.

The public relations job of the administrator might be likened to the job of field commander in time of war. The objective may be people's minds instead of enemy territory and troops, but the same rules of strategy apply: concentration of effort, economy of force, mobility, control, intelligence, and surprise.

CHANNELS OF COMMUNICATION

While most of the channels for public relations communications are familiar to the administrator, a few comments may provide some useful highlights. The following outline is an ordering of some of the major channels. In the sections that follow we will review some of these channels, considering advantages and disadvantages of each.

    A. Personal Communications
        1. Visits to constituents and influential people
        2. Telephone contacts—e.g., news tips to the reporter whose beat includes your operation
        3. Planned and unplanned contacts at social gatherings and special events—e.g., the cocktail party to meet the visiting speaker
        4. Face-to-face contacts with reporters, free-lance writers, radio and television news broadcasters
        5. Membership in civic and professional groups
    B. Mass media
        1. The press, dailies and weeklies—news releases, feature stories, news making events
        2. Radio and television—talk shows, public service announcements, newscasts
        3. Trade journals and other periodicals, including a variety of free distribution news and advertising tabloids and magazines
        4. Films and other audiovisual media
    C. In-house publications: direct mail
        1. Informational booklets and brochures

2. Newsletters
3. Special mailings
D. Other channels
   1. Bulletin boards
   2. Displays and exhibits
   3. Booths at public events such as the state fair
   4. Speakers' bureaus

Personal Communications

Even in this day of mass media and growing populations, personal contacts made with key people remain most influential in deciding many issues. A few examples illustrate the opportunities.

In the broadest sense, public relations is politics, and the classic depiction of political decisions made in smoke-filled rooms is not too wide of the mark. While smoke may no longer be an appropriate accompaniment, the chance encounter at a social gathering still may be a priceless means of establishing beneficial relationships with decision-makers and publicists. On a more official basis, the well-chosen office call or regular visit may produce results of a value far beyond the amount of time involved. In a larger organization, these seemingly casual contacts may quite properly be the result of a plan in which selected staff members are paired with these significant others so that person-to-person relations are not left to chance.

Contacts with reporters are also a case in point. A reporter's success is to a degree a function of the amount of copy or air time he or she gets before the public. If one is a newsmaker, one thus becomes a source for the reporter, of stories, tips, quotes, or background. There is a need for caution with respect to off-the-record background interviews. The reporter can feel put upon if too much is off-the-record. The interviewee can be placed in an embarrassing spot if reporters tell stories out of school. But a trusting relationship on both sides can lead to a relaxed give-and-take that may pay off in substantial benefits when one needs a public forum.

Opportunities for personal communications can present themselves by chance or by design. Contacts can be made anywhere from the Governor's Task Force on Aging to the Beaux Arts Ball. Although this may seem unduly calculating, it is a fact of life. However, it will only succeed if there is a genuine rapport and mutuality of interest. It is not a matter of exploitation but rather of genuine reciprocity. In the terminology of transactional analysis, the relationship must be adult to adult.

Administrators, however, need to view the outside contact element of their job with three reservations:

1. What is the opportunity cost of extensive outside public relations? Is it worthwhile to spend several hours a week in public gatherings when more time might be spent on internal administrative problems? There are administrators whose public image is spectacular but whose internal organization is a shambles.

2.   How does this role fit the administrator's own style? An administrator who has a penchant for external relations may do well to seek a strong insider for the number two position. An administrator who is most comfortable working within the organization may seek an externally oriented aide. One who enjoys both may want to fill the number two position with a similarly versatile person. Then a carefully planned division of labor will be needed to give each the balance they prefer.

3.   Administrators are likely to function best, as are all other people, if they lead balanced lives. If the day is filled with work and the evening and weekends are filled with work-related social functions, family, health, and perspective may suffer in the long-run. It is better to decide upon a desirable mix than to opt for any one as being preferable to the others.

Mass Media

Personal communications usually pay off in terms of specific issues. Mass communications, on the other hand, are more likely to be directed toward creating a generally favorable attitude. Such communications are most effective when they communicate facts and at the same time arouse feelings. The community is more likely to go to the barricades to preserve football than they are to protect academic freedom, partly because they care about football and also because academic freedom is an abstraction; most people find it easier to identify with football players than with scholars. People care about what happens to the football team, they know the names of the players, they know last week's score, and who the player of the week was. They rejoice or suffer with the team because it is not "they" who are out there on the field, but "we."

The academic functions of an institution can hardly hope to arouse this kind of feeling although they may get some of the reflected benefit. The purpose of mass communications is to create some modest approximation of the feelings and knowledgeable interest that are typically created by a successful program of intercollegiate athletics. This modest approximation comes as a result of communicating to the public answers to four questions about the institution.

1.   Who are we?
2.   What are we trying to do?
3.   Why should you care?
4.   How can you help?

There are four major channels that reach the general public or a significant segment thereof. We will briefly highlight some opportunities in each.

NEWSPAPERS   Among professional public relations staff, press releases are a popular means of reaching the public. Among the more effective are the well-placed feature story, usually to a single outlet, and the local-name-in-the-news type that may be carried most often by small dailies or weeklies. Many extension operations also make effective use of regular newspaper columns written by staff specialists. These serve the dual purpose of providing useful information to comparatively large numbers of readers and of giving broader public visibility to the unit. This type of outlet deserves broader use.

Good feature stories combine informational and emotional content. One of the time-honored rules of readable writing and of effective speaking is "tell a story." At the right time and place, statistics can be persuasive. At best they should be used sparingly. But from the days of the cave man, people have been interested in stories. More people can remember the parable of the good Samaritan than can recall the beatitudes. And if the story leads into a program announcement, both public relations and promotional goals may be achieved.

If broad geographical coverage is desired, one of the better points of entry to the printed page is the local stringers who cover the area for out-of-town papers. Since they are paid often on a piece rate basis, they are eager for leads that will produce a story their paper will carry. Some organizations have achieved national coverage of an activity because the stringer for a national magazine has had a story printed, which in turn, usually brings the local press in. A newsmaking event can also generate coverage not only for the event but also for activities related to the event. An open house, a centennial celebration, or a high school debate contest may provide the ideal occasion to announce a new program or to hold a press conference.

RADIO AND TELEVISION   Three kinds of station activities provide avenues into radio and television: talk shows, public service announcements, and newscasts. Most locally produced talk shows in medium-sized communities work hard to come up with enough interesting material to fill their time slot. A letter, a telephone call, or a visit to the show's producer can open the door for significant coverage if the material is newsworthy. Public service announcements serve a more limited purpose but, since stations have a legal obligation to provide public service time, the right kind of spot announcements will find a ready outlet. News stories are more difficult to get on the air simply because so many of the routine activities of any operation are not especially newsworthy; but selected projects, people, or events will receive coverage if the information is channeled to the right people.

In a large organization much of the groundwork has been done or can be done by the public relations specialist. In smaller organizations it may be a matter of the administrator's spending a little personal time getting to know the right people and giving them some of the right kind of material to work with.

TRADE JOURNALS, OTHER PERIODICALS, AND BOOKS   The outlets for special interest news and features are numerous and varied. The *Readers' Guide to Periodical Literature,* the *Ulrich's International Periodicals Directory, The Standard Periodical Directory,* and the *Ayer Directory of Publications* are just a few of the sources that regularly cover—often through convenient subject, geographic, or audience listings—the many periodicals carrying such material. In addition the number of limited circulation periodicals must swell this number to almost astronomical proportions. If the story is of particular interest to people in accounting, bookkeeping, computer science, and so on to the end of the alphabet, there are one or more periodicals serving the group in question and carrying news items and features of interest to the group. In most communities today there are also widely distributed periodicals going to every home in a given area at no charge to the recipients. They are supported by advertising revenues but depend for readership on the fact that they carry enough news and feature material to induce the addressee to open and read. Many are well-produced and well-edited and, because they are run on tight budgets, are hungry for good material.

FILMS AND OTHER AUDIOVISUALS   Although films, slide-tape presentations, and cassettes have limited utility as public relations vehicles, opportunities exist in surprising numbers. One of the better attended events at a fair was a tent with continuous showings of films. The weary fairgoer would collapse in one of the available seats and watch a fifteen- or twenty-minute film, if only to escape the crowds for a few minutes. Obviously only a large organization can have film or cassette production capabilities serving its public relations needs, but even a fairly modest operation can accomplish somewhat the same thing through slide-tape presentations. The projection equipment can be leased or purchased for a nominal amount, and a fifteen- to thirty-minute show can be repeated automatically twenty or more times a day in an airport, a shopping mall, a foyer, or a fairgrounds, reaching several hundred people each day.

In-House Publications

Personal correspondence, form letters, and direct mail promotion can be used effectively for public relations as well as for promoting participation in specific programs. When sent by first class mail, form letters typed to appear as personal may also compete effectively for attention. For example, a ''personal'' invitation to several hundred people to attend a special event will usually get a better response than a fourth class circular. Truly personal correspondence is a considerably more expensive way to go. However, such an approach may be the only route in carefully selected instances, as when dealing with small numbers—a congressional delegation for example.

Pamphlets, newsletters, and brochures can be effective both in-house and in reaching external publics. Regular mailings of newsletters, for instance, may accomplish this function, as long as cost-benefit is carefully monitored. Costs in terms of staff time, printing, and mailing need to be weighed against expected outcomes. Unless used selectively, such mailings may contribute more to the paper glut than to anything else. Some device for measuring reader response—a return coupon, a request for reader comments, or a readership poll—may give some indication of effect. Direct benefits are often difficult to measure. A striking example is that of deferred giving, in which regular communication with a selected clientele, may, years later, pay a substantial dividend in the form of a single bequest.

Other Channels

A variety of other channels may be used alone or in combination. As noted previously, animated exhibits such as slide-tape presentations are effective in the right settings. A few other examples follow in this section.

Information booths at strategic locations can provide direct contact with the public. Several continuing education organizations have staffed booths at fairs and shows where program information, brochures, and on-the-spot advising can be dispensed. Their effectiveness has been equivocal. Apart from brochures picked up by passersby, the number of contacts with those staffing the booths has been small and the cost in terms of staff time has been high. Such booths are frequently not in the choicest locations, and continuing education is not on the minds of the majority of attendees at fairs and shows. If the location is right, and the booth is effective in getting attention, the effort may be worthwhile, especially if the emphasis on continuing education is relevant for enough of the attendees—agriculture at a country fair or fitness and recreation at a sports show, for example.

Displays and exhibits—animated or not—may be useful for public relations purposes and for program promotion if, again, the location is right and the display well-done. Racks with the sign "take one," placed near a display or alone may reach a number of people, especially in airports, train stations, meeting places, hospitals, or anywhere that people spend a lot of time waiting. Conventions are fertile grounds because they are gatherings of homogeneous interest groups and because there is usually a good deal of floating about between sessions (as well as during sessions). Usually display spaces are provided and are well-patronized.

In many groups, the speakers' bureau may be another way of reaching selected publics for public relations purposes. The beleaguered program chairperson is constantly under pressure to produce another speaker at the weekly or monthly meeting. A speaker stockpile maintained by an organization may provide fodder for the knife-and-fork circuit and an outlet to the public. The effectiveness of this approach depends on the availability of quality speaking talent. A bad speaker is no advertisement for any organization. It also depends on whether the groups reached are worth reaching. Merely to supply filler for the ritual thirty minutes after the dessert is of no value to anyone. The questions that need to be answered are: "Can we reach significant constituencies by this means?" and "Can we accomplish something in this manner that cannot be better accomplished in some other way?"

Choosing the Channels

The wide range of agencies and channels that may benefit from cultivation is almost overwhelming. Consider the plight of a hypothetical director of continuing education in a small community college. She reports to the president of the college. She shares a secretary with the student adviser and her jobs include identifying the needed courses, lining up instructors, scheduling, doing the promotion, and advising potential students. She is responsible for producing an income of $150,000 a year. Not much time is left for public relations. In fact she has to jealously guard a portion of her time for family, home, and recreation in order not to get swallowed up by the job.

What is reasonable in such a situation? First, what are her public relations goals, modest as they must necessarily be? On the internal side, they are primarily to maintain good working relations with other college staff, and most of this is accomplished as part of her daily dealings with these people. As to board relations, in a small operation such as this, selected mailings, a few telephone calls, and a relatively small number of personal contacts may be enough to maintain board awareness and good will. On the external side, the primary purpose is to promote a degree of community awareness and good will. Membership in some representative civic group can be helpful but so many "representative" civic groups tend to segregate by sex and income level that this may not be worthwhile. The representative cross section may not be there. A few specific objectives may be preferable: for example, to get three or four feature stories in the local papers each year telling about interesting and successful programs, a couple of appearances on radio and television to talk about the overall program, a dinner meeting or reception for an outstanding speaker or two and possibly some news stories (prefer-ably pictures) about participants ("A new business started as a result of the course in . . ." or "Dietitians meet their continuing education requirements by attending courses at C.C.").

This may sound like a great deal of work to add to an already demanding job. In fact, the total time demand beyond what portion is directly tied to programming will amount perhaps to no more than an hour or two a week. In the long-run this may be of sufficient value to the overall program to actually save time that might otherwise be spent in extra program promotion.

The choice of channels and the amount of time and effort devoted to public relations will necessarily vary from one organization to another and from time to time. For example, radio will reach a different type of audience in a different way in a city of commuters than it will in a small city, and the amount and kind of effort will differ with the source of financial support, the political climate, and the state of the economy. Outside consultants and specialized staff may help with the fine tuning but the final decisions belong in the hands of the administration.

In this chapter we have dealt with public relations from the perspective of the unit administrator, rather than from the perspective of the public relations specialist. More so than program promotion and marketing, it is a job that cannot be delegated. Its general goal is to create a favorable environment for the organization. To accomplish this goal the organization must know who its significant publics are and plan communi-cations to reach each of them. The significant publics include the publics within the organization itself—its staff and key people in the parent organization—as well as the external publics—other organizations with similar missions, government, trade and professional associations, civic and community groups, and the general public, as well as clientele and suppliers. The general strategies for reaching these groups are essen-tially problems in communications—knowing what will be of interest to one's con-stituencies, planning the communications, getting them to the intended audience, and adapting the process to changing needs and circumstances. Good programs and willing participants are not enough to insure a healthy operation. One must constantly seek to insure a favorable environment in which to operate.

BIBLIOGRAPHY

Burke, John D. *Advertising in the Market Place*. New York: McGraw-Hill, 1973.

Cutlip, Scott M., and Allen H. Center. *Effective Public Relations*. 5th ed. Englewood Cliffs, N.J.: Prentice-Hall, 1978.

Hill and Knowlton Executives. *Critical Issues in Public Relations*. Englewood Cliffs, N.J.: Prentice-Hall, 1975.

Mechanic, David. "The Sources of Power of Lower Participants in Complex Organizations." *Administrative Science Quarterly* 7 (1962): 349–64.

Roschwalb, Jerold. "Continuing Education and the Reluctant Magicians." *Continuum* 41 (1976): 4–7.

Stephenson, Howard. *Handbook of Public Relations*. 2d ed. New York: McGraw-Hill, 1971.

CHAPTER THIRTEEN

FORECASTING AND FUTURISM

Prediction Techniques
Quantitative Methods
Qualitative Methods

WHAT DOES THE FUTURE HOLD?

Energy and Resources
Computerization and Automation
Communications and Service Industries
Lifestyle and Family Changes
The Environment

CONFRONTING THE FUTURE

Preparation
Dealing with the Future

PROGRAM EMPHASES IN THE FUTURE

THE FUTURE:
PROSPECTS
AND PROMISES

The god Apollo, having fallen in love with Cassandra, gave her the irrevocable gift of prophecy. When she proved unfaithful, he nullified his gift by decreeing that her prophecies would not be believed. Ezekiel had the same problem, complaining of people who have ears that hear not and eyes that see not. In fairness to Cassandra's and Ezekiel's detractors, it is extremely difficult for the average person to distinguish between the real prophets and the false. The credibility of prophets is generally dependent on retrospective certification. Recent reviews of the prophecies of the Oracle of Delphi give rather strong evidence that the extraordinary accuracy of the Oracle's predictions was a figment of the imagination of people writing *after* the events in question had occurred. How then does one achieve that essential administrative skill that the nineteenth century French industrialist Henri Fayol called *prevoyance?*

Two classes of future events can be disregarded with reasonable safety: those with an extremely high probability, such as sunrise and sunset, and those with an extremely low probability, such as a meteor hitting the conference center at high noon on February 28, 1988. In between these extremes, a large range of events with varying probabilities of occurrence can have significant effects on our future achievements. How can an administrator build prevoyance into that broad range between the virtually certain and the highly improbable?

We will leave the gift of prophecy to others. This chapter asks the more mundane question of how an administrator can increase his or her effectiveness in coping with the future. We will consider some of the practical problems of predicting future events and review some of the techniques employed. This will lead to an overview of some of the important areas of concern for the future, followed by suggestions as to how to respond. Some speculation as to new frontiers for continuing education and extension will also be ventured.

FORECASTING AND FUTURISM

The twin terms *forecasting* and *futurism* tend to diverge in general usage along a time dimension. Forecasters deal more often with events in the near future, and futurists deal with more remote events. Forecasting college enrollments in 1990 starts with known census data and therefore operates within certain known limits. The futurist who predicts life expectancies in the twenty-first century builds on a far more speculative foundation. The difference, which is entirely a matter of degree, depends on two things: the size of the data base and the distance from the target. Thus forecasters are more concerned with facts and figures and futurists with creative imagination. But if the prediction of next year's food supply is subject to a wide margin for error, consider the problem of predicting the food supply in the year 2000.

The hazards of building on predictions, familiar as they are, need to be underscored. What happened to Thomas Malthus's 1798 prediction that the population would shortly outstrip the food supply, or to the Ford Motor Company's sales forecast for the Edsel, is now happening to Alvin Toffler's 1970 prediction for a rapid growth in invention: *Future Shock* seems to be offset by a widespread concern with the decline of national innovativeness in the 1980s. The moral of the story is clear: unless one wants to play a game of winner take all, all bets on the future need to be hedged. Today, as always, one's view of the future depends on which prophets one believes.

From an evolutionary perspective one might conclude that survival is a matter only of mutation and natural selection—that chance is the chief determiner of survival. In this view the only way to judge who has taken the right road is after the fact. There is cause for comfort, however, because we alone of all earth's creatures conceptualize the future.

As far as we can tell from the archeological record, scientific forecasting began several thousand years ago as a means of foretelling celestial events and climatic changes. Then, as now, there was confusion between divination and forecasting. As we describe some forecasting techniques in the following section, the reader will have to decide where the line is to be drawn.

Prediction Techniques

We have previously made a somewhat arbitrary distinction, based on the difference in the time horizon, between forecasting and futurism. This distinction relates generally to the dichotomy of quantitative and qualitative techniques. The prediction of comparatively short-term events is generally greatly aided by the use of mathematical techniques. Long-term predictions are generally less able to rely on mathematical manipulations. If, for example, one wanted to predict in December the day on which the first ship will dock in the Duluth-Superior harbor in the following spring, one of the better predictions would be the average date for the last forty years. On the other hand, if one wanted to predict the comparable date a century from now, a number of qualitative considerations would enter the picture: the future state of ice control technology in the Great Lakes, the future of marine transportation, and long-term climatic changes, for example.

Just as there is no sharp distinction between forecasting and futurism, there is also no sharp line that separates quantitative from qualitative methods. Any elaborate effort at predicting the future is likely to use both. The separation is more for convenience in exposition than because they constitute distinct approaches. Both are very much dependent on a data base consisting of facts or figures or both: the first step in any attempt to predict the future is to know what is happening in the present.

Given the now considerable body of literature on forecasting and futurism, only an overview can be given here. The reader who wishes to pursue any specific method in depth can start with the references at the end of this chapter. Many of the basic methods described hereafter can be used without specialized training. Others require the help of specialists.

Quantitative Methods

The basic quantitative method is simple extrapolation. It is also probably by far the most widely used. If registrations have been increasing at the rate of 10 percent annually for the last five years, the simplest prediction for the next year is that registration will be 10 percent greater than this year. More sophisticated forms of extrapolation take into consideration such things as seasonal fluctuations, cyclical changes, and random variations. Among these techniques are trend analysis, moving averages, time series, and exponential smoothing. As the names suggest these techniques require a fair degree of mathematical preparation. The information they generate is most valid for relatively short time periods. The administrator who is preparing next year's budget may find next year's economic forecast useful and may also find a five-year projection of correspondence course enrollments useful in deciding on the press run for a study guide. The reliability of such information declines rapidly over longer time horizons; thus, these techniques belong more in the area of short-term planning rather than in the realm of the future and long-range plans.

The basic assumption underlying these techniques is that the effects that have been in operation in the recent past will persist into the future. Other quantitative techniques overcome this weakness to a degree, by dealing with two or more variables at a time. Correlation analysis and a variety of operations research techniques can help to isolate variables or to simulate conditions under which interactions take place. The Monte Carlo technique, as its name implies, can simulate a variety of outcomes when differing conditions are postulated. Although such techniques have been used most extensively in solving production and inventory problems, it is conceivable that they might have value in improving the quality of decisions about capital expenditures, staffing, and other long-term commitments when such variables as participation rate by age, expenditure rates, constraints on travel, and other factors are put into the basic equation.

The results of these techniques, of course, are no better than the assumptions and the data one starts with. The main advantages over intuitive methods are that the inputs are made more rigorously explicit and that more variables can be handled simultaneously. Even when hard data are lacking the use of subjective probabilities can bring a greater degree of clarity and order to one's projections. As a simple example, consider the use of subjective probabilities in making a decision to expand or not to expand a residential conference facility. The time horizon from concept to operation may be five years. The facility is to be financed by income over a forty-year period. Factors affecting the outcome include the growth of competition, increases in participation by clientele, operating costs, the long-range effect of mediated instruction methods, and a host of other factors. The use of subjective probabilities might be applied to projections of occupancy rates or of net income and their impact on amortization. As noted in Chapter 3, the pooling of several subjective probability estimates will, more likely than purely intuitive methods, lead to better estimates, better identification of the variables that can affect the outcome, and a more systematic approach to the final decision.

On the horizon, other mathematical techniques are being developed. Although they may have little or no immediate utility for the working administrator, they are worth watching if one wants to cope most effectively with the uncertainties of the future. For example, although most of the methods in current use deal with incremental data, a relatively new field of study is catastrophe theory, which employs the methods of topological geometry. The promising feature of catastrophe theory is its potential for dealing with discontinuous events. In a world where a telephone call can start a nuclear war or a shift in the San Andreas fault may register 8.5 on the Richter scale, futurists must include major discontinuities in their thinking. Even if the immediate practical applications are nonexistent, such developments can be a stimulus to more rigorous thinking about the future.

Qualitative Methods

Qualitative methods of predicting future developments are generally used when longer time horizons are involved. The length of time spans that are "long" or "short" vary with the subject. A twenty-year projection may be considered a short span in forestry, where even nine-inch pulpwood requires twenty or more years to mature. On the other hand, in many types of electronics manufacture a five-year old model may be an antique. Thus, as has been noted before, no clear line separates short-range planning from the future. Perhaps one reason why long-range predictions rely so much on qualitative methods is that the resulting predictions are more general. Nothing so discredits prophets as naming exact dates and specific events that fail to materialize.

This is not to suggest that qualitative methods are undesirable or fraught with error. Beyond doubt systematic approaches to predicting the future have utility and validity far beyond idle speculation. With a growing interest in predicting the future a number of systematic approaches have been developed. We describe a representative few in the paragraphs that follow.

The widely used Delphi technique has been described in Chapter 3. The procedure remains the same when the technique is employed in long-range forecasting. The principal differences are in the nature of the task assigned and the type of people who would be selected to participate. As with other methods of long-range forecasting, only history can tell us how accurate the methods will prove to be. Studies have shown that high-growth industries are more likely to use qualitative methods of technological forecasting than are low-growth industries, but the cause and effect relationship is not clear. However, if we start with the premise that the generation of alternatives is a major requisite to sound decisions, then Delphi and other methods are a step in the right direction. Furthermore the use of these methods by major industries constitutes another sort of endorsement.

The Morphological Research Method developed by the Swiss astronomer Fritz Zwicky, has been adopted by the General Electric TEMPO Center and by the Stanford Research Institute. The method, while basically simple, can become quite complex in its application. It involves five steps:

1. definition of the problem

2. identification of the parameters of the problem

3. development of a solution matrix using all combinations of the parameters—the solution set

4. a general evaluation of the solutions and selection of a manageable number of the ''best'' solutions

5. a detailed evaluation of the remaining alternatives

The outline below gives a simplified example of the first and second steps and how the matrix follows from them.

1. Problem: To predict the state of continuing professional education in the year 2000
2. Parameters
    a. Growth in the number of professionals
        (1) Decline: increase in paraprofessionals and support occupations
        (2) Steady state
        (3) Continued growth in numbers
    b. Mandatory continuing education
        (1) Increase in covered occupations and total requirements
        (2) Increase in number of subspecialties
        (3) Leveling off of mandatory continuing education
        (4) Decline in mandatory continuing education
    c. Involvement of professional associations
        (1) Supportive: encouraging educational institutions to do the job
        (2) Competitive: sharing with educational institutions
        (3) Preemptive: taking over
3. Matrix: 36 possible outcomes ($3 \times 4 \times 3$)

PATTERN (Planning Assistance through Technical Evaluation and Relevance Numbers), which was developed by the Honeywell Corporation, is another example of an industrial application. It is a specific type of the general technique known as relevance trees, and relevance trees are in turn an application of decision trees. The technique is often used for normative forecasting, in which the intent is to delineate a desired future state of affairs (with the implication that the organization intends to bring it to fruition).

The process generally starts with a brief scenario describing the state of things at some future date. This serves to provide a frame of reference and a desired mindset. It is not detailed nor need there be complete agreement as to the specifics. A panel of experts then decides on an objective and identifies possible courses of action or consequences. By voting, the panel arrives at a collective judgment of the likelihood or desirability of each of these consequences, and outlines the possible courses or consequences at this state—and so on to the desired level of specificity. Figure 13.1 illustrates a four-stage model of such a development, tracing one branch of the tree to the fourth stage.

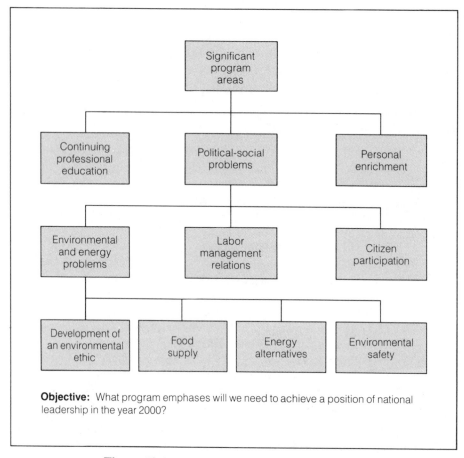

Figure 13.1. *Illustrative partial relevance tree*

For a brief overview of the potential for educational application of these and other techniques and for a detailed bibliography, the reader is referred to Richard Lonsdale's article cited in the bibliography at the end of this chapter.

All the widely-used techniques falling under the rubric of forecasting and futurism have four things in common:

1. a clear statement of objectives,

2. full use of the best data available,

3. the pooling of expert judgment,

4. a systematic method of proceeding from the objective and through the data to a set of conclusions.

WHAT DOES THE FUTURE HOLD?

A variety of conditions are going to have an impact on continuing education as well as on other segments of society. A few of these will be discussed in order to create a context for the forward-looking techniques we have been considering, and to show both how content might change and how continuing education could be brought to bear.

Energy and Resources

The limited supply of petroleum products and of some precious metals must somehow meet contemporary demands if we are to avoid serious problems. The solution is either to find alternate forms of energy or to increase conservation. Continuing education can play a very important part in energy conservation. For instance, one boiler efficiency course at the University of Wisconsin was estimated to have saved approximately $12 million in energy costs at a cost of approximately $200,000. Painless conservation practices eliminated wastes.

One effect of the energy shortage may be that more people will be participating in videocassette or cable television courses than before. Some observers suggest that enrollments in short courses will decrease in favor of in-plant and other kinds of educational experiences. Interestingly, this has not shown up in statistics so far. It may be that the need for interaction is now even greater than before, and interaction is difficult to achieve under electronic media study situations.

Every occupation has been somehow affected by the new attitudes on energy, particularly conservation and alternate energies. The latest energy information must be fed into continuing education courses to insure that they reflect the most current understanding possible.

An example of the adjustments taking place is "life cycle costing," a new subject area that has emerged as a way of taking into account the rapid increase of energy costs as opposed to all other costs. The relationship of cost to energy previously played a small role in business decisions. Equipment almost always was purchased based on its economic payback or on some form of economic justification. Now its energy efficiency as well as its ability to function independently of energy requirements plays a very important part in the decision process.

Millions of dollars are being allocated by government and industry for continuing education that minimizes the complications caused by energy shortages. The clever administrator will find ways of tapping these resources to further enhance his or her continuing education program.

Computerization and Automation

Computers, with their ability to do an enormous amount of calculations in a very short period of time, have already had a major effect on society. They can compare against memory and instructions in ways not considered possible just twenty-five years ago. This development has brought with it fears of invasion of privacy and concern about dehumanization resulting from treating persons like numbers: in some organizations, such as the university, students sometimes are known better by number than by name. These are concerns that have to be dealt with on a case-by-case basis and that have to be checked in order to maintain the standards of our society.

The computer is an amazing instrument. Its time dimensions are in nanoseconds, which is kin to the 10^{-9} seconds. One nanosecond is to a second as one second is to seven hundred years. In other words, if it takes the computer seven nanoseconds to complete a function that would take a person one second to complete, then the computer can do in one second what a person can do in 100 years.

Because almost all segments of society will interface with a computer at one time or another, the populace should have a working knowledge of computers. Computer games have already become commonplace, and computer usage is entering the primary school system. Although proponents of the efficiency of computer-assisted education have touted it as worthy of being an essential element in every school system in the United States, such a reality has not occurred. Computer-assisted education is functioning in several school systems, but it is not likely to become standard practice in all schools before the turn of the century.

Computer simulations are being used increasingly in continuing education settings. For instance, city planners can be presented with problems involving population patterns and can use data given by the computer to evaluate decisions regarding traffic flow or sewer system expansion.

Manufacturers too are finding new computer applications and using them to further automate production. In fact, before the year 2000, completely automated factories will be producing parts in quantities larger than plants of several hundred people could produce. Computer-aided design and computer-aided manufacturing (CAD/CAM) will allow pieces to be completely designed on a computer terminal with auxiliary equipment and without the aid of a draftsperson. This design will be transferred into language understood by machines able to take the next step into manufacturing. Naturally this will significantly affect personnel requirements in manufacturing.

Personnel planning therefore will be an increasingly important part in every manager's life. Today's and tomorrow's computerized automation will have effects unlike those of the mass production assembly lines of the early 1900s. The latter did not in fact reduce employment but created other jobs, which compensated for the jobs that were lost. With computerized automation, however, machines are replacing the physical and mental requirements of human effort. Manufacturing and sales requirements for such computerized systems are much less intensive than they were for the large machines necessary to replace simply the physical requirements of people.

Those who continue working around machinery will need to be far more skilled, as well as skilled in different areas than at present. Draftspersons will not be taught to do drawing on paper but on computer cathode-ray tubes (CRT).

Many continuing education administrators will be faced with insuring that the needs of the workplace are being met. Firstline supervisors will have to know how to reprogram a robot and will worry less about supervisory skills.

Continuing education administrators will also be managing by use of the computer terminal. Management information data will be readily available; the computer will be making routine decisions requiring that the administrator have a broader understanding of problems and a readiness to make decisions without a complete history of prior decision making that could direct him or her to the exact problem solution.

Communications and Service Industries

The areas that will have the largest personnel requirements in the next two decades are communications and service industries. The communication needs for message transmission, audio-video presentation and computer language development, will become even greater. With the increased capability for communications, computers will enable managers to work at home and have complete displays of activity at the office and in the factory. The manager will be able to check out process control, inventory, and any other information that the computer will have at the office. Information processing will probably command more of the personnel requirements than the telephone industry itself. Continuing education will play an important part in educating people to develop the communication skills necessary to interact with such systems and to operate such systems.

Ours will be an essentially service-oriented society. More people will be employed in this industry than in manufacturing. Caring for the elderly, the handicapped, and children will command a large part of our human resources. New fields such as home care will be developed by independent entrepreneurs. People will be spending more time taking advantage of recreational and leisure time services if present trends continue to the end of the century. Continuing education will be instrumental in providing people with both the ideas and the means for making fullest use of time off the job.

Lifestyle and Family Changes

The working mother and the single-parent family are only two indications of a changing family environment. From the history of multigeneration families, our society has moved to a situation in which many children find themselves in day care centers for at least half of their waking life. Traditional values are being challenged and families are being formed by groups not related by blood.

The lifestyles of people, some who have given up the materialistic society for a life of cutting their own wood, planting their own gardens and leading more frugal lives, are evidence that there is much less conformity to societal expectations: people are more intent on doing what they believe to be best for themselves. As we have noted, the increasing free time will make additional demands on the service industries, and lifestyles will reflect the heightened interest in entertainment, the performing arts, and, in many cases, activity-oriented learning. Such learning already plays an important part in the leisure activities of the elderly and helps middle-aged people who are seeking new careers. The continuing educator must take these different lifestyles and family situations into account in planning the time, the location, and the content of continuing education courses.

The Environment

The human ability to alter the environment is having an increasing impact on the habitability of the planet earth. From the million-year-old weapons industry through the fifty-thousand-year-old domestication of animals and on into modern times, humanity has acquired an ever accelerating ability to alter its environment for better and for worse. Even human solutions to human problems give rise to new problems. In eliminating toxins from our food supply we have introduced carcinogens. In reclaiming land for agricultural production we have destroyed much of the biomass in many areas. In increasing our comfort and convenience we have increased the threat of a greenhouse effect. By reducing infant mortality we have triggered dangerously high rates of population growth in some parts of the world. Developers have denuded hillsides, drained swamps, and "improved" river beds: by creating human habitations in one place we have made other places less habitable.

Of three possible scenarios for the twenty-first century, the worst might deal with a rapid movement toward the destruction of human habitat on earth. The best might be a combination of B.F. Skinner's *Walden Two*, Herman Kahn's technological paradise, and Edward Goldsmith's postindustrial society. The most likely scenario may lie somewhere in between. From an educator's viewpoint all three have relevance to future programming, although societal priorities arising from energy shortages and other factors may lessen the amount of time and resources allocated to education.

A catalog of issues having relevance for continuing education in the twenty-first century cannot be attempted here. A few additional suggestions for such a list hint at the magnitude of the task: trends in government expenditures, the inflation rate, life expectancy, the composition of the labor force, industrial productivity, population dynamics, patterns in recreation and the use of leisure time—to name but a few examples.

CONFRONTING THE FUTURE

Prophets from Cassandra and Isaiah to Malachi suffered from credibility problems. Forecasters and futurists contradict one another. Criteria for distinguishing false prophets from true are lacking. What can mere mortals do to confront the future?

Preparation

Given the fact that the future is inevitable, there are two attitudes we can adopt for facing it: resignation or action. From a philosopher's point of view there may be nothing wrong with resignation. Spinoza held that the only true human freedom lay in the consciousness of human bondage, and the Buddhist's paradise is Nirvana—the end of consciousness and feeling. But from an administrator's point of view, resignation means the loss of a job. For those who choose not to resign, there are three possible ways for dealing actively with the course of events:

1. a conscious effort to control events;

2. an adaptive response—making the best of what we cannot change; and

3. adventitious effects—outcomes that we influenced unintentionally—unforeseen side effects.

We control the future in a variety of ways. If we believe for example that leisure-time education is important, we may create a demand for it by skillful marketing efforts. If we believe that video disks are an effective medium for bringing programs to people, we may make it so by effective programming.

We adapt to events that we cannot or do not wish to control. We adjust fees to the market, adopt improvements in our methods when the opportunities arise, and adjust our programming to our market projections.

Occasionally our actions have adventitious effects. That is, they have consequences that we did not intend them to have or that we could not have expected. Unforeseen side effects are one type of adventitious effect. When short sugar supplies were reported in this country, many people purchased extra sugar to prepare for the future. This depleted the already short supply. As we define the course content for a given profession and, in particular, for a given course, graduates with that skill are hired by employers who utilize those skills and, in the future, report back that those are the skills required. In some cases it may be better to have different skills, but industry does adjust to what is provided.

Unplanned second and third order effects occur when, for instance, a die casting machine that makes seven-cent parts for automobiles breaks down because a worker did not provide the proper maintenance. Because of limited inventory an automobile plant that buys these seven-cent parts may have to shut down and lay off thousands of people.

Dealing with the Future

To paraphrase an old proverb: prediction is difficult especially with respect to the future. The greatest difficulty in dealing with the future is the management of risk in the face of uncertainty. Administrators differ considerably in their attitude toward risk and uncertainty. Both an excessive affinity for risk taking and a strong aversion to it can be destructive attitudes. Assuming however that one's attitude toward risk and uncertainty is not indelible, what kinds of guidelines should an administrator use in confronting the future? What follows is an effort to reflect the collective judgment of a variety of sources. As with most other advice it is to be taken with caution.

1. Use future projections for contingency planning rather than a foretaste of things to come. Future developments depend on chance occurrences as well as on an orderly unfolding. Therefore, at best, predictions should outline a set of more or less probable outcomes and a corresponding set of potential responses rather than any single response predicated upon any single outcome.

2. Pull out the stops in the early stages—sobriety can come later. In a world where improbable events occur with disconcerting frequency, creative imagination helps in generating alternatives. Brainstorming, science fiction, and free association can help, but the results should be soberly assessed in the later stages.

3. The more competent the points of view, the more likely that the solution set will include the best solution. Both in the brainstorming stage and in the assessment stage a broad and heterogeneous base of input will increase the quality of the resulting decisions.

4. Use probes whenever possible rather than a heavy commitment of resources. In most situations there is some minimal commitment of resources that will constitute an adequate test. Overcommitment can lead to costly errors.

5. Pool the risk whenever possible. Insurance does not reduce the cost of accidents. It simply spreads the risk. Cooperation among institutions can spread the cost of risky ventures, thus reducing the potential loss for each participant. Both the overtimid and the overdaring stand to benefit from cooperation.

6. Optimize in the area between decisional obsolescence and informational certainty. If there is such a thing as an idea whose time has come, there is also such a thing as an idea whose time has passed. If the time of decision is delayed until all the returns are in, that time may have passed. There is thus a moment of judgment in which the effective decision-maker balances the degree of certainty against the timeliness of the decision—and then decides.

7. Remember that any action taken in this moment of time has a future impact.

As Heraclitus said long ago, the only constant is change. Maintenance of the status quo is a decision about the future just as is the initiation of planned change.

8.   Watch the trends. The price of land never seems to come down even though it is always too high. An investment ten years ago would have been an excellent decision. Courses offered on an annual basis usually have the same growth and decline rate as that of new products. The administrator must be mindful of the trends. The clever ones will begin early in a recession to gear a public works continuing education before the unemployment rate grows to the point where the Labor Department requests proposals for retraining courses. Following the trends suggests the wise investment of time to start a proposal before the "Request for Proposal" is made. Trend watching need not be a full-time occupation but sampling the trends and studying past reactions will help predict future events.

PROGRAM EMPHASES IN THE FUTURE

As Alvin Toffler observed in *Future Shock*, people do not readily think about the future. Any do-it-yourself psychologist can demonstrate this fact. Almost any group charged with probing into the future, if given free rein, will quickly revert to retrospection. Goaded into thinking about the future, no two groups are likely to agree in their listing of topics and most certainly not in their listing of priorities. The following list lays no claim to definitiveness but is intended more for provocation. Such a listing can be a worthwhile exercise at a staff conference using brainstorming, Delphi, or nominal group technique perhaps as a means of overcoming inhibitions. The utility of such an effort is often a matter of sensitizing individuals to future problems and opportunities.

1.   *Innovation and invention.*   According to a number of indicators, innovation is declining in our society. Perhaps the law of diminishing returns is at work but, perhaps too, much of our educational emphasis is on convergent thinking—deduction, the application of formulae, and solving puzzles. Divergent thinking—generation of ideas, seeing novel applications of familiar ideas, and perceiving unusual relationships—is the basis of creative thinking. Within some limits, it is teachable.

2.   *Second (and third) careers.*   Margaret Mead, commenting on the decline of monogamy in our society, suggested that monogamy as a way of life had become less tenable because of our lengthening life span and our improved state of health. To what extent is vocational monogamy also less tenable in a society where the courts are striking down manadatory retirement laws and rules and where the threat of inflation is making early retirement less attractive? By the turn of this century, how many people between the ages of forty and fifty would welcome the opportunity to start a new career?

3.   *Participative leisure.*   Interest in spectator sports and passive entertainment must be nearing a peak. To what extent will people be seeking opportunities for participation in their leisure time activities? The trend has begun but the number of

people who might get involved in lifelong sports, arts and crafts, and civic affairs—to say nothing of interactive television and computer games—is far from the saturation point.

4. *Do-it-yourself.* Taxes come off of the top of individual income where the rate is 30 to 50 percent for average individuals. When, at the same time, a visit from the plumber or the appliance repairer takes twenty dollars off the top at the moment the door opens, interest in becoming more self-sufficient increases. Courses for the do-it-yourself householder can only become more attractive.

5. *Productivity.* Individual productivity first leveled off and then began to decline. Programmers who have something meaningful to contribute, such as utilizing technology to produce twice as many pairs of shoes per person, will continue to have ample enrollments.

6. *Ombudsmanship.* In a society beset by problems that have no simple solution, the reconciliation of conflicting views is a major challenge basically educational in nature. Teaching the skills of conflict resolution and imparting information that brings perspective, provide alternatives to the politics of confrontation.

7. *High density recreation.* Already, in order to preserve the wilderness, access is being restricted. When the rapids are so clogged with inner tubes that the canoeist cannot see the chute and the trail is so congested that no decent tent sites are left, creative recreational alternatives are needed—alternatives that preserve many of the values of trail and stream but with the ability to handle higher density use. There are educational jobs to be done in planning, development, and use.

8. *The educated health consumer.* If we do not become a nation of hypochondriacs it will not be through lack of effort by advertisers and medical columnists. Furthermore, we are approaching the point where 12 percent of our gross national product will be spent to cure us or to ward off illness. What can education do to promote wellness and to hold down health costs?

9. *Home computers.* As we have noted, we are not far from the day when most people will either have or plan to have their own computers in the home. These extremely versatile devices can be used for security, recreation, communication, and education. But to get the best use out of home computers most people will need more help than they can get from the operator manual, whose instructions seem to lose a lot in translation. Where will we go for help?

10. *Living with big government.* In spite of taxpayer revolts and citizen advocates, government continues to take more and to give less—as seen by the average beleaguered citizen. Educational programs that put their participants in better touch with their government can reduce that feeling of alienation and perhaps even lead to better government.

If the foregoing list does nothing more than inspire the reader to construct a better one, it still has done its work. The utility of this or any other list is to direct attention to the future and to forward the very practical goal of inspiring future-oriented innovative programs. The range of possible ideas extends from the specific—understanding your home computer—to the ambitious—a new career at age forty-five or fifty.

Administrators who do not confront the future, either because of an aversion to risk or an immersion in the present, put their own futures as administrators in jeopardy. Forward-looking administrators, however, will find a great deal of help available. This chapter looks at some of the tools that are available, giving a brief overview of some of the quantitative and qualitative forecasting techniques that are currently being used. It proceeds to consider some of the areas in which future studies are likely to be especially pertinent and then suggests some ways to confront the future more effectively. Finally the chapter suggests some areas in which new or expanded program efforts are likely to be most productive. Preparation for the future depends not on prophecy but on contingency planning. We cannot foretell the future, but by projecting a set of alternative developments we can be better prepared to cope with what the future may bring. And if we now implement ideas whose time is still to come, we will be one step ahead.

BIBLIOGRAPHY

Gleazer, Edmund J., Jr. *The Community College: Values, Vision, and Vitality.* Washington, D.C., American Association of Community and Junior Colleges, 1980.

Harrington, Fred H. *The Future of Adult Education.* San Francisco: Jossey-Bass, 1977.

Hencley, Stephen, and James R. Yates, eds. *Futurism in Education: Methodologies.* Berkeley, Calif.; McCutchan, 1974.

Lonsdale, Richard C. "Futures Research, Policy Research, and the Policy Sciences." *Education and Urban Society* (1975): 246–93.

Toffler, Alvin. *Future Shock.* New York: Random House, 1970.

Toffler, Alvin. *The Third Wave.* New York: Bantam Books, 1981.

Wheelwright, Steven C. and Spyros Makridakis. *Forecasting Methods for Management.* 2d ed. New York: John Wiley, 1977.

INDEX

Academic due process, 200, 202–203, 204

Accountability, standards of, 123–124

Accreditation, 159

Achievement tests, 138–139

Administration, 1–4, 130

Administrators, 12–14

Admissions
  and curriculum development, 158–159
  services, 239–244

Adult degrees, 147, *table* 148, 152

Advertising in program promotion, 109, 110–117, 118, 119–120

Advising services for students, 246–251

Advisory committees
  and community relations, 184–185
  in needs assessment, 34–36, 39
  and planning, 54, 59–60
  and program promotion, 115–116
  and public relations, 271–272

Allison, G. T., 46

Alumni, as public relations public, 267

Amenities, 56

Arrangements in programs, evaluation of, 129

Assessment degrees, 147, *table* 148, 149, 152

Associations, as public relations public, 268

Assumptions in planning, 52–53, 69

Attitudes as learning outcome, 49

Attitude scales, 137–138

Attitudinal counseling, 247–248

Attrition, control of, 159–160

Audience. *See also* Clientele
  as planning consideration, 53
  strategies to reach, 73–74

Audiocassettes, 89, 90, 160, 161, 253

Authority in organizations, 166–167

Automation, 290–291

Auxiliary enterprises and sales, 222

Base budget, 210
  defense of, 227–232
  review of, 228–230

Behavioral change in evaluation, 139–140

Board of Regents v. Roth, 203

Brainstorming, 35, 214, 295

Bramblett, Larry, 200

Breakeven point, 57

Budget. *See also* General purpose classification budget; Income budget; Incremental budget requests; Program budgeting
  control, 170, 171–172, 174–175
  cycles, *table* 217
  functions of, 208–209
  relieving income, 2
  review, 228–232
  types of, 2, 209–212

Budget Program Analysis. *See* Program budgeting

Bulletin boards, 263

Buzz groups, 35, 61

Carnegie Commission, and educational technology, 84, *fig.* 85

Case studies, as evaluation method, 141

Cassettes, 278. *See also* Audiocassettes

Census data, 22–23

Certificates in continuing education, 146, 157
  audience for, 149–150

Channels of communication for marketing, 106–107

Checklists, as planning tool, 57, 63–64
Classes, as delivery format, 81
Clientele. *See also* Needs; Needs assessment
  departmentation by, 181
  and needs assessment, 21–37
  as public relations public, *fig.* 261, 262, 272
  strategies to reach, 73–74
Cold canvass, 25
Colleagues, evaluation by, 131, 201
Collective bargaining, 203–204
College Level Examination Program (CLEP), 154, 240–241
Commission on Non-Traditional Study, 27–28, 79, 149–150
Communications industries, 291
Community
  relations, 184–185
  services, 179
Comparison groups, 135–136
Competency-based learning, 155–156
Competition
  as planning consideration, 53
  and program promotion, 105
Computers
  as educational technology, 91–92
  future of, 290–291, 296
Conferences, 80
Content
  and educatinal design, 74–75
  as planning consideration, 53–54
Continuing education
  changing leadership patterns in, 12–14
  competition between public and private institutions in, 10–12
  degrees, 152–153
  economic problems in, 10–12
  future of, 10–14, 284–297
  history of, 7–9
  professionalism in, 194–196
  units (CEU), 95, *fig.* 96, *fig.* 97, 241–242
Continuing employment status, 200
Contracts
  as income source, 221–222
  and public relations, 260
Cooperative Extension Service, 1, 5, 36, 171, 177, 183, 184, 189, 190, 194, 200, 222, 239, 269, 271
  geographic specialization in, 13
  as model for continuing education, 7–9
  as technical assistance system, 76–77
Correspondence courses
  as delivery format, 81–82
  motivation for, 96

Correspondence courses (continued)
  program promotion of, 115, 116, 119
Cost-benefit analysis
  in budget defense, 229, 230, 231–232
  in budgeting, 214–215
  in curriculum development, 160–161
  in needs assessment, 37–42
  in program evaluation, 132–133
Costs. *See also* Program budgeting
  in budget development, 216–219
  as consideration in planning, 54
  and educational design, 75
  in program promotion, 119–120
  in selecting media and methods, 95
Counseling services, 246–251
Course attendance, estimating, 29, 30, 32–33, 39–40
Credit card, arrangements for payments, 246
Credits
  and curriculum development, 158–159
  by examination, 154
  for experience, 239–240, 243–244
  modes of earning, 153–156
  nontraditional, 239–241, 243–244
Critical Path Method (CPM), 65–68
Cross-sectional evaluation, 135
Curricular programming, 145–161. *See also* Program planning, short-term
  and curriculum development, 156–159
  and modes of earning credit, 153–156
  special problems in, 159–161
  and types of offerings, 150–153
Curriculum development, 156–159

Decision making, 49, *fig.* 50. *See also* Program planning
Deferred compensation, 193
Deferred evaluation, 135
Degrees in continuing education, 146
  audience for 149–150
  and curriculum development, 157
  modes of earning credit for, 153–156
  nontraditional credit for, 239–241
  and offerings, 150–153
  types of, 147–149
Delbecq, A. L., 61
Delivery systems, 6–7, 73–98
  costs of, 95
  design of, 76–79
  educational technology in, 83–94
  formats for educational content in, 79–83
  motivational factors in, 95–98
  specialists in, 13

Delivery systems (continued)
  strategy in, 73–75
Delphi technique, 35, 61–62, 70, 214,
  286–287, 295
Demand creation, 108–109
Departmentation, bases of, 168, 180–182
Dial access, 94
Diplomas in continuing education, 146–147
Direct assessment of needs, 33–34, 39
Direct indicators, 140–141
Direct mail, 110–113
  for program promotion, 118–119, *tables*
  119, 120
Discretionary funds, 224, 225
Displays, as public relations channel, 279
Distribution of rewards
  and evaluation, 124
  and organizational authority, 167
Do-it-yourself, 296
Drucker, Peter, 49, 181
Duration as planning consideration, 56

Educational technology. *See also* Mass media;
    Radio; Television
  selection of, 95–98
  uses of, 83–94
Electrowriters, 94
End-of-course evaluations, 130–131, 135
Energy trends, 289–290
Environmental scanning, 23–24
Environmental trends, 292–293
Equal employment opportunity, 203
Evaluation. *See also* Program evaluation
  in budget reviews, 230–232
  and staff effectiveness, 201–202
Evaluative counseling, 247, 248
Exhibits in program promotion, 116–117, 279
Expenditure category budget, 210–211
Expense budget, 216–219
Experiential learning, 155–156
Expert opinion. *See also* Delphi technique
  evaluation by, 131–132
  in needs assessment, 24–25
Extension degrees, 147, *table* 148, 152
External degrees, 147–149, 155, 156
Extracurricular activities, 237–238

Faculty, 190–204. *See also* Staff
  evaluation of, 127–128
  full-time, 191
  induction and orientation of, 198–199
  qualifications of, 194–196
  recruitment and selection of, 197–198
  reward system for, 199–201

Faculty (continued)
  supplementary, 191–194
Fagaly, Robert, 172–173
Family, changes in, 292
Fayol, Henri, 283
Feedback, in evaluation, 124
Fees, as income source, 220–221
Film, 88–89, 278
Finance. *See* Program budgeting
Financial aids, 245–246
Flewellen, W. C., 200
Flexible degrees, *table* 148
Flexible entry programs, 157, 158
Float in budget management, 226
Food services, 251
Forecasting, 284–289
  in short-term program planning, 68–71
Foundations as public relations public, 267
Fourth Revolution, The, 84
Frandson, Phillip E., 8–9
Funding. *See also* Program budgeting
  in budget development, 216, 219–223
  patterns, 223–224
  and public relations, 260
  requests, 209–210
Fund management, 224–226
Futurism, 284–289

Galbraith, John Kenneth, 21
Gantt chart, 62–63
General Educational Development (GED) tests,
  154, 240
General public, *fig.* 261, 262, 271–272
General purpose classification budget, 211–212
  defense of, 227–232
Geographic dispersion
  of counseling services, 250
  in delivery system, 79
  of field staff, 170–171, 177–179
Gifts
  as income source, 222
  and public relations, 260
Goldsmith, Edward, 292
Government agencies
  as public relations public, *fig.* 261, 262,
    268–270, 274
  use of, in needs assessment, 25–26
Graduate admissions, 242–243
Grants
  as income source, 221–222
  and public relations, 260
Greenburg, Robert, 20
Group counseling, 250–251

Handouts, 116–117
Harper, William Rainey, 7
Health services, 237
Hertling, James, 20, 21
Higher Education Act of 1965, 179, 184–185
Houle, Cyril, 45, 147, 149, 152, 194
Housing services, 251–252
Human development, 4, 5–6. *See also* Needs

Income budget, 216, 219–223
Incremental budget requests, 209, 210
Independent study as delivery format, 83.
    See also Self-study
Indirect indicators, 140
Information
  about needs, cost of, 37–39
  booths, 279
  counseling, 247, 248
In-house publications, 263, 274–275, 278
Inquiries from users, 36–37
Inserts, 116–117
Institutes, 80
Instructional materials, evaluation of, 128–129
Integrated departments, 175–176
Interagency organizations, 183–185
Internal degrees, 147–149
Itinerant counseling services, 250

James, Bernard, 172–173
Job descriptions, 196–197
Joint appointments, 177
  and reward systems, 201
  and staffing needs, 193–194

Kahn, Herman, 292
Keller's Personalized System of Instruction, 79, 83,
    154, 244
Knowledge, as learning outcome, 48, 49
Knowles, M. S., 45

Laboratory courses, 92
Learning contracts, 156, 160, 243
Learning curves, 196
Learning resource centers, 78, 79, 250, 252
Legislative hearings, 270, 274
Levitt, Theodore, 102
Library services, 252–253
Licensing boards, 266
Line workers, 168–169, 171, 174
Location as planning consideration, 56–57
Lockstep programs, 157, 158
Logistics, 160
Longitudinal evaluation, 135

Lonsdale, Richard, 289
Lowe, John, 223

McClelland, David, 20
McLuhan, Marshall, 73
Magazines
  promotional advertising in, 114, 118,
    table 119, 120
  as public relations channel, 277–278
Mailing lists, 273
Malthus, Thomas, 284
Management by objectives, 202
Marketing
  channels, 110–117
  function of, in managment, 117–120
  relation to public relations, 258–259
Maslow, Abraham, 4, 17–18
Mass media, 57, 85–90
  as public relations channel, 274, 276–278
  selection of, 95–98
Matrix organization, *fig.* 176, 182
Mayo, Elton, 48
Mead, Margaret, 295
Mechanic, David, 264–265
Meetings of staff, 263
Methods as planning consideration, 54–55
Minorities, counseling services for, 248, 250
Morphological Research Method, 287
Morrill Act of 1862, 7
Motivational factors in selecting media and
    methods, 95–98
Multivariate design in evaluation, 136
Murray, H. A., 18, *table* 19

National associations, 26–27
Needs
  and decision to participate in program, 40–42
  catalog of, *table* 19
  and demand creation, 108–109
  hierarchy of, 4, 17–18, *fig.* 18
  modifying and satisfying, 20–21
  overview of, 27–28
  and program mission, 2–3
  range of, 3
  of staff, 190–196
  understanding, 17–20
Needs assessment, 21–42
  by asking clients, 27–37, 38, 39
  data costs and benefits in, 37–42
  and defining market, 105–106
  by identifying clients, 21–27
  and program budgeting, 212, 213
  strategies in, 38–39

New Educational Media in Action: Case Studies for Planners, 84
Newspapers
  advertising in, 113–114, 118
  as public relations channel, 276–277
News releases, 114–115, *table* 119, 119–120, 276–277
Nominal group technique, 61, 62, 214, 295
Nondegree curricula, 150–151
Nonparametric data, 133, 134

Objectives of program
  budgeting and, 213–216
  categories of, 133
  setting of, in evaluation, 124–127
Occupational Safety and Health Act of 1970, 49
Off-time payments, 193
Ogden, Charles Kay, 88
Ombudsmanship, 296
Open education, as delivery system, 77–78
Open University, 253
  as delivery system, 77–78
  and motivation, 96
Organizations, 165–185
  alternative structures in, 168, 171–179
  criteria of effective, 169–171
  decentralization of control in, 169, 171–174
  and departmentation, 168, 180–182
  interagency, 183–185
  problems of, 166–169
  publics of, 261–272
  span of control in, 168
  structure and function in, 166
Organized influence groups as public relations public, *fig.* 261, 262, 266–268, 271, 274
Outside review, evaluation by, 131–132
Overload payments, 192–193

Parallel rank structures, 200
Parent organization, as public relations public, *fig.* 261, 262, 264–265
Participative leisure, 295–296
PATTERN, 287–289
Peer review, 131, 201
PENNTAP, 77
Performance
  evaluation, 132–133, 243–244
  review, 201–202, 208–209
Perry v. Sindermann, 203
Persistence forecasting, 69–70
Personal communications as public relations channel, 263–264, 274, 275–276
Personal selling, 109–110

Personnel administration. *See* Staff
PERT, 51, 68
Phillips, 66, 61
Placement services, 237, 238
Planning, 56–57. *See also* Curricular planning; Program budgeting; Program planning, short-term; Workload planning
Planning-Programming-Budgeting Systems (PPBS). *See* Program budgeting
Precedence Network, 65–68
Prediction techniques, 284–289
Prescriptive degrees, *table* 148
Press releases. *See* News releases
Pricing as planning consideration, 57
Problem-centered departmentation, 180–181
Problem solving
  Cooperative Extension Model of, 7–9
  as focus of continuing education, 3–4
Procedures as planning consideration, 57
Productivity, 296
Professional associations, 266–267
Professional Development Degree (PD), 152–153
Program budgeting, 207–232
  and budget defense, 226–232
  costing in, 216–219
  funding patterns in, 223–224
  and fund management, 224–226
  and income sources, 216, 219–223
  and review, 226–232
  systems in, 210–211, 212–216
Program
  categories, 212
  content, evaluation of, 128
  control, 168, 169, 171–174
  coordination, 183–184
Program evaluation, 123–143
  cost-benefit analysis in, 132–133
  design and implementation of, 133–143
  methods of, 136–141
  objectives in, 124–127
  performance dimensions in, 132–133
  strategies of, 134–136
  those evaluated in, 127–129
  those evaluating in, 129–132
  uses of, 123–124
Program Evaluation and Review Technique (PERT), 51, 68
Program planning, short-term, 45–71. *See also* Curricular programming; Program budgeting
  approaches to, 58–62
  bureaucratic politics model of, 46
  factors affecting success or failure of, 68–71
  learning objectives in, 48–49

Program planning (continued)
  organizational model of, 45–46
  primary considerations in, 52–56
  as process, 45–58
  right time to decide in, 49, *fig.* 50
  and search for alternative solutions, 51–52
  secondary considerations in, 56–57
  tools for, 62–68
  utility models of, 46–48
Program promotion, 101–120
  as consideration in planning, 57
  defining market in, 101–107
  effective selling techniques in, 107–110
  geography and, 103–104
  managing marketing functions in, 117–120
  relation to public relations of, 258–259
  selection of marketing channels in, 110–117
Programs in continuing education
  content in, 5–6
  decision to participate in, 40–42
  delivery systems for, 6–7, 73–98
  determining scope of, 4–7
  general philosophy of, 4–5
  problem-solving focus of, 3–4
Project on Noncollegiate Instruction, 155
Promotion. *See* Program promotion; Word-of-mouth promotion
Public address systems, 263
Public relations, 257–281
  channels of communication in, 263–264, 272–273, 274–281
  scope of, 257–260
  significant publics in, 261–272, 279–281
  strategy in, 272–274

Quality control
  in curriculum development, 159
  in program promotion, 120
Quasi-experimental design in evaluation, 135–136

Radio, 161
  as educational technology, 87–88
  as public relations channel, 277, 280
Ratchford, C. Brice, 166, 169
Regulatory boards, 266
Relevance trees, 287–289
Restricted funds, 225
Results management, 202
Reward systems, 199–201
Richards, I. A., 88
Risk taking, 294–295

Sales representatives, 116

Sample surveys, 28–33, 38, 39
Satellites, 88
Schein, Edgar, 167
Self-actualization, 4, 5, 17-18
Self-evaluation, 129–130
Self-paced learning, 154
Self-study
  costs of, 95, *fig.* 196, *fig.* 197
  as delivery format, 82–83
  motivation in, 95–96
Selling techniques, 107–110
Sequencing of courses, 157–158
Service industries, 291
Short courses, 80–81
Simon, Herbert, 46
Simulators, 92
Skill as learning outcome, 48–49
Skinner, B. F., 292
Slide-tape recordings
  as educational technology, 91
  as public relations channel, 278, 279
Smith-Level Act, 7–8, 76
Social development, 4, 5
Speakers' bureaus, 279
Special interest groups, 267
Staff, 168–169, 171, 174, *fig.* 175. *See also* Faculty
  as consideration in planning, 55
  development, 202
  increasing effectiveness of, 201–204
  induction and orientation of, 198–199
  job descriptions for, 196–197
  legal issues about, 200, 202–204
  meeting needs of, 190–196
  newsletters for, 263, 278
  planning, 55, 60–61
  as public relations public, *fig.* 261, 262–264
  recruitment and selection of, 197–198
  reward system for, 199–201
  and workload planning, 196
Standard degree curricula, 151–153
Statistics, 22–23, 51
Stone, Robert, 119
Student
  activity regulation, 237, 238
  evaluations, 130–131
Student services, 235–253
  and admissions, 239–244
  counseling and advising, 246–251
  essential vs. auxiliary, 235–239
  financial aids, 245–246
  housing and food, 251–252
  library, 252–253

Study groups, 160
Subsidiary Communication Authorization (SCA), 87–88
Suppliers as public relations public, *fig.* 261, 262, 272
Supreme Court, decisions about staff, 203–204
Survey research, 28–33, 38, 39, 51

Task-focused design, 181–182
Task force organization, 181–182
Task groups, 60–61
Tax revenue, as income source, 220
Taylor, Frederick W., 182
Technical assistance models, 76–77
Telephone sales, 115
Telephonic communication, as educational technology, 92–94
Television, 161
  as educational technology, 85–87, 88–90, 93–94
  as public relations channel, 277
  slow-scan, 93–94
Thurstone, L. L., 137
Time purchase arrangements, 193–194
Timing, as planning consideration, 49, 55–56
Toffler, Alvin, 284, 295

Trade
  associations, 266–267
  journals, 277–278
Transfer credits, 155
Trial balloons, 34
Tuition, 220–221
Tutorials, 82–83, 154
1202 commissions, 183, 265–266

Unrestricted funds, 224–225
User feedback, 36–37, 124

Video disks, 89, 90
Videotape cassettes, 89–90
Volunteers, and staffing, 194
Voucher plans, 245–246

War, principles of, and planning, 70–71
Women, counseling services for, 248, 250–251
Word-of-mouth promotion, 115–116
Workload planning, 196

Zero base budgets, 209, 210
Zwicky, Fritz, 287